THE UNION OF ENGLAND AND SCOTLAND

To Helen

P. W. J. RILEY

The Union of England and Scotland

A study in Anglo-Scottish politics
of the eighteenth century

Manchester University Press
Rowman and Littlefield

©   P. W. J. RILEY 1978

Published by
Manchester University Press
Oxford Road, Manchester M13 9PL

U.S.A.
Rowman and Littlefield
81 Adams Drive, Totowa, N.J. 07512

British Library cataloguing-in-publication data

Riley, Patrick William Joseph.
   The union of England and Scotland.
   1. Scotland – History – The Union, 1707.
   2. Scotland – Politics and government – 1689–1745.
   3. Great Britain – Politics and government – 1702–1714.
   I. Title
   320.9'41'069   DA807

   UK ISBN 0–7190–0727–5
   US ISBN 0–8476–6155–5

Computerised Phototypesetting by
G C Typeset Ltd., Bolton, Greater Manchester

Printed in Great Britain
by M & A Thomson Litho Ltd
Kelvin Industrial Estate, East Kilbride

CONTENTS

Acknowledgements   *page viii*

Abbreviations   *x*

Foreword   *xiv*

I *The idea of union*   *1*

  1. Earlier union projects   *2*

  2. Impetus towards union   *6*

  3. Effects of the revolution   *8*

  4. Scottish magnate interests   *11*

  5. Scottish management under William   *16*

  6. Queensberry and the court   *19*

  7. William's conversion to union   *22*

II *The cavalier alliance*   *31*

  1. The adjournment   *32*

  2. Anne's accession and the country party   *33*

  3. The parliament of 1702   *36*

  4. Changes in the ministry   *39*

  5. Court plans for 1703   *47*

  6. The parliament of 1703   *52*

  7. Causes and consequences of the court's defeat   *59*

III *The new party experiment*   *67*

  1. Inquest on 1703   *67*

  2. The junto and the 'Scotch Plot'   *71*

3. The court's problem of 1704   73
4. The country party delegation   75
5. Seafield's new party scheme   76
6. Obstacles to court success   82
7. The parliament of 1704   96
8. Queensberry as the junto's agent   102

IV *The junto's Scottish failure*   114
    1. Criticism of the new party   115
    2. The new party in office   117
    3. Godolphin, the whigs and the act of security   119
    4. Godolphin's surrender to junto terms   121
    5. Attempts to remodel the Scottish ministry   123
    6. Argyll's *coup d'état*   129
    7. Argyll and the succession   139
    8. The squadrone's position in 1705   143
    9. The parliament of 1705   145
   10. The junto and the treaty act   151

V *Negotiations*   162
    1. The junto's conversion to union   163
    2. Junto manoeuvres to control negotiations   166
    3. Whig negotiating tactics   168
    4. The old party and the prospect of union   171
    5. The choice of union commissioners   175
    6. Previous negotiations, 1702–3   177
    7. The 1706 negotiations   182

VI *Trade and propaganda*   197
    1. Scotland's economic condition   197
    2. The political insignificance of Scotland's economy   201
    3. The Darien Scheme   206
    4. The Scottish economy and the court *v.* country conflict 213
    5. Trade as a tool of propaganda   215
    6. Arguments against union   220
    7. Unionist propaganda   233

VII *Ratification*   254
    1. The position of the old party consolidated   254
    2. Distribution of the £20,000 arrears   256
    3. Schemes to thwart the junto   259
    4. Whig precautions   270
    5. Squadrone support decisive for the union   271
    6. Party voting in the Scottish parliament   273
    7. Popular anti-unionist feeling   282
    8. Court fears of insurrection   284
    9. The union parliament   287
   10. The 'explanations'   290
   11. Last-minute manoeuvres in the Scottish parliament   293
   12. English reappraisals of the effects of union   298
   13. Ratification in England   302
   14. Harley and the union   305
   15. The measure of union   311

Appendix A   326

Appendix B   336

Bibliographical note   339

Index   341

ACKNOWLEDGEMENTS

It is a pleasure for me to acknowledge the many debts of gratitude I have incurred whilst working on this subject. Great assistance has always been forthcoming from the staffs of the Scottish Record Office and the National Library of Scotland, two of the most congenial places in which an historian can work. Public expressions of gratitude to particular individuals can be invidious but I must express my indebtedness to successive secretaries of the National Register of Archives (Scotland) who have gone to great lengths to ensure that documents not on permanent deposit were made temporarily available. Dr T. I. Rae and Mr James Ritchie of the Department of Manuscripts of the National Library of Scotland have done much to ease the problems of working from a distance on Scottish history. The guidance of Miss Margaret Brander, research librarian at Tullie House, enabled me to cope with bishop Nicolson's diary more quickly than would otherwise have been possible.

Acknowledgement is due to the kind co-operation of the duke of Buccleuch, who allowed manuscripts from Drumlanrig Castle to be deposited temporarily in the Scottish Record Office and gave permission for reference to be made to them, and to the duke of Roxburgh, who granted similar permission for manuscripts from Floors Castle. The duke of Marlborough gave permission for reference to be made to the Blenheim Papers and the marquess of Bath kindly allowed me to examine and refer to the Longleat muniments. For the general availability of the Portland manuscripts gratitude must be expressed to the duke of Portland. My thanks are also due to the directors of the Company of Scottish History Ltd for giving me their kind permission to publish in the second chapter the substance of two articles of mine which appeared in the *Scottish Historical Review* in 1965 and 1968.

I gladly acknowledge the help of the University of Sheffield in appointing me to a research fellowship which made it possible for this project to be initiated, although the final product, through a series of tediously complicated circumstances, is not only considerably belated but rather different in form from that envisaged at the time by both the appointing committee and myself.

I have received many other personal kindnesses, notably from John Simpson of the University of Edinburgh, who made available to me some of his own notes on several members of the Scottish parliament together with his copy of the union divisions conveniently tabulated from the *Acts of the Parliament of Scotland*. To him and his wife, Anne, I largely owe the recollection of many pleasant visits to Edinburgh. I am grateful to my colleague Mr A. J. Robertson who was kind enough to attempt to correct some of my misapprehensions concerning Scottish economic history, although he is far from being responsible for any remaining errors. And, as a good Scot, he would no doubt firmly dissociate himself from many of the opinions to be found in this book. My thanks are due to Mr George Rowan, who assisted with the typescript of an early draft of the work. The debt I owe to the editors of Manchester University Press is a great one and I am glad of this opportunity to acknowledge it.

Finally I must record my gratitude to my wife and family for extending to the union of 1707, at least for much of the time, the forbearance which is perhaps the due of a long-established resident ghost.

P.W.J.R.

ABBREVIATIONS

APS Acts of the Parliament of Scotland, ed. T. Thomson, ix–xi (Edinburgh, 1822–4)
Atholl Chron. Chronicles of the Atholl and Tullibardine Families, ed. John, seventh Duke of Atholl (Edinburgh, 1908)

Balcarres *Memoirs touching the revolution in Scotland, 1688–1690, by Colin, Earl of Balcarres* (Bannatyne Club, 1841)
BIHR Bulletin of the Institute of Historical Research
BL, Add. MSS British Library, Additional Manuscripts
Blenheim Papers Manuscripts of the Duke of Marlborough at Blenheim
Boyer, *Annals* A. Boyer, *The History of the Reign of Queen Anne Digested into Annals* (London, 1703–8)
Bruce, *Report* J. Bruce, *Report on the . . . Union* (London, 1799)
Buccleuch (Drum.) Muniments of the Duke of Buccleuch at Drumlanrig Castle. Particular items are referred to in abbreviated form, viz.,
Annandale 'Letters to the Duke of Queensberry from the first Marquess of Annandale'
Carstares 'Letters from Mr Carstares, 1700'
Church and State 'Queensberry Papers on Church and State'
Col. 'Colnaghi MSS.'
Pringle 'Letters from Robert Pringle, 1701 and 1702'
Queensberry Letters 'Letters to the Duke of Queensberry'
Seafield 'Letters from the Earl of Seafield, 1700–1702'
Seven Letters 'Bundle of Seven Unsigned Letters [from Murray of Philiphaugh], 1707' [*sic* for 1701]
Stair 'Letters from the Earl of Stair and the Officers of State, 1700–1706'
Union 'Letters on the Treaty of Union'
Burnet G. Burnet, *History of His Own time* (Oxford, 1833)

Caldwell Papers Selections from the family papers preserved at Caldwell (Maitland Club, 1854)
Carstares S. P. State Papers and Letters addressed to William Carstares, ed. J. McCormick (Edinburgh, 1774)

Chandler   [R. Chandler], *The History and Proceedings of the House of Commons* (London, 1741–4)

CJ   Journals of the House of Commons

Clerk, *Memoirs   Memoirs of the Life of Sir John Clerk of Penicuik . . . 1676–1755*, ed. John M. Gray (Scottish History Society, 1892)

Cobbett   W. Cobbett, *Parliamentary History of England . . .* (London, 1810)

Cowper, *Diary   The Private Diary of William, First Earl Cowper* (Roxburghe Club, 1833)

Coxe, *Marlborough   W. Coxe, Memoirs of John Duke of Marlborough; with his Original Correspondence* (London 1818)

Coxe, *Walpole   W. Coxe, Memoirs of the Life and Administration of Sir Robert Walpole . . .* (London, 1798)

CSP (Dom)   Calendars of State Papers (Domestic)

Cunningham, *History   A. Cunningham, The History of Great Britain from the Revolution in 1688 to the Accession of George the First* (London, 1787)

Defoe, *Letters   The Letters of Daniel Defoe*, ed. G. H. Healey (Oxford, 1955)

Defoe, *Review   Review of the State of the English Nation*

Donaldson, 'Foundations . . .'   G. Donaldson, 'Foundations of Anglo-Scottish Union', in *Elizabethan Government and Society*, ed. S. T. Bindoff, J. Hurstfield and C. H. Williams (London, 1961)

EHR   English Historical Review

Ferguson, *Scotland's Relations   W. Ferguson, Scotland's Relations with England: a Survey to 1707* (Edinburgh, 1977)

Fraser, *Cromartie   Sir W. Fraser, The Earls of Cromartie – their Kindred, Country and Correspondence* (Edinburgh, 1876)

Fraser, *Melvilles   Sir W. Fraser, The Melvilles, Earls of Melville, and the Leslies, Earls of Leven* (Edinburgh, 1890)

Hardwicke State Papers   Miscellaneous State Papers from 1501 to 1726, ed. Philip Yorke, Lord Hardwicke (London, 1778)

HMCR   Reports of the Historical Manuscripts Commission. These appear in the form: *HMCR Johnstone MSS*, for example

Hume, *Diary   Sir David Hume of Crossrig, A Diary of the Proceedings in the Parliament and Privy Council of Scotland, 1700–1707* (Bannatyne Club, 1828)

Int. Soc. Letters   Intimate Society Letters of the Eighteenth Century, ed. Duke of Argyll (London, 1910)

Japikse   *Correspondentie van Willem III en van Hans Willem Bentinck*, ed. N. Japikse (The Hague, 1927–37)

Jerviswood   The Correspondence of George Baillie of Jerviswood, 1702–1708 (Bannatyne Club, 1842)

Keith, *Commercial Relations   T. Keith, Commercial Relations of England and Scotland, 1603–1707* (Cambridge, 1910)

KCRO   Kent County Record Office, Maidstone

Lee, *Cabal   M. Lee, jnr, The Cabal* (Urbana, 1965)

Leven and Melville Papers   Letters and State Papers Chiefly Addressed To George Earl of Melville . . . 1689–1691 (Bannatyne Club, 1843)

LJ *Journals of the House of Lords*
Lockhart Papers George Lockhart of Carnwath, *Memoirs and Commentaries upon the Affairs of Scotland*, ed. A. Aufrere (London, 1817)
Longleat Manuscripts of the Marquess of Bath at Longleat
Lythe S. G. E. Lythe, *The Economy of Scotland in its European Setting* (Edinburgh, 1960)
Macpherson J. Macpherson, *Original Papers containing the Secret History of Great Britain* . . . (London, 1775)
Marchmont Papers *A Selection from the Papers of the Earls of Marchmont in the possession of the Right Honourable Sir George Henry Rose* (London, 1831)
Marlborough Dispatches *Letters and Dispatches of John Churchill, Duke of Marlborough*, ed. G. Murray (London, 1845)
Nicolson, Diary Bishop Nicolson's Diary, Tullie House Library, Carlisle
NLS National Library of Scotland
NUL Nottinghham University Library
Paterson, *Works* *The Works of William Paterson*, ed. S. Bannister (London, 1858)
PRO Public Record Office
RCRB *Extracts From The Records Of The Convention Of The Royal Burghs of Scotland, 1677–1711*, ed. J. D. Marwick (Edinburgh, 1880)
Riley, *English Ministers* P. W. J. Riley, *The English Ministers and Scotland, 1707–1727* (London, 1964)
Scott, *Joint-Stock Companies* W. R. Scott, *The Constitution and Finance of English, Scottish and Irish Joint-Stock Companies to 1720* (Cambridge, 1910–12)
Seafield Correspondence *Seafield Correspondence from 1685 to 1708*, ed. J. Grant (Scottish History Society, 1912)
Seafield Letters *Letters relating to Scotland in the Reign of Queen Anne* . . . ed. P. Hume Brown (Scottish History Society, 1915)
SHR *Scottish Historical Review*
Shrewsbury Corresp. W. Coxe, *Private and original correspondence of Charles Talbot, Duke of Shrewsbury* (London, 1821)
Smout, *Scottish Trade* T. C. Smout, *Scottish Trade On The Eve Of Union, 1660–1707* (Edinburgh, 1963)
Somers Tracts *A collection of scarce and valuable tracts . . . selected from . . . libraries, particularly that of the late Lord Somers* (1809–15)
SRO Scottish Record Office. Collections cited by call numbers unless otherwise stated
Stair Annals *Annals and Correspondence of the Viscount and the First and Second Earls of Stair*, ed. J. M. Graham (Edinburgh, 1875)
Swift, *Prose Works* *The Prose Works of Jonathan Swift*, ed. H. Davis and I. Ehrenpreis (Oxford, 1953)
Timberland [E. Timberland], *The History and Proceedings of the House of Lords* . . . (London, 1742–3)
Trevor-Roper, 'The Union of Britain . . .' H. R. Trevor-Roper, 'The Union of

Britain in the Seventeenth Century' in his *Religion, the Reformation and Social Change* (London, 1967)

Vernon   *Letters illustrative of the Reign of William III, 1696 to 1708 . . . by James Vernon*, ed. G. P. R. James (London, 1841)

Willson, 'James I and Anglo-Scottish Unity'   D. W. Willson, 'James I and Anglo-Scottish Unity' in *Conflict in Stuart England*, ed. W. A. Aiken and B. D. Henning (London, 1960)

Wodrow, *Analecta*   R. Wodrow, *Analecta, or Materials for a History of Remarkable Providences* (Maitland Club, 1842–3)

Wodrow, *Early Letters*   *Early Letters of Robert Wodrow, 1698–1709* (Scottish History Society, 1937)

Note

All dates have been printed as old style unless otherwise indicated, although the beginning of the year has been taken as 1 January instead of 25 March.

Spelling, punctuation and capitalisation in quotations have been modernised unless there seemed to be particularly good reasons for leaving them exactly as they appear in the original.

FOREWORD

When Anne came to the throne in 1702 the constitutional relationship between England and Scotland was that which had existed—the interregnum apart—from the accession of James VI of Scotland to the English throne as James I. Constitutionally the kingdoms were independent of each other, the sovereign of each country happening merely to be the same person. England and Scotland had little else in common. They differed in religion, in law, government, economic development and in social structure. It was only up to a point that they shared the same language. Between the two peoples, at most levels of society, there was a cordial dislike and occasionally open hostility. To each the other kingdom was the ancient enemy. The campaigns of the middle ages and the sixteenth century together with the long-established tradition of border warfare had created a firm strand in both English and lowland Scottish folklore. Within living memory Scottish troops had fought on English soil and English armies had occupied Scotland, forcing it into temporary union with England and Ireland. Scots and Englishmen had each tried to modify the religious establishment of the neighbouring kingdom.

By the beginning of Anne's reign there had been changes. Scottish nobles and gentry were adopting the more affluent English style of life. Increasingly they were prepared to face the discomforts, even perils, of the Great North Road to visit the English court for political or social advantage. They were well known at posting inns in Stamford, Ferrybridge and York. Scottish regiments had fought the French in William's war and were to do so again under Marlborough. In London there existed a thriving, though socially aloof, community of expatriate Scottish merchants. Yet the lack of amity between the two peoples had not noticeably decreased. The Scots looked on the English as selfish and arrogant, an impression which English attitudes did much to reinforce. Harley took an habitually unflattering view of the Scots as a people, despite his family alliance with the earl of Kinnoull. Nor did he attempt to conceal it. In 1703 he referred, in a revealing phrase, to Scotland's 'lame arm to beg by'. But then, English ministers saw the Scottish nobility and gentry at their importunate worst and Harley as secretary and then lord treasurer saw more than most. In persuading the queen in 1712 to create twelve new peers to lessen court dependence on the Scots he expressed himself irritably to Dartmouth on the Scottish nobles' expectation of being paid for every vote. Harley's opinion of the Scots was a not uncommon one. Swift had dinner with lord Dupplin and others. He reported to Stella: 'We were treated by one colonel Cleland, who has a mind to be governor of Barbados and is laying these long traps for me and others to engage our interests for him. He is a true Scotchman . . .' The fact was that Scottish nobles and gentry in England were frequently living beyond their means, in some instances well beyond, so their solicitations tended to be rather blatant and marked with an urgency that excited attention even amongst their English contemporaries who were by no means diffident about asking for favours. In the country at large popular acquaintance with the Scots was by way of the ubiquitous pedlars, suspect as strangers and, on account of their scanty stock coupled with tenacious sales technique, arousing a near-contemptuous dislike. When sergeant Kite listed to captain Plume his five new recruits they were 'the strong man of Kent, the king of the gypsies, a Scotch pedlar, a scoundrel attorney and a Welsh parson', all characters of some stature in the folklore of the time.

By the time of Anne's death the constitutional position had been drastically changed by the treaty of union of 1707 on which the present United Kingdom rests. Theoretically each of the kingdoms of England and Scotland lost its separate existence and its own parliament. Both were merged into one kingdom of Great Britain, with one parliament at Westminster. That was not how it appeared at the time. It seemed to many that Scotland sacrificed her independence by giving up her own parliament and accepting some representation in that of England, a view more realistic than the legal one. Whatever it was that created better relations between the English and the Scots—shared experience, industrial revolution, empire, Sir Walter Scott and all his works—it was certainly not the treaty of union. By the end of the eighteenth century the general attitudes of the two peoples towards each other were changed scarcely, if at all.

So, then, an obvious question arises: how did there come to be a union in the first place? It is noteworthy that the question did not assume any great importance for historians until the union seemed to

be a going concern, during the last century and earlier in this, by which
time Sir Pertinax Macsycophant had been replaced as the fictional
stereotype of the Scot by Mac, the dour, dependable Scottish chief
engineer. Union could then be looked upon as a perfectly natural
evolutionary development. Its apparent success seemed to rule out
other possibilities, so that most have assumed the creation of the United
Kingdom to have been only a matter of time. Some have postulated too
much continuity of policy, too much statesmanlike vision and too much
integrity on the part of the union's principal actors for anybody's good.
As Dr Ferguson has said of Trevelyan and Pryde, they 'regarded the
union as . . . just such an honest solution untarnished by sordid motives
as they might themselves have reached . . .' Politicians of the reigns of
William and Anne were not in fact standing upright in the shadow of
Mr Gladstone, fortified by devotion to principle. Only Harley acquired
and possibly deserved the nickname 'the trickster' but few others had
earned the right to call him that. Most of them progressed across the
political scene, furtively or brazenly, with the determination to be
nobody's fool and no aim in mind beyond securing office with
consequent profit. Transactions emerging from such an atmosphere
will not be explained by ruling straight lines of causation between two
points, talk of generosity healing old wounds, or by an excess of charity
at the expense of accuracy. The union was made by men of limited
vision for very short-term and comparatively petty, if not squalid, aims.
In intention it had little to do with the needs of England and even less
with those of Scotland, but a great deal to do with private political
ambitions. A very few of the union's creators were pragmatic men who,
despairing of the existing relationship within the union of crowns, acted
for want of better and fear of worse. If it seems that this book squats too
lengthily by their cold hearths picking over decayed and crumbling
gossip or gnawed and calcified ambitions it is justified in that there is
no other way of approaching the spirit in which the union was made.
Cynicism and cackling malice are better guides than reverence to the
politics of that, or perhaps of any other, time. Scrutiny of the
contradictory aims of both Englishmen and Scots in the period before
1707, the motives which prompted them and the outcome of their
efforts, so frequently at variance with their intention, leads only to the
conclusion that for those who took part the union of the kingdoms was
no more than a solution to very limited, even parochial, difficulties.
And even so it was a largely fortuitous occurrence. The chapters which
follow will lend some support to this assertion.

CHAPTER ONE
The idea of union

A crowd of people was at the palace of St James's on 23 July 1706 when copies of the proposed treaty of union were presented to the queen. Those commissioners who had taken part in the negotiations attended, together with the usual assemblage of courtiers. Two copies of the treaty, one for each of the kingdoms, were separately presented by Cowper, the lord keeper of England, and Seafield, the lord chancellor of Scotland. Seafield, seldom if ever at a loss for words, made his presentation with a speech delivered fluently and without notes. Cowper embarrassed everyone but himself by trying to recite his speech from memory. He 'miserably mangled it' and finally, pulling a script from his pocket, he read it 'with great composure of mind'.[1] The queen made a gracious reply.

Obstacles, and large ones, had still to be surmounted. As yet the treaty had been ratified by neither of the parliaments but, for the moment, the fact that the commissioners had reached agreement seemed in itself a success.

Subsequently the two parliaments were to accept the treaty with some few amendments and a great deal of noise signifying little. The United Kingdom came into existence on 1 May 1707, more than a century after James VI and I had tried to turn a union of crowns into a union of kingdoms and failed. Why had the politicians of Anne's reign been more successful? Why, for that matter, had they wanted a union at all?

When the commissioners had first met to begin negotiations on 16 April 1706 there had been the usual exchange of formal speeches and compliments. Seafield, for the Scots, told the English commissioners: ' . . . We are convinced that a union will be of great advantage to both . . . and we are the more encouraged to expect success in this treaty by the good disposition appeared in the parliament of Scotland for it and by the friendly proceedings in the last session of the parliament of England which gave general satisfaction . . .'[2]

But Seafield was telling rather more than the truth. The 'good disposition' said to have appeared in the Scottish parliament of 1705 had been far from unanimous even amongst those who voted for the treaty project; the 'friendly proceedings' in the English parliament owed more to the tactical needs of domestic politics than benevolence towards the Scots. Seafield, however, was not on oath and was doing no more than make concessions to a sense of the momentous and a feeling for what was proper. Others used similar language. Those who spoke or wrote in this way about the union of 1707 were not necessarily hypocrites because they shared in what has been described, justifiably, as 'probably the greatest "political job" of the eighteenth century'.[3] Of course they might have been. Some of them undoubtedly were. Others had been caught up genuinely in an atmosphere of co-operation—a delusive condition with a brief past and no future.

This residual evidence of cordiality is in part responsible for the myths surrounding union. There have been other causes. Contemporaries imposed their own spurious pattern on events. Politicians, as always, disseminated high-minded justifications of what they did, claimed credit for a foresight they did not possess and seemed ultimately to swallow their own propaganda. The results deserve close scrutiny, submerged structures of apparent significance being frequently no more than shadows in green water. Human incompetence, deceit and a whole procession of plans gone awry are not easily reduced to geometricalities. There were aspects of the union which neither Seafield nor anyone else would have dared to mention publicly in 1706. What was the almost unavowable for contemporaries became for later commentators the disregarded; yet it is closer to the reality of the union than any idea of a bargain between the kingdoms for the benefit of both.

1   Earlier union projects

On the surface the entire episode of the Anglo-Scottish union would seem to lend itself to clear-cut explanations: the 'manifest destiny' view that a union of the whole island was inevitable,[4] the idea that a steady process of cultural assimilation had political union as its natural outcome, or even that union was 'a political necessity for England and a commercial necessity for Scotland'.[5] Such interpretations carry little conviction, despite strong support from august quarters. James VI and I, addressing the English parliament, pronounced that union with Scotland was a blessing ' . . . which God hath in my person bestowed upon you . . . Hath he not made us all in one island, compassed with one sea and of itself by nature indivisible? . . . And now in the end and fullness of time united in my person, alike lineally descended of both crowns.'[6]

Nevertheless, although this view was much expounded at the time and, with rather less excuse, has been implied since, there is no natural law which decrees that only one political system should exist within what seems a geographical unity. Nor does cultural assimilation of itself lead necessarily to political fusion.

The most powerful incentives to the union of England and Scotland have always been political: security and ease of government, considerations present throughout the whole catalogue of union projects. Any ruler who thought he was strong enough tried to impose unity on the island. Such designs had their origin in the need for military security or cravings for dynastic aggrandisement and invariably the policy was foisted on the nations from the top. There was no growth of fraternal sentiment at the roots. The distribution of forces dictated that union schemes were planned mostly in the south, from Agricola, through Edward I and the Tudors, to Cromwell. The sixteenth century saw English rulers persistently striving towards union. To the Tudors the sealing off of Scotland from French influence was a vital objective of English policy which union seemed the best way of achieving. And such a union would have put an end to the continual distraction of border warfare.[7] Both Henry VIII and Protector Somerset made strenuous attempts to achieve union through conquest, disguising their motives—inadequately, as it proved—by diplomacy and propaganda.[8] The extent of their failure led Elizabeth and her ministers to abandon the strategy of frontal attack; their objective remained, nonetheless, unchanged.[9]

Waiting for a union of crowns as a consequence of James IV's marriage to Margaret Tudor was not a policy to commend itself to the impatient but it was the only realistic one. Such a union was always a more likely outcome than conquest. For most of the sixteenth century the crowns were never separated by more than one life and at the time that was only a fragile barrier.[10] The crowns were joined eventually in 1603 by the accession to the English throne of James VI of Scotland.

Since one person then ruled on both sides of the border this event in
some ways simplified the relations between England and Scotland. The
kingdoms had one foreign policy. Border fighting sharply declined and
consequently there was a dramatic increase in the prosperity of the
border counties.[11] James, though, was far from content with this
limited prospect.

An obvious policy for any monarch was to consolidate and centralise
in the interests of power and efficiency, a process commonplace at the
time throughout Europe.[12] But James was concerned with more than
practicalities. He was a man vouchsafed a glimpse of the awesome
potential which lay in the title 'king of Great Britain', its owner mighty
in stature amongst the rulers of Europe and God's chosen instrument
for healing the breach between catholic and protestant.[13]

There were foundations on which to build. Although the island
comprised more than one kingdom the term 'Great Britain' was
already respectable usage.[14] By the beginning of the seventeenth
century English culture had begun to infect Scotland's ruling order and
clerical classes.[15] James now contemplated for this suppositious entity
not only one king but one kingdom, one law and one religion, so he
induced both England and Scotland to begin negotiations to this end. It
soon became clear that many were actively opposed to the project
whilst the rest lacked enthusiasm. The negotiations, not surprisingly,
failed. English merchants professed to fear Scottish commercial rivalry
and shied away from the Scottish pedlar as from a virulent strain of
plague. At the beginning of the seventeenth century such alarm, if
honestly felt, was ludicrous. Courtiers were already uneasy at the
behaviour of some of James's Scottish followers and claimed to live in
dread of being overwhelmed by a swarm of hungry Scots moving south
to devour their fees and salaries. After such trepidation it was an anti-
climax to discover that the Scots lacked any desire for a closer union
with England. They were jealous of the visible signs of their
independence: religion, the 'fundamental laws, ancient privileges,
offices, rights, dignities and liberties of the kingdom'. English
commercial competition threatened to ruin Scotland. Nobody seemed
able to conceive of any benefit to the island as a whole save that of
removing the debilitating effects of internal strife. James's subjects were
manifestly out of sympathy with his ambitions and he had to resign
himself to the mere possession of both crowns.[16]

But if the union of crowns removed some threats to security it also
produced substantial complications. In 1603 there was created a

system of three kingdoms—England, Ireland and Scotland—within which the political forces were finely balanced. For such a structure to function effectively there had to exist one dominant power, either through the crown's imposing its will on all kingdoms alike or through the primacy of a particular kingdom. One or the other was necessary, since the structure's equilibrium was capable of being upset with surprising ease. The cruder manifestations of this are notorious: the strength added to Charles I's position by Wentworth's rule in Ireland, the advantage the English opposition gained from the Scottish rising against Charles in the bishops' wars, the embarrassment caused to the commonwealth government by Scotland's acceptance of Charles II as king. For the elimination of such tensions the logical remedy was complete union.[17] Once only in the seventeenth century was it applied: in the military emergency of the early 1650s, when it resulted from the Cromwellian conquest of both Scotland and Ireland and the incorporation of the three kingdoms into a united political system with one parliament. However, the political structure of the protectorate, despite its military capacity, was not sufficiently stable for union to be fully exploited. It was furthermore too short-lived. But administratively it was tidy and within that limited context offered sufficient advantage to make its passing in 1660 a cause of regret to some who realised the problems of governing the kingdoms separately. Clarendon wrote of the dismantling of the Cromwellian union: 'It might be well to question whether the generality of the [Scottish] nation were not better contented with it than to return into the old road of subjection [to their nobles]. But the king would not build according to Cromwell's models.'[18] As the century progressed more was to be heard of the power of the Scottish nobility.

A notable part in persuading Charles II to revoke the Cromwellian union was played by Lauderdale, soon to be managing Scotland for the king. Ironically it was he who, to serve the crown's political ends in England and at the same time advance his own influence, seems to have promoted the next scheme of union. A corps of disciplined Scottish members was to be introduced into Westminster and their voting strength unleashed on the English country opposition. Since such intentions could hardly be made public, a complicated subterfuge was resorted to. Resentment against the English navigation acts and at the trade recession caused by the Dutch war of 1664 allowed advantages for Scottish trade to be put forward as the motive. But English politics were concerned at least as much with rivalries at court as with contests between crown and opposition. Lauderdale's rivals had no wish to see his influence at court advanced by whatever method. Charles II, willing enough to be made a powerful monarch as long as he personally was not too much put about, had no fancy for stirring up unnecessary trouble, and so the 'grand design' of union was allowed to collapse.[19]

2 *Impetus towards union*

Such projects did, however, lay down, amongst those with first-hand experience of Anglo-Scottish problems, a very thin substratum of opinion in favour of union. The executive in England became increasingly convinced, especially after 1688, of the need for union to reinforce the court's position at Westminster. The approach of the English ministers was more circumspect than Lauderdale's but their faith in the ultimate objective was strengthened by the knowledge that after the revolution of 1688 Scotland had become ungovernable. The achievement of union was thus one of the aims borne in mind by the English court, and that entirely for political reasons. Furthermore, some Scottish officers of state were gradually coming to be of the same mind as the English.

But to say this is not to draw a firm line of causation between the court's realising the necessity of union and the eventual negotiation of the treaty. An absolute crown would have proceeded on the grounds of administrative and political logic to unite the kingdoms. The crowns of England and Scotland were not absolute but depended on the strength and inclinations of English and Scottish ministers. The English had no knowledge of, and little time for, Scotland save when the Scots made themselves a nuisance. Even then they preferred to keep Scotland quiet by hand-to-mouth expedients. Their resolution wilted at the difficulties more radical measures would create. Some would take up the union idea in the hope of making their own political task easier, or to increase their own power. Far more thought they stood to lose: their places, their influence, or they feared being outmanoeuvred and doomed to see their rivals established in power for the foreseeable future. Only when public need coincided with private advantage, which was rarely, did the union policy make progress. So such schemes were always blocked in one or other kingdom by those who preferred to take their chance in the jungle of Anglo-Scottish politics.

Yet this jungle—it was nothing less—for those who had any permanent responsibility for governing the two kingdoms with as little friction as possible became the most important argument in favour of union. Some Scots might pride themselves on their legal independence. Amongst the more realistic, though, it was taken for granted that considerations of security would not allow England to stand by and see the dynastic connection severed, not even when the death in 1700 of Anne's sole surviving child provided a legal opportunity for eventual separation. Indeed, the very fact that the English would resist Scottish independence injected an important element into the situation and gave some Scots an impetus towards union; the state of the Scottish economy and the views of the Scottish people were alike irrelevant. Certainly there were economic circumstances to justify union as a possible means of increasing trade—there was no certainty about it—but they had little to do with the union policy. Hindsight clearly shows that Scotland was caught in a serious economic crisis more likely to worsen than not. Some Scottish merchants were the victims of the economic nationalism developing in Europe and the consequent high tariff barriers which injured Scotland as a primary producing country with little bargaining power. The merchants had suffered damage from the French wars. The nation at large had lived through the famine years of William's reign. All these experiences gave cause for concern but it is too much to expect that Scotsmen knew the reasons for the wider and more serious crisis. Rival propagandists at the union were not in agreement even on matters of fact, far less over causes and remedies. Some denied the existence of any crisis at all. Any discernible economic weakness could always be put down to a temporary recession. Even had the reasons been diagnosed for what was at the time no more than an alleged economic decline, it is difficult to see how those merchants whose trade was supposedly harmful to the nation would, or even could, take remedial action. It is no easier to understand, given the nature of Scottish politics, why any cause of economic recession, however objectively established, should predispose a Scottish parliament to support union. Up to a point the parliament could handle conflicts of internal economic interest. Members were prepared to legislate against the importation of Irish foodstuffs. They had taken action in wrangles between wool growers and cloth manufacturers. But any topic which involved the court as a political interest and made allegiance or opposition to it an issue at once banished practical judgement in favour of factional loyalty. Union was such an issue, and since the final initiative for it came from England, its success being due to the English political situation, the ultimate motivation for union was entirely political. The Scottish court party would, if suitably gratified, undertake almost anything the English ministry demanded. Trade was hardly more than a propaganda argument for embracing or opposing a union designed for quite other reasons.

The union of 1707 arose from a crisis of security for England. It was a crisis produced by far more than uncertainty over the Scottish succession after the death of the duke of Gloucester. What was at stake, and would continue to be so whether the issue of succession were resolved or not, was the governability of Scotland. Developments since the revolution had shown that some Scottish problems—those of managing the kingdoms in harness, of containing the rivalry of the great nobles and of cushioning the antagonism between presbyterians and episcopalians—could be solved only by merging both kingdoms within one unit of government. Scotland had been ungovernable for much of the time since 1688. Its administration had for long periods been in a state of paralysis. By the end of William's reign the government had reached an *impasse* as the king's management of Scotland was seen to be on the point of collapse. This, together with political problems at Westminster which set a beleaguered English court musing on Scottish relief columns, led William to recommend union to parliament. Union was virtually the king's last resort. All other methods of governing Scotland had failed.

3   *Effects of the revolution*

The revolutionary settlement of 1689 and 1690 had contributed to this breakdown. The abolition of the standing committee of the 'articles' had reduced the influence of the court, greatly affecting the conduct and tractability of the Scottish parliament. Instead of a nominated committee preparing all business, parliament each session elected a number of *ad hoc* committees which were not as easily controlled. The range of parliamentary resources must have been affected too by the events of 1689 and 1690, when the activities of the 'club' had demonstrated the power of a concerted and determined opposition.[20] Sometime members of the 'club', most having long since turned courtiers, were active in politics till well after the union. All of them remembered, to whatever purpose, the lesson of those years.

Even so, the infirmity of human nature made possible the management of parliaments. The Scottish parliament was no exception. Certain conditions, though, were prerequisite. There had to be a united Scottish ministry acting with the full support of the English administration. The voice from England had to speak loudly, firmly, without discord and it had to be dominant in the English parliament. These conditions for the most part were lacking until 1706.

The significance of English affairs was shown by the political importance of the Scottish religious settlement of 1690. A presbyterian system had been imposed which left the church in the hands of sixty or so ministers dedicated to the principles of dogmatic presbyterianism—this in spite of the breadth of the religious spectrum in Scotland even when the catholics had been discounted. William, the English court and the convocation of Canterbury gave some encouragement to Scottish episcopalians, showing an inclination to insist on their being tolerated to at least the degree extended to English presbyterians. But in Scotland, in 1690, political considerations were decisive. The court had to accept a stringent presbyterian settlement. Zealots, filled with exaltation at the prospect of doing the Lord's work, were then able, despite William's disapproval, to purge the church by devious and underhand means.

Although the Scottish bishops had rejected William's overtures at his accession[21] there seemed no essential reason why either conform clergy or episcopalians should have been enemies of the new government. A majority, in the genuine belief that church government was neither here nor there, would, given the chance, have conformed just as easily to the new revolutionary establishment as they had to the previous one, but for the most part they were denied it. Many, if not already jacobites, soon became so, driven, they claimed, by the discriminatory style and the sweeping purges of the new church establishment. However, political manipulation was at least as much to blame. Successive waves of political opposition to the court made use of the episcopalians and their problems without caring much about either. Their reasons were tactical. Scottish politicians scrambling for office had no hope of success if they confined their efforts to Scotland, ministries being overturned not in Edinburgh but at the English court. So political malcontents were overwhelmingly tempted to pose as champions of fair play for Scottish dissenters to ingratiate themselves with the English tories who felt strongly about the plight of Scottish episcopalians. In face of this, Scottish courtiers invariably found themselves at a disadvantage. Such religious views as the Scottish ministry privately cherished had to be subordinated to the fact of the legal establishment whatever courtiers managed to do, unofficially or even secretly, to mitigate the lot of the episcopalian and conform clergy.[22] Consequently the usual routine of opposition was to approach the English tory ministers to stigmatise the Scottish court as 'presbyterian bigots' and 'hot men' alienating the loyalty of the episcopalians.

So a recurrent pattern developed. Officers of state were 'hot men' and persecutors, whilst the opposition stood for tolerance. Once the opposition had clawed a way into office it was their turn to be labelled 'bigots' by the excluded. The first marquess of Tweeddale had embraced and renounced many causes during his career but early in William's reign, from the political wilderness, he was a defender of the episcopalians; later, as lord chancellor, he was a 'hot man'. The second duke of Queensberry's career followed a similar course although for short periods, greatly to the envy of his rivals, he succeeded in combining both roles. George, lord Melville, followed the process in reverse. Having, as lord high commissioner to the Scottish parliament in 1690, passed the act setting up the presbyterian church establishment,[23] he qualified as a 'bigot' and was attacked as such. Once displaced and in opposition he was found, albeit rather self-consciously, amongst the 'episcopalians'. None of this deceived any Scottish politician for a moment. To them it was all part of a game whose rules they well understood. The only people to be misled were those Scottish episcopalian clergy who needlessly drifted into jacobitism and those tory leaders at Westminster who thought they had allies in Scotland amongst those 'of the Church of England persuasion' as the episcopalians were said to be.[24] There was in fact no hope of toleration for episcopalians within a separate Scottish kingdom, since they seemed to pose too great a threat to both political and religious establishments. They could be accommodated only within a full union. But in the meantime, as a consequence of this tactic, the English tories incorporated Scotland into their own schemes and aimed at a political victory there for those they deluded themselves into thinking were 'Scottish tories'. This objective, founded as it was upon a massive misapprehension, could do nothing but increase the tensions already inherent in Anglo-Scottish relations.

Like others in England the tories were to discover painfully that the most important consideration for the generality of Scottish politicians was personal advantage in official salary, perquisites and influence. For this they would embark on one policy or another, sometimes with a prospect of success, more often with none at all; as long as they could attain power, gain credit for any achievement and lodge the blame for failure with their opponents they felt they had acquitted themselves well. The same objectives justified the sabotage of whatever policies might be in train, irrespective of their merit. Inaccurate information was fed back to the English court. Lying and misrepresentation were tactics used frequently and blatantly; forgery to discredit rivals was by no means unknown. Reputations for corruption were easily and deservedly acquired but little opprobrium was attached to them. One of Queensberry's advisers in 1698 thought a corrupt president of session preferable to one with a dominant personality.[25] Baronial power struggles continued in Scotland stark and undisguised long after they had been given, in England, a more respectable veneer. Later, during the pamphlet war at the union, the earl of Cromartie advanced the argument that union would put a stop to such dishonesty and political malpractice.[26] He was in a position to know about such tactics, having himself been a skilled practitioner in that field.

4   Scottish magnate interests

Full, and even extravagant, use of such dubious methods was made by the Scottish magnates, the 'nobility of the first rank', leaders of the powerful interest groups in Scottish politics. After the revolution, when the parliamentary grandees had been thinned by popery and jacobitism, there were really four such interest groups which counted and which it was unwise to neglect. There were the Douglases, who looked at this time to the dukes of Queensberry, the Hamilton family interest represented by Anne, duchess in her own right, but led in parliament by her husband and, later, her son, the Murrays under the marquess and then dukes of Atholl and the Campbells under their chieftains, the earl and subsequently dukes of Argyll. Their followings were not wholly family groups but widespread political connections, each magnate having his sphere of territorial influence which could override family ties. Anne, duchess of Hamilton, had married into the Douglas family so that her husband, the third duke, and her son, the fourth, were related to the dukes of Queensberry, their political rivals. The first duke of Atholl and the fourth duke of Hamilton were jealous competitors and also brothers-in-law. Thus where noble families were powerful enough to be a threat to each other, or even if they maintained a traditional enmity, family ties counted for no more than they did amongst sovereign princes. Lesser noble families who represented no challenge to the magnates could be accepted as part of the interest and were often enough content to remain in near dependence as did the lords Bargany on the house of Hamilton or Mar, Wemyss and Northesk on Queensberry. Nevertheless the family element was strong. A mere name could render its owner suspect to a rival group. Sir James Murray of Philiphaugh was a firm Queensberry man, one of the second duke's most trusted henchmen, but special undertakings were required of him that he had shed all partiality for Atholl.[27]

These magnate interests were even more than products of family loyalty or territorial dependence and even more than parliamentary followings. They were business propositions for the magnates, career structures for politicians and lawyers, associations for personal advancement and, not least, protection agencies. Profit featured very prominently in their calculations. For many of the nobility and gentry the most vital economic interest was the financial by-product of politics. Gains from industrial and commercial enterprise seemed inadequate without the rewards of office, the contracts obtained through court influence and the advantages in litigation which sprang from attachment to the dominant group. Magnate wealth was not founded on coal, salt or black cattle. The Queensberry fortune did not emerge from land and sheep but from the proceeds of major office-holding by the first and second dukes successively, both avaricious men. There were other peers who needed the money. Government service was the salvation of the Findlater estate, redeemed only by Seafield's success as a court manager. Mar and Wemyss had industrial and commercial interests but were initially driven into politics by heavy mortgages.[28] Deprivation of favour could be ruinous. In William's reign Breadalbane had been unable to visit Edinburgh on the king's business without an official protection against arrest for debt,[29] whilst the penury of the earls of Home bordered on the desperate.[30] The fourth duke of Hamilton, who had not held office at all, and Atholl, who had spent only short periods in the court, were both heavily in debt. It is true that Hamilton did not have the family estate at his disposal during his mother's lifetime and that she outlived him. On the other hand, had he come into the inheritance there is a strong probability that he would soon have been even more in debt than he was accustomed to be. At one time or another all these peers focused their hopes on court favour and office.

Although nobody remained untouched by hope of profit there was, it must be said, more to politics than that. What of the opposition magnates, countrymen and jacobites, who had to resign themselves to spending much, if not all, of their time in a political empty quarter? They were certainly not courting debt for its own sake. Even the jacobites, although they had their sticking point, were prepared to snatch at official salaries given the chance. Opposition was, of course, aimed at demonstrating a nuisance value that it was worth the court's while to neutralise, but there were other motives. In part it originated in sheer resentment which circumstances often transformed into the chief cause of protest. Then the opposition settled down implacably to a campaign of harassment for its own sake.

So the profits of office, although coveted and whenever possible seized, were only a part of the *raison d'être* of the magnate interests. The different aspects were nevertheless linked. Political influence brought profit but as part of a circular process. Wealth made possible the establishment of an interest. The magnates aspirant of William's reign—Melville, for example—feathered their nests and were glad of the money but they had also been attempting to establish new monopolies of political power. The pursuit of money and the pursuit of power were inseparable but each existed as a motive in its own right. When, in the reorganisation after the union, Mar lost his job as secretary of state, he was compensated by a generous pension for the duration of the queen's life, but his loss of political influence led to withdrawal symptoms and he was soon intriguing for a return to office.[31] There were many such 'busy' men, nature's insiders, who were unhappy away from the centre of affairs. The drive towards political power and prestige as ends in themselves was demonstrated frequently by the Scottish magnates in their personal vendettas. Political prestige counted for at least as much as profit and in the last resort it could be decisive. A magnate preferred to tower in opposition rather than be a mere partner in the administration. At least from the outside a magnate could indulge to the full his urge to harass his rivals and feel the exhilaration of being cheered by the Edinburgh crowd.

Reinforcing the starkness of this choice—that between a monopoly of power and recourse to opposition—was the system of clientage. Those who wished to get on, or at the least keep out of trouble, found themselves incorporated, sometimes willy nilly, into one or other of these networks of dependence. The allegiance of some was dictated by family or territorial relationship. The dukes of Argyll and Atholl, clan chieftains, their position reinforced by the hereditary jurisdiction which made them not only landlords but virtually chief constables and judges, were intolerant of political deviation amongst their rank and file. The influence of Hamilton and Montrose began with land and family. In time the Hamilton interest was swollen by the discontented who wanted a magnate as leader whilst Montrose benefited temporarily because he seemed a natural focus for those who disliked the second duke of Argyll. Other, occasionally more dedicated, support came from young men anxious to get on. Entering on a public career necessitated enlistment under one or another set of colours. Seafield, as plain Mr James Ogilvy, attached himself naturally to his relative the third duke of Hamilton under whose protection he made his first steps—to a knighthood and the post of solicitor-general.[32] For obvious reasons the Queensberry interest attracted more followers of this kind than did others. The second duke of Queensberry's interest was based partly on family connections—he was particularly incensed when his relative Morton let him down in 1704—but became more of a voluntary association than the rest. The long period of influence enjoyed by himself and his father led young lawyers hoping for advancement and nobles seeking an allowance to attach themselves willingly to the duke in the belief that they were investing in a certainty. Queensberry made use of his place at court to expand his following. He sought out potential dependants for encouragement: Murray of Philiphaugh, Clerk of Penicuik, Boyle of Kelburn and of the nobles, Mar, Wemyss and Northesk. It was understood that such connections were to be personal, allegiance being owed to the duke rather than to the court. Stair, after the Glencoe enquiry had damaged his reputation, chose to attach his family to Queensberry. He himself became the duke's guide and counsellor. The whole Dalrymple family benefited because, for the time being, Stair had invested his political interest wisely. Inevitably some of the weaker brethren, together with some of the more shrewd, tried to hedge their bets. Strained relations between Queensberry and the court, as in 1704, led to some panic and frenzies of calculation.

Members of an interest looked to their leader for services and protection. In a kingdom where the judiciary was greatly influenced by political considerations the latter was especially important. A lone traveller could be set upon by thieves masquerading as the judiciary, stripped and robbed, all through due process of law. Such was very nearly the experience of the first marquess of Tweeddale under both Charles II and James. Driven to law with what he thought was a cast iron case, he was the victim of a judicial sharing out by the president of the court of session and members of the privy council.[33] But ministries were sensitive to allegations of unfair treatment if the charge was made by somebody whose voice in parliament was loud enough to make an impression. So, whether court or opposition, it was better to proceed in convoy. Everyone who could think of nothing better, and few could, had a vested interest in staying loyal to one group. Even Seafield, when pursuing his policy of remaining independent of the magnates, felt at times very exposed.

Peers of the calibre of Queensberry or Hamilton were even more than 'nobility of the first rank'. They were symbols of group solidarity. A magnate's following had invested in him a large amount of capital in time, energy and loyalty. Each was a figurehead without whom an entire clientage structure would collapse to the detriment of all its members. If it was at all avoidable this could not be allowed to happen. Clients did all they could to prop up their leader's prestige, as Queensberry's in 1704–5 and Hamilton's after his behaviour had damaged his credit seemingly beyond repair.

Collaboration between these grandees for any length of time was impossible. The second duke of Queensberry and the first duke of Argyll worked together longer than most, a collaboration which owed something to a certain naivety on Argyll's part. Even this period of restraint was not without jealousy or incident. Men of their social calibre and political pretensions were not at all interested in co-operation save on their own terms. Their ultimate objective was a monopoly of the apparatus of patronage and administration. For Queensberry the attainment of this objective appeared to be almost a psychological necessity, but this quirk did not create the problem. It merely intensified it. Magnates entertained no scruples over disrupting government for their own ends. Loyalty to their family interest and their own self-advancement were their primary concerns. They squabbled over places and precedence. They kept up a continual rumbling of resentment at fancied slights. Everything else—the interest of the crown, efficiency of management, Anglo-Scottish security and the well-being of Scotland—took second place. The misfortune was that no interest was powerful enough to dominate Scotland unaided yet each was sufficiently strong to cause some disruption. Given favourable conditions—a Scottish 'country' grievance and a dissident English group at Westminster strong enough to provide hope and encouragement—the disruption could be massive. In fact the Scottish magnates could neither rule the country themselves nor would they allow anyone else to do so. Scotland was not large enough to contain family rivalry on this scale.

5   *Scottish management under William*

By the end of his reign William had had his fill of their competing ambitions. Ever since the revolution he had adopted various devices to harness the magnates in the service of stable government. His lack of success had been almost total. He had even brought to the surface other dangers which magnate dominance had tended to obscure.[34] At his death the Scottish court party had been brought to a state in which it was unable to fulfil its task of dominating parliament.

Immediately after the revolution William, from necessity rather than choice, tried to make use of the third duke of Hamilton as an instrument of Scottish government. At the time Hamilton was too powerful to be ignored. But the King regretted this venture, as most people regretted their dealings with Hamilton. Whatever the duke's underlying personal qualities, and there was no general agreement over these, nobody claimed he was an easy man to work with. He could produce an amalgam of equivocation, obscurity of intent and strident self-assertion that was notoriously difficult to combat.[35] His employment was in itself a guarantee that his clamour for favours would be incessant and that all the other magnates would be in opposition. By 1690 William felt well rid of him.

The king's next attempted solution to the problems of Scottish management was to speak encouragingly to the magnates whilst employing lesser men who might reasonably be expected to be modest in their demands and grateful for what they received: second-rank nobility and lawyers of varied status and intensity of ambition. But these 'motley ministries' left the court extremely vulnerable and were no less productive of internal strife than magnate government. Some lesser families were blatantly on the make and strove for a foothold quite as tenaciously as the magnates fought to maintain their power. In the process they could be equally disruptive of stable rule. Had Scotland remained a separate monarchy a different attitude to government might have emerged during the seventeenth century. Magnates and others might conceivably have become imbued with some sense of responsibility for the well-being of the kingdom. But real power lay elsewhere, in England. Office represented profit and patronage, not responsibility. Government was there only to be exploited. The magnates had enough power to exploit it and others tried to acquire the same capacity. Melville had seemed unassuming enough when appointed secretary of state after the revolution but he had a rapacious family to provide for. He set out to establish a monopoly of the machinery of government, make a fortune and join the ranks of the magnates.[36]

Ambition on this scale brought him into conflict with the ever-vigilant Dalrymples, 'a family that will swim with everybody but not hazard sinking with any' as they were later characterised.[37] Their rivalry paralysed the ministry. The Dalrymples' later contest, between 1692 and 1696, with Tweeddale as lord chancellor and James 'Secretary' Johnston had the same effect. Annandale, too, proved a constant irritant to all administrations, his ambitions outstripping his power and ability. His aspirations to a dukedom, the lord chancellorship and control of the treasury were a great burden to him and to everybody else. In all directions his advance was always blocked, which left him full of jealousy and a great inclination to rock whatever boat he happened to be in at the time. And, throughout this period, the magnates loomed constantly in the background, allied, whatever minor favours they had received, with the opposition to the ministry. As long as they were excluded from political power their intention was to render intolerable the lives of the Scottish courtiers.

By 1696 it was plain that any arrangement which denied the magnates the lion's share of influence was quite unworkable. The time appeared to have come for this to be acknowledged. The task of absorbing them into the court and giving them a major role in government seemed to have been made deceptively smoother by the changes amongst the great nobility since the revolution. Hamilton had died in 1694, leaving as his successor his son, the earl of Arran. Argyll had pronounced himself to be dedicated henceforth to business. Whilst not prepared to abandon too precipitately the notorious irregularity of his life he was ready, at least up to a point, to preserve appearances. The eldest son of the marquess of Atholl, earl of Tullibardine,[38] had taken over the political leadership of the Atholl interest whilst his father chose to stay in the background. Even more significantly, the first duke of Queensberry had died in 1695, bringing into the forefront of Scottish politics his son, formerly earl of Drumlanrig and now the second duke. It looked as though almost a new generation of magnates had emerged, co-operating for the moment whilst in opposition, serving notice that they did not intend to be ignored for much longer.

On the assumption, completely unjustified, that if a magnate alliance had functioned in opposition there was no reason to doubt its feasibility in office, William and his advisers concocted the ministry of 1696. Tullibardine, Queensberry and Argyll were employed as colleagues. Lesser men were used to preserve the balance: Marchmont as lord chancellor, Seafield as secretary of state,[39] with one or two more of similar status. It was made clear to them that they were not to tread on the magnates' toes. Marchmont was to conduct himself towards them with 'deference'.[40] Gestures were even made towards the Hamilton family. Selkirk, one of the third duke's sons, already had a post in William's household; two others were gratified: lord John was made general of the mint and lord George was created earl of Orkney.

That such a coalition was expected to survive indicates that the king was taking some dubious advice. The future was to make clear how little he understood the motivation of Scotland's higher nobility. Tullibardine set out from the first to gain control of the court. But, in trying to outmanoeuvre Argyll and Queensberry, he overreached himself and by 1698 they had driven him out of the ministry straight into opposition, an achievement which reduced the strife within the court at the cost of strengthening the malcontents. There already existed the nucleus of a 'country' opposition smarting over the dismissal two years earlier of Tweeddale, 'Secretary' Johnston and others to make room for the magnates. The Tweeddale interest had for some time been enlarged through the minorities of Roxburgh, Rothes and Haddington. The first marquess had exercised a kind of guardianship over their political interests and with it had accepted their local feuds in addition to his own. Tweeddale himself had a standing and unpleasant rivalry with Melville's family to which was added Rothes's conflict with the same interest over who should dominate Fife. Roxburgh and Douglas of Cavers were in competition for control of Roxburghshire. Both Melville and Douglas were in alliance with Queensberry and the court. Such personal considerations sharpened the edge of the opposition which, in 1698, was being led by Tweeddale's son, the second marquess. They were now joined by those leaving the court with Tullibardine. Shortly afterwards Arran, recently created fourth duke of Hamilton, after an indirect approach to Queensberry angling for a share of court influence and patronage,[41] received a dusty answer and went straight into the opposition just as it was settling down to exploit the Darien catastrophe. The collapse of a Scottish colonial venture to which the English had shown hostility provided a cause which aroused sympathy throughout Scotland. An opposition comprising the Hamilton, Atholl and Tweeddale interests, presented with such a cause as Darien, was almost too strong for the ministry. The court survived the crucial parliamentary sessions of 1700 and 1700–01 but only with the greatest difficulty and by a narrow margin. Everything indicated that the next session, due to meet in 1702, would be impossible to manage unless the ministry's approach was radically changed. It was this prospect of further humiliation which opened the king's eyes to the nature and magnitude of the Scottish political problem.

6 *Queensberry and the court*

After the departure of Tullibardine in 1698 the court party remained a coalition. With Queensberry, Argyll and the Dalrymples were the survivors—men who had managed to keep office through the various changes in the ministry. These last had little sympathy with the dominant interests. So it was first of all against these men, and then against Argyll himself, that Queensberry began to move with a view to establishing himself as the unchallengeable court leader. His success was so remarkable that Cockburn of Ormiston told Carstares in 1700: '. . . let Queensberry have the use of this government to drive his designs and purposes till it ruin; some of us cannot, nor will not, follow Queensberry . . .'[42] And, at that time, Queensberry was ostensibly allied to Argyll.

Preferment after preferment had been gained for Queensberry–Dalrymple men. Advantage had been prised even from adversity. During the Darien uproar the Queensberry group had created the myth that the duke was the mainstay of the Scottish ministry and that only he stood between the court and disaster. William seemed naively prepared to accept this claim, perhaps because it matched the erroneous appraisal of Scottish affairs current amongst his advisers. They, and therefore William, had seen Queensberry as the ideal person to overcome divisions in Scotland. Although his family's connections were episcopalian the duke himself was of impeccable revolutionary standing. He had been the first Scotsman of note to join William after his arrival in England. His alliance with Argyll seemed to indicate that he was not only willing enough to co-operate with others but acceptable to the presbyterians.

Argyll suddenly realised that during the years of their 'partnership' he had gained little but his elevation to a dukedom whilst Queensberry and the Dalrymples had made enormous gains. When, against his expressed wishes, a vacancy in the court of session was filled by Stewart of Tillicoultry, a Dalrymple man, he was at last stung into rivalry. His response was to assert himself as the leader of the presbyterian interest in the ministry making firm representations against the promotion of any whose sole loyalty was to the Queensberry interest.[43] Philiphaugh reported to Queensberry: ' . . . a letter from the earl of Argyll to my lord president which I saw the other day which is dated the 14 of this [June 1701] wherein the earl does not only insist upon his former allegiance [*sic* for 'allegation'] of your grace's breaking engagements to him but as I remember says that if your grace continued to him as formerly this had not fallen out and one thing makes the matter harder to be adjusted is that the whole scheme has been laid without him and he meets with no yielding in any point and this he must think not equal . . . nor ought any one man to put himself in balance with all the rest . . .'[44]

Partly as a consequence of this breach Queensberry began to experience a certain sluggishness on the part of the court in carrying out his recommendations. It was not that the duke was being deprived. He still had his successes. There was merely a gap between his demands and what the king was prepared to grant. For one who had earlier told Mar that his aim in seeking power was to make use of it for the good of his friends,[45] the situation now that some of them could not be gratified was frustrating[46] and could create damage, since the leader of a political interest was expected to deliver. Queensberry went into a sulk and began his usual talk of resignation and a quiet life.[47] His dependants felt a crisis to be imminent and were seriously concerned since all the support they had invested in Queensberry could be at risk were he to abandon himself to obstinacy, spite and recrimination. Urgently they advised him to concentrate for the time being on keeping what he had and not to push at once for more gains. He should tell the king with dignity that the sole object of his requests had been William's service. Meanwhile it was possible that Argyll would discredit himself if given enough rope.[48]

The dispute between the two magnates became notorious. Roderick Mackenzie, secretary of the Africa Company and a man who made it his job to know what went on, wrote: ' . . . Queensberry and Argyll [are] absolutely at odds about the disposal of vacant posts to their respective friends so that some of their promises must fail . . .'[49] That

was how the situation looked from the outside. From inside the court the quarrel took on the colour of a dispute over the management of the next parliament, due to meet in 1702, but in fact it was a struggle for predominance within the court party. Argyll was in a reasonably strong position to compete because, although his motives were no more elevated than those of Queensberry, he had a certain rationality on his side. Argyll wanted to come to terms with some of the opposition by giving the lord clerk register's place to Hamilton of Whitelaw. Queensberry wanted it for Murray of Philiphaugh. Argyll's contention was that more than ten or twelve of the opposition would change sides with Whitelaw and support the vote for a standing army.[50] As far as managing the next parliament went there was some sense in this proposal even though Argyll's real concern was more with the recruitment of prospective allies to oppose the Queensberry interest.[51]

For his part, Queensberry was in the grip of an obsessive desire to gain promotion for Philiphaugh whether or not success would sabotage the next parliament. Of far more importance to Queensberry was keeping out Whitelaw, anathema to himself and the Dalrymples. Yet for the management of the 1702 parliament Queensberry could think of nothing more constructive than nibbling round the edges of the episcopalians in opposition, attempting in the process to oblige some of his own relatives. He obtained a pension of £500 a year and a place on the privy council for the earl Marischal.[52] Carmichael, secretary of state and a man increasingly worried by Queensberry's behaviour, remarked: ' . . . the earl of Marischal's pension is dissatisfying to many here; and some are of opinion it will be to no purpose, that it will not fix him . . .'[53] There was no reason at all why Marischal's pension should have fixed him. He was a member of the jacobite opposition who in 1700 had declined to support the ministry for £300 a year and his attitude to the ministry if not to its money remained unchanged. Queensberry must have known this and disregarded it. What he had in mind was the strengthening of his own interest in the court rather than the court's interest in parliament. Queensberry's behaviour reflects no credit on him as a minister of the crown but he was unfortunate in being in a position where his defects were spotlighted. His urge to have his own way and frustrate the aims of his opponents became more marked as time went on but in this he differed only in degree from the other magnates. It had been said of the situation in 1690: 'D[uke] Hamilton was not satisfied with his interest in the government, unless he had been chancellor, and had a greater share of his friends in the public judicatures . . .'[54] Nor had Argyll any qualms about pitching his own claims very high and he could, if thwarted, attain heights of rage which rendered him foam-flecked and bloodshot for an unhealthy length of time. All were dedicated to the same cause: control of the Scottish court interest. None of them was prepared for very long to take just a share of the pickings. For Scottish magnates any talk of managing the parliament was a tactical manoeuvre and no more.

However, to William in the autumn and winter of 1701 and 1702 the problem of managing the Scottish parliament was a vital one. By that time there was no excuse for failure to sum up the situation in Scotland. In terms of sheer technical management there was something to be said for handing Scotland over to one interest large enough to keep control, but the interest would have to be either big enough to cope with this task unaided or otherwise capable of forming stable alliances with others. Queensberry's interest, in the face of opposition from Hamilton, from the Atholl interest, from Tweeddale and now from Argyll, was not strong enough to manage. What appeared to be his own plans for the next parliament did not inspire confidence. And he had amply demonstrated that he would not work with anyone save on his own terms, which would certainly be unacceptable, hence William's hesitation over giving Queensberry any further increase in influence. But to employ anyone else was pointless, since Queensberry would move immediately into opposition. Within the existing structure there was, in truth, no solution. Magnate rivalries had made Scotland ungovernable, and this had become apparent to William at a time when the death of the duke of Gloucester, Anne's last surviving child, made it necessary for the Scottish succession to be settled so that the link between the kingdoms was maintained.

7 William's conversion to union

When Scottish affairs called for decision William's usual course had been to let things slide until the last possible moment and even beyond. But now, increasingly, the truth was being forced upon him that the only escape from the Scottish predicament, and perhaps even from some of his English problems too, was through a full union of the two kingdoms. Apart from the inherent logic of this course, pressure in its favour was building up on William from two directions: from Scottish courtiers concerned with the technicalities of management and from English politicians who were already envisaging union as a possible means of recovering their former status at Westminster.

In Scotland, as elsewhere, William's preference was to employ men he regarded, although sometimes mistakenly, as a-political functionaries. His reliance on the 'nobility of the first rank' had been forced upon him rather than deliberately chosen. His own inclinations had led him to make use of such men as Sir John Dalrymple, James Johnston and Seafield. It was the last of these who had ultimately developed into the superlative example of a servant of the crown, as far as possible detached from magnate struggles. Seafield had progressed since the revolution when, as Mr James Ogilvy, he had been just another younger son with native wit, legal training and very little else. His father, the earl of Findlater, was a good-natured Scottish peer with a heap of debts and a taste for serious reading which unfitted him for coping with his financial plight. James proved to be the only hope for the family's solvency. This and his own ambition had led Seafield into some curious shifts: spokesman for James in the convention, involvement in jacobite conspiracy as a member of the 'club', solicitor-general in 1693 taking improper fees in collusion with the lord advocate[55] and Tullibardine's acolyte as joint secretary in 1696. His capacity as a manager and tactician had been revealed when he became president of the 1698 parliament and gradually, as a Scottish minister, he developed his own approach to his exercise of office. And he, like the first marquess of Tweeddale, Johnston, Marchmont and the first earl of Stair, had gradually become convinced that the only way to manage Scotland lay through full union with England.[56] It was a conviction that came, sooner or later, to everyone who had to handle Anglo-Scottish affairs. The split between Queensberry and Argyll in 1701 could only have reinforced his belief.

In England, though, most politicians were quite indifferent to the vagaries of Scottish politics. Certainly they saw no point in union. A proposal for union in 1695, introduced into the lords to quieten the uproar over the Scottish act legalising the Africa Company, received short shrift.[57] By 1699 and 1700 the position had changed. From the treaty of Ryswick William and his whig ministers had been in trouble with the commons. As the tory opposition conducted a successful campaign against the court the whigs became progressively less able to conduct business. Much to William's chagrin they had already suffered defeat over the reduction of the standing army. During their tenure of office the whigs had lost some of their solidarity. They were not altogether easy over William's conduct of foreign affairs and its possible domestic repercussions, which could further damage their position. The court was to suffer even more humiliation through the act of settlement in 1701 with the limitations it placed on the prerogative. In Scotland the Darien agitation had reached its peak and the tory opposition seemed to be trying to open another political front there, giving encouragement to the country party.[58]

Suddenly there appeared signs of a whig initiative in favour of union. Unofficial soundings were taken and individual Scotsmen were led to think that union was being favourably considered.[59] Union, of course, would have solved the succession problem but it did not escape notice that revival of the project also coincided with ministerial difficulties in the commons. The whigs were outnumbered there and the position was being further eroded by an opposition campaign to purge the house of revenue officials. Very probably Jack Howe summed up the court and whig motives correctly when he said they wished '. . . to bring in 30 or 40 Scotsmen into the house to supply the places of so many revenue officers that were to be dismust [sic]'.[60] It is possible, too, that a union proposal was to be an additional line of defence should the tories take up the cause of Caledonia to embarrass the court. Without question the plan was sabotaged by the tory peers in spite of the whig majority in the lords on which the court had banked to give it a better chance of success. The court was disappointed. 'The king,' Argyll told Annandale, 'did intend to move an union by some of his managers and signified so much to his cabinet council. This took wind and earl Peterborough having notice of it was resolved to prevent the court, and [it] is thought to ruin the success of the project, though on other occasions he professes a regard to the Scots nation, did bring it into the house, by introducing the book writ, the title whereof carries a good aspect[61] but withall has many things in it to be condemned and carrying, as they say, a brag to the English nation, and he reading those places concluded with an overture of an union, which indeed has, I fear, disappointed it . . .'[62]

Peterborough received some mixed verbal support: from tories such as Normanby who shared his motives, from whigs who were beginning to see union as the salvation of their party and from Godolphin, whose administrative mind had appraised its advantages. Others were cautious. Rochester said he wanted time to think about it, and Halifax, whilst being careful not to disapprove of the scheme, was chiefly concerned to give the impression of having had no prior notice of it.[63]

In the commons, the tory majority, to ensure full attendance to defeat any such proposal, refused all leave of absence to members.[64] The high tory view was plain. '. . . Sir Edward Seymour said it was not now a proper time, he thought, to debate the union betwixt England and Scotland, but, if ever it should be debated, he should oppose it for this reason: that a woman being proposed to a neighbour of his in the country for a wife, he said he would never marry her, for she was a beggar, and whoever married a beggar could only expect a louse for her portion . . .'[65]

The union project was resurrected in the following year, this time under tory auspices and as a tactical diversion. The whigs were attempting to recover their former position by recourse to one of their favourite devices: the imposition of loyalty oaths. They were proposing the abjuration of King James. To many tories this was a far from congenial proposal, and to deflect it Nottingham stood up to assert that the best means of ensuring the protestant succession was a union with Scotland. A proposal to give the whigs what they had been hankering after, at least since 1699, was a curious one to emanate from a tory but Nottingham thought he knew what he was about. A proposal, after all, was not an accomplished fact. Furthermore he made a stipulation: before negotiations for union began there ought to be an election in Scotland to ensure that the parliament there did really represent the nation. Nottingham's views rested on the usual tory misapprehensions concerning Scotland. He hoped that an election would change the complexion of the Scottish parliament to the advantage of those he had been led to think were his episcopalian friends—'Scottish tories'. If a Scottish election fulfilled Nottingham's expectations and tory strength continued to grow in England, a union might well appear more attractive to the high church party, bringing not only party political advantages but the prospect of a united episcopalian kingdom.[66]

William was expecting another war with France yet at the same time, to give even the appearance of coping with the commons, he had had to make concessions to the tories. A combination of a French war, a tory ministry and the Scottish succession unprovided for seemed to promise a cheerless future, so the king and the remaining whig interest in the court were quick to take up Nottingham's initiative, but on their own terms. In what was to be his last message to parliament William recommended to their consideration a union with Scotland. However, he envisaged no previous election. The old convention parliament, in being since 1689, was to be the instrument of union. If this scheme could be pushed through there was a chance that the arrival at

Westminster of what were regarded as sound Scottish 'whigs' could buttress the position of both the crown and the junto lords during the forthcoming war. The whig lords denounced proposals for the dissolution of the Scottish parliament as an untoward interference in the affairs of another kingdom.[67] The resulting situation was part of William's legacy to Anne and her ministers. Administrative convenience and the court's political advantage alike pointed firmly to union, but many private interests were opposed to it. Unfortunately for the court, and for some later interpretations of union, the private interests were politically more effective and capable of putting a stop to the whole project. They did so, in defiance of the court, till 1706.

What has to be examined here is the subterranean process whereby one political accident and miscalculation after another eventually produced the circumstances under which the English court was able at last to have some of its own way. The manoeuvres embarked upon were devious in the extreme. Blatant self-interest was frequently involved. Nevertheless the labyrinthine episode has to be traced in its entirety if the achievement of union and the character of the agreement are to be understood.

It is possible to argue that the political circumstances which gave rise to the union are immaterial, since they merely brought about the treaty in 1707 instead of at some other time: that the weakness of the Scottish economy or the gradual acceptance of English habits by the Scottish landed order, or both, would at some stage have led to a treaty. This is a proposition incapable of proof. Indeed, given the state of Anglo-Scottish politics in the early eighteenth century, a far more likely outcome of failure to negotiate union in 1707 would have been an English invasion and conquest of Scotland, with or without a civil war. As one commentator wrote in 1702, the Scots could talk of separation as much as they liked but England was not going to stand by and watch them introduce to the island 'a petty prince of Savoy with a pretension to the whole', nor a viceroy from France.[68] Such intervention could have produced union of a kind—it had done so before—but it would have been a union with vastly different consequences from the one finally negotiated. And neither conquest nor civil war would have owed anything to the economic plight of Scotland.

Notes

[1] Clerk, *Memoirs*, 62-3.
[2] *APS*, xi, 164-5.
[3] W. Ferguson, 'The making of the Treaty of Union of 1707', *SHR*, xliii (1964), 110.
[4] Rightly given short shrift by Dr Ferguson, *art. cit.*, 89-90.
[5] W. R. Scott, 'Scottish industry before the Union' in *The Union of 1707. A Survey of Events*, ed. P. Hume Brown (Glasgow, 1907), 101.
[6] Willson, 'James I and Anglo-Scottish Unity', 44.
[7] Lythe, 193-4.
[8] I am indebted to my colleague, Dr M. L. Bush, for generously providing me with references on this topic. Examples of the propaganda material used include: Society of Antiquaries, Proclamations, Proclamation of [31 Jul. 1547]; 'A Declaration, Conteynyng The Just Causes and considerations, of this present warre . . .' (1542), printed in *Early English Text Society*, Extra Series, xvii (London, 1872), 191–206; James Harryson, 'An Exhortation to the Scottes to conforme themselves to the honorable, Expedient, & godly Union . . .' (1547) in *ib.*, 207–36; 'An Epistle or exhortacion, to unitie and peace, sent from the Lord Protector . . .' (1547) in *ib.*, 237–46; 'An Epitome of the title that the Kynges Majestie of Englande hath to the sovereigntie of Scotlande . . .' (1547), 247–56; John Hooper, 'A Declaration of Christ and his Office . . . Original Dedication To the most noble and victorious prince Edward, duke of Somerset . . .' in *Early Writings of John Hooper* (Parker Society, 1843), xi-xiv. For other references to this propaganda campaign see Donaldson, 'Foundations', 312–13 and 313 n . 1.
[9] Lythe, 193.
[10] Donaldson, 'Foundations', 312–13.
[11] Lythe, 199.
[12] Trevor-Roper, 'The union of Britain . . .', 445–6.
[13] Willson, 'James I and Anglo-Scottish unity', 41–55.
[14] Donaldson, 'Foundations', 313–14.
[15] *Ib., passim.*
[16] The negotiations are summarised in Lythe, 204–15, and Bruce, *Report*, i, 30–127. See also Keith, *Commercial Relations*, 9–19. For exercises in unionist argument see Sir William Conwallis, younger, *The Miraculous and Happy Union of England and Scotland* . . . (London, 1604); *The Works of Sir Francis Bacon*, ed. Basil Montague (London, 1826), v, which contains Bacon's speeches and writing on the topic; Sir Thomas Craig, *De Unione Regnorum Britanniae Tractatus*, ed. C. S. Terry (Scottish History Society, 1909); I. H[ayward], *A Treatise of Union of the two Realms of England and Scotland* (London, 1604) and *The Joyful and Blessed Reuniting the two mighty and famous Kingdoms* . . . (*Oxford, [1605]*); *John Gordon, Enotikon Or A Sermon Of the Union of Great Brittannie* . . . (London, 1604); [Sir John Skinner?], *The Mirror of his Majestie's present Government* . . . (London, 1604).
[17] This argument is set out by Trevor-Roper, 'The union of Britain'; see also

P. J. Pinckney, 'The Scottish representation in the Cromwellian parliament of 1656', *SHR*, xlvi (1967), 106.

[18] Quoted Lee, *Cabal*, 35. See also *ib.*, 35–7.

[19] See *ib.*, 43–69, for a reconstruction of this episode. For a summary of the negotiations: Bruce, *Report*, i, 185–230. Note William's subsequent remarks on union: Burnet, *History*, i, 512, Dartmouth's note (h). Ferguson, *Scotland's Relations*, chap. 8, *passim*, rejects Lee's interpretation in favour of the view that Lauderdale was with the utmost reluctance obeying the king. Charles, for his part, was keeping his ministers individually occupied with various tasks to distract them from his private foreign policy. Dr Ferguson could be right, though, as he points out, the evidence for this entire episode is circumstantial and to accept the union projects of 1668 and 1670 as part of a 'design' of some kind connected with Anglo-Scottish relations, prompted most likely by Tweeddale with the king's approval, seems a more economical explanation. Tweeddale, although his preferences varied according to circumstances, certainly regarded union as a means of attaining stronger monarchical rule in England or a more 'liberal' rule in Scotland.

[20] James Halliday, 'The club and the revolution in Scotland, 1689–90', *SHR*, xlv (1966), provides an analysis of the 'club' opposition. See also P. W. J. Riley, *King William and the Scottish Politicians* (Edinburgh, 1979), chap.2.

[21] W. L. Mathieson, *Politics and Religion in Scotland, 1550–1695* (Glasgow, 1902), 348–9.

[22] See *CSP (Dom), 1691–2*, 62–3, 'Memorial concerning affairs in Scotland', [1691].

[23] Macpherson, App., 195–8, Melville to the king, 29 April 1691 [*sic* for 1690].

[24] *HMCR Finch MSS*, ii, 392–3, Sir George Mackenzie to Nottingham, [Jul. or Aug. 1690].

[25] Buccleuch (Drum.), Col., bundle i, fragment of a memorial to [Queensberry], [1697 or 1698].

[26] *Two Letters Concerning the Present Union From A Peer in Scotland To A Peer in England* (1706).

[27] Buccleuch (Drum.), 'Seven letters', [Philiphaugh] to [Queensberry], 7 Aug. 1701.

[28] *The Earl of Mar's Legacies to Scotland* ... (ed.), the Hon. Stuart Erskine (Scottish History Society, 1896), 141–2; Sir W. Fraser, *Memorials of the Family of Wemyss of Wemyss* (Edinburgh, 1888), iii, 176, Weymss to Cromartie, 2 June 1709.

[29] *Leven and Melville Papers*, 530, Breadalbane to Melville, 17 Sep. 1690.

[30] BL Loan 29/xlviii, 955, Home to [Oxford], 5 Nov. 1713; *ib.*, 987, same to [same], [1713].

[31] Riley, *English Ministers*, 118, 145–6.

[32] *Seafield Corresp.*, intro., xxii.

[33] NLS, MS 7026, 61 [Tweeddale] to Yester, 3 Mar. [16]68 [*sic* for 1686] for a summary of his embarrassment over the affair of the £10,000 bond. This

episode can be traced in *ib.*, *passim*, and reflects little credit on anybody involved.

34 The role of the magnates in Anne's reign will be apparent in later chapters. Assertions concerning William's reign are documented in Riley, *King William and the Scottish Politicians, passim.*

35 See Polwarth's opinion of him: Japikse, ii, 15–21, 12 Feb. 1687.

36 SRO, James Johnston's Letter Book, SP3/1 (no pagination), Tweeddale to [Johnston], 23 Feb. 1692.

37 SRO, GD 220, G, Graham of Gorthie to Montrose, 3 Dec. 1715.

38 Lord John Murray until 1696, when he was raised to the peerage in his own right.

39 Then still respectively Lord Polwarth and Sir James Ogilvy.

40 Buccleuch (Drum.), Letters, xiv, Murray to Queensberry, 7 May 1696; *ib.*, Ogilvy to same, 22 May 1696; *Carstares S.P.*, 319–21, Ogilvy to Carstares, 24 Jul. 1697.

41 BL Add. MSS 6420, 3, president Dalrymple and Philiphaugh to [Queensberry], 12 Dec. 1699.

42 *Carstares S.P.*, 608, Ormiston to Carstares, 10 Aug. 1700.

43 Buccleuch (Drum.), Seven Letters [Philiphaugh] to [Queensberry], 7 Aug. 1701.

44 *Ib.*, [same] to [same], 21 Jun. 1701.

45 SRO, GD 124, Box 16, MM849/4, 25 Oct. 1701.

46 *Ib.*, MM849/2, Mar to Queensberry, draft, 31 Jul. 1701; *ib.*, MM849/3, Queensberry to Mar, 12 Aug. 1701.

47 Buccleuch (Drum.), Letters, xvi, Annandale to [Queensberry], 1 Oct. [1701].

48 *Ib.*, Seven Letters, [Philiphaugh] to [Queensberry], 8 Jul. 1701; *ib.*, [same] to [same], 7 Aug. 1701; *ib.*, [same] to [same], 22 Jul. 1701.

49 SRO, GD 205, Letters from Individuals, R. Mackenzie to W. Bennet, 11 Jun. 1701.

50 Buccleuch (Drum.), Stair, Sir D. Dalrymple to [Queensberry], 8 Sep. 1701.

51 *Ib.*, Seven Letters, [Philiphaugh] to [Queensberry], 7 Aug. 1701.

52 *Carstares S.P.*, 704, Ormiston to Carstares, 29 Jul. 1701.

53 *Ib.*, 701, Carmichael to Carstares, 29 Jul. 1701.

54 NUL, Portland collection, PwA 2441/7q.

55 *Carstares S.P.*, 159–61, 170–7.

56 NLS, MS 7029, 92v., Tweeddale to Johnston, 15 Oct. 1695; *HMCR Johnstone MSS*, 108, Johnston to Annadale, 10 Apr. 1699; *Marchmont Papers*, iii, 178, Marchmont to Seafield, 7 Oct. 1699; *Carstares S.P.*, 581, Seafield to Carstares, 30 Jul. 1700.

57 *HMCR Lords MSS*, N.S., ii, 6 n., 12 Dec. 1695.

58 *Carstares S.P.*, 556, Philiphaugh to Carstares, 11 Jul. 1700; *ib.*, 621 J. Stewart to Carstares, 17 Aug. 1700.

59 *HMCR Johnstone MSS*, 108, Johnston to Annadale, 10 Apr. 1699;

Marchmont Papers, iii, 199, Marchmont to Pringle, 23 Dec. 1699; NLS, MS 7104, 16 [lord B. Hamilton] to Gleneagles, 28 Dec. 1699.

⁶⁰ Quoted in D. Rubini, *Court and Country, 1688–1702* (London, 1967), 173. See E. Hughes, *Studies in Administration and Finance, 1558–1825* (Manchester, 1934), 281–4.

⁶¹ *An Enquiry into the Causes of the Miscarriage of the Scots Colony at Darien* (Glasgow, 1700).

⁶² *HMCR Johnstone MSS*, 115, 20 Jan. 1700. See *HMCR Lords MSS*, N.S., iv, 106–7.

⁶³ NLS, MS 7021, 5–6, lord B. Hamilton to Tweeddale, 11 Jun. [*sic* for Jan.] 1700. Pringle was left with the feeling that the lords were well-disposed: *HMCR Marchmont MSS*, 152, to Marchmont, 15 Feb. 1700.

⁶⁴ Vernon, ii, 444, Vernon to Shrewsbury, 27 Feb. 1700.

⁶⁵ E. M. Thompson (ed.), *Correspondence of the Family of Hatton*, (Camden Society, 1878), ii, C. Hatton, 20 Jan. 1699/1700.

⁶⁶ Burnet, *History*, iv, 557–8; H. Horwitz, *Revolution Politicks* (Cambridge, 1968), 164–5; *HMCR Roxburghe MSS*, 154, 155; *HMCR Marchmont MSS*, 154.

⁶⁷ *Ib.*, 155, Seafield to Marchmont, 3 Mar. 1702.

⁶⁸ [B. Fairfax], *A Discourse upon the Uniting Scotland with England* (London, 1702).

CHAPTER TWO

The cavalier alliance

William's death proved to be a significant event in Anglo-Scottish relations. Circumstances in England and Scotland combined to create a situation of intolerable complexity. At the public level in the new reign the two kingdoms were brought into confrontation with more prestige at stake even than during the Darien crisis. Less well advertised but more important were the possible side effects on the internal politics of each of the kingdoms. In Scottish politics William's inactivity had bordered on the irresolute but there had been no mistaking the fact that he was king. When he chose to assert his will it had produced some effect and when he made no decision, which was frequently, nothing much was done. Anne was unlikely to maintain the same position. Her lack of confidence and experience made her more dependent on her English ministers. English politics were to impinge more directly on Scotland and, moreover, to be seen to do so. The pretence that Scotland was ruled by a Scottish sovereign through Scottish ministers would be exposed as an even thinner fiction than hitherto. With William had died the influence of Portland and Carstares. As advisers and intermediaries they had interpreted the Scottish scene for William and consequently their views had carried great weight. Scottish courtiers had been conscious of the undesirable aspects of this arrangement but it had been far more discreet than their having to make representations direct to English ministers.

The very identity of these ministers made a difference to Scotland. William had been driven to make concessions to the tories but Anne's accession brought the tories back in strength. For the sake of appearances Devonshire and Somerset were left in office, as magnates rather than whigs, but more tories were brought in to reinforce those appointed at the end of the previous reign. Godolphin and

Marlborough, as Anne's managers, tories by inclination, raised no objection to these appointments, though they did have some qualms. The tories were notoriously averse from wars with the French, particularly if they involved large-scale continental operations of the kind William had embarked on and Marlborough was contemplating. The managers were for the moment soothed by promises of tory support, but even so, the appointment of Normanby, blinkered and obtuse, as lord privy seal made them wonder whether things had not been taken too far. The bulk of the tory party, high anglican, xenophobic and suspicious of courts, could make life difficult. However, these new ministers—Nottingham, Rochester and their like—were the men who looked benignly on any Scotsman claiming to be an episcopalian and were determined to have elections in Scotland sooner rather than later so that the episcopalian voice could be heard.

1 The adjournment

The procedure to be followed on the death of William had been laid down with seeming precision by the act of security of 1696.[1] If parliament stood adjourned at the time of the king's death, as it did in 1702, then it had legally to meet within twenty days and could remain in existence for up to six months unless there was at once a new election. Anne's Scottish ministers had no taste for either alternative. With more or less reluctance the English accepted what was less a considered judgement than collective indecision in the face of practical difficulties. Reconvening the old parliament would have led to the resumption of the full-scale opposition from the last reign which the ministry was still too divided to cope with. Twenty days must have seemed a ridiculously short time for the Scottish court party to regain some composure. There would be objections in Scotland to a war with France in view of the inevitable losses to merchant shipping from which the Scots had suffered in previous hostilities. Only the year before Philiphaugh had impressed on Queensberry the unpopularity to be incurred by anyone who gave even the appearance of supporting a declaration of war. At the time he doubted whether a quorum of the council could be raised to sign such a declaration. He had advised that, if war appeared necessary, Scotland should remain non-belligerent until French acts of hostility against an officially neutral Scotland produced a demand for war.[2] In 1702, then, it seemed easier to have war declared on Scotland's behalf before a parliament met in

Edinburgh to face a *fait accompli*.

So Scottish ministers in London accepted the ingenious suggestion that they could keep to the letter of the act of 1696 by a notice of adjournment's being issued within twenty days rather than a summons to parliament. Lawyers amongst them had misgivings about its legality and even more about its advisability but practical considerations overrode their doubts. A warrant was issued adjourning parliament to 26 May, the queen 'having many important affairs to settle which we cannot possibly adjust in so short a time . . .'[3]

2 Anne's accession and the country party

The English ministers had problems enough of their own. As usual they would have preferred to ignore Scotland whilst bearing union in mind as a long-term solution to its major problems. The tories of 1702 were no exception. In the time available they had little choice but to let the Scots have their own way. It was understood, though, that the old parliament was to transact essential business only. The English tories intended to postpone serious adjustments in Scotland until new elections should reveal the episcopalian predominance they believed existed.[4] So Scottish opposition leaders who went to London to ask for the immediate election of a new parliament received no satisfaction.[5] 'Secretary' Johnston, sniffing round the court for gossip and opportunity since his dismissal in 1696, was puzzled by the tories' motives for allowing parliament to meet at all. Being of a suspicious cast of mind, he could think of no other reason than that they were giving the presbyterians enough rope to hang themselves.[6]

The Scottish opposition had concluded that whatever the complexion of affairs in England they were going to have to campaign as vigorously as ever for changes in Scotland. Victory was not going to be handed to them. No help was to be expected from the English whigs, who opposed new elections in Scotland for fear that the tories' calculations might be correct. So the Scottish country party adopted the old tactic of appealing to the English tories in terms of religion.[7] They represented the issue as a struggle between a selfish presbyterian ministry trying to preserve its dominance at all costs and episcopalians who wanted merely to be heard and tolerated. By 1702 this was even more of a fabrication than ever. Scottish ministers were afraid of losing their jobs, they were apprehensive that elections would return the opposition in greater numbers, but they were far from being all

uniformly bigoted presbyterians. And anyway, there were at this stage
few episcopalians in the parliamentary opposition, though many were
content to allow the fiction to be used if that was the only way to obtain
a new election.[8]

This odd turn of events placed Queensberry in a potentially
hazardous situation. Originally he had represented the 'episcopalian'
wing of the ministry. By the court presbyterians he was still viewed in
that light, so to be attacked as the leader of a bigoted presbyterian
ministry was a new experience for him. However, the opposition rather
overdid things. They were determined to discredit Queensberry
completely with all shades of opinion and, since consistency of
argument was not greatly esteemed in Scottish politics, the duke was at
one and the same time represented as a last-ditch presbyterian and as
an episcopalian. But, in the short term, Queensberry was able to turn
to advantage this ambiguity in his position. To the English tories he
posed as the spokesman of the sober episcopalian interest and
represented the presbyterians in the ministry—the more committed of
his opponents whom he had long been trying to dislodge—as the major
obstacle to reconciliation in the church. Queensberry, the story ran,
had been doing his best but his rivals were a millstone round his neck.
By 1704 he had undergone a cautious transformation, emerging as the
defender of the presbyterian establishment against episcopalian
aggression. Queensberry could play the religious game as well as the
next.

If this presbyterian–episcopalian alignment was a fiction the talk of
union, which was becoming an ingredient in Scottish politics as well as
in England, was hardly less spurious. The Scottish opposition had
owed, not its existence, but its cohesion and identity to the issues
arising from the Darien collapse. Darien, though, could never be more
than a transitory grievance. When the project of Caledonia was
manifestly defunct and its further discussion became academic it would
also be dead as a political issue. Consequently, unless a substitute
could be found, the opposition would be drained of some of its vigour.
In fact the next step sprang logically from the Darien episode. The
argument over Scotland's right to New Caledonia had led inexorably to
the question of sovereignty—an issue with much more staying power.
As Melville had told Carstares at the height of the crisis, the opposition
was beginning to argue that the king must have his reasons for refusing
an act which asserted Scotland's right to colonise Darien. Then '. . . his
reasons do either concern Scotland, or are exotic as to Scotland. If the

first let us know them; we will be ready to comply with his greater wisdom. If they do not concern Scotland, then, they say, this gives ground for an unanswerable argument, that the crowns of England and Scotland are incompatible, seeing it is not to be supposed that, where the interest of England and Scotland do irreconcilably interfere, the king must act in favours of England . . .'⁹ This was a line of thought that by 1702 had been further elaborated. The opposition had begun to talk of a treaty with England to guarantee Scottish independence and liberty of trade. Any repetition of English interference with such projects as Darien, in the unlikely event of any further undertaking, would have to be made impossible. This objective was quite clear but the accompanying talk of 'freedom of trade' was far from precise. 'Freedom of trade' was a concession useful to mention but dangerous to define. It was better as a hazy cluster of advantages which England might conceivably be brought to allow. Hints were in circulation of the possible fringe benefits from such a treaty: compensation for the Darien losses and such tariff concessions as could be squeezed out of the English under threat of keeping open the Scottish succession. Perhaps because union was being spoken of, if not too vigorously promoted, in England this policy was referred to as one of 'union', though the opposition's idea of a union was a complete delusion created by propaganda. It was a visionary bargain which would bring Scotsmen a triumph over the destroyers of their trade and allow them to dip their hands into the bottomless wealth of England. This chimerical goal was initially created for the credulous and ill-informed. The less naive assumed that England would never agree to union on such terms, so that the Scottish court, the opposition's real target, would have at some point, on English direction, to oppose the project. Then the opposition would be able to pose as moderate and responsible supporters of the only solution to Anglo-Scottish problems compatible with Scotland's dignity. The ministry would appear as unreasonable and unpatriotic, dragging their feet over a fair bargain with England. A general though unspecific concern for trade, therefore, and an enthusiasm for a treaty were useful weapons for an opposition to aim at the court and the more effective for their lack of precision.

Before the session of 1702 the court was already being charged with unpatriotic intentions, amongst them a design to defeat 'a union'.¹⁰ The court was extremely vulnerable to gossip, in particular the recurring rumour that the ministers were acting against the queen's own wishes. It did, after all, seem unlikely that a high tory queen with a high tory

ministry in England should be countenancing the reassembly of the old
convention parliament. The talk was so persistent that Queensberry
was driven to obtain an official denial from the queen: '. . . We
understand that reports are spread about that we are dissatisfied with
the late measures taken by us for the administration of the government
of Scotland. These reports are unfounded and injurious to our honour,
and we regard those who spread them as disaffected to our service . . .'[11]
But it had little effect. The Scottish court was going to have to suffer a
great deal more from this weapon. If an English ministry could be
made to appear divided, then the opposition contended that the Scots
were not fully supported. This, that or the other English faction was
said to be in the ascendant and determined to change policy in
Scotland whilst the queen, despite her public face, was really in
sympathy with them against ministers claiming to speak in her name.

3 The Parliament of 1702

So the old convention parliament was summoned yet again for the
session of 1702. The outcome was decisive for the fate of the old court
party and for Scottish politics until the union. Both ministries, English
and Scottish, hoped that the parliament could have a brief sitting, with
business kept to the bare minimum. The queen's title to the throne was
to be ratified, supply granted and an act passed for negotiating a union
in accordance with the proposal bequeathed by William. To soothe the
presbyterians, confirmation of the church settlement was to be
permitted and, for the sake of English sensibilities as well as to gratify
Scottish episcopalians, Queensberry's instructions as commissioner
permitted him '. . . to allow such of the episcopal ministers as shall
apply to qualify themselves to be admitted and have our protection
. . .'[12] This affected the situation no more than when William had said
much the same thing.

However, the parliament did not go as the court had planned. Led by
Hamilton, the country opposition, to the strength of seventy-four
members, seceded in a body before the session was opened on the
ground that the meeting was illegal. It is easy enough with hindsight to
say what Queensberry ought to have done. To have discontinued
proceedings at once would have been an acknowledgement of defeat.
Undoubtedly the best course would have been to hold a brief official
session passing some token act or no act at all and then to have
adjourned immediately afterwards. Queensberry chose the worst

possible course. He continued with the full session and, with only the rump present, acted as if nothing untoward had happened. The queen's title was ratified and acts for supply and appointing union commissioners were passed.[13] A complete abandonment of the session, admitting defeat, would probably have led to fewer complications. From the start the legality of the session had been dubious and the court's position based largely on bluff. Now the bluff had been called, the court's prestige had collapsed and the opposition had been given a bonus in the shape of another major grievance. With some justice and a great deal of confidence they could now insist that parliament's proceedings were invalid. It was a stance that they adopted with some zest, openly denouncing as illegal the rump's vote of supply and planning a campaign to refuse payment. And what applied to the cess affected equally parliament's other proceedings, including the ratification of the queen's title. The session had left a mess which was in urgent need of clearing up.

Among the debris was an intensified crisis within the ministry. During the previous year Philiphaugh had advised Queensberry against settling the succession. He added: 'I'm confident your grace will be far from undertaking any such thing. I hope you will continue of the same opinion I have heard your grace declare, to wit, that this nation should not make one step that way, before the case existed, unless England gave us good conditions as to our liberty of trading ...'[14] This view of putting pressure on England was extremely limited—not to settle the succession 'before the case existed'—and its demands modest—freedom for any Scottish company to trade in accordance with its charter—but it does indicate an awareness of the bargaining power of the vacant succession. However, Queensberry's resistance proved to be negotiable rather than determined.

Queensberry's instructions in 1702 allowed him to pass an act imposing an abjuration of the pretender, and he had thought of doing this as a matter of course. But opinion within the rump and the ministry was divided. The difference of opinion coincided with the split between the Queensberry faction and those within the court who had been in opposition to the duke at the end of William's reign. When news of this proposal leaked out there was a threat that, if necessary, seceders would return to outvote the court over abjuration. Some Queensberry men actually canvassed jacobite support to make defeat certain. Consultation with Stair and other intimates led Queensberry to put it to the officers of state that an abjuration would be better avoided, since its main effect would be to force a public vote and expose the division of opinion within the court. In spite of Queensberry's efforts the split was brought out into the open. The person immediately responsible was the earl of Marchmont, whom Queensberry had been trying to oust from his post of lord chancellor in favour of one of his own followers for the last four years of William's reign. Marchmont had been attached in one way or another to the opposition to Queensberry for even longer. He had succumbed to inflexibility of mind and long-windedness of speech but always commanded respect. Now, at Queensberry's proposal, he at once expressed the disquiet of the presbyterians. He was so insistent on the abjuration vote's being put to parliament that Queensberry asked him to give his word not to introduce it on his own initiative. Marchmont declined but said that if Queensberry as commissioner gave him a direct order then he would obey. Behaviour was very stiff on both sides. Queensberry gave him the formal instruction which seemed called for, in spite of which Marchmont at the house's next sitting moved the abjuration. His motion was carried by a mere four votes, which, in a rump composed entirely of courtiers, was a defeat. Feelings were so bitter that, to prevent open strife within the court party, Queensberry in some haste adjourned on 30 June 1702.[15]

Marchmont's action, ill-advised and wrong-headed though it was, had been born of a long period of resentment. It was the culmination of the jealousy with which he and the 'presbyterian' wing of the court had watched Queensberry's power grow in the last reign. Marchmont, Ormiston and their sympathisers had no affection for the duke's supporters, regarding them not only as political rivals but as virtual jacobites. To Marchmont jacobitism was a potent menace in Scotland. He suspected, perhaps rightly, the motives which had prompted many to oppose abjuration despite their argument that abjuration would weaken Scotland's bargaining power, which sounded patriotic enough. Now, with a tory ministry in England which included Queensberry's friend Rochester, it seemed that the duke was on the way to obtaining the full power he had failed to acquire under William. So the formal proposal of an abjuration was aimed at Queensberry, to expose his following for what Marchmont was convinced it was—crypto-jacobite. He could see no other valid reason for opposing the abjuration, and said so. It was in such circumstances, with the two wings of the old court alliance publicly divided, that important questions had to be answered. How could the damage of 1702 be rectified? There would

have to be an election, but when? How was the court interest to be
reorganised?

Both Queensberry and his opponents in the court, though for
different reasons, were against precipitate elections. Marchmont and
his sympathisers wanted a further meeting of the old parliament in
August 1702, just before the expiry of the six months' limit, to pass an
abjuration to discourage open jacobite participation in the elections.[16]
In England, the junto whigs, deprived of influence but with no desire to
see Scotland in the hands of the tories' allies, supported this scheme.
The proposal was quite impracticable. One illegal session of
parliament had done enough damage and another could only make
things worse. Nor was there any reason to suppose that the abjuration,
so disruptive in June, would be any less so in August. This was the
English ministry's conclusion, and the convention parliament, elected
in 1689, was at last dissolved on 8 August 1702. Queensberry,
dominated by the fear that any change would be for the worse, and the
'presbyterians', professing to be on the brink of a jacobite *coup*, alike
had to accept the fact of new elections. Only the anti-court groups in
Scotland and the English tories were satisfied.

4 Changes in the ministry

Obviously some changes were needed if the opposition was to be
managed. The general reaction to the secession of 1702 and the
widespread hostility to the cess showed the seceders had a
disconcerting amount of support in the country, yet the queen's title
had to be ratified and a legally indisputable vote of supply obtained. At
some stage, whether earlier or later, an arrangement would have to be
made with some part of the opposition.

The Scottish country party leaders did their utmost to persuade
English ministers that they, or some of them, should be admitted to
office, and throughout the 1702 session they had kept in close touch
with the English court. Godolphin was one who had never been fully
convinced of the regularity of the 1702 parliament and as its
management was bungled, he was confirmed in his opinion.[17] The
opposition leaders thought him, for one, worth talking to. Another
significant figure in this episode was Nottingham, a high churchman,
firm to the Hanoverian succession but concerned, as he had always
been, about the fate of Scottish episcopalians. When members of the
Scottish opposition approached him in the name of episcopacy he

proved most receptive. His name was soon closely linked with hints to country party leaders that, were they to appear in London, there was a possibility of some agreement between them and the court. Such rumours made presbyterian placemen increasingly wary and suspicious.[18] Marchmont urgently enquired about the current influence of his English connections at court. However, the presbyterians could do little but hope for the best, since, for the time being, affairs were out of their control.

In 1702 the duke of Queensberry, as in the last years of William's reign, was the pivot of Anglo-Scottish relations. For the benefit of tory ministers in England he was making episcopalian noises although he knew very well that the sort of toleration the Scottish episcopalians wanted could not be risked. Consequently he was wary of precise undertakings and was outbid by those offering to do more for the episcopalians, though their motives were political rather than religious. Queensberry talked to suit everyone but was reluctant to act or even recommend action. His agreement to elections in 1702 had come after some hesitation. Others had had no such doubts. Some were enthusiastic for broadening the base of the court party, a scheme which Queensberry, rightly, saw as a threat. He wanted only such changes as would benefit his own influence so, for the time being, although his personal position was central to the problem of management, he let others make the running.

One who was very willing to run as far and as quickly as necessary, perhaps even further, was George Mackenzie, viscount of Tarbat, who made the first challenge to Queensberry's position. Tarbat was widely mistrusted, and with very good reason, being one of the most slippery of Scottish politicians. Yet he had a talent for conviviality which people often found engaging even when they suspected, or knew, that he was scheming against them. His mind was volatile in the extreme. He continually generated ideas and projects, mostly inconsistent with each other but always connected, however deviously, with his own welfare. These ideas were usually presented under the cloak of broad and abstract political, even philosophical, principle. He spoke and wrote so earnestly in whatever role took his fancy that it was, and on occasion still is, difficult to determine what his exact aims were. He could be Tarbat the vigorous, determined manager. Then he could be swiftly transformed into the infirm elder statesman, claiming all the wisdom of experience and the detachment consequent on withdrawal from active politics. It was not that he was dishonest, though for much of the time he certainly was, but rather that for him honesty was not a relevant criterion of conduct. When in 1693, he had been caught again, for the third time in his career, falsifying parliamentary minutes as lord clerk register, no action was taken against him. The generality of members tended to the view that a propensity to forgery was his affliction as others had the stone.[19] Although he never incurred general dislike, as a practical politician he was taken less seriously in Scotland as time went on. He produced alternative schemes of government almost as involuntarily as a spider spinning a web, and anyone who approached too closely and credulously was liable to become enmeshed in his fabrications. Alexander Cunningham, who knew him, had it that he was 'long looked upon as a state mountebank'.[20] In Scotland he might well have been, although even there none could ignore him on account of his political interest. Now he was to re-enter politics, stimulated by an English audience to whom he was not so well known, to bring off one more major confidence trick. This time his victims were the English ministers and in particular Nottingham.

Tarbat's attitude to the parliament of 1702 was an excellent example of his tactical capacity when he was on form. He deprecated questions about the legality of the session. If the queen said it was a parliament, then it was a parliament, and that was the end of it. At the same time he indicated that she might conceivably have been ill advised.[21] Astutely, he kept apart from the seceders but preserved his family interest with them through the secession of his brother, Roderick Mackenzie of Prestonhall. He sat in parliament long enough after the secession to demonstrate that he was not challenging its authority but then stayed away to protest against the act ratifying the presbyterian church settlement. Thus he avoided association with parliament's decisions whilst establishing his credentials with Nottingham and others as a politically moderate episcopalian. After the session he was well placed to write to London offering advice in the role of a non-party man, a despiser of sordid manoeuvres and the unscrupulous advancement of private interests.

The English took him at his face value and summoned him to court. He hastened south with a zest surprising in one who, in William's reign, as a way out of his embarrassments, had pleaded old age and infirmity. Once in England he placed his influence squarely in opposition to that of Queensberry. Tarbat wanted a drastic revision of the Scottish ministry to come to terms with the seceders.[22] He seems to have judged that a subsequent election would allow him to pose as the

leader of the Scottish episcopalian interest and to run off with some of
Queensberry's clothes. The thought of such changes before an election
induced alarm or caution amongst the rest of the Scottish ministers.
Signs and portents of that kind could be mischievously used and
disastrously interpreted. The fact that Anne had a tory ministry in
England created speculation enough. Too much conjecture would
certainly strengthen the country party, and nobody in the existing
court interest wanted that: not Queensberry and certainly not Seafield,
who believed in change only to attain a specific end—not in change for
its own sake, as Tarbat sometimes seemed to do. The presbyterians in
the court had been willing to come to terms with Whitelaw but did not
relish the sort of adjustments that were now being mooted. A
compromise of sorts was reached at the presbyterians' expense.
Marchmont was to be the first sacrifice. His open defiance over the
abjuration at last gave Queensberry, whose resolution was unfaltering,
sufficient excuse to press for his dismissal. He wanted to replace
Marchmont by one of his own clients; instead the office of lord
chancellor went to Seafield, who was in no sense a Queensberry man.
Indeed, as the eyes and ears of the crown in Scotland, Seafield was
entering on the period of his greatest influence in Anglo-Scottish
politics. He was the trusted adviser of Godolphin and Harley—their
institutionalised substitute for Carstares's influence on the late king.

Seafield's political loyalties were to the crown. Much earlier than
most he had the prescience to see that men of his rank could not
compete in strength with magnates. Joining a single magnate interest
as some did was a possibility, but this was to enter into bondage unless
one belonged to a family as influential and active as the Dalrymples.
Instead, Seafield built up an interest on an altogether different
foundation: his personal ability and his proved trustworthiness as a
crown manager. This gave him in time a position outside, and even
above, magnate squabbles, which he viewed with some detachment.
During the previous reign he had developed conventions which limited
his operations. Adjustments in Scottish politics were related strictly to
the management of the next session of parliament. Seafield's task was
to give advice on what was needed to provide a court majority.
Whatever was finally agreed between the English and Scottish
ministers he considered binding until parliament adjourned. The
adjournment brought the season for further advice and adjustment.
Amongst his ministerial colleagues this bred a certain mistrust. Seafield
was with them, usually taking the full burden of management, but he

was not really of them. They operated as political *banditti*; to Seafield they represented a hazard for the crown. Within his own conventions Seafield betrayed nobody. In England there was already a respectable tradition which allowed permanent civil servants, secretaries of boards such as Lowndes, Burchett and Blathwayt, to hold their posts for the sake of administrative continuity despite ministerial changes. As members of parliament, whatever their private views, they voted for the court interest. This tradition was not developed in Scotland, yet Seafield acted in accordance with it. He functioned as a permanent civil servant with Scotland as his 'department'. Lockhart's gibe that the lord chancellor was a blank sheet for the court to write upon was just as true of any civil servant who also had a function in politics.[23] Seafield was being judged as merely another Scottish politician when, by Anne's reign, he had become something rather different.

The office of secretary, which Seafield vacated on his promotion, went to Tarbat—an unwelcome appointment for Queensberry, his colleague as the other secretary of state. Subsequently the duke lost no opportunity of trying to discredit his colleague and to have him removed on one friendly pretext or another ostensibly for Tarbat's own good.[24]

But Queensberry did succeed in having some of his own way. Selkirk, who had joined the seceders, was dislodged at last from the post of lord register, to be replaced by Murray of Philiphaugh, whose appointment gave Queensberry a long-delayed satisfaction.[25] To prevent alarms and conjectures the changes were not to be announced till after the elections. No further decisions were to be made until the results were known. In that this was aimed at quietening rumour and speculation it was a gain for the existing court interests. The changes were announced in November and, significantly, Tarbat accepted the agreement only with reluctance.

After the elections the English court and its Scottish advisers had to think about managing the next session of parliament, planned for the spring of 1703. Taking off a sufficient number of the opposition without losing more court supporters than could be spared was always the problem. In the winter of 1702 and 1703 there were two aspects to it: the composition of the new ministry and the court's policy for the 1703 session. Queensberry's position could have been threatened by either and he was prepared to fight to retain his influence.

Most Scottish politicians either wanted changes or had become resigned to them. The difference lay in the adjustment each group was prepared to accept. Queensberry's aim had not faltered since William's reign: the extension of his own power within the court. If he realised at all that narrowing the ministry into a mere Queensberry interest would make parliament impossible to manage he betrayed no recognition of the fact. The probability is that, compared with his own private concern, he accorded it a very low priority. He had been against the admission of Tarbat to the ministry and he was opposed to any compromise with the country party. Indeed, he was prepared to try to block, to the extent of threatening resignation, the appointment of anyone whom he found uncongenial.[26]

Nevertheless it was plain that if ministers were to make any showing at all in parliament some understanding would have to be reached with people outside the court. Those, such as Nottingham and Seafield, who favoured negotiations with the opposition found their efforts strengthened by the more purposeful elements of the country party. In order to apply pressure to the court they had started a campaign of refusal to pay the cess voted in 1702.[27] James Johnston knew that ministers were anxious to drive a bargain with the opposition and he urged Tweeddale and others to go to London to make their views known. So, in the autumn of 1702, Tweeddale went to see how far the court was prepared to go to meet the opposition's demands. The second marquess of Tweeddale had never had a head for business. In the past his father had bemoaned his inability to cope with people and had tried, with very little success, to push him to the front. Now his own son, Yester, writing from Scotland, prompted and exhorted him to action but with no greater effect than his grandfather had produced. Yester's expectations were modest enough. He thought that for the moment they had to settle for what they could get. To his father he wrote that he longed 'to know those changes that have been so long expected. But I am persuaded, as your lordship writ, that at best it will be but an hotch-potch business. However, I would have this knot of courtiers broke at any rate . . . the not paying of the cess is the only game we have to play . . .'[28] And again, '. . . we hope that none will be so far imposed upon as to break off from the party upon dishonourable terms, but do not expect neither that people should refuse all employments because they get not all their will . . .'[29] But Tweeddale proved to be stiff-necked, holding out obstinately against all compromise. He refused to accept a place on the treasury board unless Queensberry was completely excluded from all financial management and an investigation begun into past administration. Under the circumstances this was unrealistic, so Tweeddale, with a few civilities from the court, returned empty-handed.

But the opposition to Queensberry consisted of more than Tweeddale and his following. The election results had sharpened the old 'episcopalian' tactic and it was being used by Tarbat from within the court itself. He was to write of the large number of Scots with 'great hopes of an equal and no bigot ministry'.[30] What he wanted was to purge the ministry of such of the old 'presbyterian' interest as had no great personal following. In this he had the support of Queensberry. But Tarbat wanted them out to show what he could do for the episcopalian interest, whilst Queensberry bore them a grudge for opposing his attempts in William's reign to engross the court. Over the dismissals, therefore, there was agreement. Marchmont had already gone. He was followed by Melville, Leven, Cockburn of Ormiston and Maxwell of Pollock. Argyll and Annandale, both identified with the presbyterian cause, remained undisturbed. Not even Queensberry had the strength to dislodge Argyll, but the differences between the two dukes had not been composed. Their rivalry was merely to be pursued on a different pretext. Queensberry would have been relieved to see the back of Annandale, who had been not only his political opponent at least since 1694 but also his rival for the control of Dumfriesshire. Annandale's political weight did not approach that of Argyll but, as friend or foe, he was almost impossible to deal with for any length of time. Most thought him untrustworthy and inconsistent. Occasionally, but only occasionally, they maligned him. He was a blatant, even high-handed, turncoat who could execute a *volte-face* in mid-sentence without changing the tone of his voice. It was always a nice point of calculation whether Annandale was safer as an apparent ally or as an open rival. It seems to have been felt in 1703 that he was better left where he was.

Once the purge had been carried out Queensberry was quick to take the credit where he thought it would do any good. He made much of the fact '. . . that he has turned out some eminent presbyterians . . .', wrote Sir Alexander Bruce, 'And yet I hear that unthankful presbyterian party are apt to misconstrue it, not considering that he did not turn them out as such but purely for a reason that any wise man will [descry], viz., because he had others to put in their places, of whom he was more persuaded they were more firmly devoted to his particular interest . . .'[31] Queensberry, despite his reluctance to do much for episcopalians, was competing with Tarbat for the role of their defender, at least in English eyes.

So much for appearances. The real pattern of the settlement shows in the nominations to the vacant posts and the new commissions of the judicatures on 4 February 1703. Tarbat's brother, Mackenzie of Prestonhall, one of the seceders, was made lord justice clerk and, against all the opposition Queensberry could bring to bear, the post of privy seal was given to Tullibardine, between whom and Queensberry was a deep and possibly irrational animosity. In addition, Tarbat's son and Tullibardine's father were put on the privy council and exchequer. By these appointments the interests opposed to Queensberry made some inroads into the court. Yet if any single interest benefited from the changes it was that of Queensberry and the Dalrymples. Prestonhall's appointment was balanced on the same day by that of Queensberry's brother[32] as governor of Edinburgh castle. In the treasury Queensberry's influence was predominant. If the nominal appointment of Prince George is discounted, ten were added to the exchequer commission, of whom six belonged to the Queensberry–Dalrymple alliance. On the pretext of expanding the 'episcopalian' element Queensberry's share of places had been increased as never before since the peak of his campaign under William. He had managed against the apparent odds to turn Tarbat's impetus to his own advantage. To have endured obloquy as the kingpin of a 'bigoted' presbyterian ministry and, as a result, to have expanded his influence as the champion of the episcopalians must surely rank as one of Queensberry's major political triumphs. Some of the duke's rivals had been forced into the ministry, it is true, and seemed likely to prove objectionable, but the dismissed ministers had also been a nuisance to him. Moreover the newcomers were in the position of odd men out. As early as January 1703 Bennet of Grubet had remarked about the new coalition, if that is what it was, '. . . the pins are so hard screwed up that some strings must crack and disorder the harmony of the present concert . . .'[33] He proved to be right.

Queensberry seemed to have most to fear from Tullibardine, the representative of a magnate interest in long-standing rivalry with his own. He was, moreover, fresh from the opposition into which Queensberry had pushed him in 1698. Since Darien Tullibardine's position in the country party had been somewhat eroded by Hamilton and Tweeddale, whose interest in the Africa Company was greater than his, so that going back into the ministry could have been the means of re-establishing his personal position. He might even make ground by setting himself up as the country party's spokesman within the court. This was certainly the pose he adopted. To the English tories he was a court supporter and the episcopalians' friend;[34] to the country party he tried to demonstrate that 'Tullibardine was Tullibardine still nothwithstanding of the seal.[35] These were difficult roles to combine, as he discovered when he had to back hastily out of the no-cess campaign and explain away his retreat to his former associates. One could, it seemed, be both 'presbyterian' and 'episcopalian' but to be both court and country was infinitely more precarious.

5 Court plans for 1703

Once the composition of the Scottish ministry had been decided there remained the further problems of parliamentary aims and tactics. There were some overriding considerations. Godolphin had some firm views which Marlborough seems to have been content to approve.[36] These English requirements had to be accepted as the basis of any plans. The 1702 fiasco had forced Scotland on their attention and the issue had to be dealt with. The queen's title had to be legally ratified, the cess voted in 1702 had to be paid and if possible a further supply granted. Otherwise some flexibility was permissible. Both Godolphin and Marlborough accepted, perhaps surprisingly, that any attempt to settle the succession or pass the abjuration in the 1703 parliament would be undesirable. There could have been only one reason for this: the urgency with which both men wanted a union of the two kingdoms. William's initiative had led to negotiations over the winter of 1702–1703. They had collapsed, although the fact was never officially admitted and technically they were merely adjourned.[37] Yet the problems which had driven William to support union seemed about to become more, rather than less, pressing. Both men wanted Scotland neutralised so that it could be forgotten and attention focused on the conduct of the war. So when it was argued, as in 1702, that the settlement of the succession or an act of abjuration would throw away Scotland's bargaining power, Godolphin and Marlborough felt constrained to accept this view whether or not they relished it.

The fact was that neither of them relished it. Godolphin was apprehensive about jacobite activities. Queensberry's enemies had not been slow to blame the jacobite inclinations of his supporters for his attitude to the succession. Marlborough was suffering from his wife. Sarah, speaking with the voice of the junto, wanted the succession in Scotland settled and left neither her husband nor the queen in any doubt of it. Under such pressure Godolphin hedged and nurtured thoughts about some means, vague and unspecific, of disavowing the pretender without actually abjuring him. Both men had good cause to feel uneasy. Their conniving at such a policy in Scotland could endanger their domestic position. Should anyone in the Scottish parliament propose, as a private venture, the succession or abjuration, forcing the ministry to be at the least noncommittal, the court's conduct could be made to appear inept or, more probably, sinister. If the junto should embark on a campaign to embarrass the court, as they were to do in late 1703 and the spring of 1704, they would be able to make great play with the Scottish succession.[38] Politicians in both kingdoms understood very well this connection between Scottish affairs and English party politics, and the managers had to bear it constantly in mind.[39]

In 1703 Nottingham and the court tories were also committed to union. In fact, Godolphin and Marlborough apart, they were almost its only champions in England. Rank-and-file tories developed a roaring in the ears at the very mention of union with a presbyterian kingdom. The whigs, knowing they could expect no benefits from union whilst in opposition, had abandoned the idea.[40] The court tories, however, thought they glimpsed opportunities for themselves in union. If the project could be carried with Scottish episcopalian support their position as an English court party might be strengthened and retained into the foreseeable future. Their reasoning was essentially similar to that of the whig courtiers in William's reign. So for the moment the tory leadership was prepared to co-operate with the managers.

However, regardless of the differences of opinion and the tensions within and without the court, the new parliament had somehow to be controlled. The main preoccupation of Seafield and a few others, seriously concerned with the technicalities of the operation, was the situation to which the 1702 elections had given rise. Management presented an even more difficult problem owing to the appearance of a strong third party of self-styled 'cavaliers'. A number of jacobites, non-jurors under William, had been encouraged by Anne's high tory preferences and her status as King James's daughter to entertain delusions of political advantage if not of grandeur. Conditional loyalty to Anne, they decided, would not overburden their consciences. Accordingly some of them had taken the oaths to qualify for election and a number of jacobite peers had decided to attend parliament. In 1703 this cavalier party, reinforced by a few jacobite sympathisers from

the former country party, was seventy strong. Those of the country
party accepting the leadership of Hamilton and Tweeddale numbered
about sixty. The largest single group, with, at full strength, between
ninety and a hundred votes, was the court. Even so it had no complete
majority, a fact which plagued Scottish managers till the union.
Moreover the group of recently dismissed ministers and their close
supporters, although still optimistically looked on as courtiers, were not
completely to be relied upon. Under these circumstances, if the court
was to succeed in anything, it urgently needed a bargain with one of the
other groups. The failure to make terms with Tweeddale meant certain
opposition from the country party. There remained one possibility: a
court–cavalier alliance. Whatever objections could be made to such a
bargain, and obviously there were many, it is difficult, given the court's
aims and the urgency attaching to them, to see any alternative.

Tarbat, Tullibardine and Seafield each accepted this policy, though
for different reasons. Tarbat thought the scheme likely to advance his
own interests and furthermore emotionally satisfying. He rushed into it
dizzy with excitement and optimism. Tullibardine, notwithstanding
earlier professions of new-found presbyterian conviction, discovered the
Atholl political interest no longer amongst the country party but, since
their emergence as a separate group, with the cavaliers. His choice was
therefore made for him and he espoused the cavalier alliance with
enthusiasm. But for Seafield any such collaboration was a mere
business transaction, the court gaining the cavaliers' votes for essential
measures in return for strictly limited concessions.

Negotiations for such an alliance were begun and by March 1703 the
earl of Home, leader of the jacobite 'Mitchell's Club', was trying to
persuade cavaliers to pay the cess and support the ministry. As
subsequent events showed, the cavaliers were already agreeing not only
to pay the cess but to accept the legality of the disputed 1702
parliament, to ratify the queen's title and to bring in a further vote of
supply. They were promising support for the whole of the court's
essential business for 1703. In return the cavaliers were to be offered
some insignificant concessions. Legislation on which the cavaliers could
not at least decently abstain was to be avoided. A gesture or so was
made to give them a general impression of the court's goodwill. The
queen wrote to the Scottish privy council in February about the
treatment of episcopalians. Anne merely expressed a wish that
episcopalians should 'be protected in the peaceable exercise of their
religion, and in their persons and estates, according to the laws of the

kingdom . . .',[41] which introduced nothing new. A proclamation of
indemnity was issued for crimes committed against the crown since
1689. It was intended mainly to indemnify those who had not hitherto
recognised the revolution settlement or the turning of the convention
into a parliament in 1689. Six men with cavalier connections were
added to the privy council, although two of them, Dunmore and
March, were Queensberry men first and cavaliers second. Finally, it
seems likely, from Queensberry's instructions as commissioner, that
the court agreed not to obstruct an act allowing separate episcopalian
worship in meeting houses if such should be proposed.

All this was most embarrassing for Queensberry, who was caught in
a net partly of his own construction. His excuse that he had been
hitherto prevented by the presbyterian element in the ministry from
helping the episcopalians now seemed to have evaporated and at a time
when he found himself with men prepared to go much further than he
to gratify the episcopalians. He could not afford to be outbid for the
favour of the English tories yet at the same time there was little that
could be safely done for episcopalians in Scotland. Queensberry
thought toleration inexpedient and Godolphin agreed with him. The
court badly needed presbyterian votes and therefore could not offend
the presbyterians. Murray of Philiphaugh emphasised this to
Queensberry, '. . . I think it not prudent unnecessarily to provoke a
considerable party in the nation when by a little caution and
management they may be kept quiet. I think her majesty has other
affairs ado than either to make the rest of Scotland episcopal or the
north presbyterian . . .'[42] Queensberry did not need to be warned. An
uproar in Glasgow when, on the strength of the queen's letter,
episcopalians tried to hold a dissenting service, irritated him. He
accused them of having provoked a riot to discredit the presbyterians.
As secretary of state he wrote formally to Seafield saying that the queen
expected the privy council '. . . to hinder any provocation to be given by
the dissenting clergy to whom by her royal letter directed to their
lordships [of the privy council] she promised protection only in their
actings as allowed by law . . .'[43]

Despite these substantial reservations, however, Queensberry, to
preserve favour with the tories, continued to speak as if he
wholeheartedly supported the alliance. He was not prepared to do any
more. But even Seafield, whose approach was calculating enough,
thought the cavalier alliance, as far as it went, should be a reality and,
unless the session of 1703 was to be an even greater debacle than the

preceding one, he was right. If the price of cavalier support was no more than the avoidance of objectionable legislation and the mere introduction of a toleration act, then the alliance was cheap. If the toleration failed, as it was almost certain to do, then parliament could be adjourned. The court would have achieved its objectives and no promise would have been broken.

For Queensberry, though, the policy could be no more than a charade. Mere talk to gain Nottingham's support was easy, and if it would also engage the cavaliers so much the better. But he had to think of the presbyterian votes, and rather than take the risks involved in any further commitments to jacobites he intended to conduct the session of parliament as if the old convention parliament had not been dissolved.[44] He thought it necessary, for instance, to ratify not only the legality of the 1702 parliament but that of all the sessions from 1689, an undertaking quite uncongenial to the cavaliers. Such a course would retain the allegiance of part of the court but gain that of nobody else. On these terms the 1703 session was doomed before it had begun but for the time being Queensberry kept his reservations to himself. Blame for any failure could afterwards be laid on the newcomers to the ministry whom Queensberry could truthfully claim to have had foisted on him.

Queensberry's instructions as commissioner merely disguised the gulf between him and those who agreed with Seafield. There were too many loopholes. The essential business of the parliament was explicitly ordered but acts for ratifying the presbyterian church establishment and allowing episcopalian ministers to have meeting houses were merely permitted. There was, too, a curiously worded financial provision which was significant. Country party thoughts, or at least propaganda, had taken a reformist turn. Early in 1703 one of their meetings had issued a declaration of intent: to enquire into and rectify the civil administration, which they implied was riddled with corruption and embezzlement. They had also indicated their determination to restore to the crown all the grants 'nibbled' in the last reign. To some in the queen's service this savoured of a threat. Queensberry, in particular, had no relish for this sort of thing, especially since Philiphaugh, one of his advisers, had to rebuke him for securing extra grants for himself and denuding the treasury so that other salaries could not be paid.[45] The duke had never been modest in his demands and was understandably disquieted and unco-operative when Tarbat and Tullibardine proved to be greatly taken with the idea of investigating the financial administration of William's reign. Agreement was eventually prised out of him. But subsequently he was found, as secretary of state, drafting the proposed indemnity in such a way as to pardon in advance anyone guilty of irregularities concerning public money since the revolution. This, at least, was rectified at the last moment but the commissioner's instructions on the topic were vague: 'You are to endeavour to procure an act clearing and asserting the jurisdiction of our exchequer or what relates to our revenue'.[46] In the event a very reluctant Queensberry had to be coerced into having the subject raised in parliament at all.

6 The parliament of 1703

These ill-assorted queen's servants, already in disagreement, were to face, in May 1703, the new Scottish parliament which, quite accidentally, exposed Anglo-Scottish difficulties in a more public fashion than before.[47] The basic problems, still almost unmentionable, remained unaltered; but the form they were to take till the union was further defined.

The initiative came from what was left of the country party, a nationalist opposition but nationalist only because it was the opposition. Their ostensible policy sprang from the fact that a charge of subservience to English interests was the easiest one to level against any Scottish ministry. In 1703 their immediate plan was to continue the previous year's campaign, attacking the legality of the 1702 parliament, but they intended also to advance towards objectives pursued since Darien. These concerned Scottish sovereignty: legislation to place the kingdoms on a more equitable footing and to ensure that any future Scottish sovereign would be chosen without English influence.[48] England was to be deprived of the power to prejudice Scottish interests as she was believed to have done over Darien, hence the attempt to impose 'limitations' on the crown possibly before, but certainly after, the queen's death. There were perhaps a very few members of the country party who believed in this policy. Apart from Fletcher of Saltoun—the 'patriot'—they are not easy to identify. Most, and certainly the leaders, were not interested in settlements, merely in disrupting parliament and embarrassing the ministry to get jobs for themselves. A patriotic stance was their obvious strategy.

But in 1703 they were the smallest group in parliament and there seemed no reason why they should have attracted support from anyone else. Obviously they could expect no backing from the court. The cavaliers were already too set on the vistas which seemed to be opening before them. To gain office, influence in Scottish politics and toleration for episcopalians they were ready to profess devotion to the queen, do the court's bidding and help to carry business in parliament.

The disruption which provided the country party with its backing in votes emanated from the court itself. Apart from Queensberry's personal following and the newcomers, the court comprised a few permanent 'insiders', of whom Seafield was the most notable, and what remained of the presbyterian interest. These presbyterians, always ill-disposed to Queensberry, held the key to the situation in 1703. Those still in employment were led by Argyll and Annandale, supported by the lord advocate, Sir James Stewart. The last had a thoroughly deserved reputation for venality and shiftiness but as time went on was professing more and more rigorous presbyterianism. The recently dismissed ministers with such following as they could muster made up the rest of the presbyterian group and their relationship to the court was as yet undefined. The court managers professed to hope they would do their 'duty' and continue to support the ministry's policy, but this seemed over-optimistic. Marchmont and the others resented their dismissal, and the spectacle of an alliance between the court and the jacobites alarmed them. As they saw it, the court–cavalier alliance could not be allowed to achieve the kind of success which might cement it and give it more power. The alliance had to be broken, and they planned to discredit the cavalier party by showing it up for what it was—a jacobite party opposed to the revolution. Another prospect they had in mind was the embarrassment of Queensberry, for whom their affection was slight. By forcing him to declare publicly which side he was on, some, at least, of his talk would be exposed as dishonest and whatever credit he still retained with the episcopalians might altogether disappear.

The cavalier alliance gave the court the initial advantage of surprise over the country party. Hamilton and his followers had their tactics rendered useless and the country party was massively outvoted. The queen's title was ratified and the legality of the 1702 session established. The next step was to be the introduction of an act for supply and, if that passed, the court's official business would have been completed. In accordance with Seafield's programme, parliament would then have considered the proposal for toleration, and as this was virtually certain to fail, parliament could then have adjourned. For the time being the cavaliers would have served their purpose.

But neither the presbyterians nor the country party intended supply to pass without a struggle. The country party wanted no vote of supply at all, whilst the presbyterians could not allow such a vote to pass with open cavalier support for fear of the political consequences. Both groups prepared diversionary plans to block any supply. Presbyterians within the ministry had drafted an act ratifying the legality of the convention parliament and all its proceedings since the revolution. For the country party Tweeddale moved that parliament should give priority to constitutional changes necessary to preserve religion and liberty. Argyll and Annandale then applied direct pressure on Queensberry. They told him that unless their act was given preference over supply they and the court presbyterians would support Tweeddale's motion. It was plain that if Queensberry was to postpone an open defeat over supply he must abandon the cavaliers or adjourn. He might just as well have adjourned, since defeat was assured either way, but Queensberry was never very good at counting heads and he decided to break with the cavaliers.

He told the cavalier leaders he would have to let the presbyterians have their way, at which they were somewhat taken aback and they professed themselves to be 'much stumbled'. To increase their freedom of manoeuvre they decided rather reluctantly to support Tweeddale's motion, which would allow the introduction of a variety of measures. At this, since it was going to pass handsomely anyway, the court let Tweeddale's motion through without a vote.

Immediately a number of varied acts were handed in for debate. In the hope that once the presbyterians were satisfied they would help to vote supply Queensberry gave precedence to their proposed acts. In the meantime he tried to soothe the cavaliers, since he needed their support. He assured them that such 'presbyterian' measures were necessary for the queen's service and that they should be patient about toleration, to which parliament would attend in due course. Up to a point this plea was successful. The cavaliers, in spite of everything, collaborated to a surprising extent. They accepted the confirmation of the presbyterian church settlement; they acquiesced when the house ratified the turning of the 1689 convention into a parliament. Where they finally called a halt was at declaring it treason 'to impugn or endeavour by writing or malicious or advised speaking or other open act or deed to alter the claim of right'. This, arguably, made it treason to advocate episcopalianism in any way. Hamilton of Whitelaw, in fact, with the full weight of his legal reputation, asserted that this was so. The cavaliers' refusal to accept this was critical for both the court–cavalier alliance and the ministry. All the presbyterians within the court together with the Queensberry interest supported it, but those most active in arranging the cavalier alliance—Seafield, Tarbat, Atholl[49] and Prestonhall—spoke against the act. Seafield, as chancellor, had no vote, but Atholl and Prestonhall voted against it and Tarbat, typically, abstained. The act was voted and proved to be the end of the cavalier alliance. When the cavaliers' act for toleration came to be read disillusionment was complete. Predictably it received little support, generated a disturbance in parliament and was wisely not proceeded with.

All this completely transformed the parliamentary situation. The house was fragmented. The country party retained its determination to press for the reduction of English influence. The cavaliers split in various ways, all feeling the urge to vent their spleen on the court but some restrained by a dislike of damaging the prerogative lest there should ever be a Stuart restoration. Such respect for the monarchy accounted for the existence of a group of cavaliers, nicknamed the 'flying squadron', who proved susceptible to Seafield's persuasive talents. They agreed to give the court some slight assistance—against, for example, limitations within the queen's lifetime. But for the most part the cavaliers, resentful at what they saw as Queensberry's betrayal, took to opposition in order to disrupt proceeedings. Joining with the country party, they adopted a quite spurious pose of injured patriotism. Their subsequent nationalist posturing has to be viewed in the light of their earlier readiness, in return for promised favours, to support an English-inspired ministry in carrying its legislative programme. 'Patriotism' was rummaged out of the attic to suit the circumstances.

A separate Hanoverian group made an appearance, centred on Marchmont and the other ex-ministers. In collaboration with court presbyterians they had tried earlier to bring about the Hanoverian succession by some legal sleight of hand. They had proposed the repeal of the act of succession of 1681 in so far as it was inconsistent with the claim of right. Since this act asserted as fully and emphatically as possible the principle of direct hereditary succession and since the claim of right debarred popish successors, such a measure could conceivably have effected a Hanoverian settlement without any express vote. Its probable outcome and certainly its intent were both realised and, by a majority of twenty-four, parliament ordered that it should lie on the table. At this the Hanoverian group seemed to calculate that once the country party was satisfied over limitations they might perhaps consent to settle the succession on the house of Hanover. So, preferring a limited Hanoverian succession to the dangers of no succession at all, they prepared to collaborate with the country party in voting limitations. Only when it became clear that there was no possibility of settling the succession in the 1703 parliament did this group assist the court in fending off some of the wilder proposals of the country party. In particular they helped to defeat the anti-monarchical demands of Fletcher of Saltoun, which few of the country party were in favour of anyway although prepared to vote for them. Fletcher wanted something which bordered on a republic whilst the country leaders merely sought employment. That aims were for the most part merely tactical did not prevent feelings running high in parliament through the reactions natural in such an assembly, violence of language being seldom in practice countered by the soft answer. The young men of the country party, Roxburgh and Rothes for instance, determined to make a showing early in their parliamentary careers, postured and orated in the name of liberty and justice. Tweeddale screwed himself up to the point of speaking like the leader he was supposed to be, whilst Hamilton was by turns disdainful and indignant. All were genuinely infuriated by the court's tactics of engineering long debates and long adjournments to gain time. But, at bottom, what mattered to most of the opposition was the bargain they hoped to make, sooner or later, with the English court, so that from the very beginning the strategy of the Hanoverians had been misconceived.[50]

The hopelessness of the Hanoverian cause in 1703 was fully demonstrated by the reception given to Marchmont's act intended to settle the Hanoverian succession subject to limitations on the power of the crown. Once members realised its purport, Seafield had difficulty in keeping the house quiet long enough for the act to be read. The proposal was rejected with great contempt and rowdiness from the country and cavalier parties; Marchmont was refused permission even to have its rejection noted in the minutes. The courtiers could do nothing but keep silent and hope for the best.

Otherwise the ministry remained split. Seafield and Tarbat, for their separate reasons, each wanted to salvage something from the wreckage of the cavalier alliance. Tarbat was emotionally attached to it and afraid of spoiling his reputation with the English tories. Seafield merely wanted the court to reach an adjournment without being excessively mauled. Queensberry and Argyll, on the other hand, were trying to behave as though the opposition did not exist, Queensberry to avoid admitting past mistakes and Argyll to give the impression that he and the presbyterian interest had the power to manage parliament without assistance. General mistrust prevailed amongst the ministers, with an understandable desire to take out insurance policies against parliament's eventual outcome, whatever it might be.

These parliamentary splinterings meant that for much of the session the country party could take the initiative with their programme. This was an opportunity they had no right to expect, since their support was coming mainly from people completely unsympathetic to their professed aims. Any such development had been dismissed by Queensberry earlier in the session as unworthy of consideration. He had reported to the English court a possible 'conjunction of the cavaliers and some of our disobliged former friends and others with the duke of Hamilton', but he concluded that 'their interests and principles are so different and incompatible [that] they can never join in particulars that can straiten me any way'.[51] Queensberry was right about the conflicting interests and principles but disregarding the negligible influence that principle exerted on political behaviour. Even the single issue of whether one accepted the revolution or not was of limited effect in a situation where, whatever their ultimate objectives, the prime intention of all opposition groups was to embarrass the court. In 1703 a number of groups found themselves in this position and so were able to combine their nuisance value. The alliance, nevertheless, was quite fortuitous.

Yet from the parliament of 1703 emerged the act anent peace and war and the act of security, both forced on the court by this ill-assorted opposition and both important links in the chain of events leading to the union. The former act vested in the Scottish parliament, for the future, the final decision on Scotland's declaring war. The prospect disquieted Godolphin but, despite his private remonstrances to the Scottish officers of state, the queen was advised to let it become law. The act of security was intended to lay down the conditions under which the next successor to the Scottish throne was to be selected, conditions which would ensure that the choice was free of English influence. For the English the alarming part of this act was the 'communication of trade' clause. By this provision the separation of England and Scotland was envisaged on the death of the queen unless, in the meantime, the Scots had been granted, amongst other things, full freedom of trade with England and the plantations. The act savoured of aggressive nationalism and seemed very like an attempt to dictate terms to England. Ironically this menacing clause had no part in the country party's original proposal. What they originally had in mind was the safeguarding of Scotland's future trade projects against English interference, harking back once again to Darien. So in an attempt to ensure that sufficiently stringent limitations were placed on the crown without delay in 1703, Roxburgh proposed that the two crowns were to be separated at the queen's death unless the limitations were law by the end of the session. It was to fend off this time limit that the 'communication of trade' clause was introduced, not by the opposition but by the court as what seemed to some a bright tactical idea. Much to the ministry's embarrassment, however, the clause was taken up by the opposition, not as it stood but tacked to Roxburgh's original proposal, the time limit being extended beyond 1703 to Anne's death. Thus the court had gained time but at the cost of lending the act of security an ominous aspect and, perhaps more significantly, introducing a 'communication of trade' into the country party's demands. Some Scottish ministers, being well aware of the danger, had frightened themselves by what they had done. Officers of state who had concurred in the original proposal, or even actively advised it, were suddenly very quick to disclaim all responsibility. Queensberry's chief concern was that he should be in possession of collective advice in favour of the clause signed by all but himself. Argyll and Annandale, who had favoured the proposal, not only voted against it but registered a formal protest.

The English ministry was determined that the queen should not give assent to any act containing such a clause. Despite the Scots' contention that the act was necessary to pacify parliament, the English, for reasons of domestic politics, declined to give way. Nottingham declared that no Englishman dared advise the queen to give the royal assent to such an act.

A further product of this session appeared in England to be of some significance: the wine act, allowing the importation of foreign wines, generally understood to be French although this was not specifically mentioned. If French wines were imported they would have to be brought in indirectly by way of another state to keep within the law, although doubtless there were merchants who looked forward to a quietly profitably trade with France. In some English circles the act was seen as yet another provocation from the Scots. It was, in intention, nothing of the kind. The act had been sanctioned by the English ministry, its main purpose being to replenish the Scottish civil list out of which official salaries were paid. The main source of the civil list income was customs revenue, greatly depleted by the war and the consequent prohibition on French wines. So the act was a financial measure to make provision for ministerial salaries and pensions which could not otherwise be paid. The court, assisted by some burgh members interested in the wine trade, by the flying squadron's preferring the wine act to limitations, by Hanoverians who had given up hope of the country party's ever settling the succession on Hanover, and by some cavaliers hoping for easier contact with France, managed to carry the act against strong country opposition. This brief interlude gave the court one of its few successes. Immediately afterwards the country party intensified its campaign for limitations, with every hope of seriously disturbing if not defeating the court. Queensberry's only way of escape was to adjourn parliament without a vote of supply and in September he was finally driven to this.

7 Causes and consequences of the court's defeat

The session of 1703 had produced dramatic results. Viewed as texts, in isolation, the act anent peace and war, the act of security and the wine act appear to accord very well with the view that they were nationalist in inspiration. It is easy to represent them as weapons to force the English to compromise over Darien and other outstanding issues. The reality was quite different. These acts were not due to the calculated policy of any particular group, much less of parliament as a whole, since no one had envisaged what came about. Fletcher of Saltoun's intentions were clear but he was one of the incorruptibles, a visionary, unconcerned with compromise. The bulk of his colleagues of the country party rejected his vision outright although relishing its nuisance value. Their interest lay solely in making a noise and embarrassing the court. Some of the parliament's proceedings, the acts of peace and war and security in particular, were concerned with the very basis of Scottish sovereignty but save for the peculiar circumstances of the session even this principle would have been inadequately supported, attracting no more than the sixty or so votes of the country party. And they would have been motivated not by patriotism but by committed opposition. Roxburgh, of all people, declaring his readiness to demand justice, sword in hand, has to be taken less than seriously.

However, in England only the acts of the 1703 session attracted attention. A temporary and ill-assorted opposition majority had contorted and bawled its way into a position which surprised most of its members and considerably embarrassed some of them. This confusion was not appreciated in England, where the illusion of institutional solidarity was dominant. A direct challenge seemed to have been issued by the Scottish parliament. And, in a sense, from the point of view of Anglo-Scottish relations, the origin of the acts was of less importance than the fact that they had been voted. It would have been a pitiful opposition which failed to masquerade as patriots claiming quite undeserved credit for the acts voted. For those who had supported the country party for unsavoury motives there was no other way to justify, publicly, what had been done. It creates a better impression to own up to patriotism, even in excess, than to malice, jealousy and resentment. So the apparent intention of the acts filtered into the opposition programme as good propaganda and a useful device for obstruction. Court proposals could be blocked by a counter-demand for a treaty with England to safeguard Scotland's position. Any treaty proposed could be rejected as unsatisfactory. When necessary, it could be argued that any measures at all should be preceded by limitations, misuse of the power of the crown under English influence being the fundamental cause of Scottish misfortunes. Altogether the parliament of 1703 had been a windfall to the opposition. Not only had it produced a court crisis but during the session the lines of their own future policy had been revealed to them.

The roots of the court's debacle were very deep but one of the most easily traced was the encouragement given to the cavaliers through the intrigues of 1702 in London. From this sprang many of the subsequent problems of management and the unsuccessful attempts made to solve them. The failure of the court–cavalier alliance had been only a symptom of the ministry's quandary. Since whatever hope there was of an alliance with some of the country party had been destroyed—by Tweeddale's intransigence and Queensberry's determination to remain in power—logic seemed to dictate as the only solution the court–cavalier alliance. At least Seafield thought so. And in that such success as the court could claim in 1703 was due to this scheme he was right. Without it the queen's title would have remained in doubt and the legality of the 1702 session would have been denied. The traces of cavalier support that Seafield contrived to retain throughout the session enabled the court to emerge less mangled than might otherwise have been the case. What had been badly underestimated were the probable effects of the scheme on the presbyterians. Their known antagonism to both Queensberry and the cavaliers and its link with the rivalry in the court between Queensberry and Argyll makes their reaction, with hindsight, appear natural. Perhaps it ought to have been foreseeable at the time. Even so it is difficult to see what other course could have been taken but to accept the risks involved. In the circumstances of 1703 there was no complete solution to the problem of managing the Scottish parliament.

The irresponsibility of Queensberry's conduct typifies the nature of the Scottish problem. When he at last faced the parliament his predicament can excite sympathy but it was one he had done much to create by his complete disregard of the problem of management. He had contributed greatly to the court's defeat. Moreover his reactions in defeat indicate the order of his priorities. What came first in his scheme was not the future success of court policy but his determination to load his opponents with the blame for failure.

When the cavaliers were forced out of the court alliance Queensberry was quick to misrepresent the cause, which he ascribed to disagreement amongst ministers. He placed this on record by asking for a letter from the queen ordering the officers of state to obey his instructions. The queen wrote formally to this effect.[52] His main target was Atholl, his rival, whom he wished to discredit. The act of security had originated in a straightforward court proposal to provide for continuity of government should Anne die before the succession had been agreed. Atholl was put up as court spokesman to introduce this formal measure, on the strength of which Queensberry later tried to blame him for the act as eventually voted, complete with opposition amendments.[53] When the court was considering its hazardous 'communication of trade' amendment to Roxburgh's proposal Queensberry tried to persuade Atholl to propose it in parliament.[54] This and other circumstances led Atholl and Seafield to suspect, with reason, that he was preparing to shift the blame should anything go wrong.[55]

Quite apart from their habitual enmity there had been differences between the two magnates during the parliament. They were not such as to mark out Atholl for the deluge of criticism to which he was subjected. In most of his conduct he was allied with Seafield, who for the most part was not attacked and certainly not with the same venom. Queensberry magnified Atholl's various quirks and lapses. To maintain his 'country' image Atholl had refused to accept the ratification of the 1702 parliament and when the vote was taken he was at his father's funeral, which seemed to provide him with a face-saving exit.[56] Queensberry complained that Atholl had broken the undertaking to support the measure and that his father's funeral should not have interfered with his duty.[57] Stories to Atholl's disadvantage, sometimes bordering on tittle-tattle, were fed back to London. When the marquess returned to Edinburgh after his father's funeral he was accused of showing disrespect to the lord commissioner by not visiting him as his first call. Atholl denied it but it hardly seems to matter whether the story was true or not.[58] There was much more complaint of a similar kind. However, the really important issue at the time seemed to be that of Atholl's dukedom. Before the 1703 session patents had been issued for Tarbat to be an earl and Atholl to be a duke. The patents were to be retained by Queensberry until the end of the session. Atholl suspected rightly that Queensberry was trying to delay the issue of his patent until a similar one had passed for the titular head of Queensberry's own family—the marquess of Douglas, a minor. But this was one of Queensberry's lesser aims. Just as in William's reign he had been indignant over Hamilton's promotion, he was extremely resentful that Atholl should be made a duke at all. If he could have got away with it he would have stopped the issue of the patent. In the correspondence between Edinburgh and London, even at the height of the parliamentary crisis, a disproportionate amount of energy was devoted to this topic. Queensberry, who had written to Nottingham hardly at all on the subject of parliamentary affairs, suddenly communicated with him at length in denunciation of Atholl and his patent for a dukedom.[59] He wrote to the queen on the same subject accusing Atholl of, among other things, jacobitism.[60] Both men seemed to have reduced national politics to the level of a primary school quarrel. But for them this was the substance of politics. What counted for Queensberry and Atholl, as for most others, was not whether the court succeeded in managing parliament or not but who should control the court interest and the disposal of patronage.

It is in this context that one has to view the so-called 'Scotch plot'. Towards the end of the 1703 parliament Queensberry, as lord commissioner, wrote confidentially to the queen indicating that he had information showing the entire parliamentary opposition to be part of a jacobite conspiracy. He did not wish to divulge the source of this disclosure unless ordered to do so, but he affirmed, 'God knows whether the story be true or false but my author is a man of quality and integrity that I dare assure your majesty there is neither mistake nor trick on his part . . .'[61] The person thus referred to was the already notorious Simon Fraser, whom few others would have described in such terms. Fraser was prepared to implicate Atholl—his own enemy and Queensberry's—in the plot. How far Queensberry was acting in good faith is open to doubt, whatever qualifications he made. The story fitted precisely his own immediate requirements. It provided an explanation of sorts for the size of the opposition in a parliament he had claimed would be easy to manage. There was a chance of its discrediting Atholl. Queensberry's opponents did not hesitate to charge him with having used the fabrications of a double agent for his own political advantage.[62] Even Seafield, who was not personally ill-disposed to Queensberry, referred obliquely to 'the contrivances and actings of some'.[63] And afterwards, when it suited him, even Queensberry was to claim that he had given little credit to the informer.[64] The most charitable thing which can be said about Queensberry's behaviour was that at the end of a long and probably exhausting session he was rendered over-credulous by a desire to find a scapegoat for the failure. If charity is abandoned one is left to contemplate a most unsavoury manoeuvre.

The session of 1703 had presented the English court with a major problem. One of the most threatening facets of this was that the junto whigs had sniffed the possibilities of using Scottish affairs to advance their own interest in England. Queensberry's credit had not stood high with them before but now he seemed finally to have taken sides against the Scottish 'tories', so the whigs joined in his defence. Their official version of the events of 1703 was that Queensberry would have succeeded in handling parliament had he not been deserted by Atholl, Tarbat and Seafield, who were virtual jacobites.[65] This was a travesty of what had happened in Edinburgh but, together with the 'plot', it was to provide the junto with ample ammunition for the forthcoming session of the English parliament.

Notes

[1] *APS*, x, 59.

[2] Buccleuch (Drum.), Seven Letters, 5 Aug. 1701.

[3] *CSP (Dom), 1702–3*, 7, 19 Mar. 1702; *Marchmont Papers*, iii, Marchmont to the queen, 1702.

[4] Buccleuch (Drum.), Pringle, 3 Jun. 1702; *ib.*, Stair, Rochester to [Queensberry], 3 Jun. 1702; BL, Add. MSS 29588, 43, Seafield to Nottingham, 4 Jun. 1702; *Jerviswood*, 10, Johnston to Baillie, 13 Feb. 1702/3.

[5] *Carstares S.P.*, 714, Marchmont to Carstares, 31 Mar. 1702.

[6] *Jerviswood*, 3, Johnston to Baillie, May 1702.

[7] Buccleuch (Drum.), Letters, xvi, [Carstares] to [Queensberry], 27 May 1702.

[8] Wodrow, *Analecta*, i, 15, 17; *HMCR Johnstone MSS*, 119–20, P. Johnston to Annandale, 13 Mar. 1702; *HMCR Hamilton MSS, Supp.*, 149, Hamilton to Marlborough, 16 Mar. 1702.

[9] *Carstares S.P.*, 514, Melville to Carstares, 4 Jun. 1700.

[10] Buccleuch (Drum.), Letters, xvi, [Carstares] to [Queensberry], 21 and 27 May 1702.

[11] SRO, GD 26, xiii, 67/4, Queensberry to Leven, 21 May [1702]; *CSP (Dom), 1702–3*, 99, the queen to Queensberry, 3 Jun. 1702.

[12] Buccleuch (Drum.), Church and State, May 1702.

[13] *APS*, xi, 16, 20, 26.

[14] Buccleuch (Drum.), Seven Letters, 5 Aug. 1701.

[15] *Marchmont Papers*, iii, 242, Marchmont's memorial, 1 Jul. 1702; BL, Add. MSS 6420, 7, Pringle to [Queensberry], 2 Jul. 1702; *Carstares S.P.*, 714, Philiphaugh to Carstares, 4 Jul. 1702; *HMCR Laing MSS*, ii, 63, Seafield's memorial, 10 Jul. 1704; SRO, GD 220, G, Boyle to Montrose, 28 Jun. 1702.

[16] The following account of the preparations for managing the 1703 parliament is an abridged version of an article: P. W. J. Riley, 'The formation of the Scottish ministry of 1703', *SHR*, xliv (1965), 112–34, modified in the light of further evidence of Queensberry's general policy. Documentation has been restricted to new evidence and the identification of quotations.

[17] Buccleuch (Drum.), Letters, xvi, [Carstares] to [Queensberry], 3 Jun. 1702 and Riley, *art. cit.*, 115 n. 5.

[18] *Caldwell Papers*, i, 195, Denham to W. Hamilton, 17 Mar. 1702.

[19] *Carstares S.P.*, 170–7, Johnston to Carstares, 16 May 1690 [*sic* for 1693].

[20] Cunningham, *History*, i, 326.

[21] Buccleuch (Drum.), Letters, xvi, Tarbat to [Queensberry], 8 Jun. 1702.

[22] *Jerviswood*, 7, Johnston to Baillie, 21 Nov. 1702; BL, Add. MSS 29588, 214, Tarbat to Nottingham, 12 Sep. 1702; NLS, MS 7021, 64, Bruce to Tweeddale, 18 Jan. 1703; *HMCR Portland MSS*, viii, 110, [Carstares] to [Harley], 15 Sep. 1702; *Seafield Letters*, 115, Hamilton to W. Keith, 7 Aug. 1702. For examples of Tarbat's 'objective' appraisals see *ib.*, 123, 'The Present State of the Scots Divisions' [1703], and 129, 'Characters of Families' [1703].

[23] *Lockhart Papers*, i, 52.

²⁴ SRO, GD 248, Box 5/2, Misc. correspondence to and from the earl of Seafield, Queensberry to Seafield, 6 Mar. [1703].

²⁵ See above, p. 21.

²⁶ *HMCR Laing MSS*, ii, 47–50, [*c*. Feb. 1704].

²⁷ See above, p. 37.

²⁸ NLS, MS 7021, 56, Yester to Tweeddale, 19 Nov. 1702.

²⁹ *Ib.*, 58, same to same, 28 Nov. 1702.

³⁰ BL, Add. MSS 29588, 457, Tarbat to Nottingham, 9 May 1703.

³¹ NLS, MS 7021, 68, Bruce to Tweeddale, 11 Mar. 1703. The author of *The State of Scotland Under the Past and Present Administration With Relation to England, &C.* (1703) takes a similar view of the changes.

³² Earl of March.

³³ SRO, GD 205, Letters of Sir W. Bennet, Bennet to Dirleton, 26 Jan. 1703.

³⁴ BL, Add. MSS 29588, 496, Atholl to Nottingham, 25 Jun. 1703.

³⁵ SRO, GD 205, Letters from Individuals, R. Mackenzie to Bennet, 28 Jan. 1703.

³⁶ Apart from the possible threat it represented to his campaigns or the likelihood of its being an objective for a French landing Marlborough seems to have had little interest in Scotland or its affairs: see Henry L. Snyder, *The Marlborough–Godolphin Correspondence*, 3 vols. (Oxford, 1975), *passim*. On one of the rare occasions when the duke cautiously ventured an opinion on Scottish policy, viz., that Queensberry be dismissed in 1704, Queensberry had been out of office for almost a month.

³⁷ See below, p. 182.

³⁸ See below, pp. 71–2. For an example of the propaganda use made of the reluctance to settle the Scottish succession see *Somers Tracts*, xii, 617.

³⁹ Blenheim Papers, B2/33, [Harley] to [Godolphin], 20 Sep. 1703, e.g., and Riley, *art. cit.*, 505 n. 5.

⁴⁰ See below, pp. 178–9.

⁴¹ Boyer, *Annals*, i, 207–8; NLS, MS 7021, 73, Bruce to Tweeddale, 25 Mar. 1703; SRO, GD 248, Box 5/2, Misc. correspondence to and from the earl of Seafield, Queensberry to Seafield, 17 Mar. [1703]; Wodrow, *Early Letters*, 257–61, Wodrow to L. Campbell, 1 Apr. 1703.

⁴² BL, Add. MSS 6420, 8, to [Queensberry], 16 Mar. 1703.

⁴³ SRO, GD 248, Box 5/2, Misc. correspondence to and from the earl of Seafield, Queensberry to Seafield, Mar. 1703.

⁴⁴ The parliament had been adjourned in June and dissolved in August.

⁴⁵ BL, Add. MSS 6420, 8, 16 Mar. 1703.

⁴⁶ *CSP (Dom.), 1702–3*, 671, 2 Apr. 1703.

⁴⁷ What follows is summarised from P. W. J. Riley, 'The Scottish parliament of 1703', *SHR*, xlvii (1968), 129–50, where the evidence for the conclusions can be found.

⁴⁸ W. Ferguson, 'The making of the Treaty of Union of 1707', *SHR*, xliii (1964), 90 *et seq.*, was the first to stress the importance of sovereignty as an issue in 1703.

[49] Atholl died at the beginning of this parliament and his son, Tullibardine, must henceforth be referred to by this title.

[50] I am fully in agreement with Dr Ferguson (*Scotland's Relations*, 206–7) that there was 'angry intransigence' in the parliament of 1703 but would contend that it sprang from motives rather more petty than nationalism. In view of Ferguson's own low estimate of political motivation in Scotland, with which I obviously agree, this seems a more likely explanation. What should come as no surprise to an historian—but to me, at least, frequently does—is the extent to which politicians can become worked up over something about which they care very little.

[51] *HMCR Laing MSS*, ii, 14, Queensberry's memorial, [29 May 1703].

[52] *CSP (Dom.), 1703–4*, 3, 5 Jun. 1703.

[53] *HMCR Laing MSS*, ii, 13, Queensberry's memorial; BL, Add. MSS 6420, 13, [Queensberry] to the queen, 11 Aug. 1703; *ib.*, 15, [same] to same, 25 Sep. 1703; *ib.*, 24, 'Memorial concerning my Lord Privy Seal', [1703]. Cf. Seafield's version of the episode in *HMCR Laing MSS*, ii, 19, to Godolphin, [29 May 1703].

[54] See above, p. 58.

[55] *HMCR Laing MSS*, ii, 33, Seafield to Godolphin, 28 Jul. 1703; *ib.*, 30, Atholl to [Godolphin], 23 Jul. 1703; BL, Add. MSS 6420, 10, 20 Jul. 1703.

[56] *Ib.*, 24, 'Memorial concerning my Lord Privy Seal', [1703].

[57] *HMCR Laing MSS*, ii, 10–15, Queensberry's memorial, [29 May 1703].

[58] BL, Add. MSS 28055, 29, Atholl to Godolphin, 10 Jun. 1703.

[59] *Ib.*, 29588, 494, 20 Jun. 1703. See also *HMCR Laing MSS*, ii, 22–3, [Seafield] to [Godolphin], [Jun. 1703].

[60] BL, Add. MSS 6420, 15 [Queensberry] to the queen, 25 Sep. 1703.

[61] *Ib.*, 13, [same] to same, 11 Aug. 1703.

[62] See below, pp. 68–9.

[63] BL, Add. MSS 34180, 40, to Godolphin, 30 May 1704.

[64] *Seafield Letters*, 77, Seafield to Godolphin, 26 Aug. 1705.

[65] Vernon, iii, 238, Vernon to Shrewsbury, 15 Oct. 1703.

CHAPTER THREE

The new party experiment

The consequences of the session of 1703 and Queensberry's allegations of widespread jacobitism proved so painful for the court that it sought relief in some major but extremely delicate political surgery. The operation failed, leaving Godolphin's position as court manager virtually intolerable.

Despite what the English took to be great concessions—royal assent to the act anent peace and war, for example—there was little to show in return and the Scottish parliament had ended in uproar. No supply had been forthcoming. The court had hoped that the union commission might be renewed. In fact the commission had been squashed and the prospect of union had receded.[1] A further casualty had been the tories' vision of managing Scotland through an alliance with the episcopalians, or cavalier party as the political episcopalians had proved to be. Whatever lingering illusions were still cherished by a few tories, politicians of Nottingham's calibre must have realised that they had reached a dead end.

1 Inquest on 1703

For the English managers the problem now was to secure the link with Scotland and obtain supply in the next parliament. The recent session was of interest to them only in so far as it affected future arrangements. But those Scots alleged to have been in the plot wanted the events of the session raked over to vindicate themselves and re-establish their eligibility for employment. Queensberry wanted no enquiry. He aimed at triumph by assertion, affirming that failure had been the fault of almost everyone else, whereas he, if fully supported by other ministers, was confident of success in a subsequent parliament.

He went further. He claimed to believe that, if parliament were to meet again on 12 October, to which date it had been officially adjourned, it would grant supply. Indeed, he said that only the reluctance of the other officers of state had prevented his proposing it.[2]

Queensberry could not have believed this. If, as he alleged, he was the victim of a gigantic jacobite conspiracy, there was little hope of its evaporating between September and October. And anyway it seems most unlikely that a parliament which had sat from May to September without approaching supply, and had been adjourned to restrain it from objectionable measures, would reappear in October completely changed in heart. Queensberry wanted to re-establish belief in his fitness to continue as commissioner by comparing himself favourably to others in terms of devotion to the queen's service. Such changes as he proposed were brazenly designed to remove his personal opponents from the ministry and replace them with his own followers.[3]

Amongst those he tried to blame for the failure of 1703 were Seafield, Atholl and Cromartie,[4] who to clear themselves wanted an inquest in the presence of the queen and her English ministers. They were anxious to hear from Queensberry himself the allegations they suspected he had secretly made against them. Queensberry wished to evade such an embarrassing confrontation.[5]

No attempt had been made to investigate the 'plot' thoroughly in Scotland. On the contrary its supposed existence had been kept a close secret. With the assistance of a pass issued by Queensberry, Fraser had been able to take a highland jaunt; with a passport issued by Nottingham on Queensberry's recommendation he had since returned to France having every reason to be satisfied. When the 'plot' was exposed at the end of 1703 it was not by Queensberry, who had been satisfied with casting suspicion on his rivals in a private letter to the queen. But Fraser's intrigue was known to Robert Ferguson, 'the plotter', who warned Atholl of what was going on. Then Balcarres, a former jacobite exile enlisted for the court by Queensberry, had spoken unwisely of the pass issued to Fraser, whereupon Queensberry, to justify himself, had cited his own letters to the queen by way of official warrant. Thus began a demand for a full investigation which found Queensberry unprepared, there being an embarrassing lack of evidence.[6] Some of his friends, though, Stair and Balcarres in particular, seeing political advantage in the 'plot', and realising that silence would get them nowhere, took up the story publicly and with zest. Balcarres talked of discoveries about to be made on the strength of which he was offering five hundred to five in guineas that Queensberry would increase his influence at court.[7]

So Queensberry had to brazen it out. The country party believed that he had tried to create just enough vague suspicion about his rivals to allow himself a clear field in Scottish affairs.[8] Some of his supporters had certainly thought along these lines and Queensberry's own actions seemed to point to the same intention. When Sir John MacLean, newly arrived from France, was interrogated by the council, Queensberry opposed Atholl's being present on the ground that he might be implicated.[9] As it happened MacLean's evidence discredited Fraser, as a result of which he later claimed to have been maliciously harassed by young Argyll on behalf of 'the Queensberry club'.[10] Meanwhile Queensberry's immediate concern was to keep the situation vague and be all things to all men. His aim had not wavered in the least since 1696: the achievement of complete dominance in Scottish patronage and affairs. He secured his continuation as lord high commissioner with pay and allowances until long after the parliament had been adjourned.[11] Then he wanted authority to compel the obedience of other ministers along the lines of his arrangement with William in 1700.[12]

But probably because stories of the 'plot' were increasing in circulation the English managers decided on a disputation before the queen. Despite all Queensberry's attempts to prevent it a 'Scots council' met in Anne's presence on 18 January 1704 where Atholl spoke his mind about Queensberry, reading a lengthy memorial about the 'plot' and attacking Queensberry's method of investigation.[13] Most of the talking on Queensberry's behalf seems to have been done by Stair even though the duke was present. He insisted that there was a plot involving influential persons. When Atholl demanded proof Stair could only repeat his assertion. Before the meeting closed Atholl's son and Stair had quarrelled to such an extent that the queen had to intervene to prevent a duel.[14]

Now that Atholl could claim to have been unjustly accused, there being a complete dearth of evidence, he increased the pressure against Queensberry. Selkirk wrote to tell him, '. . . you have more in your hand now than Scotsman ever had, so I hope you will make good use of it. I am sure if the triumvirate[15] agree, you may have *carte blanche* from the queen, and dispose of matters as you please, so now it depends on you whether this nation shall continue to groan under Queensberry's government, or be forever free of it . . .'[16] He meant, of course, that it rested with Atholl whether the Murrays and the Hamilton interest were going to topple Queensberry or not. Atholl thought he had a chance. He challenged Queensberry so vehemently over his actions in 1703 that Tweeddale thought none but Queensberry would have borne it so 'christianly'.[17] Atholl hoped for the co-operation of Seafield and Cromartie, looked upon by some as members of his 'party' against Queensberry.[18] But they had little in common save a desire to clear themselves of charges arising from the recent parliamentary fiasco. Their other aims were very different. Both were thought to be backsliding in the campaign against Queensberry, for which the more zealous members of the country party scorned them. In the council meeting when the Queensberry men accused them of collaborating with the opposition they had merely justified themselves, resting on 'self defence and declaring they were of no party; (I suppose) they meant except the uppermost', according to Roderick Mackenzie.[19] Lord John Hay thought they wished only to keep their jobs.[20] He may have been unfair even to Cromartie, though it is doubtful. He was certainly unfair to Seafield.

There was little basis for co-operation between Cromartie and almost anybody else, but he was certainly not going to stick out his neck gratuitously to further Atholl's interest, which was what seemed to be expected of him. Seafield was in a different category, his position being more secure than Cromartie's and the basis on which he operated fully appreciated by Godolphin. Whatever happened he was unlikely to lose his place. If, after receiving advice, the English managers had for whatever reason decided that Queensberry was to be commissioner to the next parliament, Seafield would have accepted it and been in his place as chancellor to execute whatever policy had been agreed on. So, although he had to defend his actions in the 1703 parliament, that was the limit of his common ground with Atholl.

Seafield's preoccupation, like Godolphin's, was with future management. He knew that Queensberry could not hope to carry a majority in parliament on his own terms. But at least Queensberry had a considerable following within the court. Atholl had none. And, whatever he might pretend, Atholl's parliamentary position was not strong amongst the opposition. Though his territorial interest and highland following made him a magnate his connections were with cavaliers and episcopalians. After the 1703 session he could not hope for cavalier support should he become a minister; nor could he expect much encouragement from the country party, most of whom followed

Hamilton or Tweeddale. The real nature of his interest was driving him to follow his father's example, making the most of his jacobite connections whilst pretending otherwise. In early 1704 it had not quite come to that, but already it was obvious that Atholl was not the man to manage the next parliament. How the next parliament was to be managed was a question on which Seafield's ideas were already taking shape.[21]

2 The junto and the 'Scotch Plot'

The urgency of the problem was increased by events in English domestic politics. Scotland had become a crucial problem in English affairs through the junto's realisation that the 'Scotch plot' was an issue they could exploit for the session of 1703–4, enabling them to attack the ministry's conduct of affairs and, possibly, to drive the earl of Nottingham out of the ministry.

Through their small majority in the lords the whigs were able to use the 'Scotch plot' to castigate the ministry in the name of almost every whig principle. They claimed to fear danger from France, threats to the protestant succession and the revolution, jacobite conspiracy passing unnoticed or, worse still, disregarded, under the noses of ministers, to say nothing of the alleged concealment of treachery by the court and, in particular, by Nottingham. The junto had been given a rare opportunity and they made the most of it.

The queen's telling the lords that she had information of 'ill practices and designs carried on in Scotland by emissaries from France' was the signal for the whig offensive. In December 1703 the whig majority began to order the seizure of persons supposedly connected with the 'plot' and set up a committee consisting entirely of whigs to question them.[22] Rumour was used to prejudge the issue. Even before the investigation was properly begun the junto lords were letting it be known that there had been a 'plot', although no evidence had so far appeared to justify this belief.[23]

The tory majority in the commons retaliated by questioning the lords' right to conduct such an enquiry.[24] The lords set out precedents, asserting that the enquiry was essential, Nottingham's report on the seizure and examination of persons coming from France being so unsatisfactory.[25] Evidence of clandestine trafficking between France and parts of Britain came to light, though what it amounted to is open to question: there was always cloak-and-dagger activity between

Britain and the continent. To some people it was almost a sport. The committee attached great importance to 'letters ... written in a Gibberish language, wherein the conspiracy is said to be contained'.[26] But the entire investigation, whether of persons or papers, produced evidence of nothing more than this secret but fairly routine voyaging across the Channel, none of which could really be dignified, then any more than at any other time, with the name of 'plot'. It certainly bore no relation to anything alleged by Queensberry.

However, the lords were in no way deterred by this deficiency from voting some stern resolutions which formed the basis of an address to the queen. They resolved that there had been a dangerous conspiracy to raise rebellion in Scotland and bring about a French invasion in the interest of the prince of Wales. Nothing, they asserted, had given so much encouragement to this as the succession's not having been settled in Scotland. Accordingly they wished the queen to have the succession decided, after which the lords would do all they could to bring about a union of the two kingdoms.[27] The drift of this was apparent to those who understood the language of party politics at Westminster. A tory pamphleteer observed in 1704 that '. . . there is a party in the house of lords who will needs manage all the affairs of England and meddle in the affairs of Scotland too, which is none of their business . . .'[28] The junto was using Scotland to put pressure on the court. The administration's policy in Scotland—avoidance of the succession and concentration on union—had to be condemned. The junto was now reversing the order of priority. The whig lords had to be seen to be dictating to the court, posing as guardians of the protestant succession the settlement of which in Scotland would suit them much beter than union. By affirming the reality of the 'plot' they were deliberately leaving open to suspicion the Scots supposedly implicated.

The court's Scottish policy standing condemned, the lords then passed a vote of censure on Nottingham for his alleged remissness in not having properly examined Sir John MacLean nor having prosecuted Ferguson 'the plotter'.[29] Soon afterwards Nottingham resigned and went into opposition. Being a man who set great store by consistency, he continued to profess an academic belief in union but his attitude was similar to that of the Scottish opposition: in support of union but opposed to any practicable terms.[30]

3 The court's problem of 1704

The court, meanwhile, was left confronting the junto over Scotland. Godolphin and Marlborough, having connived at leaving the succession open, were vulnerable. The Scottish parliament seemed to have rendered the union policy impracticable for the foreseeable future. In such circumstances the court had no choice but to accept the policy of succession, if possible without seeming to have been forced into it. The queen's reply to the lords' address was terse: she had some time ago decided to settle the protestant succession in Scotland as the best way to union.[31] That the court had already decided on succession, if only to anticipate the inevitable junto demand, seems to have been true[32] but the statement could not have carried much conviction.

However, the junto's campaign had been only partially successful. Until the enquiry into the 'plot' had started the English managers seemed unable to think of any way of handling the next parliament save through a *rapprochement* between Queensberry and the ministers with whom he was in dispute, this in spite of the fact that the 'plot' had left far too many people professing themselves slandered and outraged for Queensberry to be likely to succeed. It was possible, as a well-informed correspondent of the marquess of Montrose thought, that Queensberry knew too much about court policy for him to be dropped with safety,[33] but this was before the lords' enquiry was fully in progress. During the lords' investigation Queensberry's usual combination of private assertion and public discretion had to be temporarily abandoned. To clear himself over his dealings with Fraser he had to perform more openly, and his behaviour endeared him neither to the court nor to those Scots who were being accused of jacobitism. He told the junto what he knew about court policy in Scotland, on account of which he was accused of 'having betrayed their secrets to the lords' making them in consequence 'very pushing and insulting'.[34] In addition he tried to pass all responsibility to the court by emphasising his willingness, if asked, to give the source of his information. It was true that he had offered to name Fraser but he had made it clear that in the interests of security he was most reluctant to do so. During the course of the enquiry there might well have been other indiscretions. From the enquiry Queensberry at length emerged as an ally of the junto, much to the distaste of the court managers, who looked on him as unfit to be employed.

Yet despite the court's aversion it was not easy to think of any

alternative. Queensberry was backed by a considerable lobby. The
junto had already cast him in the role of leader of the revolution party
in Scotland—the obvious man to carry the succession.[35] There seemed
to be no other feasible choice. The young duke of Argyll, recently
succeeded to the title, was 'mighty brisk and forward', insisting on
having all his father's places, but was as yet an unknown quantity in
politics.[36] Carstares, although dislodged from his former position, had
retained some influence with individuals and was using it in
Queensberry's favour.[37] In fact, whatever the queen and her English
managers wanted, Queensberry had been the dominant interest in the
court party for so long that if he said he could carry the succession it
was not going to be easy to reject him. Queensberry's followers had too
much at stake to allow him to fall without a struggle. Any readjustment
was likely to be painful for them and particularly so for his close allies,
the Dalrymples. Common repute had it that Stair, the head of that
family, was acting as Queensberry's *eminence grise*, having established
something of an ascendancy over him.[38] So, prompted perhaps by Stair
but certainly with the concurrence of all his followers, Queensberry
declared categorically that he could carry the succession in parliament.
Baillie of Jerviswood wrote to his wife: '. . . The succession is the
present measure; but whether the court be in earnest a little time will
discover. However, the duke of Queensberry undertakes it frankly, and
will be the man employed in all probability, for the lords who support
him[39] will have it so . . .'[40]

Queensberry wanted very badly to be commissioner again, otherwise
he ran the risk of losing money, status and employment. He had no
wish to see his interest damaged, for such would be the probable result
of his being supplanted. He was no more anxious to suffer than were his
supporters who had invested their careers in his advancement. But the
Queensberry interest had less excuse for their claims than had the
junto, who appeared to be starkly ignorant of Scottish affairs. To
anyone with knowledge of Scotland it was obvious that Queensberry
could not command a majority in parliament whatever policy he
undertook. The English court suspected it. Seafield knew it. And so did
Stair, who seems to have made in London a suggestion for overcoming
the problem of the Scottish parliament: to pay the Scottish army with
money from England and not call parliament again till the queen's
death. This story must have leaked from a council meeting and gained
wide currency. The topic was officially evaded but the fact never
denied.[41] In part it was the notoriety of this suggestion that led to a

country party delegation's being sent to London.

4 The country party delegation

During the enquiry into the 'plot' Atholl had felt increasingly isolated at court. Consequently he wrote to Scotland asking for country party support to reinforce his efforts against Queensberry and incidentally lend credence to his pose as the country party spokesman in the ministry. His plea and the news of the lords' proceedings on the 'plot' decided Hamilton to call an opposition meeting at Steele's tavern on 16 February 1704. It was a predominantly country party affair with a mere scattering of cavaliers present. The meeting decided to send Roxburgh, Rothes and Baillie of Jerviswood, leading members of Tweeddale's interest, to London as a delegation to ask the queen to call parliament and allow a Scottish investigation into the 'plot'. They were to oppose the advice she had allegedly been given to pay Scottish forces with English money as inconsistent with the liberties of the nation and they were to ask that Queensberry should not be made commissioner.[42] Other possibilities were realised. Eglinton wrote to Cromartie: '. . . I am very hopeful these that are sent will make frank offers of their service to the queen, and so give encouragement of good success in parliament, which may make it meet soon . . .'[43]

Curious circumstances attended this choice of delegates. Lockhart, who was at the meeting, thought the selection had been rigged by Hamilton and others.[44] Already in London, at Seafield's request, was Belhaven, Hamilton's relative and supporter, at this time the duke's channel of communication with the court. And, as it happened, these three delegates were exactly the people Seafield wished to see. On their arrival in London the delegates were taken to kiss the queen's hand, not as was usual by one of the secretaries but by Seafield himself. An audience was arranged for the following week,[45] by which time the delegates had been fully briefed by their Scottish sympathisers in London. The day before the audience Baillie had decided that the only way to dislodge Queensberry was for some of the country party to go into office, and he wrote to Tweeddale, who always willed the means of gaining office but tended to shy away from the prospect of employment. Baillie told him that if all honest men were of Tweeddale's mind nothing could be done.[46]

At the audience the queen heard with attention what the delegates had to say. She assured them that the affair of the 'plot' would be laid

before the Scottish parliament. Although careful not to deny the fact of
the proposal attributed to Stair she did say she would not have taken
such advice. As they made their way out from this inconclusive
audience the delegates were unexpectedly called back from the bottom
of the stairs. The queen wanted to tell them she had decided to settle
the succession in Scotland and sounded them about their attitude
towards it. They affected caution. As delegates, they said, they were
unable to answer but would consult the persons who sent them. The
queen asked them to think it over and the audience ended.[47] But
delegates or not, the country party mission, during their stay in
London, were bidding against Queensberry. Most people, except the
junto, knew that Queensberry was promising too much, but the
country party delegates thought there was a chance of settling the
succession if the court conceded some limitations on the power of the
crown. There the discussion had to rest, because it was not certain
whether the court would accept limitations and, if it did, how extensive
they would be. Furthermore, although Roxburgh, Rothes and Baillie
were all connected with Tweeddale and Marchmont, they could not
make promises for either. So the delegates returned to Edinburgh,
where they reported to their constituents of the opposition meeting and
denied any knowledge of decisions taken in London. In view of what
happened later Lockhart denounced this as utter perfidy, which seems
unjust. It may be granted that Roxburgh and Rothes were two young
peers on the make in politics and that Baillie could be evasive enough,
but all they had done so far was take part in confidential negotiations
which might or might not prove fruitful and so were merely exercising
necessary discretion.[48]

5 Seafield's new party scheme

In the meantime as a possible way out of their difficulties Godolphin
and Marlborough were turning to Seafield's plan for the next Scottish
parliament. The new scheme had germinated in Seafield's mind as his
previous undertakings expired when the session of 1703 ended in
failure. Towards the end of the session a clamour had arisen from
Argyll and the presbyterians for affairs to be run on a strict revolution
basis. They meant, of course, that they wanted to monopolise the court.
This was no solution and Seafield warned against it: '. . . If there is a
dangerous faction in any of the two kingdoms and another of the same
kidney in the other it would seem dangerous to take that party's advice

in choosing the officers and servants and these trusted with power and forces in that other kingdom . . .'[49] This was a rather involved way of telling the English court not to trust completely the opinion of either the junto or the presbyterians on Scottish affairs. The drift of his argument became clearer: '. . . the late king, being induced upon mistakes and misinformations, did choose to settle his government in Scotland on a party, a lesser party and an angry party. Several were put in whose former practices had not been very conformable to the revolution principles, and many were put out who were firm in these principles . . .'[50] By November 1703 Seafield was in frequent consultation with the queen and her English ministers whilst Queensberry was showing signs of uneasiness. Seafield gave nothing away but wrote for Belhaven to come up to London.[51]

What Seafield had been urging on Godolphin from late 1703 was a dramatic change in Scottish politics involving some very devious management. The court needed a majority. In 1702–3 a court–country alliance had been blocked by Queensberry, and the only remaining possibility, if it amounted to that, a court–cavalier alliance, had been sabotaged by presbyterian pressure. The events of 1703 pointed inexorably to the fact that a court–country alliance had to be reconsidered. If Queensberry was again prepared to block that without proposing any realistic alternative then Queensberry would have to go. Neither he nor his junto backers could produce any feasible suggestions. The old recipe of Queensberry's running the court party and hoping to take off the opposition was ludicrously inadequate. All his promises notwithstanding, Queensberry in 1704 had no chance of settling the succession or, indeed, anything else.

Seafield's plan involved the creation of a new court party without Queensberry. The duke and his immediate associates were to be replaced by other leaders bringing more support, though the bulk of the existing court interest had otherwise to be left as far as possible intact. Godolphin was attracted to the plan, which would permit him to assert his independence of the junto. Under junto pressure he had accepted the settlement of the succession but he had no wish for the whigs to dictate also the composition of the Scottish ministry. Moreover such a new court interest could conceivably be directly responsive to Godolphin's wishes, a vast improvement on having to take into account what Queensberry would or would not stand for.

The complications were substantial. If a court–country coalition should be created without Queensberry, who would be the lord high commissioner to the next parliament? There appeared no comparable figure in the court party. Of the magnates with country affiliations either Hamilton or Atholl would create more trouble than he was worth. There was no one else but Tweeddale, whose personal probity was held in high enough esteem, but his personality had its drawbacks and, anyway, it was by no means certain that he would accept.

But if Queensberry were not appointed, what in the meantime was to be done about him? He was a secretary of state and, serving month and month about with Cromartie, a main channel of communication with Scotland. The secretaries shared a secretary–depute, Sir David Nairn, a confirmed Queensberry man. Since Queensberry could hardly be expected to co-operate in the annihilation of his own political interest he had to be kept in ignorance of the court's intentions, but it was going to be very difficult to engineer a new political structure behind his back. The obvious solution would have been his dismissal but Seafield thought this inadvisable until the future was clearer. His reasons were devious. If Tweeddale proved to be resolute in his refusal of office, as, with his quirky personality, he might well, the entire scheme could collapse and then whether it liked the idea or not the court might have to fall back on Queensberry. On the other hand, should the scheme go according to plan, Queensberry in office and expecting to be commissioner could be less dangerous than Queensberry rejected and out of court. There was a further bonus. As Seafield later told Godolphin, '. . . It has been of great advantage to us that *Queensberry* stood in all his employments till matters were brought this length, for the fears of his continuing has engaged a great many to be for *the queen's* interest, and the measures proposed . . .'[52]

There were several aspects to the plan. The key was to persuade the Tweeddale interest, or the bulk of it, to accept a share in managing the settlement of the succession. This task was left to Seafield. One of the scheme's weaknesses was the Tweeddale interest's lack of experience in office and Seafield thought of bringing in James 'Secretary' Johnston, his former colleague of William's reign, to reinforce them. Johnston, tending his gardens at Twickenham, still kept a watching brief at court for Tweeddale, the son of his ally of the 1695 parliament.[53] Others of the country party outside the Tweeddale interest had to be persuaded if possible to support the plan. The operation was to be conducted jointly by Seafield, Godolphin and, once their co-operation was assured, by the Tweeddale group. And when Queensberry was dismissed, if it ever came to that, the support of the old court interest had nevertheless to be

retained for the new managers. It was to be the special task of
Godolphin to apply the necessary pressures from the top.

Even after Roxburgh, Rothes and Baillie had been sounded the court
gave no clues to its course of action, the risk of unsettling too many
people being excessive. Lord Ross, for instance, a fairly minor figure,
had started a move to reshuffle the government for his own greater
glory towards which the court was sagely non-committal.[54] He was
appointed commissioner to the general assembly of the Church of
Scotland in March 1704, providing him with some gratification and
securing his future support without betraying the court's intentions.
After all, the employment of Ross in such a capacity defied
interpretation.

Cromartie had not been taken into the court's confidence, and
wisely. However, some vibrations seem to have reached him—he had
sensitive antennae—and his reaction was typically brazen. Hitherto his
theme had been the continuance of the cavalier alliance and
consultation with such 'episcopalian' stalwarts as Aberdeen and
Breadalbane.[55] Then suddenly, in March 1704, he wrote to
Marlborough in very different terms, recommending Johnston as the
man who might save the situation.[56] Coming from Cromartie this was
quite monstrous. As it happened the scheme had already been
arranged between Godolphin, Marlborough and Seafield with
Johnston brought in for consultation, some time in March before
Marlborough left for the continent.[57]

Before the scheme could progress Seafield had to make further
contact with the Tweeddale group, but this had to be deferred until the
end of March, Queensberry's month 'in waiting', Seafield's formal
instructions having to go through the secretary's office. Cromartie had
now to be let in on the secret, and as soon as he took over as secretary
'in waiting' Seafield's instructions were rushed through, dated 5 April
1704.[58] Queensberry's followers had been chagrined that no decisions
in their favour had been taken during March, and Queensberry himself
was worried. Early in April he told Seafield that if any plans were being
kept secret from him he would resign and Seafield, on the point of
leaving for Scotland to negotiate the duke's downfall, did what he could
to pacify him for the time being.[59] To keep Queensberry inactive for so
long had been no mean achievement.

Two sets of instructions had been drawn up: one open and one
secret. The former commanded Seafield to go to Scotland and let it be
known that the queen wanted the succession settled on Sophia and

intended to employ only those who would support that. Promises could be made at Seafield's discretion and if necessary he was allowed to use his open instructions as his credentials.

The secret instructions were more specific, reflecting the negotiations with the country party delegation at court. Seafield was to see Tweeddale and let him know that the queen was prepared to make him commissioner to the 1704 parliament to pass the succession, afterwards giving him a good post. To help him Tweeddale was allowed to grant reasonable limitations on the power of the crown. Rather than have the succession fail the court would allow parliamentary nomination, after the queen's death, of officers of state, privy councillors and judges as Charles I had agreed in 1641. Other concessions were offered: triennial parliaments, a place act and legislation to ensure impartial justice, presumably by reform of the court of session. On the strength of all this countrymen were to be persuaded to join the court or, in the last resort, to stay away. Should Tweeddale accept the post on these terms Seafield was to give him full collaboration. Promises could be made to Tweeddale's immediate followers when they had agreed fully to the scheme: Roxburgh to be a secretary of state, Rothes the governor of Edinburgh castle or whatever else would satisfy him, and Baillie treasurer-depute. Seafield was to settle with Tweeddale the timing of these appointments.

Meanwhile the most stringent security precautions continued to be observed. Johnston was wary even of going to see Godolphin lest it give rise to conjecture. Cromartie, as secretary, was acting as personal messenger between Godolphin and Johnston with a great show of secrecy, though what he let out in obscure conversational references was probably quite sufficient to frustrate the court's purpose. Speculation was certainly rife: Portland had already told Burnet that Tweeddale was to be commissioner[60] and Queensberry had become more restive though Godolphin reported that he was keeping him in 'a tolerable humour'.[61]

Seafield, meanwhile, found Tweeddale inclined to pessimism and reluctant to be commissioner. He thought that too many countrymen had been upset by the lords' proceedings on the 'plot' to accept the succession policy. But the pressures on Tweeddale were strong. He was the leader of an interest whose function, whatever his private inclinations, was to open a way into office for himself and his followers. Others rather than Tweeddale were responsible for the offer's having been made and if, for temperamental reasons, he was disposed to refuse, his chief followers were not, and he knew it. So finally, with Seafield exercising his persuasive talents, Tweeddale agreed to accept office. At this point Yester, Roxburgh, Rothes and Baillie were taken officially into consultation and, with Seafield, settled their preliminary requirements for management. To save Tweeddale's face more subterfuge was called for. The entire scheme was to be presented as the English ministry's initiative without previous consultation. Tweeddale asked for a letter offering him the post of commissioner as if it were the first he had heard of it. This was for him to show to Hamilton and Atholl to help him fend off allegations of underhand bargaining when he tried to convert them to the succession. Johnston was to be at once appointed lord clerk register and the new managers wanted some alterations in the privy council. All patents and commissions in the process of being passed were to be stopped. All nominations to office, except for the appointment of Johnston and Tweeddale, were to be secret until the end of the session unless, to increase confidence in the new managers, an announcement became necessary. The new men accepted the need to retain the support of the old court party but reluctantly and with reservations. Particularly they were insistent that Leven should have no post until after the session, since it would greatly disoblige Rothes, Leven's great rival in Fife. Finally Tweeddale asked that Argyll be sent down to Scotland to ensure that his dependants followed the court in parliament.[62]

Once the arrangement with Tweeddale was about to become public and official, Seafield asked for Godolphin's protection against Queensberry's malice. Only the queen's service, he said, had brought him into this scheme, which seems to have been the truth. He was risking his own interest when he could have lain low and done as he was told. Instead, to find a way out of a political *impasse*, he had set afoot a project extremely hazardous to himself.

Seafield's calculations were theoretically sound. As he was later to say, an alliance between the court and country parties was the only way to achieve a majority. Such a coalition did carry the union in 1706 and 1707. But in 1704 the scheme was technically too difficult, the main obstacle being that of leadership. At that time Queensberry had ruled himself out as a possible manager yet in the face of his opposition nobody else could succeed. By 1706 there was a difference. Queensberry had been sufficiently rehabilitated to function again as leader and a court–country alliance could be brought about on a different basis. It is a virtual certainty that in 1704 no one could have succeeded but Seafield's scheme offered the only and very slim chance. This slender possibility was ruined by Queensberry's opposition, which administered the *coup de grâce*, by a clear divergence in aim which appeared between the new managers and Godolphin and also by inexplicable mismanagement in London.

6 *Obstacles to court success*

Plans initially went awry over the timing of Queensberry's dismissal. Once Tweeddale had accepted the commissioner's place, his warrant should have been issued immediately during April when Cromartie was 'in waiting'. Queensberry could then have been dismissed. Instead nothing was done. Queensberry was allowed to take over again as secretary 'in waiting' in May and the warrant had to go through his hands,[63] creating unnecessary difficulties. Seafield had to correspond with Godolphin by way of Cromartie;[64] Godolphin was driven to setting up a separate channel of correspondence through the postmaster at Berwick by arrangement with the postmaster-general.[65] More seriously, throughout May, Queensberry accumulated a disproportionate number of rewards for himself and his followers, creating doubt in Scotland about where favour really lay. As usual such doubts had unfortunate consequences.[66] By whatever agency this situation was allowed to develop, it was exploited as a means of undermining confidence in the new managers and of maintaining Queensberry's credit. There is self-congratulation in a surviving list entitled 'Papers passed by the duke of Queensberry in the month of May last being the last month of his waiting'.[67] At the end of May Queensberry and Nairn were both dismissed,[68] Cromartie remaining as the sole secretary with Alexander Wedderburn, appointed by the Tweeddale group, functioning as his depute,[69] but by this time great damage had been done.

However, there were causes of failure more fundamental than the mistiming of Queensberry's dismissal. Seafield's aims, accepted by the Tweeddale group, differed significantly from those of Godolphin. The lord treasurer, with the junto breathing down his neck, wanted quick results. He had no real appreciation of the complications of Scottish affairs, which exasperated him as Scottish and Irish politics have always exasperated the English. On the other hand, Seafield and the Tweeddale group—the 'new party' as they were being called—were acutely aware of the size of their task and the fact that it could be accomplished only in the long term if at all. Seafield's objective was not so much the passing of the succession as the construction of a court majority in the Scottish parliament. As many as possible of the country party had to be split irrevocably from the opposition and attached to the court. Patronage might win over a sufficient number to give general support but only time would allow them to contemplate settling the succession without loss of face. In 1704 the settlement of the Hanoverian succession aroused no enthusiasm at all in the country party after the parliamentary excesses of the previous years. So the succession policy was badly timed. The new party shared Seafield's vision, though not necessarily for the same reasons. Naturally they were aware of its wider advantages but they were more impressed by the possibility of their entering upon the Queensberry inheritance as the dominant interest in Scottish politics. This seemed a prize worth having.

The point recurs in letters from Edinburgh: '. . . *if the business of the succession must be carried on*', Seafield wrote to Godolphin, 'then the queen will be obliged to be very plain and positive with all the servants . . .'.[70] Johnston agreed.[71] To Seafield the immediate settlement of the succession was an irrelevance which intruded upon and would probably jeopardise his long-term aims. He reported to Godolphin in July: '. . . the old [court] party is positive they cannot believe that the queen is in earnest if men at the head of an opposition to her are continued in her service. But the managers have prevailed with them to have patience at least till the breach betwixt the new party and the cavalier party be wider, and open and declared, which will be very quickly, and which will cement the old party and the new party, and which is the only sure foundation upon which the settlement of this nation can be built whether it be built this summer or not . . .'[72] Later in his report he reverted to the same point: '. . . a letter should be written encouraging my lord Tweeddale and those joined with him to do their best, and assuring them, that in such a case, though they should not succeed at this time they would have the continuation of her majesty's countenance and favour, which letter may be shown to g.g. and p.p.,[73] for they too have got the same notion, that if they can make the business [of the succession] fail they shall be the men that the queen must have recourse to; which they have been told is ridiculous, for the breach being once made betwixt them and the new party they will have no strength but what the present ferment gives them which will blow over before another session . . .'

This difference in emphasis between Godolphin and the new Scottish managers was not the only one. Their judgements over how far particular individuals could be depended on did not coincide. The original intention had been to take off as many countrymen as could be persuaded to follow Tweeddale whilst retaining such of the old court as were thought to be dependable. Tweeddale and Godolphin disagreed over how far some members of the old party could be trusted. The new party's requests for changes were not extravagant although occasionally ill-advised. They wanted Annandale dismissed from the presidency of the council, for which there was some excuse. Annandale's capacity for causing trouble was almost unlimited and old animosities lingered between him and the country party. Tweeddale also asked that some of the Queensberry group be removed from the privy council on the grounds that they were 'obnoxious' and not easy to do business with.

To fill these gaps the new party hoped to gain the support of both Hamilton and Montrose, each of whom commanded a worthwhile parliamentary interest. Neither would commit himself to support of the succession, but even so, with the long-term objective of the court–country alliance in view, the new party thought that some gratification might be a good investment. They asked for both to be added to the privy council.[74] For the rest they proposed to leave places vacant so that some would vote for the court in expectation.[75] Godolphin lacked sympathy for these proposals,[76] and the reason is not readily apparent. Montrose was just emerging into politics as an unknown quantity and might well have seemed an obvious man to recruit, yet Seafield's original instruction represented the limit of Godolphin's willingness to enlist him. Montrose was to be assured of the queen's regard for him, which she would not like him to forfeit through opposition.[77] Whether this was intended as an inducement or a threat was not clear. Hamilton was in a different category, since everybody knew his reputation and he was likely to be more trouble in the ministry than in opposition. But this hardly represented Godolphin's assessment of Hamilton's usefulness, since, even whilst rejecting the new party's request, he was entertaining illusions of his own about the duke.[78] Rather does it seem that if Godolphin wanted Hamilton in the court at all he preferred a direct bargain with him to an arrangement between the duke and the new party, probably to avoid new and possibly unmanageable concentrations of power in Scotland.

To build up a reputation for consistency and to attract country support, the new party had fantasies of acting as a 'country party ministry'. This, as Atholl had discovered, was a posture difficult to maintain, involving as it did a withdrawal from political reality. The prospect alarmed Seafield. One of the initial inspirers of this attitude had been Johnston, drafting in London versions of the queen's letter hostile to the old court and with little bearing on the political situation in Scotland. Seafield felt obliged to tell Godolphin privately that no good could come of gratuitously offending the old party[79] His prescription for Johnston was total immersion in Scottish politics and he asked for him to be sent to Edinburgh as soon as possible.[80] It proved an effective cure, exposure to the Scottish climate modifying Johnston's ideas considerably.[81]

Even so, throughout the session of 1704 the new managers showed themselves intent on preserving their country party image. Tweeddale refused allowances on the scale to which Queensberry had been accustomed. He had, he said, opposed exorbitant claims in others and would not be guilty of the same offence himself.[82] Once the session had begun he would not resort to the tactical adjournments which the country party had condemned in Queensberry's time.[83] To Godolphin's consternation he announced from the throne his continued support for the act of security, having no intention at all of changing his mind merely because he was in office.[84] And when a point was reached at which Godolphin thought the session had gone on far too long for anybody's good,[85] Tweeddale continued to let parliament conduct business with a country party flavour to it. One of his motives was the hope of being able to end the session without ill feeling but he also wanted to build up a store of country party goodwill.[86] The latter aim sprang from a gross miscalculation but Tweeddale tried hard. Parliament worked through the reports of the accounts committee, meat and drink to the opposition but most unpalatable to some of the old court.[87] Tweeddale wanted to allow a triennial act and a place act, gratuitously, without any *quid pro quo*, moving Godolphin to protest that it would merely encourage the opposition in their 'insolent presumption'. Even though deferring to Godolphin's opinion Tweeddale gave tacit encouragement to a place act and an act increasing the representation of barons. Finally and much to Godolphin's relief he succeeded in bringing the parliament to an end without any untoward disturbance.[88] The session had lasted almost two months, much of it having been taken up with 'patriotic' business.

This striving to maintain a country stance in office indicates an extraordinary degree of naivety. Johnston apart, nobody connected with Tweeddale had had any previous experience of parliamentary management. Tweeddale's character was such that his behaviour need occasion no surprise. Roxburgh and Rothes were both very young, with a tendency to affectation. Baillie was diligent rather than commanding. All were employed as the court's last hope. Tweeddale was honest enough but his supporters had wanted jobs. Their problem had been how to gain them without renouncing too blatantly their opposition views and completely forfeiting their credit with the country party. They fancied they had the formula by accepting succession with stringent enough limitations to satisfy the country opposition, so being able, as managers, to claim consistency with their earlier politics. They were so preoccupied with keeping up appearances that they failed to recognise the minimal influence exerted by principle in deciding political alignments. Country parties were not in opposition because they believed in 'patriotic' principles. Their 'patriotism' was an outcome of opposition. For most country members all that had happened was that the court had taken off Tweeddale and some of his followers, thus making them fair game. There was no reason for Hamilton and Atholl to welcome Tweeddale's appointment; nor did they. Seafield had shared none of these new party illusions but he was bound for the session, no other course remaining open to him save collaboration with the new party. He had to try to exert on their management as much influence as would serve his and the court's main purpose.

Godolphin had always known it was possible that the opposition might make a fool out of Tweeddale but, despite Seafield's warnings, he too was a victim of self-deception. He was misguided enough to think that the old court party, once relieved of Queensberry's dominance, would prove, even without drastic action on his part, a reliable instrument of policy. His own undertaking in the scheme had been that of trying to retain the allegiance of the court party after Queensberry's dismissal and in his efforts to achieve this he probably conceded too much. Regardless of Seafield's pleas for time domestic pressures forced him to insist on the succession's being attempted in 1704. And although he often reiterated his readiness to comply with the new party's reasonable requests, his interpretation of 'reasonable' circumscribed Tweeddale's powers and helped to destroy the credibility of the new managers and their policy. What the new party asked for was not exorbitant but it was enough for Godolphin to accuse them of abandoning themselves to past resentments and a desire to 'mystify and discourage' people.[89] He advised them to cultivate habits of calmness and moderation.[90] Behind all this lay his own resolution not to dismiss from the privy council anyone he hoped might support the succession, although such hopes were largely unfounded.[91] Tweeddale's complaint that he lacked proper support[92] and Seafield's strong hints that Godolphin did not realise the damage some of the old party could inflict left the lord treasurer unmoved.[93] And neither Seafield nor Tweeddale then knew the full extent of Godolphin's indiscretion. He had entirely broken his promise to the new party by allowing Leven to kiss hands as governor of Edinburgh castle and master of ordnance, the appointments not to be announced till after the session.[94] He told Seafield that whatever optimism he might feel over Scottish affairs was due to the support he expected from Leven and the Hanoverians.[95] Godolphin then tried by an additional instruction to Tweeddale to head off further complaints from Edinburgh. He was to demand, in the queen's name, that all officeholders should declare for or against the succession.[96] No one who failed to declare for the succession was to be employed. This was a directive easier to issue than to carry out. It was particularly difficult for Tweeddale, who was not a dominant personality and already somewhat unnerved. What could Tweeddale, or indeed anyone else, say to people who declined to answer and spoke of having discussed their attitude with the queen and Godolphin, to whom Tweeddale was referred? A few brisk dismissals on the spot might have helped but no one could be dismissed without Godolphin's express permission.[97] So it is difficult to sympathise fully with Godolphin's exasperation during the parliament when he wrote wildly of the queen's refusing to accept supply from those who so obstinately rejected the general good,[98] or with his readiness to blame the country opposition, who had merely acted true to type, rather than Queensberry's men, who had been the main cause of his disappointment.[99] This hysteria passed in time and he achieved a more rational view.

The failure of the scheme was due more than any thing else to the attitude of the magnates, which meant that the effort expended in trying to gain support elsewhere was wasted. Amongst the country party the managers could hope to influence only those who were of Tweeddale's own interest and with something to gain from his promotion.[100] For the rest the men who counted were Hamilton, Atholl and Queensberry.

The court's letter to Tweeddale offering him the post of

commissioner might have spared him embarrassment but as a means of influencing Atholl and Hamilton it was useless.[101] Neither was interested in the advancement of any save himself. Each of them had a jacobite face to put on if country support faltered or shrank, and whereas they could oppose the succession as countrymen, they could hardly support it and pass as jacobites.

Atholl had some cause to feel aggrieved. He had made the biggest single effort against Queensberry at court after the 'plot', in the winter of 1702–3. Moreover, it was initially at his request that the country party delegation had gone to London, so it seemed to him that the Tweeddale group had gone behind his back. Quite understandably he felt slighted. In the hope of not alienating him completely the new party kept him as lord privy seal, but to no good effect. Up to the last possible moment he remained in London doing his utmost to thwart arrangements with the new party.[102] After that there was no hope of his co-operation. He planned to sabotage the succession policy, although he kept his intentions vague,[103] claiming in the meantime that the new party was conspiring against him and inflicting slights upon him, although the slights were largely his own invention.[104] Golophin did gauge Atholl's attitude correctly. He thought he should be dismissed at once and he offered the post of privy seal to Tweeddale. When the new party still declined to dismiss him Godolphin was incensed.[105] The new party in wanting to avoid allegations of harsh treatment and unjustified dismissal were setting too much store by appearances. Atholl was going to oppose. He needed no excuse and if he did he would invent one. Belhaven thought that if Atholl were dismissed he would have no one to blame but himself and he was right.[106] Atholl's dismissal would at least have shown that the managers meant business.

Godolphin had correctly assessed Atholl's intentions but entertained false hopes of Hamilton. He had thoughts of persuading Hamilton to vote for succession by a personal arrangement, by-passing the new party, and in 1704 he employed Belhaven as an intermediary for this purpose.[107] Superficially Hamilton's position was unlike Atholl's. Having no office he had no claim to be consulted but he nevertheless shared Atholl's aims, both wishing to dominate Scottish politics. To them Queensberry was the real rival and now that, for the time being, he was out of the way Tweeddale seemed a trifling obstacle to be brushed aside. Another disastrous session and the court might find itself driven back on either one of them—or, at least, so they calculated. Hamilton had seemed to indicate that his support for the succession would depend on a direct and substantial bargain between him and the English court. He would wait, he said, to see what Belhaven and Johnston had to tell him when they came to Scotland.[108] On finding that Belhaven had no power to make bargains Hamilton thought of talking things over with Atholl before coming to a decision,[109] in the meantime giving Godolphin a vague assurance of his readiness to support what he took to be the queen's interest.[110] There was no room left for doubt about Hamilton and Atholl's intentions.[111] They would behave as excluded magnates had always behaved, either in person or by proxy. Finally, for that session, Godolphin was driven to taking all favourable references to Hamilton with a pinch of salt and quietly had his mail intercepted.[112]

But the key to the situation was held by Queensberry, whose shadow, even in dismissal and apparent disgrace, lay darkly on Scottish politics. Hamilton even invoked him as an excuse for not supporting the ministry as mere caretakers doing Queensberry's work for him. The list of favours granted to Queensberry during his last month in office made this idea quite plausible.[113] It was, nevertheless, untrue. If Queensberry could be kept out and affairs made to succeed without him, he was out to stay.

Throughout the parliament of 1704 Queensberry's policy, as distinct from what he said, was quite consistent. His aim did not at all differ from that of Hamilton and Atholl. Each wanted to control the court. Over the winter of 1703–4 Queensberry had done all he could to avoid losing office. It was important both for him and his following that he should remain commissioner even though parliament should prove to be another disaster. Failure could be blamed on someone else but the dominant position, once lost, was not easy to recapture. The court regarded sceptically his optimistic assessment of his prospects for 1704 but the junto whigs seem to have taken them at their face value. Since the 'plot' they had come to look on him as the leader of the 'whig' interest in Scotland. Marchmont, Ormiston and Sir John Maxwell might have disabused them of this fantasy had they been consulted but they were not. So the whig lords exerted all the pressure they could to support Queensberry for the post of lord high commissioner.[114] As Queensberry came to suspect that developments to his detriment were afoot he tried wrecking tactics, threatening to resign[115] although, no matter how serious this prospect appeared to some, resignation was one of the last things Queensberry was likely to inflict on himself. Indeed, he drew up and countersigned Tweeddale's commission, putting as

good a face on it as possible, wishing Seafield and the queen's affairs all
success.[116] But men of Queensberry's status did not accept such
changes with humility and submission. Even had Queensberry himself
been so inclined, which he was not, his followers would have actively
resented it for the sake of their own careers. From the time of his
dismissal his objective was to sabotage the new court scheme.

He was assisted by the court's need to keep his following as well
disposed to the succession as possible. Contrary to Scottish political
practice he was treated courteously after his dismissal. This, and the
spate of grants directed towards the Queensberry interest, moved the
new managers to protest. It was the old story. If Scottish management
were to be efficiently conducted favour could flow in no more than one
channel.[117] To breach this rule was to court disaster.

One grant, which again demonstrated Queensberry's lack of
restraint where public money was concerned, was to take on some
lasting political significance. The warrant was for the payment of what
purported to be his salary and expenses as commissioner and secretary
of state during the previous session and was so extravagantly phrased
that Cromartie, who had to countersign it, felt moved to protest. It
seemed to continue Queensberry's expenses as commissioner to the
parliament of 1703 up to Whit Monday 1704, whilst Tweeddale's
commission was for the 1704 session only. Furthermore, Queensberry's
allowances had priority over the army's pay and, in spite of the
warrant's specifying payment at the rate of £1,500 a year in two equal
instalments until the full amount of over £16,000 was cleared,
Queensberry had been given a single warrant for an immediate
payment of £1,500.[118] Godolphin had the wording of the warrant
changed but Queensberry wanted his money and wrote to Seafield
asking him to see his warrant through the Scottish treasury. The duke
indicated that if payment were forthcoming he would feel able to do all
he could to see that the queen's affairs went well.[119] This money
became one of his obsessions and more was to be heard of it.

Retiring commissioners were usually provided with a pardon, or
'exoneration', to cover any technical illegalities or oversights that might
have occurred during their tenure of office. Queensberry's exoneration
was couched in such all-embracing terms as to excite comment,
especially since his handling of the 'plot' was yet to be investigated by
the Scottish parliament. The exoneration met with resistance but, since
Queensberry seemed unlikely to get his expenses in the near future,[120]
Seafield, feeling obliged to placate him in some other way, used his

authority as lord chancellor to have it passed.[121] It did not, of course, placate Queensberry at all. He zealously continued his campaign of sabotage against the new ministry.

Damaging rumours were started. The idea that Queensberry was not at all out of favour was vigorously circulated not only by his supporters but also, for different reasons, by Hamilton. Queensberry, the story went, had been laid aside reluctantly by the court till the 'plot' blew over. The new managers were not a new court interest, only caretakers, so that any support for them would be a bad investment.[122]

Another, more enduring, rumour was reported to Godolphin by Seafield. Some of the queen's servants in league with the cavaliers 'have propagated the doctrine that the queen acts only in compliance with the house of lords, but that neither she nor her ministry are in their minds for the present measures; [and] that they have undeniable proofs of this from those that have been in the business with the queen or her ministry . . .'[123] Thus began the story of the queen's 'secret and revealed wills' which Cromartie felt called upon to denounce at the beginning of the 1704 parliament.[124] It became the Queensberry group's major rationalisation to explain away their opposing the succession in 1704, and later perpetuated by Sir John Clerk of Penicuik, who might even have come in time to believe it.[125]

However, there was no doubt that, in 1704, both Godolphin and Marlborough wanted the succession settled to lessen the pressure on them in England. The only member of the English court actually named as opposing the succession was Robert Harley[126] and if this was true, as it might have been, it was no more than a private venture aimed at the junto, Harley being unaware that the junto lords were quietly strangling their own avowed Scottish policy to serve higher priorities.[127]

There were reasons enough for Queensberry wanting to ensure the new party's failure but only one could be mentioned publicly to excuse his lack of co-operation: fear of being attacked over the 'plot'. This alleged apprehension was groundless, as both he and his followers knew.[128] Queensberry was later to say as much. True, the new party felt obliged to make indignant noises but they were too dependent on old party support to let any enquiry get out of hand, and anyway, Godolphin had made it perfectly clear to them that the 'plot' was to be buried.[129] It was the old party itself which tried to keep the 'plot' a live issue to serve their own purposes. Leven professed to feel threatened by the new party on account of the 'plot'.[130] The Dalrymples claimed to be concerned for the sake of both Queensberry and Stair, the latter having actively propagated the story. The new managers gave them assurances with which Sir Hugh and Sir David Dalrymple pronounced themselves satisfied. 'But,' Seafield reported, 'according to the method of the family my lord Stair upon this is shut up two hours with duke Hamilton, and since that time the other brothers fall back, and the duke owns himself unconcerned whether we begin with the plot or not. In short the bargain seems to be that the dukes shall drop the plot provided the Dalrymples in conjunction with others of Queensberry's party will drop the succession. . . . but they will act as they ever did upon double views . . . In short if the queen has any hold of that family it is to be made use of, for here none can have any hold of them.'[131]

Beyond all doubt it was the Queensberry interest which defeated the succession in 1704. Yet Queensberry was playing a double game not only with the English court but even with members of the old party. He could hardly be honest to those who were committed Hanoverians. As it was, after the event, Leven complained that many of Queensberry's followers had opposed the succession and that the duke himself had not gone to Edinburgh to lead them in support of it. Queensberry protested that out of office he had no control over his group and that anyway Leven was the only person to have suggested that Queensberry's going to Scotland would have done any good. Had it been possible to help the revolution cause by being in Edinburgh he would have ridden north, even though, in his then state of health, it had killed him.[132] Amongst all this there was merely a hint of the truth: '. . . If things did not go as is proposed the blame would be laid on me and if all went well I should have none of the credit and other people's interest would be secured by our having done their business. However, I do assure your lordship that I do very little value my own interest in respect of the general good . . .'[133] Later he wrote again to Leven: '. . . I . . . let things take their fate and this was thought the properest method at this juncture by all our friends here . . . at the distance I am it is really my opinion that to have made things easy at this time to the new ministry was to strengthen and exalt those who are enemies both to the present constitution and ourselves and as to what has now passed among you I know not what friends there may think but those here who are looked upon as the firmest to the constitution and the protestant succession approves of every step and thinks it better and safer both for the successor and ourselves than any settlement could have been expected at this time . . .'[134] Queensberry was right to this extent: the failure of the succession in Scotland was greeted by Halifax with glee in which, presumably, his junto colleagues shared.[135]

More honest was Queensberry's letter of 1 July to Mar: '. . . nothing is so necessary as diligence and union [amongst the Queensberry party]; and if . . . [the new party] are disappointed . . . and other matters fail, we may soon see the face of affairs alter to our advantage . . .'[136] So, led by Mar in close touch with Queensberry,[137] a phalanx of the duke's men opposed the succession[138] and then embarked on a campaign of harassment against the new managers. Queensberry thought this commendable, deploring the conduct of those who had given any support to the new party. He presented Mar with detailed advice on how to conduct the opposition, emphasising especially the importance of blocking supply: 'if they fail in the supply it will be a far greater disappointment [than the succession] and will show to everybody the weakness of the present undertakers; so you ought to bend your whole strength there . . .'[139] Yet even to Mar he could still protest '. . . all I wish for, now that I am out, is to be able to live quietly like a gentleman at home and sometimes to divert myself with my friends'.

Seafield was under no illusions about what was happening. '. . . The duke of Queensberry's friends do all they can to make the business fail, and are resolved, some of them, to be against it and some of them to be absent. All which is the effect of assurances from London that if they can make the business fail in my lord Tweeddale's hands, he is to be restored again. Plain language should be used to him for, notwithstanding his pardon, he is more ways than one at the queen's mercy . . .'[140]

But this was in the sphere of magnate politics. At a humbler level some members of the parliament were disorientated, the main landmarks having disappeared: Queensberry out, his followers in opposition, Tweeddale and his country group suddenly styled the 'new party' and, in league with Seafield, acting as the court interest. These rank-and-file members could always muster a fair assortment of King Charles's heads but these, within a secure framework of personal and court allegiance, could be tolerated. But for a man who preferred to be with the court because it was safer the question arose of which was the court? How would a country party man fare by supporting Tweeddale? Would he in time acquire a share of court favour or would he be despised by court and country should Tweeddale prove to be a nine-day wonder and Queensberry came back in? How could anyone be sure that Tweeddale was not merely being made a fool of by the English?

What many needed until the situation became clearer was a simple slogan to cling to for safety. This was one of Seafield's worries as he wrote to Godolphin: '. . . there are indeed great divisions. Some desires [sic] places, others against the succession, some for a communication of trade before declaring. Some few for a union. Some for resentments . . .'[141] There had always been some, if not many, for a union, at least in theory. Communication of trade did not in itself command much support and was spoken of largely as a result of its introduction into the 1703 session. There were always resentments. But for opposition opinion the most useful bond by far was the demand for a treaty with England. It sounded businesslike and equitable. It was also vague and committed nobody to anything. Both Cromartie and Seafield recognised it as a delaying tactic. By what Seafield called 'these national and plausible propositions' the opposition leaders stiffened opinion in favour of putting off the succession.[142] '. . . Those who are against us are unified if they pretend to be for a previous treaty with England for advantages in point of trade'.[143] On neither side were the leaders saying what they meant. The opposition talked of trade and a treaty; the court claimed that the best way to achieve such aims was by limitations and settlement of the succession. The latter were making the best of the task they had been given; the former were trying to sabotage their efforts. All the rest was talk. Some rank-and-file members wanted nothing so much as a justification for voting against the succession or the ministry. For the more hesitant the vague demand for a treaty had attractions in offering an escape which would not expose them to the wrath of either side.

Apart from plain doubts about which side to back there was more than a little honest resentment amongst members of the old court party. Many of them had soldiered on since the revolution, voting for the court of the day, and with more or less patience had taken their places in the queue for preferment. They had borne the burden of Darien and 1703 only to find the erstwhile opposition brought into the vineyard not as labourers lately arrived but as managers. Forfar, a peer of the old party whose intellect was not highly regarded, but who had given consistent support, felt he deserved a post, especially when, as he put it, men of various principles—he might as well have said 'any Tom, Dick or Harry'—were coming in.[144]

The situation had been deliberately made so obscure that even some of Queensberry's own henchmen were uncertain what to do for the best. Could they have been sure that his eclipse was temporary they would have gone unhesitatingly into direct opposition to the new party, but if he were really finished they had no intention of inviting the same fate. This was the earl of Glasgow's attitude. After the session of 1703 he thought he had detected the drift of policy and wrote to tell Carstares that settlement of the succession was the only measure which would do any good.[145] When Queensberry seemed to be on the way out Glasgow spoke in more general terms of his loyalty to the revolution.[146] During the crucial succession vote he stayed away, afterwards spending time and energy in self-justification.[147] By the end of the 1705 session he was virtually professing himself, cautiously and untruthfully, a jacobite.[148] He still voted for union in 1706.

Cromartie was his usual shifty self. He had been in the scheme earlier than most but the new party placed little trust in him and Cromartie knew it. Their success would mean, sooner or later, his departure from office. Consequently whilst his support for succession was ostentatious he did what he could to undermine confidence in the Tweeddale group. His utterances were tinged with pessimism, containing hints that failure would be due to bad management and disregard of his advice. He voted for the succession, claiming to have brought another member to do the same, and persuaded six more to abstain, statements which one could either take or leave.[149]

But also Tweeddale had less success with the country party than he had expected. Seafield at first gave credit to the new party's assurance that they could bring about forty members into the succession.[150] On the following day he amended this to thirty-five.[151] In the event it proved to be twenty-four, excluding Tweeddale, as commissioner, and Johnston, who had not been in the previous parliament.[152] Even so, had the old party strength held, the twenty-four would have turned the scale, but the number was a disappointment. Aside from any general reasons for this lack of support, the new managers were not really men to win friends and influence people. One of the allegations against them was that they were a narrow and exclusive clique[153] and although there was malicious exaggeration in this it contained some truth. A group so long in opposition suddenly entrusted with the leadership of their former rivals would have found it difficult not to take refuge in a self-conscious exclusiveness—the 'diffidence' so frequently mentioned in the correspondence of Seafield and Godolphin.[154] This apart, Tweeddale had never been very adept at getting on with people and time had made no improvement. Johnston reported a not untypical incident: '. . . duke Hamilton and the other heads of the opposition

went in a body to wait on the commissioner, but he sent them out word
that if they had business with him they must make another time, for he
was making his dispatches of what had passed in parliament. This
provoked them mightily . . .'[155] He also refused, as commissioner, to see
Carstares or any delegation led by him—an aversion traceable to 1696
and the dismissal of Johnston and Tweeddale's father.[156] It was
understandable but neither politic nor proper.

There were ways in which Johnston proved more of a liability than
Tweeddale. It had seemed a good idea to bring in a man of political
experience, with knowledge of both kingdoms, to strengthen the new
party management. But times had changed. Johnston was not now
appearing in Edinburgh as a former active revolutionary and William's
secretary of state. He seemed no more than an anglicised expatriate
sent from London to manage a Scottish parliament. He proved to be
quite out of touch with Scottish affairs and his mere presence aroused
resentment.[157] In parliament he was treated with scant respect.[158] His
colleagues were so concerned about the hostility to him that they
thought it inadvisable to invite further irritation by his making speeches
in the house.[159] But to have the lord register, and the man popularly
taken to be the chief manager, sitting mute in parliament brought him
into further ridicule. In his cabinet minutes for 18 July 1704 Harley
noted, 'Johnston laughed at.'[160] Johnston himself soon realised that his
unpopularity made him useless to the court in Scotland. His wife had
become unnerved by large stones being thrown through the bedroom
windows[161] and he asked for leave to return to England.

7 The parliament of 1704

Disaster quickly overtook the new party's venture. The whole pattern
of the 1704 session was set by the defeat of the succession proposal.
Parliament met for business on 11 July, when the queen's letter was
read indicating that the succession ought to be settled and asking for
supply.[162] As an inducement Tweeddale referred in his speech to the
powers he had been given for passing a wide range of acts: for
safeguarding liberties, righting wrongs and encouraging trade.[163]

The opposition's only interest in all this was tactical: how to stop the
court from carrying out its plan—whatever it was. Their first move
came almost at once, its only object being to block the succession as
soon as possible.[164] Seton, younger, of Pitmedden, made a proposal: no
successor was to be nominated in the coming session but limitations

were to be passed to strengthen Scotland sufficiently to be able to negotiate on equal terms a federal union with England.[165] Seafield thought this a tactical blunder, since it gave the opposition's game away. In his opinion the opposition's best policy was to press for a treaty with England, a proposal which all those in doubt could support, '. . . but by this [proposal] it appears plainly that the design is only to stop the settlement without any project of advantage to Scotland. They are so sensible of this that I believe they will not pretend to maintain this resolve . . .'[166] Seafield was right. The opposition had been embarrassed by Seton's rather blatant wrecking manoeuvre and it was allowed to drop. But Hamilton now felt the situation to be so critical that his opinion of a treaty underwent an abrupt change. He had been heard speaking of any proposed treaty as 'damnation' but suddenly professed to see such a treaty as the kingdom's salvation. Countrymen and others seized on the 'patriotic' idea of a treaty each as a way out of his own particular dilemma: which horse to put his money on, or on what pretext to oppose the new party.[167] So on 13 July the agreed opposition strategy was put into operation. Hamilton made a proposal vague enough to be supported by anyone, including the jacobites: '. . . that this parliament will not proceed to the nomination of a successor until we have had a previous treaty with England in relation to our commerce and other concerns with that nation'.[168] The managers succeeded in gaining a delay but had little hope of defeating the proposal.[169] Pressure on individual members was mounting. There was some dissatisfaction in the political nation over the undoubted arrogance of the English in settling their own succession and then expecting Scotland to follow suit as a matter of course. There were extenuating circumstances but in the context of Anglo-Scottish relations they seemed irrelevant. Tweeeddale told Godolphin and the queen that the nation was in an excitable state; most shires and burghs, however prompted, had drawn up instructions to their members against settling the succession in that parliament.[170] These instructions would seem to indicate a massive opposition attempt to organise what national resentment there was.

Against such a 'patriotic' proposal the new party managers had only one argument to use, the one Seafield had already been using in his private conversations with members: that limitations, with the successor named, would be just as powerful a bargaining point in negotiations with England as an open succession. When parliament met again on 17 July Rothes proposed the court's alternative: '. . . that this parliament will immediately proceed to make such limitations and conditions of government for the rectification of our constitution, as may secure the religion, liberty and independency of this nation, before they proceed to the said nomination; and that afterwards they should take the duke of Hamilton's resolve into consideration'.[171]

There was a six-hour debate over which proposal should be considered first. Towards the end, Sir James Falconer of Phesdo moved that the two proposals should be combined, which proved, to the court's great discomfiture, a popular suggestion.[172] Perhaps anything which promised an end to a six-hour debate would have been acclaimed and on a vote the joining of the two motions was carried by one hundred and twenty-one to seventy-nine. The resulting composite motion was then passed by a majority of fifty-five.[173] There was a clear voting pattern. The court minority included the twenty-four members of the country party who had adhered to Tweeddale, Johnston, voting in his capacity as lord clerk register, such of the old party as were strong Hanoverians, Marchmont and Leven amongst them, and other old court men who were not personally dependent on Queensberry. With the majority were those of the country party who had chosen to stay in opposition, the cavaliers and Queensberry's personal following. Of the last-named group some thirty were said to have voted with the opposition whilst yet others abstained,[174] lacking, in the event, the nerve to oppose directly the court of the moment. Glasgow was one absentee, and Morton, whose defection greatly irritated Queensberry and Mar.[175] The conclusion must be that with the support of Queensberry's men the succession would have passed. It was, indeed, apparent to most people at the time.[176]

The passing of the composite resolution blocked the succession policy for 1704. All that was left for the court was to try to obtain supply. Their efforts to squeeze out of parliament as much unappropriated cess as they could on the lowest possible terms occupied the rest of the session. The contest pivoted on the relationship between the act of supply and the act of security, reintroduced in 1704. Hamilton had made only one commitment to the court—a promise to vote for supply. When the time came he proposed a derisory two-month cess. The justice clerk suggested a grant of twelve or fourteen months' cess,[177] at which Hamilton promptly abandoned talk of supply and took up limitations, reintroducing the act of security voted in the previous session. The 'communication of trade' clause had been omitted, since his resolution seemed to have made it redundant.[178] After the act's first reading Tweeddale said that although his personal attitude to the act was well known he would have to seek further instructions, an announcement which parliament received with surprising good humour, once more turning its attention to supply. Seafield and Cromartie's private soundings had revealed that a majority would settle for a very modest six months' cess, so the managers pushed for this and carried a first reading by sixteen votes.[179] At this the opposition tried unsuccessfully to tack supply to the act of security, but the division of opinion was so close that a compromise seemed desirable. Its eventual form was Roxburgh's proposal that both acts, supply and security, should lie on the table till the queen's pleasure were known, an expedient not in principle far removed from tacking. The device succeeded by eighteen votes.[180] A fairly consistent majority in favour of these supply compromises seems to indicate a body of opinion anxious to combine 'patriotic' sentiments with such token gestures of goodwill to the court as might afterwards substantiate claims to have voted 'honestly'.

However, Roxburgh's compromise placed the issue of the act of security once more in Godolphin's lap. The managers had expected the act to reappear and had tried in advance to persuade Godolphin of the need to pass it. His decision seemed vital for the long-term aims of the new party experiment, in which Seafield had always had more faith than in the immediate settlement of the succession. These wider aims were stressed once again by Tweeddale, Seafield and Johnston in a joint memorandum,[181] arguing that some gesture was needed to bring over the thirty or so 'well-meaning' country men who had not joined the new party. The act of security could serve the purpose. But more immediately there was the problem of the army. Without supply the forces would have to be disbanded, and supply was dependent on the act of security. Meanwhile, the campaign which was to take Marlborough to Blenheim was approaching its climax. The outcome was uncertain and intelligence reports indicated the imminence of a French invasion. Godolphin's predicament was unenviable. The pressure on him to allow royal assent to the act of security was increased by representations from the managers. Their arguments were persuasive. Unless the act were passed the new party would lose all credibility and would disintegrate. No basis would then exist for the formation of a court majority in the future and the entire scheme of 1704 would have been a waste of time. Nothing less than the act of security would satisfy the country party, and the managers played down what might, to the uninformed English, appear to be disadvantages.[182] They also failed to add that there was no guarantee that royal assent to the act would at all impress the country party.

Godolphin's views on the session's prospects had tended to be pessimistic. Such hope as he allowed himself was based on his faith in Leven and the old party men. With the disappearance of any immediate prospect of settling the succession he began to regard Seafield's long-term aims more favourably, since he had nothing else to cling to. Already he had directed Tweeddale and Seafield to make plans to reconcile the old and new parties, forming a new court party which could be relied upon to do as it was told.[183] To Leven he wrote more generally. He told him that the parliament would not have been wasted if it united all who supported the succession, since such a coalition provided the only hope of success.[184] There was more than an echo of Seafield in this.

Even so, Godolphin did all he could to avoid making a decision over the act of security—understandably, since he ran the risk of creating an impossible situation whatever he did. Whether they accused him of betraying English interests, defying the Scottish parliament or allowing the disbandment of the Scottish standing forces in an emergency, his critics would show no mercy. As the Scottish managers tried to prepare him for the act's becoming an issue he suggested, with excessive, even desperate, optimism, some alternatives to be offered in return for supply. If an act of security became unavoidable then it should merely set out the method of choosing the successor on the queen's death.[185] Such speculations were being rendered daily more unrealistic, Hamilton having reintroduced the old act of security. Under great pressure, Godolphin with grave misgivings and some reservations, gave permission for the act to be touched with the sceptre. He strongly urged that the objectionable clause envisaging the possible separation of the kingdoms should be left out.[186] But, as Tweeddale had told him, this was not feasible[187] and as soon as Godolphin's reluctant and heavily qualified permission to give assent arrived the commissioner lost no time in extricating himself from the *impasse* in parliament. On 5 August he touched with the sceptre both the act of security and the act of supply. It can hardly be said that he had much choice. The opposition was already contemplating changes in the act of security which would have made it not only objectionable but revolutionary. The ministry had hastily to start a rumour that they intended to modify the act before it passed, stampeding Hamilton into insisting that the act should pass as it stood. Tweeddale was very relieved to oblige.[188] Nevertheless the court party was showing increasing signs of uneasiness. In the previous session Annandale had made a protest against the act of security as an obstacle to the protestant succession. He protested again in 1704 but now joined by a whole list of old party men insuring themselves for the future.[189]

Tweeddale, with thoughts of cultivating country party goodwill, felt obliged to prolong the session until it could be adjourned to the general satisfaction, however uncongenial the business. It was this prospect which caused trepidation at the English court: that parliament might, for instance, begin nominating commissioners to negotiate the proposed treaty with England, a bad precedent, tending to undermine the power of the crown.[190]

The question of nomination was of course bound to be raised. Opinion on the subject amongst the managers was divided. The majority, including Tweeddale, Seafield and Johnston, thought that an immediate nomination would be undesirable, leading to a choice of commissioners whose main aim was the sabotage of any agreement. A minority favoured immediate nomination with the despairing argument that if—the implication was 'when'—negotiations failed, it would be obvious where the blame lay.[191]

However, projects for nominating commissioners came to grief, not through the managers' tactical skill but because Queensberry's supporters were resolved to secure his nomination. They made separate approaches to the new party and to Hamilton and Atholl, offering to carry any list which included Queensberry. Queensberry's unacceptability was one of the few things on which Tweeddale and the opposition were agreed, so as a diversion Belhaven brought in the 'plot', arguing that they could hardly nominate to a treaty commission anyone accused of complicity in the 'plot' unless officially cleared. Atholl and Hamilton, to exclude Queensberry, fell in with this argument and a fairly innocuous resolution about the 'plot' was passed instead.[192]

But still, to preserve what was by this time a wholly imaginary country aura, the managers allowed the session to drag on whilst the accounts were examined, all good entertainment though doubtless uncomfortable for individuals. But when the opposition began to talk about a place act and increased representation for the barons Seafield managed to divert the house to an act allowing the export of wool from Scotland.[193] Such acts were always unpopular in England, providing notorious opportunity for the export of smuggled English wool to the continent. Because of this the act has been looked on as yet another dart planted in England's flesh by the Scottish parliament. Some of the ministry did try for the opposition's benefit to represent the wool act in this guise but such efforts were mere exercises in propaganda to distract attention from more embarrassing proposals.[194] Apart from this tactical function the act was no more than a further round in the perennial struggle between Scottish wool growers and the manufacturing interest. The latter favoured prohibition to restrict the market and bring down the price of wool, but in times when cash was short the wool growers' voice was heard more sympathetically, since the export of wool improved the trade balance.[195] The latter was the situation in 1704. The act had its first reading on 9 August and received the royal assent on the 25th.[196] So in intention the wool act was concerned with Scotland's internal economic rivalries, though, once it was passed, it acquired an added significance. English opinion received it unfavourably as yet another hostile measure and since hostility is to some extent in the mind of the recipient this aspect carried some weight.

By this time even some of those immersed in the business of parliament thought the session unduly prolonged. From London, it appeared endless and Godolphin became increasingly restive until at last Tweeddale took the opportunity of a quiet spell to adjourn on 28 August.[197]

8 Queensberry as the junto's agent

The plan contrived by Seafield for this session had been successfully frustrated by Queensberry's followers. On the succession they had either joined the opposition or abstained. They appeared with Hamilton to vote no more than two months' cess though they knew the treasury was exhausted.[198] They had favoured the tacking of supply to the act of security. When six months' cess was approved they engineered a petition from army officers who had been clothing their regiments for fourteen months at their own expense. Their motive was not solicitude for the officers, whose arrears, after all, dated from Queensberry's administration, but to have as much of the new supply as possible appropriated for almost any reason they could think of.[199] And they were successful. All but £12,000 was earmarked for army debts and the maintenance of three frigates for convoy duties.[200] When

Tweeddale proved easy-going over the range of business permitted, the Queensberry group went out of their way to prolong the session, introducing acts to which they were not remotely sympathetic. Murray of Philiphaugh urging on parliament a place act, and an act for increased representation of barons was an incongruous spectacle.[201] Only the threat from Hamilton and Atholl to enquire into the 'plot' forced the Queensberry group to support the new party,[202] ironically, since this was one of their pretexts for opposition. Despite their protestations of good faith after the session, Queensberry's men had been engaged in a deliberate campaign to sabotage the new party and the English court. Over the proposed nomination of treaty commissioners Queensberry wrote to Mar: '. . . I wish matters may be so managed that this may not be the occasion of duke Hamilton or any of his party's joining with the court and get them a victory at last, which yet they have had no great reason to brag of. And for this end, pray be earnest to keep all our friends in town till the parliament be up . . .'[203]

None of this was in the least unusual. It was merely the old magnate game: an excluded interest showing how much damage it could do in parliament. Queensberry, whatever his claims, was not strong enough to carry the court's policy in parliament but he had sufficient influence to obstruct anyone else, defeating the succession partly through the backing of the junto, who managed to create sufficient doubt concerning the court's policy. Halifax was fairly explicit to Portland: 'The great affair in Scotland is at an end, and is finished in a most shameful manner for the court. It was never known at any time that the ministers made so sad a figure as they did upon this occasion and if the lords here have the mortification to see the measures were taken for Scotland quite contrary to their opinion and endeavours, they may likewise have the satisfaction to see the success has not justified the ministers but vindicated their [lordships'] judgments . . .' The junto objected not to the limitations, which would at least have been a logical position. In Halifax's opinion the best move the new party made in the entire session was that of trying to get parliament to consider limitations rather than a treaty. He made it clear that their quarrel was with persons rather than policies.[204]

The whig lords resented the court's wilful independence in not picking the managers they had supported. Now their efforts were to be directed to placing the blame on the English court and the new party, not on Queensberry. Indeed, the whigs, as became increasingly apparent, preferred succession to fail in Scotland rather than be carried by Godolphin's chosen agents, so giving an anonymous tory pamphleteer an opportunity which seemed to him worth developing. Both the whigs and the Dutch were against union, and the chance of hitting both at once was too good to miss. So, sincerely or not, he took up the cause of union, professing to think it the best way of settling the Hanoverian succession in Scotland. He hinted that the junto had been the chief obstacle to settling the succession. 'It belongs not to me to say by what arts and methods that miscarried in the last session of the Scottish parliament . . .'[205] Part of the truth, at least, had been suspected.

Notes

[1] *HMCR Laing MSS*, ii, 61–3, Seafield to Godolphin, [8 May 1703 (incorrectly dated by the editor 8 Jul. 1704)].

[2] BL, Add. MSS 6420, 15, [Queensberry] to the queen, 25 Sep. 1703.

[3] Buccleuch (Drum.), Col., memorandum [1703–4].

[4] Tarbat received his patent as earl of Cromartie after the 1703 parliament.

[5] SRO, GD 220, A, Atholl to Montrose, 9 Dec. 1703; *ib.*, GD 204, 41, Tweeddale to Rothes, 9 Dec. 1703.

[6] SRO, GD 220, unsigned letters, [   ] to Montrose, 13 Dec. 1703.

[7] NLS, MS 7021, 81, Sir A. Bruce to Tweeddale, 7 Dec. 1703; *ib.*, 83, same to same, 11 Dec. 1703.

[8] *Ib.*, 87, same to same, 19 Dec. 1703; *ib.*, 89, same to same, 21 Dec. 1703.

[9] *Ib.*, 83, same to same, 11 Dec. 1703.

[10] Fraser, *Cromartie*, i, 249, Sir J. MacLean to Cromartie, 11 Jul. 1704.

[11] BL, Add. MSS 39953, 35, Cromartie to Godolphin, 7 Jun. 1704.

[12] SRO, GD 205, Letters from Individuals, Mackenzie to Bennet, 9 Dec. 1703. See Riley, *King William and the Scottish Politicians*, chap. 8.

[13] NLS, MS 7021, 79 [   ] to Tweeddale, 2 Dec. 1703; BL, Add. MSS 27382, 99–100 (Atholl's memorial).

[14] *Atholl Chron.*, ii, 20, Tullibardine to the duchess of Atholl, 20 Jan. 1704; *ib.*, 21, same to same, 27 Jan. 1704.

[15] I.e. Atholl, Cromartie and Seafield.

[16] *Atholl Chron.*, ii, 13, 18 Oct. 1703.

[17] SRO, GD 205, Letters from Individuals, Mackenzie to Bennet, 30 Nov. 1703; *ib.*, same to same, 9 Dec. 1703; *ib.*, GD 204, 41, Tweeddale to Rothes, 9 Dec. 1703.

[18] *Atholl Chron.*, ii, Selkirk to Atholl, 18 Oct. 1703; SRO, GD 205, Letters from Individuals, Mackenzie to Bennet, 2 Feb. 1704.

[19] *Ib.*

[20] NLS, MS 7021, 91, to Tweeddale, 24 Feb. 1704.

[21] See below, p. 76 *et seq.*

[22] *LJ*, xvii, 348, 352, 353–4. The committee consisted of Devonshire, Somerset, Somers, Sunderland, Townshend, Wharton and Scarborough.

[23] NLS, MS 7021, 85, Bruce to Tweeddale, 14 Dec. 1703.

[24] *CJ*, xiv, 259–60.

[25] *LJ*, xvii, 371–4, 389.

[26] *Ib.*, 360–502, *passim*; H. Horwitz, *Revolution Politicks* (Cambridge, 1968), 191–6, deals with this episode in so far as it concerned Nottingham.

[27] *LJ*, xvii, 505–6, 554.

[28] *Several Reasons Why the Succession Ought not to be Declared by This Parliament, And All Objections to the contrary Answered . . .* (1704).

[29] *LJ*, xvii, 523–4.

[30] See below, pp. 303–4.

[31] *LJ*, xvii, 557.

[32] Hume, *Diary*, 146–7; *Marchmont Papers*, iii, 263, Baillie to lady Grizell Baillie, 9 Mar. 1704.

[33] SRO, GD 220, Unsigned letters, [   ] to Montrose, 13 Dec. 1703.

[34] *Marchmont Papers*, iii, 263, Baillie to lady Grizell Baillie, 9 Mar. 1704; SRO, GD 205, Letters from Individuals, Mackenzie to Bennet, 17 Mar. 1704; *HMCR Laing MSS*, ii, 47–50, 'Grievances to the duke of Queensberry's ministry and reasons against his being longer continued in the ministry' [1704].

[35] NLS, MS 7021, 85, Bruce to Tweeddale, 14 Dec. 1703; *ib.*, 87, same to same, 19 Dec. 1703; *Marchmont Papers*, iii, 263.

[36] SRO, GD 205, Letters from Individuals, Mackenzie to Bennet, 11 Nov. 1703.

[37] *Ib.*, same to same, 30 Nov. 1703; *HMCR Portland MSS*, viii, 114, [Carstares] to [Harley], 23 Oct. 1703.

[38] SRO, GD 205, Letters from Individuals, Sir A. St Clair to Bennet, 8 (?) Sep. 1703; *ib.*, GD 220, Unsigned letters, [   ] to Montrose, 13 Dec. 1703. See above, pp. 14, 69.

[39] I.e. the junto.

[40] *Marchmont Papers*, iii, 263, 9 Mar. 1704.

[41] Fraser, *Cromartie*, i, 219, lord Haddo to Cromartie, 17 Feb. 1704; *ib.*, 220, Sir K. Mackenzie to Cromartie, 17 Feb. 1704; *Marchmont Papers*, iii, 263; *Lockhart Papers*, i, 87–8.

[42] NLS, MS 1032, 5, Hamilton to [Orkney?], 8 Feb. 1704; Fraser, *Cromartie*, i, 219, Haddo to Cromartie, 17 Feb. 1704; *ib.*, 218, Eglinton to same, 17 Feb. 1704; *Lockhart Papers*, i, 92–4.

[43] Fraser, *Cromartie*, i, 217, 10 Feb. 1704.

[44] *Lockhart Papers*, i, 92–4.

[45] SRO, GD 205, Letters from Individuals, W. Jamieson to Bennet, 9 Mar. 1704.

[46] NLS, MS 7021, 93, Baillie to Tweeddale, 7 Mar. 1704.

[47] *Marchmont Papers*, iii, 263.

[48] *Lockhart Papers*, i, 96–7; SRO, GD 205, Letters from Individuals,

Mackenzie to Bennet, 6, 12, 20 Apr. 1704; BL, Add. MSS 34180, 32, Seafield to Godolphin, 27 Apr. 1704.

[49] *HMCR Laing MSS*, ii, 38–41, memorial of 16 Sep. 1703; BL, Add. MSS 34180, 23, Seafield to Godolphin, 18 Sep. 1703; *ib.*, 25, same to same, 22 Sep. 1703.

[50] *HMCR Laing MSS*, ii, 42–5, Seafield's memorial, *c.* 1703.

[51] *Seafield Corresp.*, 365, J. Philp to Findlater, 2 Nov. 1703; SRO, GD 205, Letters from Individuals, Mackenzie to Bennet, 11 Nov. 1703.

[52] *Seafield Letters*, 11, Seafield to Godolphin, 11 May 1704.

[53] *HMCR Laing MSS*, ii, 57–9, same to same, Jun. 1704. See Riley, *King William and the Scottish Politicians*, chap. 4.

[54] *Ib.*, 96–7, 1704; BL, Add. MSS 28055, 111, Ross to Godolphin, 25 Jul. 1704.

[55] *Ib.*, 29589, 277, Cromartie to Nottingham, 8 Oct. 1703. A detailed scheme which bears all the marks of Cromartie's contriving appears in *HMCR Laing MSS*, ii, 45–6.

[56] *Seafield Letters*, 159, Cromartie to [Marlborough], 28 Mar. 1704.

[57] BL, Add. MSS 34180, 32, Seafield to Godolphin, 27 Apr. 1704; *ib.*, 50, same to same, 9 Jun. 1704; *ib.*, 28055, Johnston to Godolphin, 6 Aug. 1704.

[58] *HMCR Seafield MSS*, 194–5.

[59] BL, Add. MSS 34180, 14, Seafield to Godolphin, 7 Apr. 1704.

[60] *HMCR Laing MSS*, ii, 50, Johnston to [same], 17 Apr. [1704]; BL, Add. MSS 39953, Cromartie to Godolphin, 7 May 1704.

[61] SRO, GD 248, Box 2/1, Godolphin's letters, Godolphin to Seafield, 20 Apr. 1704.

[62] BL, Add. MSS 34180, 32, Seafield to Godolphin, 27 Apr. 1704; *ib.*, 36, same to same, 29 Apr. 1704; NLS, MS 7121, 20, Tweeddale to same; 18 May 1704.

[63] SRO, GD 248, Box 5/2, Misc., Godolphin to Seafield, 11 May 1704.

[64] BL, Add. MSS 34180, 32, Seafield to Godolphin, 27 Apr. 1704; *ib.*, 36, same to same, 29 Apr. 1704.

[65] SRO, GD 248, Box 2/1, Godolphin's letters, Godolphin to Seafield, 17 May 1704.

[66] BL, Add. MSS 34180, 54, Seafield to Godolphin, 28 Jun. 1704; *ib.*, 50, same to same, 9 Jun. 1704.

[67] Buccleuch (Drum.), Church and State, [1704].

[68] *Carstares S.P.*, 727, Nairn to Carstares, 1 Jun. 1704.

[69] Fraser, *Cromartie*, i, 237, Seafield to Cromartie, 30 May 1704; NLS, MS 7121, 24, Tweeddale to Godolphin, 3 Jun. 1704; BL, Add. MSS 34180, 44, Seafield to same, 3 Jun. 1704; *ib.*, 39953, 37, Cromartie to same, 10 Jun. 1704.

[70] *Ib.*, 34180, 36, Seafield to same, 29 Apr. 1704. My italics.

[71] *Ib.*, 28055, 90, Johnston to same, 8 Jul. 1704.

[72] *HMCR Laing MSS*, ii, 63–7, Seafield to same, 10 Jul. 1704. The same view appears in *ib.*, 72–6, unsigned memorial, 18 Jul. 1704.

[73] Most probably Hamilton and Atholl.

[74] *Seafield Letters*, 11, Seafield to Godolphin, 11 May 1704; NLS, MS 7121, 20, Tweeddale to same, 18 May 1704; *ib.*, 24, same to same, 3 Jun. 1704.

[75] Fraser, *Cromartie*, i, 237, Seafield to Cromartie, 30 May 1704.

[76] See below, pp. 86–7.

[77] NLS, MS 7102, 11, 5 Apr. 1704.

[78] See below, pp. 88–9.

[79] *HMCR Laing MSS*, ii, 57–9, 'Memorial for your lordship's private information', Jun. 1704.

[80] BL, Add. MSS 34180, 44, Seafield to Godolphin, 3 Jun. 1704; *ib.*, 50, same to same, 9 Jun. 1704.

[81] *Ib.*, 56, same to same, 6 Jul. 1704; *Seafield Letters*, 13, same to same, 6 [or 5] Jul. 1704; SRO, GD 248, Box 2/1, Godolphin's letters, Godolphin to Seafield, 17 May 1704.

[82] *HMCR Downshire MSS*, i, pt. 2, 831, W. Penn to Sir W. Trumbull, 22 May 1704.

[83] *HMCR Laing MSS*, ii, 63–7, Seafield to Godolphin, 10/11 Jul. 1704. This was a reference to Queensberry's adjournment tactics in 1703.

[84] See below, p. 98 *et seq*.

[85] SRO, GD 248, Box 2/1, Godolphin's letters, Godolphin to Seafield, 10 Aug. 1704.

[86] BL, Add. MSS 34180, 78, Seafield to Godolphin, 27 Aug. 1704.

[87] *Ib.*, 80, same to same, 29 Aug. 1704; *APS*, xi, App., 56: *HMCR Portland MSS*, iv, 107, 10 Aug. 1704.

[88] NLS, MS 7121, 36, Tweeddale to Godolphin, 22 Jul. 1704; *ib.*, 46, same to same, 21 Aug. 1704; *ib.*, 7104, 94, Godolphin to Tweeddale, 31 Jul. 1704; BL, Add. MSS 34180, 80, Seafield to Godolphin, 29 Aug. 1704; *APS*, xi, App., 59. Despite his desire for an harmonious adjournment Tweeddale had on occasion lost his temper when he demanded repeatedly that Seafield should adjourn, which 'he prudently declined' to do: SRO, GD 124, Box 16, 'An account of what passed in the parliament of Scotland, 1704', 12.

[89] SRO, GD 248, Box 2/1, Godolphin's letters, Godolphin to Seafield, 25 May and 8 Jun. 1704.

[90] *Ib.*, same to same, 17 May 1704; *ib.*, same to same, 25 May 1704; *ib.*, Box 5/2, Misc., same to same, 9 May 1704; NLS, MS 7104, 79, Godolphin to Tweeddale, 22 May 1704.

[91] BL, Add. MSS 34180, 40, Seafield to Godolphin, 30 May 1704.

[92] NLS, MS 7121, 22, Tweeddale to Godolphin, 30 May 1704.

[93] BL, Add. MSS 34180, 40, Seafield to Godolphin, 30 May 1704; *ib.*, 44, same to same, 3 Jun. 1704; SRO, GD 248, Box 5/2, Misc., 24 Jun. 1704.

[94] See above, p. 81. *HMCR Laing MSS*, ii, 44–6, Leven to Godolphin, 26 Sep. 1704.

[95] SRO, GD 248, Box 2/1, Godolphin letters, Godolphin to Seafield, 28 Jun. and 13 Jul. 1704.

[96] NLS, MS 7021, 101, same to Tweeddale, 20 Jun. 1704; *ib.*, 7102, 17, the queen to same, 21 Jun. 1704.

[97] BL, Add. MSS 28055, 88, Tweeddale to Godolphin, 8 Jul. 1704.

[98] NLS, MS 7104, 83, Godolphin to Tweeddale, 15 Jul. 1704.

[99] *HMCR Bath MSS*, i, Godolphin to Harley, 19 Jul. 1704.

[100] SRO, GD 205, Letters of Sir W. Bennet, Bennet to Dirleton, 22 May, 5 and 10 Jun. 1704.

[101] See above, p. 81.

[102] SRO, GD 248, Box 2/1, Godolphin's letters, Godolphin to Seafield, 20 Apr. 1704.

[103] *Ib.*, Box 5/2, Misc., Atholl to Seafield, 21 May 1704; *ib.*, GD 205, portfolio 9, Belhaven to Godolphin, 13 Jun. 1704; *Seafield Letters*, 11, Seafield to same, 11 May 1704; *ib.*, 136, Atholl to same, 11 Jul. 1704; *ib.*, 137, same to same, 18 Jul. 1704; *Atholl Chron.*, ii, 30, same to countess Orkney, 18 Jul. 1704; *ib.*, 36, same to Godolphin, Oct. 1704; *HMCR Portland MSS*, iv, 99, Leven to Harley, 11 Jul. 1704.

[104] *Atholl Chron.*, ii, 29, Atholl to the duchess, 6 Jul. 1704; *ib.*, 26, same to Cromartie, 24 May 1704; SRO, GD 248, Box 2/1, Godolphin's letters, Godolphin to Seafield, 30 Apr. 1704; BL, Add. MSS 39953, 33, Cromartie to Godolphin, 7 May 1704. *Cf.* Seafield's claim that Atholl had done better financially than he seemed to think: *ib.*, 34180, 48, to Godolphin, 9 Jun. 1704.

[105] NLS, MS 7104, 83, Godolphin to Tweeddale, 15 Jul. 1704; *ib.*, 85, same to same, 18 Jul. 1704; SRO, GD 248, Box 2/1, Godolphin's letters, same to Seafield, 20 Jun. 1704.

[106] SRO, GD 205, portfolio 9, Belhaven to Godolphin, 29 Jun. 1704.

[107] *Ib.*, same to same, 3 and 13 Jun. 1704.

[108] *Seafield Letters*, 11, Seafield to same, 11 May 1704; BL, Add. MSS 34180, 40, same to same, 30 May 1704.

[109] SRO, GD 205, portfolio, 9, Belhaven to same, 3 Jun. 1704.

[110] *Ib.*, Hamilton to same, 24 Jun. 1704. See also BL, Add. MSS 34180, 44, Seafield to same, 3 Jun. 1704.

[111] SRO, GD 205, portfolio 9, Belhaven to same, 29 Jun. 1704.

[112] *HMCR Bath MSS*, i, 57, Godolphin to Harley, 9 Jun. 1704.

[113] SRO, GD 205, Letters of Sir W. Bennet, Bennet to Dirleton, 10 Jun. 1704; BL, Add. MSS 34180, 50, Seafield to Godolphin, 9 Jun. 1704.

[114] See above, pp. 73–4. NLS, MS 7021, 85, Bruce to Tweeddale, 14 Dec. 1703; *Marchmont Papers*, iii, 263; SRO, GD 26, xiii, 67/12, Queensberry to Leven, 25 Jul. 1704; NUL, Portland collection, PwA 942, Halifax to [Portland], Aug. 1704.

[115] BL, Add. MSS 34180, 14, Seafield to Godolphin, 7 Apr. 1704.

[116] SRO, GD 248, Box 5/1, Letters to Seafield, Queensberry to Seafield, 9 May 1704; *ib.*, Box 5/2, Misc., same to same, 13 May 1704.

[117] *Ib.*, Box 2/1, Godolphin's letters, Godolphin to Seafield, 23 May 1704; *ib.*, same to same, 8 Jun. 1704; BL, Add. MSS 34180, 40, Seafield to Godolphin, 30 May 1704; *ib.*, 48, same to same, 9 Jun. 1704; *ib.*, 50, same to same, 9 Jun. 1704; *ib.*, 54, same to same, 28 Jun. 1704; *ib.*, 28055, 90, Johnston to same, 8 Jul. 1704.

118 *Ib.*, 39953, 35, Cromartie to Godolphin, 7 Jun. 1704; Fraser, *Cromartie*, i, 239, same to same, 9 Jun. 1704.

119 SRO, GD 248, Box 5/2, Misc., 22 Jun. 1704.

120 See below, p. 129.

121 SRO, GD 205, Letters from Individuals, Mackenzie to Bennet, 1 Jun. 1704; BL, Add. MSS 34180, 44, Seafield to Godolphin, 3 Jun. 1704.

122 *Ib.*, 28055, 107, Johnston to Godolphin, 22 Jul. 1704.

123 *HMCR Laing MSS*, ii, 63–7, 'Memorial of the present state of affairs', 10–11 Jul. 1704.

124 *APS*, xi, App., 39–40.

125 Clerk, *Memoirs*, 52–3.

126 NLS, MS 7121, 28, Tweeddale to Godolphin, [14 Jul.] 1704; BL, Add. MSS 28055, 103, Johnston to Godolphin, 19 Jul. 1704; *Jerviswood*, 35, Johnston to Baillie, 13 Jan. 1705.

127 See below, pp. 103–4.

128 *HMCR Mar and Kellie MSS*, i, 230, Queensberry to Mar, 14 Sep. 1704.

129 E.g. SRO, GD 248, Box 2/1, Godolphin's letters, Godolphin to Seafield, 17 and 25 May 1704.

130 *Seafield Letters*, 152, Leven to Godolphin, 20 Jun. 1704; *ib.*, 13, Seafield to same, 6 [or 5] Jul. 1704; *HMCR Portland MSS*, iv, Leven to Harley, 20 Jun. 1704; *HMCR Bath MSS*, i, 58, Godolphin to Leven, 28 Jun. 1704.

131 *HMCR Laing MSS*, ii, 63–7, 10–11 Jul. 1704.

132 SRO, GD 26, xiii, 67/11, Queensberry to Leven, 1 Jul. 1704; *ib.*, 67/12, same to same, 25 Jul. 1704.

133 *Ib.*, 67/11, same to same, 1 Jul. 1704.

134 *Ib.*, 67/12, same to same, 25 Jul. 1704.

135 NUL, Portland collection, PwA 942, Halifax to [Portland], Aug. 1704; NLS, MS 7121, 42, Tweeddale to Godolphin, 6 Aug. 1704.

136 *HMCR Mar and Kellie MSS*, i, 228, Queensberry to Mar, 1 Jul. 1704.

137 *Ib.*, 227, Mar to lady Mar, 16 Jun. 1704.

138 Viz., Bute, Duffus, Dupplin, Dunmore, Galloway, Kellie, Mar, March, Northesk, Primrose, Rosebery, W. Douglas of Dornoch, A. Horsbrugh of Horsbrugh, W. Morison of Prestongrange, J. Murray of Bowhill, J. Pringle of Haining, J. Sharp of Hoddam, J. Stewart of Sorbie, R. Stewart of Tillicoultry, W. Stewart of Castle Stewart, W. Alves (Sanquhar), J. Clerk (Whithorn), W. Cultrane (Wigtown), G. Dalrymple (Stranraer), R. Douglas (Kirkwall), J. Urquhart (Dornoch). All voted for Hamilton's motion. There were also significant absentees, e.g. Elphinstone, Garnock, Glasgow, Morton, Rollo, W. Dalrymple of Glenmuir, A. Douglas of Egilshay, *et al.*

139 *HMCR Mar and Kellie MSS*, i, 228, Queensberry to Mar, 1 Aug. 1704.

140 *HMCR Laing MSS*, ii, 63–7, 10 Jul. 1704.

141 BL, Add. MSS 34180, 54, 28 Jun. 1704.

142 *Seafield Letters*, 13, Seafield to Godolphin, 6 Jul. 1704; BL, Add. MSS 39953, 41, Cromartie to same, 4 Jul. 1704.

143 *Ib.*, 34180, 58, to same, 8 Jul. 1704. Baillie made the same point, saying

'he was for limitations before going upon a treaty because limitations might procure us a treaty whereas a treaty might disappoint us of limitations': SRO, GD 124, Box 16, 'An account of what passed in the parliament of Scotland, 1704', 17 Jul. 1704.

[144] *HMCR Laing MSS*, ii, 59, 1704.

[145] *Carstares S.P.*, 723, to Carstares, 27 Nov. 1703.

[146] SRO, GD 26, 127/1, Glasgow to Leven, 11 May 1704; *ib.*, 127/2, same to same, 18 May 1704.

[147] *Seafield Letters*, 179, same to Godolphin, 12 May 1705.

[148] *HMCR Bute MSS*, 619, to Bute, 1 Oct. [1705].

[149] SRO, GD 248, Box 2/1, Godolphin's letters, Godolphin to Seafield, 5 Jun. 1704; BL, Add. MSS 39953, 41, Cromartie to Godolphin, 4 Jul. 1704; *ib.*, 43, same to same, 6 Jul. 1704; *ib.*, 49, same to same, 11 Jul. 1704; *ib.*, 53, same to same, 18 Jul. 1704.

[150] *HMCR Laing MSS*, ii, 63–7, 10 Jul. 1704.

[151] *Ib.*, 67–8, Seafield to Godolphin, 11 Jul. 1704.

[152] Boyer, *Annals*, iii, App., 41–4. The list of the new party of 1704 given by Lockhart (*Lockhart Papers*, i, 98–9) is inaccurate. He appears to have confused the Tweeddale group of 1704 and its allies with those who were ultimately to form the squadrone in 1706–7. For the latter see Appendix A. Those who voted with the new party in 1704 were: Belhaven, Haddington, Rothes, Roxburgh, Ruglen, Selkirk, Sir W. Hamilton of Whitelaw, James Johnston (lord clerk register), Sir W. Anstruther of Anstruther, G. Baillie of Jerviswood, W. Baillie of Lamington, W. Bennet of Grubbet, J. Brodie of Brodie, J. Cockburn, ygr., of Ormiston, R. Douglas of Strahendrie, R. Dundas of Arniston, Sir J. Home of Blackadder, Sir J. Houston of Houston, J. Sinclair, ygr., of Stevenson, P. Bruce (Coupar), A. Edgar (Haddington), J. Spittal (Inverkeithing). Tweeddale, as lord high commissioner, did not vote.

[153] BL, Add. MSS 28055, 120, [Carstares] to Harley, 27 Jul. 1704; *ib.*, 111, Ross to Godolphin, 25 Jul. 1704; *HMCR Laing MSS*, ii, 81, [   ] to Ormiston, 25 Jul. 1704; SRO, GD 205, portfolio 9, Belhaven to Godolphin, 3 Jun., 29 and 31 Aug. 1704.

[154] E.g. SRO, GD 248, Box 2/1, Godolphin's letters, Godolphin to Seafield, 25 May 1704.

[155] *HMCR Laing MSS*, ii, 76–8, Memorial, 20 Jul. 1704; *Jerviswood*, 35, Johnston to Baillie, 13 Jan. 1705.

[156] *HMCR Portland MSS*, viii, 128, Carstares to Harley, 8 Jul. 1704. Riley, *King William and the Scottish Politicians*, chap. 5.

[157] *Seafield Letters*, 138, Atholl to Godolphin, 22 Jul. 1704; Saltoun was quoted as speaking in parliament to the same effect: Hume, *Dairy*, 145.

[158] *Seafield Letters*, 137, Atholl to Godolphin, 18 Jul. 1704; SRO, GD 205, portfolio 9, Belhaven to same, 26 Jul. 1704; BL, Add. MSS 28055, 120, [Carstares] to Harley, 27 Jul. 1704; *HMCR Portland MSS*, viii, 141, same to same, 25 Aug. 1704.

[159] *HMCR Laing MSS*, ii, 70–72, Seafield to Godolphin, 18 Jul. 1704.

[160] BL, Loan 29/9.

[161] BL, Add. MSS 28055, 128, Johnston to Godolphin, 6 Aug. 1704.

[162] *APS*, xi, 125–6.

[163] *Ib.*, App., 38.

[164] *Lockhart Papers*, i, 100.

[165] Boyer, *Annals*, iii, 21.

[166] *HMCR Laing MSS*, ii, 67–8, Seafield to Godolphin, 11 Jul. 1704.

[167] BL, Add. MSS 28055, 126, Johnston to Godolphin, 3 Aug. 1704.

[168] *HMCR Laing MSS*, ii, 68–70, Seafield to same, 14 Jul. 1704; NLS, MS 7121, 28, Tweeddale to same, [14 Jul. 1704].

[169] *HMCR Laing MSS*, ii, 68–70, Seafield to same, 14 Jul. 1704; SRO, GD 205, portfolio 9, Belhaven to same, 16 Jul. 1704.

[170] NLS, MS 7121, 30, Tweeddale to same, 18 Jul. 1704; *ib.*, 32, same to the queen, 18 Jul. 1704.

[171] Boyer, *Annals*, iii, 21.

[172] *HMCR Laing MSS*, ii, 70–72, Seafield to Godolphin, 18 Jul. 1704; *Seafield Letters*, 137, Atholl to same, 18 Jul. 1704; *Lockhart Papers*, i, 101.

[173] NUL, Portland collection, PwA 942, Halifax to [Portland], Aug. 1704; *HMCR Laing MSS*, ii, 70–72, Seafield to Godolphin, 18 Jul. 1704; NLS, MS 7121, 30, Tweeddale to same, 18 Jul. 1704. Belhaven confused the two votes: SRO, GD 205, portfolio 9, Belhaven to Godolphin, 18 Jul. 1704. Boyer, *Annals*, iii, 33. *Ib.*, App., 41–4, gives a division list which is probably that for and against joining the two motions. Boyer includes Tweeddale and Seafield in the minority although as commissioner and chancellor they did not vote. If this correction is allowed for his list produces a vote of 122:82, i.e. an opposition majority of forty. Such other evidence as there is suggests that the list can contain few, if any, inaccuracies.

[174] Fewer than thirty have been identified although much depends on how one defines Queensberry's personal following: see above, p. 93 n. 138. *Ib.*, 38–40, prints an extract from the views of 'an ingenious Scotch gentleman who seems to be well versed in the affairs of his own country' which provides an admirable summary of the reasons for the new party's failure. In cynicism it is the equal of any modern account constructed, however biliously, from contemporary evidence. He estimates that thirty-two or thirty-three old courtiers voted for Hamilton's motion.

[175] *HMCR Mar and Kellie MSS*, i, 228, Queensberry to Mar, 1 Aug. 1704.

[176] A point made, for example, by a memorialist in *HMCR Laing MSS*, ii, 72–6, 18 Jul. 1704.

[177] *APS*, xi, App., 41; Hume, *Dairy*, 141; *HMCR Laing MSS*, ii, 76–8, Memorial, 20 Jun. 1704.

[178] Hume, *Diary*, 143–4, and above, p. 97.

[179] Hume, *Dairy*, 144–5, says twenty-two votes but others have it as sixteen: e.g. BL, Add. MSS 39953, 57, Cromartie to Godolphin, 22 Jul. 1704. See also NLS, MS 7121, 34 Tweeddale to same, 22 Jul. 1704; *ib.*, 36, same to the queen, 22 Jul. 1704.

[180] Hume, *Dairy*, 146–7; *HMCR Laing MSS*, ii, 83–5, Memorial by Tweeddale, Seafield and Johnston, 26 Jul. 1704.

[181] *Ib.*

[182] NLS, MS 7121, 38, Tweeddale to Godolphin, 26 Jul. 1704; *ib.*, 40, same to same, 1 Aug. 1704; *HMCR Laing MSS*, ii, 88–9, Seafield's memorial, Jul. 1704; BL, Add. MSS 34180, 64, Seafield to Godolphin, 26 Jul. 1704; *ib.*, 28055, 114, Johnston to same, 26 Jul. 1704; *HMCR Portland MSS*, iv, 104, Seafield to Harley, 26 Jul. 1704.

[183] SRO, GD 248, Box 2/1, Godolphin's letters, Godolphin to Seafield, 25 Jul. 1704; NLS, MS 7104, 91, Godolphin to Tweeddale, 25 Jul. 1704.

[184] Fraser, *Melvilles*, ii, 187, 27 Jul. 1704.

[185] NLS, MS 7104, 92, Godolphin to Tweeddale, 28 Jul. 1704; SRO, GD 248, Box 5/2, Misc., same to Seafield, 28 Jul. 1704.

[186] NLS, MS 7104, 94, same to Tweeddale, 31 Jul. 1704; Fraser, *Cromartie*, i, 253, Wedderburn to Cromartie, 31 Jul. 1704.

[187] NLS, MS 7121, 40, 1 Aug. 1704.

[188] *Ib.*, 42, Tweeddale to Godolphin, 6 Aug. 1704; SRO, GD 205, portfolio 9, Belhaven to Godolphin, 6 Aug. 1704; *HMCR Laing MSS*, ii, 89–92, Seafield's memorial, 6 Aug. 1704.

[189] The list of protesters: *APS*, xi, App., 54. See also *Lockhart Papers*, i, 100.

[190] SRO, GD 248, Box 2/1, Godolphin's letters, Godolphin to Seafield, 10 Aug. 1704; *Seafield Corresp.*, 378–9, Wedderburn to same, 12 Aug. 1704; NLS, MS 7104, 87, Godolphin to Tweeddale, 12 Aug. 1704.

[191] BL, Add. MSS 28055, 126, Johnston to Godolphin, 3 Aug. 1704; *ib.*, 39953, 67, Cromartie to Godolphin, 6 Aug. 1704; NLS, MS 7121, 42, Tweeddale to same, 6 Aug. 1704; *HMCR Laing MSS*, ii, 89–92, Seafield's memorial; SRO, GD 205, portfolio 9, Belhaven to Godolphin, 6 Aug. 1704.

[192] BL, Add. MSS 34180, 74, Seafield to same, 10 Aug. 1704; *APS*, xi, App., 55; *Lockhart Papers*, i, 106; *HMCR Mar and Kellie MSS*, i, 229, Queensberry to Mar, 15 Aug. 1704.

[193] BL, Add. MSS 34180, 76, Seafield to Godolphin, 21 Aug. 1704.

[194] See, e.g., *Letter to a member of Parliament concerning Manufactures and Trade* (1704), quoted Keith, *Commercial Relations*, 189.

[195] Smout, *Scottish Trade*, 215–16.

[196] *APS*, xi, App., 55, 66.

[197] BL, Add. MSS 34180, 80, Seafield to Godolphin, 29 Aug. 1704.

[198] *HMCR Laing MSS*, ii, 78–80, same to same, 22 Jul. 1704: NLS, MS 7121, 46, Tweeddale to same, 21 Aug. 1704.

[199] *APS*, xi, App., 42.

[200] Vernon, iii, 264, Vernon to Shrewsbury, 18 Aug. 1704.

[201] *APS*, xi, App., 59; NLS, MS 7121, 46, Tweeddale to Godolphin, 21 Aug. 1704; BL, Add. MSS 34180, 78, Seafield to same, 27 Aug. 1704.

[202] *Ib.*, 74, same to same, 10 Aug. 1704.

[203] Buccleuch (Drum.), Church and State, Abstract of Letters, St[air] to [Queensberry], 7 Aug. [1704]; *HMCR Mar and Kellie MSS*, i, 229, 15 Aug. 1704.

[204] NUL, Portland collection, PwA 942, Halifax to [Portland], Aug. 1704.
[205] *Great Britain's Union And The Security Of The Hanover Succession Considered . . .* (London, 1705).

CHAPTER FOUR
The junto's Scottish failure

Political manoeuvres concerning Scotland centred next on the parliamentary session to be held in 1705. The entire episode was to be a tangle of miscalculation and deceit involving the internal politics of both kingdoms. From it emerged a situation in which the junto, despite all their efforts, were trapped into accepting the union policy. Godolphin, who had schemed to regain his freedom of action, succeeded in advancing union but at the price of allowing control of negotiations to pass to the junto.

The events of the 1704 session did not substantially change Seafield's views on the management of Scottish affairs but after the adjournment the situation was undeniably different. During the parliament Seafield had scrupulously observed the terms of the agreement with the new party. It was possible that adjustments would afterwards be called for, either because they were necessary or merely because the English court wanted them. Seafield began to prepare himself for such an eventuality, which could involve his estrangement from his new party colleagues. A note of caution entered his correspondence. He advised the court that if changes were contemplated the fact should be kept secret, at least for some time.[1] Though he still believed that a coalition between the old and new parties was the only possible basis for a majority in parliament, he had come to think that private interests and personal jealousies prevented their achieving this for themselves so that Godolphin would have to dictate terms to them[2] much as William had imposed the coalition of 1696. But Godolphin in the meantime agreed to keep private letters to Seafield separate from any official correspondence so that Tweeddale could be kept in the dark.[3]

1   Criticism of the new party

Both parties knew that the eventual settlement would be made in London and both angled for the support of Seafield,[4] whose standing at court was well known. Preliminary skirmishing took place, involving the usual exercises in self-justification and denial of any merit to rival groups. Tweeddale's feeling was that, lacking the patronage necessary to increase their influence in parliament, the new party had done as well as they could. He complained that, of those in office, Seafield and Johnston were the only ones to show zeal.[5] Others who had been allowed to keep their employments had done nothing. There was some justice in this claim. Despite their many errors and dubious motives, the new party had at least tried to do what was expected of them so their conduct needed less ingenuity to explain than did that of their opponents. Old courtiers and some countrymen were ready with extremely disingenuous explanations of their own behaviour. It was suddenly revealed that Hamilton, out of sheer loyalty, had had drafted an act for a treaty which allowed the queen to nominate commissioners and had been ready to introduce it into parliament.[6] Atholl associated himself with this and thought he could hardly be blamed if the commissioner chose to adjourn just as the act was to be brought in.[7] Some critics of Tweeddale and the new party scheme would have been more impressive had they offered a feasible alternative, but they did not. Cromartie was very free with criticism yet, despite 1703, he still hankered after the cavalier alliance.[8]

The old party's arguments were contradictory to the point of stupidity. What had happened in 1704 made it quite obvious that the new party could not control parliament, but nothing could disguise the fact that the old party was no less incapable. Yet the Queensberry group's defection was to be somehow Tweeddale's fault. The new party was to receive no credit even for its two dozen votes. They were blamed for the place act and the barons' act but there was no mention of Queensberry's men having pushed both measures as hard as they could.[9] According to Leven the new party could have had a majority had they permitted Queensberry's friends to join them, whatever he meant by that.[10]

A surprising aspect of this campaign of denigration was the readiness of Melville's family to follow Queensberry, to whom they owed neither gratitude nor obligation. But local rivalries made them implacably hostile to Tweeddale, Rothes and Roxburgh, and they probably judged that their only hope of further advancement lay through Queensberry and the junto. So Melville's family damned the new party, collectively and individually, as an unsavoury crowd of mercenary politicians. Stable government in Scotland, they argued, depended on the revolution party, which, as a minority, had to be supported from the outside. They identified not only themselves with this party but also, notwithstanding much evidence to the contrary, the Queensberry group. And it would have been better had they made up their minds whether they were a minority or a majority.[11] Both assertions were made.

Other old party men snarled around like jackals. Annandale declared that the new party lacked any desire to settle the protestant succession.[12] Carstares blamed them for having made no preparations to manage parliament.[13] Queensberry's group stressed their own numerical strength beyond all credence.[14] They represented themselves as victims of Tweeddale's thirst for vengeance whilst claiming to be strong enough to dominate parliament.[15] They blamed Tweeddale for allowing the act of security to pass although they themselves had supported it, and Queensberry in the previous session had himself asked permission to give it the royal assent as a necessary measure. They could not agree whether the new party had stopped the nomination of treaty commissioners maliciously, to prevent Queensberry's inclusion, or whether the Queensberry men themselves had stopped it out of loyalty to the crown for fear that parliament might make a wrong choice. Both claims were advanced. There was uncertainty whether the six months' cess had been gained unwisely by trading the act of security or whether Mar was to be congratulated for obtaining the cess to pay off army arrears.[16] At one point they showed a brief inclination to justify their opposition as a reaction to Queensberry's dismissal. Subsequently they judged Queensberry's alleged inability to control his followers when he was out of office to be a safer explanation.[17]

None of this affected the real problem in the slightest. The old party, whether led by Queensberry or anybody else, did not have a majority. And Queensberry remained determined, if not restored to office, to maintain a deadlock in Scottish affairs. This was quite within his capacity. He exhorted Mar to go to London to give his version of what had gone on in parliament, ' . . . and to give a true account of the weakness and mismanagement of the new ministry . . .'[18] Before going up, though, Mar was, on Queensberry's behalf, to reach an

understanding with Hamilton and Atholl for a magnates' self-denying
ordinance: all were to stay out and engage in further sabotage should
Tweeddale continue to be employed.[19] This apart, Queensberry
retained his obsession with the payment of his arrears, which anyone
could be forgiven for taking to be his main concern. If he were given this
money he would, he said yet again, retire quietly to Drumlanrig.[20]

2   *The new party in office*

Godolphin, well briefed by Seafield, gave these stories little credence.
He was in no doubt what had happened and there emerged one small
crumb of comfort for him. The session of 1704 appeared to have given
him a tactical advantage over the junto. After the hue and cry over the
'Scotch plot' in the house of lords[21] he had capitulated to the junto's
demands by trying to settle the succession in Scotland. The failure of
1704 gave him an opportunity to call, in public, the junto's bluff. By
making support for the succession the test of qualification for office in
Scotland he could settle the Scottish ministry afresh. Junto clients who
had opposed—the Queensberry men, for instance—could be removed.
The new party men who had supported the succession could be
appointed, thus producing a ministry more dependent on the English
court than Queensberry, under existing conditions, was ever likely to
be. Whatever they thought or, privately, said the junto could hardly
complain in public.

English rather than Scottish politics were in the forefront of
Godolphin's mind in making the decision. But then he began to view
the arrangement with characteristic gloom. Possibly he regarded the
reconstitution of the Scottish ministry as no more than a very
temporary gesture of defiance at the junto. He was, after all, under
permanent threat from a junto majority in the lords, a hazard that
Harley, in the commons, did not have to face. For Harley had
welcomed the move as a spirited response by the court.[22] Godolphin,
though, wrote to Leven, without enthusiasm, to tell him that the queen
resolved to remain firm to the succession policy, '. . . endeavouring to
cement and unite all those who concurred in that measure . . . What
effect this may have in Scotland, either now or hereafter, I cannot
pretend to judge . . .'[23]

Leven's appointment to Edinburgh castle was made known and
Cromartie was provided for as justice-general, but other offices were
filled by members of the new party and their allies. Seafield reluctantly,

though without rancour, became joint secretary with Roxburgh, his post as chancellor being given to Tweeddale. Atholl was dismissed as lord privy seal to make way for Rothes. Hamilton of Whitelaw, by turns supporting and opposing the court since 1689 in the hope of achieving high judicial office, was finally made lord justice clerk. Baillie of Jerviswood became treasurer-depute in a treasury commission dominated by the new party. William Bennet of Grubbet was appointed muster-master.[24]

Political expediency led to one exception to the general rule. The new party badly needed more parliamentary strength and for this reason they were anxious for the support of Montrose. Family interest and tradition destined this young peer to be a rival to Argyll. He was friendly with the young lords of the new party, all being much of an age. His stepfather was in the Tweeddale interest. As 'nobility of the first rank' he would be an asset to the new party. Montrose himself was keen to obtain an office which he thought no more than his due but he was, for whatever reason, rather less anxious to give undertakings for his future behaviour;[25] he was notoriously uncommunicative even to his friends,[26] but the new party wanted his support so badly that they were prepared to take him, more or less, on his own terms and he was found a place in both exchequer and privy council.[27] An attempt was made to procure even more. The queen had recently bought out the duke of Lennox from his hereditary offices of admiral, chamberlain and lord of the regality of Glasgow for the sum of £3,000.[28] The new party had marked out the lord high admiral's place for Montrose but here the pressures of English politics were felt. Changes could not exceed what Godolphin felt able to defend to the junto. Tweeddale wrote to tell Montrose that, support of the succession in 1704 being an essential qualification, the queen could not at once give him a major post but, on the strength of assurances for the future, she would make him lord high admiral as soon as English affairs permitted.[29] Montrose had, in fact, declined to give any assurances at all but, even so, the new party was desperate enough to overlook this.[30] Other support was forthcoming from Marchmont, long since disenchanted with Queensberry and, as Baillie's father-in-law, friendly with the new party. His attachment was strengthened by the appointment of his son, Sir Andrew Hume, to the court of session.[31]

3   Godolphin, the whigs and the act of security

But Godolphin had reason to be worried about the impact of Scottish affairs on the political situation in England. With the resignation of Nottingham the court had but recently shed its high tory skin and was showing no haste to take on a whig complexion. Once the parliamentary session began pressure could be expected from both sides, Scottish affairs providing an excellent excuse for an attack on the ministry, particularly since the act of security had received the royal assent. The attack itself was mounted for domestic reasons, with Scottish affairs as no more than a device. Seafield told Carstares: '. . . the division here [in England] is like to bring in Scots affairs before the parliament . . .'[32] Vernon had similar views: '. . . two acts of [the Scottish] parliament passed in the last session, viz., about arming the country and exporting wool, are to be made handles, so far as they will go, to the mortifying our ministry . . .'[33] One pamphleteer was moved to speculation about the act of security debate in the lords, '. . . whether it was to keep a great man or two in awe by threatening them with it; or whether to make better terms for themselves . . .'[34]

The act of security was a promising issue over which to attack Godolphin.[35] Even in its emasculated form, without the communication of trade clause, it could be represented as a hindrance to the succession and a threat to English security. And the junto had this great advantage: that the real issues behind the court's Scottish policy could hardly be ventilated in open debate.

The junto made the most of the situation. They were the better able to do so since it was immaterial to them whether there was a settlement of the Scottish question at all as long as the blame for failure could be laid elsewhere. Their object was to use the act of security to blackmail Godolphin and extract the greatest possible advantage to themselves in both English and Scottish politics. The lord treasurer's vulnerability to whig pressure as a result of this act became notorious in both kingdoms. During the 1705 session the junto lords were afraid lest the Scottish parliament should grant a supply so generous as to slacken their hold on Godolphin, as Roxburgh told Baillie: '. . . If a three-year cess is brought in and carried, it will do *the old party* no small hurt with *the whigs* . . .'[36] This opinion had a long life. Even at the time of the union negotiations there were those who believed Godolphin to be engaged in no more than an exercise to relieve the unpleasantness the act had brought on him.[37] And after 1707 Somers was reported to have

claimed that the union's only purpose had been to save Godolphin from
the consequences of his folly over the act of security.[38] If Somers did say
this he was not telling the truth but it would seem that the junto wanted
Godolphin's responsibility for the act to be remembered.[39]

The attack on Godolphin opened in the lords early in the session of
1704–5 and at first it seemed likely to make his position untenable.
With junto help he could repel tory attacks and if the tories were on his
side he could hope to withstand any unreasonable clamour initiated by
the junto. With both against him he was defenceless. In this session
both parties were eager to demonstrate how much damage they could
inflict if they chose. Haversham, backed by Nottingham, began the
debate for the tories. They wanted to censure Godolphin[40] and the
whigs joined them. Since the real issues of the act of security could not
be mentioned, Godolphin, according to Dartmouth, '. . . talked
nonsense very fast, which was not his usual way, either of matter or
manner; but said much as to the necessity of passing the [Scottish]
money bill . . .'[41] There was not much else he could say but he did
affirm that 'their meddling in . . . [Scottish] business would do but
harm; whereas if they would let it alone, he believed the queen might
easily bring the affairs of that country to a happy settlement, and had
employed men that were both able and earnest in't . . .'[42]

But whig aims did not include a Scottish settlement, however
favourable to England, if it were brought about by means of which they
disapproved. Dartmouth reported what he saw and heard: '. . . I saw
lord Wharton discoursing very seriously with lord Godolphin, and from
him went to lord Somers, and both afterwards to lord Halifax . . . and
the whigs . . . diverted the whole debate; he having, as we afterwards
understood, delivered himself entirely into their management, provided
they brought him off . . .'[43] The complete bargain could hardly have
been concluded in so short a time and in public, though doubtless the
subject was broached. Roxburgh's version was that '. . . This affair is
delayed . . . by the means of *Somers*, in order to get a thorough
conjunction betwixt *the lord treasurer* and *the whigs* . . .'[44] But attitudes
fluctuated. The lords, Johnston noted, '. . . are to and fro, as matters
are off or on betwixt them and the court'.[45] In the commons, too, the
subject was raised by John Smith for the junto whigs and, as in the
lords, it turned into a general attack on the court. The tories, in
particular, were anxious to seize any opportunity to heal the split in
their party which had been crippling their effectiveness since the tack.[46]

4   Godolphin's surrender to junto terms

In time the court and the whigs seem to have worked out a bargain to include both Scottish and English affairs. The outcome was that the court accepted another change in Scottish policy and submitted to the appointment of the junto's nominee for the post of lord keeper. Nathan Wright had acquired an unsavoury reputation and the time had certainly come for him to go. But Anne's expressed preference was for a 'moderate tory' to fill the post,[47] instead of which Cowper was appointed, and the next day at St James's Dartmouth met Godolphin, who '. . . seemed desirous I should understand, that it had not been done with his approbation, which I did not doubt, knowing it was part of his penance for having passed the Scotch act of security . . .' [48]

Throughout the whole of this parliamentary crisis both parties directed their attacks specifically at Godolphin. The tories, being in a weaker position in the lords, were more blatantly destructive, having nothing in mind but disruption. The whigs wanted to squeeze out of Godolphin what they could and since they had good prospects of success they could assume a more constructive pose but it remained no more than a pose. What they had in mind was the passing of the succession in Scotland before the court's policy of union could meet with any success. But the succession was to be carried by junto nominees and no one else, so they were demanding the dismissal of the Tweeddale group and the reinstatement of the old party. As a beginning Halifax, whose understanding of Scottish affairs was meagre, went out of his way to blame Johnston for all Anglo-Scottish difficulties from 1695 to 1704. Over the composition of the ministry Godolphin was able to delay but otherwise he had to accept at once the whig policy of coercing Scotland. The junto's public justification for this coercion was that proceedings in Scotland 'seem to tend to an exclusion of the Hanover succession, rather than the coming into it . . .' [49] With great hypocrisy they adopted the attitude that it was not at all proper to interfere in Scottish affairs but that England had every right to demonstrate to the Scots the dangers of separation. Godolphin had no choice but to accept this.[50]

The precise nature of the coercion can be judged only from the alien act as it eventually passed, which, in some respects, differed from the way it was portrayed both at the time and subsequently. Contemporaries thought of it as declaring the Scots alien, and prohibiting the importation of their coal, cattle or linen unless they had

arranged either for the negotiation of a union or for the settlement of
the succession by 25 December 1705.[51] This seems to have been the
impression the whigs wished to convey, but it was an inaccurate one.
The alien act which became law—'an act for the effectual securing the
kingdom of England from the apparent dangers that may arise from
several acts lately passed in the parliament of Scotland'[52]—referred in
its preamble to the desirability of union and did make provision for
negotiation, but the penalties specified in the act were to be consequent
solely on the Scots' failing to settle the succession. It was intended to
force the settlement of the succession whilst making encouraging noises
about negotiation and union. The various parties to the act were
obscuring their real intentions and conducting the debate in largely
fictitious terms. Despite the camouflage, however, it was clear at the
time that the court preferred union and the junto disliked it. Somers
wrote to Marchmont implying that union was impracticable,
significantly, because, as the most eminent of the convinced
Hanoverians, Marchmont was thought to be a key figure if the
succession was to be settled in Scotland.[53]

The whig lords achieved their real aim in the alien act rather
obliquely. The bill as originally voted in the lords did authorise the
appointment of English union commissioners and allowed a similar
Scottish appointment as an alternative to settling the succession. When
this bill went to the commons it was resolutely ignored, despite a
reminder from the lords.[54] Ultimately the commons insisted on drafting
their own bill, sponsored by junto whigs. The main difference between
the two was that in the commons' bill the penalties were consequent
upon failure to settle the succession. The original alternative of
appointing union commissioners was omitted.[55] When at length the
revised version reached the lords it was accepted as it stood and
received the royal assent on 14 March.[56] The junto whigs, not for the
only time, were showing one face in the lords and another in the
commons. In the lords they were ostensibly carrying out their part of
the bargain, extricating Godolphin from his predicament by calling off
the whig attack and passing the alien act in terms which, presumably,
the court had approved. Then, the whigs in the commons first of all
kept Godolphin uneasy by leaving the issue open and subsequently
passed an act rather different in character from that agreed.

The junto succeeded in keeping Godolphin on tenterhooks but they
had once again misjudged the Scottish situation. Despite their talk of
moderation and the impropriety of interfering in Scottish affairs they

had taken up a big stick, which proved very unpopular in Scotland.[57] Not that warnings had been lacking. The new Scottish ministers had counselled inducements rather than threats to procure the succession.[58] Marchmont was persuaded to write to his whig acquaintances in protest against the alien act but without effect.[59] The danger of threats was constantly mentioned in debate by the English tories but the intervention in almost anything of Rochester, Haversham and Jack Howe was enough to arouse the junto's suspicions.[60] Nevertheless, the penal clauses had eventually to be repealed before any co-operation was forthcoming from the Scots.[61] It was a *volte-face* which the junto was to execute smoothly and without embarrassment.

Whatever Godolphin's private misgivings on his bargain with the whigs he could for the time being see no other way of extricating himself from his difficulties. With all the burdens of a wartime administration he was probably relieved to survive one parliamentary session at a time. Moreover, in everybody's mind were the forthcoming English elections of 1705, which were likely to be crucial. Failure to tack an occasional conformity bill to the land tax bill had led to some disintegration amongst the tories. The split between 'tackers'—extreme tories—and 'sneakers', who had failed to vote for the tack, had made court management in the commons easier than usual during the session of 1704–05. A group of unattached tories had emerged prepared seemingly to go along with the court. Misled by the ease of management in the commons after the tack, the court hoped to have tackers, looked on as wild tories, replaced by moderate whigs and moderate tories[62] who would, they thought optimistically, strengthen the court's central position. The whigs' aim was rather different. They intended to use an electoral alliance with the court to eliminate tackers and secure the return of junto whigs, thus changing in their favour the party balance in the commons. Such an understanding might well have had a place in their bargain with Godolphin, each party to the arrangement hoping to turn it to advantage and emerge from the election stronger than before.

5 Attempts to remodel the Scottish ministry

The junto lords were not content merely to foist on Godolphin their coercive policy for Scotland. They had no intention of tolerating the existence of the new ministry any longer than necessary and maintained pressure on Godolphin for the re-establishment of the old party led by Queensberry. Events proved that they were able to undermine both the Scottish ministry and Godolphin's will to support it.[63] Their success was due in part to the new party's weakness but it owed much to the junto's capable opportunism.

Roxburgh, in London as secretary of state, was despondently aware of the whigs' machinations aimed at his own and his colleagues' dismissal.[64] The new party ministry was vulnerable, having no secure power base. Members of the old party who constituted the bulk of the court's voting strength were not going to risk anything for an arrangement which left the Tweeddale interest with all the jobs. If, by the next Scottish parliament, the new party were still in office, whatever policy they might attempt would certainly be opposed again by the Queensberry faction, and probably by others as well. This would mean yet another defeat for the court. Some solution had to be sought but there was no obvious course. Seafield and Roxburgh were reported to be having differences over management,[65] the new party's chief aim being to hold on to office, whilst Seafield had to think of controlling the next Scottish parliament. Seafield still believed a coalition between the new and old parties to be necessary as the only way of achieving a court majority but thought some adjustment vital to secure more old party co-operation. With this conviction he had, since the adjournment, carefully preserved his links with members of the old party.[66] Developments within the Scottish ministry were making changes unavoidable.

Tweeddale, compared with most Scottish politicians, was fairly scrupulous in his dealings but his deficiencies were considerable. All his public enterprises were distinguished by almost unqualified failure. Even his own followers were driven to admit that he was not competent to function as chancellor.[67] Sooner or later something would have to be done about him, they knew, especially since Seafield had stepped down in deference to him and was now reported to be wanting his job back.[68]

Hamilton of Whitelaw died in December 1704, after a very brief period as lord justice clerk. The vacancy was inopportune but the new party tried to make the best of it, hoping to increase their own interest by bringing in Ormiston, though Seafield was not in full agreement. Whitelaw had been both a lord of session and lord justice clerk. Seafield had promised to acquire the next vacant gown for Sir Alexander Ogilvy of Forglen, his relative and election manager in the north-east. A compromise was reached which involved separating the two posts. Forglen was to be lord of session whilst Cockburn of Ormiston, hitherto

as resentful of the new party as of almost everyone else,[69] was to be
placated by appointment as lord justice clerk with an additional
pension of £200 a year.[70] Ormiston had other views. He intended to
have both posts, which, in view of the new party's arrangement with
Seafield, was awkward. Ormiston was in a strong position to exert
influence independently of them. As a supporter of the revolution
interest and a self-styled ally of the whigs he appeared to the junto an
ideal instrument to make the first breach in the new party ministry.
Even Godolphin was favourably disposed to him if only because they
had in common a dislike of Queensberry.[71]

Ormiston felt himself on strong ground and began to entertain
delusions of grandeur. When the new party offered to increase his
proposed pension to £300 a year to reconcile him to their scheme he
was contemptuous.[72] His confidence was justified and he acquired both
posts, as he said, in spite of Roxburgh. After this, to impress the
English, he took to posing as a man of considerable Scottish interest
having at his disposal some of the main props of the new party: Rothes,
Haddington and Montrose, whilst retaining influence in the old
party—the key therefore to an alliance between the two groups.[73] To
enhance his own status he openly derided the new party's deficiencies.
They had, he claimed, confined their schemes 'within the number of
five or six persons . . .',[74] an opinion which Godolphin was pleased to
hear, since it confirmed some of his own suspicions.[75]

Ormiston's *coup* and associated gossip brought the scent of change to
the old party and produced a consequent hardening of their attitude.
Philiphaugh declared himself against an alliance of any kind between
the two parties, which seemed to leave the new party even more
precariously situated than before.[76] To face a new session of parliament
they needed more voting strength, and quickly. Some of their
requirements were sufficiently obvious. Roxburgh judged Seafield to be
reliable but he did want to be chancellor again and any new
arrangement had to take this into account.[77] They had to try again to
bring Montrose to a more definite commitment.[78] For the rest, the new
party's appraisal suggested alternatives: either they could attempt a
closer relationship with the old party, paying the necessary price in
offices, or they could seek to make terms with Hamilton. Whichever
alliance they chose involved a complete breach with the rival interest.
But neither alternative offered any prospect of success, whatever
illusions the new party entertained in their private musings. Hamilton
would not serve in a subordinate position, nor was such a reunion of the

old country party strong enough to manage parliament unaided. Any arrangement with the old party which ignored Queensberry was doomed, and Queensberry wanted payment of his outstanding expenses from the Glasgow customs before he would contemplate discussions. Even then he would be content with nothing short of restoration to his former position in the old party. Yet the new party's plight was such that they were driven to investigating even such improbabilities.

Hamilton was waiting for offers of a scale that no one at all was willing to contemplate. In doing so he was overrating his own value. He had a great nuisance potential in opposition but he would be valuable to the court only in conjunction with, and in subordination to, other interests.[79] Hamilton envisaged rather different arrangements. Johnston had discussed the possibility of Hamilton's being employed but found his demands likely to be extravagant, beginning with the payment of his debts, at which Johnston abandoned all thought of the project.[80] He commented, '. . . Hamilton's friends are so gross as to intimate to great men here that he is *chambre à louer*. But for all that's to be done now, I find it's thought scarcely worth the while to make the purchase'.[81]

At quite an early stage Roxburgh[82] had been thinking of yet another possibility: that of reaching agreement with two of the major interests of the old party. If Argyll and Annandale could be brought in on strictly defined terms, sections of the old party might adhere more firmly to the court alliance, although Roxburgh was very reluctant to approach Annandale.[83] Baillie thought the proposal better than nothing but he did not relish the obvious difficulties. Initially someone would have to talk to Tweeddale, who was quite happy as chancellor and saw no reason for change. Gaining Argyll was very likely to lose them Montrose, which would reduce the new party to insignificance as a separate interest. Even so, Baillie thought Argyll preferable to Queensberry, and his reasons are illuminating. The new party should try to keep most of the offices whilst passing the blame for any failure on to Argyll, whom the new party was going to try to use.[84]

But the great shadow on the wall was that of Queensberry. Since he had the junto's support and substantial voting power, the new party ministers knew that his employment might become an unavoidable necessity, although they hoped it would not come to that, and so did Godolphin and Marlborough.[85] Roxburgh had even tried to sound out Queensberry's attitude in case they had to cope with him in the ministry, though some of their supporters were outraged at the prospect. Selkirk told Roxburgh, 'he was *duke Hamilton's* brother, and *that he* would never set up *Queensberry*, who he knew desired nothing so much as to brew his hands in their blood'. Roxburgh 'told him I was as little for setting up Queensberry as he, and was as much against his appropriation; but that it was necessary to gain him to do the business . . .'[86]

The queen was vehemently opposed to Queensberry and unwilling even to contemplate his being in office again. She was unwilling even to order him in 1705 to go to the Scottish parliament.[87] When, despite all objections, it became necessary to employ him again, Anne protested bitterly: 'As to the duke of Queensberry, though he is none of my choice, I own it goes mightily against me, it grates my soul, to take a man into my service that had not only betrayed me, but tricked me several times, one that has been obnoxious to his own countrymen these many years and one that I can never be convinced can be of any use . . .'[88] Her surrender on this point was one of the many humiliations which built up her resentment to the level it had reached by 1708.

But early in 1705 the new party was trying to strengthen the court's position without involving Queensberry. Seafield was hoping to convince the old party that the proposed arrangement was desirable. To Carstares he argued in favour of employing some of Queensberry's party, but not the duke himself. Taking him in would at once throw the entire Tweeddale interest into opposition, and management would remain impossible.[89] Seafield was probably right no matter what hopes Roxburgh might have entertained of collaboration with the duke.

In selecting Argyll as their instrument for the 1705 session the new party were trying to use the only feasible alternative to Queensberry in the old party—the only other court magnate. Argyll's father, the first duke, had worked for a long time in some degree of unwitting subordination to Queensberry before turning rebellious in 1701. It was not at all certain that John, the second duke, would be content with his father's status. When he succeeded to the title in 1703 he had been peremptory in demanding all his father's offices. In the following year the new party, in sore need of his support, had done all they could to satisfy him. When the lords of session had raised objections against admitting Argyll to his father's place as an extraordinary lord at the age of twenty-five Seafield as chancellor had overruled them. Argyll felt under no obligation and, in as much as he was attached to any group, remained with the old party.[90] By December 1704 he had made plain his opinion that some of the new party ministers should be dismissed, business being impossible without some of the four dukes in office.[91] He was certainly thinking of neither Hamilton nor Atholl. It is even doubtful whether he had Queensberry in mind.

Roxburgh's project involved Argyll's appointment as commissioner for the parliament of 1705 with Annandale as one of the secretaries of state. Tweeddale was to give up the chancellorship to Seafield and become instead president of the council. Inevitably the new party would be less prominent, but they were to keep some offices, preserve their existing country party support and, in conjunction with Seafield, mould policy by putting pressure on Argyll.[92] Looked at with hindsight, the whole project seems naive but the new party had to try to work with some other interest and whatever choice they made the outcome might have been much the same.

In the end the new party had to be forced into adopting the Roxburgh plan. Seafield became restive at Tweeddale's inability or reluctance to see the point of readjustment and tried to frighten the new party into acquiescence by professing an alarmist view of their prospects. He pointed out to Roxburgh that the new party could not manage alone, as everyone knew, and that Godolphin could be greatly tempted to employ the old party again. It would satisfy the whigs, make Godolphin's life easier and if the old party failed again then Godolphin could afford to take a very detached view of the situation which developed.[93] Seafield did not really believe that the old party had to be entirely restored, but, since the new party leaders did little but twitter with indecision,[94] they had somehow to be forced into activity.

It rested finally with Godolphin, prompted most likely by Seafield, to take the initiative. The brisk, confident tone in which Godolphin wrote to Seafield was certainly assumed for the occasion with the aim of frightening the new party. And Godolphin laid down the law. The new party had little authority, and such as they had was being used to mortify the old party to the prejudice of the queen's service. It was, he thought, time to put an end to this 'wilful obstinacy'. He then proposed that the project Roxburgh had earlier canvassed be acted upon immediately, Seafield becoming chancellor, 'lord Annandale to be secretary, lord Tweeddale president of the council, the duke of Argyll to be declared commissioner and to be acquainted with it first by yourself, that you may have the government of him as far as he is capable of being managed ...' Marchmont, he thought, could be made commissioner to the general assembly, and other details could be worked out in Scotland. In order for this general scheme to succeed, Queensberry would have to be satisfied over his money despite his behaviour and the queen's predictable reluctance. He brushed aside the possibility of objections from the new party. If they stayed then all well and good, but if they resigned '. . . I am apt to think their places might be filled with those who would be perhaps more useful than themselves, but I agree it would be better if they please to continue and not bring things to that extremity . . .'[95] This offhand statement that the new party was not indispensable was far from being true, and Godolphin knew it. The whole letter is consistent with Seafield's previous warning, issued *via* Roxburgh, and intended to impose the projected scheme on the new party, in particular upon Tweeddale. The letter was, in fact, written for Seafield to show. Roxburgh, who had acquiesced in the scheme and probably initiated it, covered his own tracks by blaming Seafield: '. . . *Seafield* is without doubt, *the greatest villain* in the world . . .'[96]

The proposal for Argyll's inclusion placed Queensberry in a dilemma. His followers had advised him that his best policy was to stand aside, refusing a post even if offered it, to demonstrate to the court his indispensability. Another *débâcle* in 1705 would undoubtedly mean the new party's dismissal and make Queensberry's recall on virtually his own terms unavoidable.[97] Now the Argyll project introduced a complication and even posed a threat. It opened up the possibility of Argyll's replacing him as the old party leader. Queensberry was so obsessed with money that officially he agreed to support the scheme in return for payment of his allowances,[98] but even so he did what he could to dissuade Argyll from taking the post.[99] Argyll might conceivably succeed and Queensberry's future could be at risk.

Queensberry and the junto had been alike taken aback at the offer to Argyll and even more by his acceptance, but they rallied, and each contrived to extract something from the situation. Queensberry's price had been the payment of his arrears,[100] after which he lay low until the time came for useful action in his own interest. The whigs' intentions soon became apparent.

6   Argyll's coup d'état

Argyll was taken to see the queen by Roxburgh and Seafield, to kiss hands formally on his appointment as commissioner. As soon as the ceremony was over Argyll erupted, much to the discomfiture of both secretaries, and insisted that Annandale, not Marchmont, should be commissioner to the general assembly. At the time the queen declined to commit herself but Argyll eventually had to be given what he wanted.[101] His clamour for immediate changes in the Scottish ministry grew louder and more insistent. Even before kissing hands he had told Leven that there would be at least five vacancies: the whigs would insist on Johnston's dismissal and four lords of the treasury would go.[102] Later he added Baillie and Roxburgh to the list of those to be removed.[103] The English court and the new party were both discovering that they had taken a tiger by the tail. The court had hoped that Argyll would obey his instructions, go to Scotland, consult all office-holders regardless of party and reach some agreement to co-operate. But Argyll, backed by the junto and given detailed advice by Wharton and Queensberry, demanded changes even before he went to Scotland, threatening resignation unless he had his own way.[104] Annandale, characteristically, professed goodwill to Baillie and Seafield whilst urging on Godolphin that the ministry should be more 'of a piece'.[105] Resisting this combined pressure was a strain on the court.

Seafield reported from Scotland his own misgivings. If Argyll insisted firmly enough on a clean sweep of the Tweeddale group the old party might support him merely to get places, regardless of what happened in parliament. Philiphaugh for one would obstruct any plan for an alliance unless he were reinstated as lord clerk register, so if there were to be any chance of the Queensberry group's being amenable Johnston had to be dismissed.[106] The English court offered him up as a sacrifice for the greater good. He was replaced as lord register by Philiphaugh—a victory for the Queensberry group and the junto[107]—and Argyll had still not left London. But then the court managed for the time being to hold out and insist that Argyll should go to Scotland and begin consultations before any further changes.[108]

The new party leaders in Scotland knew from Johnston how the situation was developing in England. They were too well acquainted with old party feeling in Edinburgh to entertain illusions that they would receive any consideration other than could be wrung out of either them or Argyll by sheer blackmail. Their doubts concerning the intentions of the English court put them in a continual dither of conjecture. Support from Godolphin might have been their only hope and they had no wish to antagonise him gratuitously, so they avoided recriminations. But Argyll's intentions were clear to them all, save

Tweeddale. Tweeddale had not been allowed to know of Argyll's tantrums in London. It could have been that he was less of a liability when kept in ignorance. Tweeddale was stiff-necked and, as Baillie said, prone to commit himself in haste without consultation and then it was very difficult to persuade him to retract.[109]

Baillie had made up his mind over what the new party's attitude should be. Unless Argyll and the old party agreed to co-operate, the new party should wash their hands of the whole scheme and remain entirely passive, leaving all responsibility to the new commissioner.[110] They might, of course, be dismissed, so they had also to make provision for that possibility. If it became known that they had acquiesced in the original scheme it would lose them all their country party interest and leave them weak and isolated.[111] So, if possible, they should try to increase their strength and bargaining power by making sure of Montrose's allegiance while they were still in office and had some influence.[112] They thought of pushing through Montrose's commission as lord high admiral at the same time as Argyll's own warrant.[113] Roxburgh, still secretary, pressed hard for this, fearing that Montrose might be alienated from the new party when he heard of Argyll's appointment.[114] The object was to present Argyll with a *fait accompli*, and earn Montrose's gratitude and support. But the affair was bungled. Presumably to spare Godolphin some embarrassment from the whigs' probable reaction, the court decided that Montrose's appointment was not to be made known until all the Scottish ministers were in Scotland so that the initiative would seem to be entirely theirs though, in the meantime, Montrose could be told privately that his commission was being passed.[115] But all this led the new party into dubious tactics. Since Argyll was certain to be very annoyed by a commission granted to Montrose after his own appointment as commissioner, the commission was falsified to seem to have been passed prior to Argyll's appointment.[116] This was later to be a source of trouble.

Contention took place at the outset over Argyll's allowances as commissioner. As a condition of his accepting the post, Argyll had insisted on having allowances on the same scale as Queensberry,[117] giving Tweeddale an opportunity to adopt a high-principled attitude. Tweeddale, still chancellor, refused to pass Argyll's warrant. 'I cannot blame him for this,' Baillie told Johnston, 'it being what we formerly complained of, and what he himself would not accept of—neither are we much concerned to keep measures with . . . [Argyll] at the rate he drives . . .'[118] This helped Tweeddale's 'country' image but enraged

Argyll, becoming one of the many issues over which he threatened to resign.[119]

It was in this situation, with the Scottish ministry demoralised by dissension and the prospect of drastic changes, that the affair of the English ship *Worcester* reached its tragic climax. The *Worcester*, captain Thomas Green, master, had put into a Scottish port for shelter in 1704. Roderick Mackenzie, the over-zealous secretary of the Scottish Africa Company, had at once thought of seizing the ship and cargo on some pretext as part compensation for his company's losses, and by deception and force he succeeded in taking possession of the ship. Whilst the ownership of the vessel and its cargo was being decided by legal process, rumours, flimsily based on the boasting of drunken sailors, began to circulate that the master and crew had committed piracy against Scottish ships. They were put on trial and found guilty by a Scottish court. The decision was reached by what would seem to have been due process of law, although it is virtually certain that the entire crew was innocent.[120] All were condemned to death, and in Edinburgh and its surrounding districts there emerged a determination that the men must die. It was seldom that Scots had Englishmen at their mercy. In view of the court's sentence, righteous anger seemed justified and was duly displayed. An act of judicial vengeance was demanded for the accumulation of wrongs the Scots felt they had suffered at the hands of the English. When Seafield arrived in Edinburgh, newly appointed lord chancellor, to face a problem which was none of his making, the *Worcester's* crew were awaiting execution. He was one of the few people to come out of the episode with any credit, though he received little or no help from any group '. . . Both the parties,' he wrote, 'have so much endeavoured to preserve their popularity in this matter that I have truly had extraordinary difficulty as ever I had in any affair of my whole life . . .'[121]

In England there was not only indignation at events in Scotland, there was evidence that the condemned men were innocent. At least one of the alleged victims of Green's crew had been seen alive and well. Anne indicated her wish that a reprieve be granted for the further evidence to be taken into consideration, so the Scottish privy council was under pressure from London. But in Scotland the mass agitation was greater and more immediate. To vote for reprieve was to invite a lynching. The council took temporary refuge in technicalities. The queen's pleasure had not been signified by her personally but by a letter from Argyll as commissioner. The council could agree that this was not a sufficient warrant and they requested a direct order from the queen.[122]

Each party aimed at giving the other the responsibility whilst itself avoiding all blame. Baillie rejoiced that the new party had a chance to take the popular side against reprieve.[123] When the queen wrote and herself urged reprieve the old party members, for the most part, stayed away from the next council meeting. Any rejection of the queen's letter was to be left to the new party, which at once changed its tactics to take swift advantage of the old party's unco-operative attitude. Instead of opposing a further reprieve, they supported it to show their rivals as backsliders.[124] Everyone would have been greatly relieved if a clear order for reprieve had been forthcoming from London rather than a mere recommendation.[125] Scottish opinion was so incensed meanwhile that even Seafield began to worry about the effect a further reprieve might have on the chances of managing the next parliament.[126] The utmost that can be said to excuse this general cynicism is that most, if not all, of the privy council were at the time convinced of the guilt of Green and his crew, [127] so, the sentence having presumably been deserved, the question of whether to reprieve or not became one of political expediency. And ministers were in physical danger. Baillie later wrote, '. . . had these persons been never so innocent, the council could not have saved them without endangering their [own] lives, besides other inconveniences . . .'[128]

The issue had to be faced on 10 April 1705. Seafield called a meeting to make a decision on reprieve and summoned as many privy councillors as possible to Edinburgh. Most decided in favour of discretion. Like the nobleman who gave a feast, Seafield received a variety of excuses. Belhaven, who prided himself on his courage and plain speaking, thought the council could manage without him. Northesk pleaded insufficient notice. Roxburgh was having trouble with his leg. Tweeddale was occupied with private business. Cockburn of Ormiston was unable to travel because his son was using all the horses.[129] Seafield and the few who answered the summons walked to the council chamber through the angry Edinburgh mob which seemed likely to lynch them if they granted a reprieve. At their meeting they were well aware of their danger. Out of the fourteen councillors present only seven were prepared to vote at all, including Seafield, who gave his casting vote as chancellor for reprieve. But, for the reprieve to be valid, it had to be signed by a quorum of nine. Seafield offered to sign if enough abstainers would join him to make the reprieve legal. This appeal produced a total of seven offering to sign, but no more, so Green and two of his crew were condemned to be executed the following day.[130] After the meeting, on a mere rumour of reprieve, Seafield's coach was attacked and he had to take refuge in Sir Gilbert Elliot's house.[131] The three Englishmen were duly hanged after which popular interest subsided and the rest of the crew were subsequently reprieved.

The *Worcester* episode was used to discredit the new party, in Scotland by Argyll and his allies, and in England, where the whigs ran it for all it was worth. Annandale took it upon himself to be very severe on the new party, blaming them exclusively for the tragedy whilst justifying his own inaction in the most lofty terms.[132] Some of the new party had certainly abdicated responsibility and none of them proved himself a hero. But exactly the same can be said of the old party, whose members had formerly been the most prominent and vigorous in the prosecution of Green. The most sordid aspect of the affair was the general readiness to use the lives of the *Worcester's* crew for political advantage.

The main confrontation came when Argyll arrived in Edinburgh, the English court fully committed to his appointment as commissioner and his equipage provided at great expense. Although instructed to consult all the queen's servants and to make recommendations only with their advice, he closeted himself with Annandale, Leven, Glasgow and Philiphaugh, all of the old party, who, not surprisingly, decided that all the new party should be dismissed. Their recommendation was couched in general terms: that the ministry would be 'ever feeble so long as it was not of a piece', and, according to Glasgow, who, like Annandale, had a talent for justifying at the drop of a hat the most abrupt changes of direction, the court's failure since 1702 had been due to mixed ministries.[133] This was either stupid or dishonest or, conceivably, both. Philiphaugh, more sanely, thought that if the new party remained in office they would appear to be the basis of the administration and the old party mere superstructure, whereas the opposite was true.[134] He was right, of course, but he was still offering no answer to the question of how the court was to muster a parliamentary majority if it pushed the new party back into opposition.

The fact was that Argyll had gone north fully determined, with the junto's backing, to have the new party out. This was an aim which the old party would be tempted to applaud whatever the parliamentary consequences and their support was all Argyll needed to spur him on. Being a man prone to personal abuse and misrepresentation, and averse from rational argument, Argyll's initial report to Godolphin consisted of little more than vituperation against the new party. He blamed them for every mishap in the queen's service over the past year. Another of his grievances was the harsh treatment he claimed they had meted out to him personally. He later reciprocated by refusing to pay their arrears of salary, which seemed to restore him to some peace of mind.[135] The climax of his denunciations was formal advice to the queen that those whom he had consulted 'unanimously agreed that it was absolutely necessary your majesty would be pleased to put your government entirely on a revolution foot by removing the new set . . .',[136] thus reviving the 'Scotch plot' libel that the new party were jacobites.

What worried Godolphin and the court was that Argyll had declined to have any dealings with the new party and had not even consulted Seafield, thus disregarding his instructions. The Scottish court was swiftly contracting to nothing more than the old party, which, unaided, could not command a majority. Seafield advised Argyll to ask the new party for assurances of support and only when they refused would it be time to talk of dismissals. Argyll said it was too late to join the parties and again threatened to resign.[137]

Godolphin was by now showing signs of agitation. He had been ready to accept some new party dismissals if that would strengthen the old party's allegiance whilst not completely alienating the new party. He had not been prepared for Argyll's insistence on a complete purge. The queen 'desires nothing more than to see a plain scheme by which her measures may succeed . . .', Godolphin told Leven,[138] but what she was getting from Argyll was far from that.

Harley was deputed to draft a letter from the queen to Argyll to emphasise his responsibility for the consequences of what he proposed. He was to call together all those of whatever party still in office and ask for an undertaking that they would acquiesce in the court's policy. Only those who declined were to be dismissed and no vacancy was to be filled before the queen had been consulted. Argyll was asked for specific assurances that his proposed measures would succeed,[139] but he was too slippery to be caught by that. Unless he had a completely free hand he threatened to resign and actually went to the length of sending to the queen what, with some imagination, could be taken as a letter of resignation.[140] But even if the court should give him his own way entirely he still refused to guarantee success. It was the court, he claimed, which had put everything at risk by their delay in turning out the new party, which should have been done before he left London.[141] He now knew that by threatening resignation he could virtually dictate to the court. The appointment of another commissioner would unhinge any remnant of the original plan and, besides, there was no money left to equip another. Consequently Argyll's threats of resignation became more frequent and took on a certain monotony. On his appointment there had been some talk of his being given an English peerage. Suddenly, in the middle of the dispute about dismissals, he demanded his peerage patent immediately, although he was prepared for it not to be made known till after the parliamentary session. Unless the court sent the patent he would resign.[142] Again the court had little choice but to give way.

And meanwhile relations between Argyll and the new party became, if that was at all possible, worse. The new party, with Seafield's connivance, still hoped to manipulate the passing of Montrose's commission even after Argyll's arrival in Edinburgh. Unforeseen hitches, though, brought the affair to the notice of Argyll, who stopped the commission. This was not, he said, out of animosity to Montrose, but to teach a lesson to those who thought to pass commissions without his knowledge.[143] Montrose appealed to the queen but Argyll did not give way on the grounds that Montrose would not acknowledge any obligation to him as commissioner, which was true enough. Montrose would not accept favours from Argyll. The court again found itself powerless to intervene[144] and abandoned the struggle. The allocation of places was decided in Scotland by Argyll and the old party.

But the process of distributing offices introduced Argyll to difficulties of which he had been completely ignorant when demanding wholesale dismissals. And, although covetous of office, the old party leaders too became increasingly and uncomfortably aware that they still lacked a majority and perhaps ought to revise their attitude to the new party. They tried to secure new party votes at a lower price. The president of session—Stair's family being prominent amongst Argyll's advisers—was despatched to Baillie with an offer of a place in the treasury in return for his support. Baillie rejected this out of hand.[145] Endeavours were then made to cut off new party stragglers and Haddington, for one, was persuaded into some kind of compliance with the new ministry.[146] Argyll was forced into second thoughts about Montrose, its seeming necessary to sacrifice personal animosity to political expediency. Glasgow went to ask if Montrose would accept the presidency of the council but Montrose declined.[147]

When these approaches to the new party met with very little success the old party and Argyll decided on a wholesale purge, regardless of its effect in parliament. They had remained in close touch with the junto, who had at every stage been told what was being demanded from the court and why. The junto had collaborated fully. They had discouraged Argyll from resigning with the argument that resignation could only drive Godolphin back to the new party.[148] So, even if they failed in parliament, which seemed more than likely, the old party felt sure of the junto's backing and protection.[149]

In the meantime the new party had abandoned themselves to lengthy but inconclusive discussion of whether they should all resign together if any one of them should be dismissed,[150] though in the event they were given no choice, being purged in their entirety.[151] Their places were filled, much to the queen's distaste, by old party men. Anne made no secret of her bitterness at being forced to break all her promises to Tweeddale and his followers.[152] So the old firm was back but now, seemingly, led by Argyll instead of Queensberry. This development made Queensberry very wary and although he was proposed for the offices of privy seal and lord of the treasury he waited on developments and kept his intentions to himself.

Appointments to the vacant offices created within the old party dissensions which became more serious with time. Annandale, for one, was disobliged. In conversation with new party men he had exuded goodwill and reassurance but behind their backs no one had been firmer than he for their dismissal. What modified his views was his growing jealousy of Stair's influence on Argyll. This, and a proposal to put Stair's son-in-law, Loudoun, in the secretary's office, enraged him.[153] He began to think he detected traces of Queensberry's lingering influence, which soured him, since he had himself indulged in unlikely fantasies of supplanting Queensberry as leader of the court party. This lay behind his objections to the appointment of Philiphaugh as lord register.[154] He denounced Philiphaugh and the whole tribe of Dalrymple into whose hands Argyll seemed to be falling.[155] The suspicion occurred to him that the whole scheme had been merely a plot to secure the aggrandisement of Stair's family. As this fancy became transformed into conviction he began to deny having ever been in favour of wholesale dismissals.[156] Such accumulated resentments were to lead directly to Annandale's opposing the union in 1706.[157]

Ormiston, too, was dissatisfied. He was occasionally borne up by visions of himself dominant in Scottish affairs although his schemes frequently left him still the odd man out. In the hope of getting his own way he had been highly critical of the new party but as offices were being distributed he, too, suddenly began to claim that he had never supported great changes.[158]

Ignorant of the parliamentary state in Scotland and perhaps even intentionally misled by old party men anxious to regain office, the junto must have felt that they now had reason to expect to achieve their aim.[159] Their part in sabotaging the Scottish project of 1704 had been due not to any dislike of the succession but to concern for their higher priority of maintaining pressure on Godolphin. A Scottish ministry dependent on Godolphin rather than in league with the junto meant more freedom of action for the English court than the whigs cared to see. So their objective for 1705 was the same as that of the previous year—to obtain settlement of the succession in Scotland but, more important, by a ministry of their own choice.[160] In the existing state of English politics a union was one of the last things they were prepared to contemplate. Now, they thought, there could be no excuse for union.[161]

Argyll had gone north committed to the succession, and two ministers—Annandale and Ormiston—who had been in closest touch with the junto gave it firm priority.[162] In view of this the junto lords felt safe in pressing for Argyll to be given money to pay off civil list arrears, creating a favourable disposition amongst Scottish members of parliament. Argyll himself had asked for the money to be available.[163] This one requirement now seemed all that was necessary to ensure success.

But once in Edinburgh, Argyll was exposed to the bleak aspect of the Scottish political scene. Then, since his main aim was to strengthen his own personal interest by some success in no matter what direction, the junto were to find him as difficult to deal with as the court had done. And the crux of the whole business was that in 1705 a settlement of the Scottish succession was not feasible. The old party men in Edinburgh knew this and had tried to convert the junto to the alternative of an act allowing negotiations for a treaty with England.[164] They had no success. Seafield told Godolphin: ' . . . I believe that the party in England are for pressing the succession, but, as I wrote formerly, my lord Stair and the lord register are very sensible that it will divide Queensberry's friends and that it will not succeed . . .'[165] Godolphin must have relished the situation. All the old party's talk in London about the chances of settling the succession had been taken by the junto at face value. Now such tactical promises were to prove beyond the old party's capacity whilst the junto were to suffer for their own credulity.

The English court, though, was comparatively carefree. Godolphin had been in favour of union but the succession policy had been forced on him by the junto. Except as a way out of English parliamentary difficulties he had no attachment to it. In 1704, with a ministry of his own choosing, in defiance of the junto's declared wishes, he had not dared to risk any double-dealing for fear of the political consequences in England. When the court had failed through no fault of its own the repercussions had been severe enough. But in 1705, having bowed to the junto's demands as presented by Argyll, the English ministers were able to adopt a more detached, even a relaxed, attitude. They could talk of succession, since that seemed to be acceptable, whilst waiting for events to take their course. Godolphin made his attitude plain to Johnston. He would accept the changes in Scotland but keep his mind on union as part of an 'after game'.[166] This was to be one of the rare situations in which the junto found themselves at a disadvantage.

7   Argyll and the succession

The predicament was explained to Argyll in Scotland by his old party advisers and later by Seafield. Since succession could not be carried in the parliament of 1705 the only practicable policy was to try to obtain an act allowing negotiations for a treaty with England. This counsel was sound but, as so often in Scottish affairs, it had nothing to do with the merits or otherwise of the policy. Dismissing the new party had reduced the court vote and since the old party had not had a majority since the 1702 elections it could not hope to carry anything by itself. In the previous year the succession had been defeated by Hamilton's resolution in favour of a treaty. Queensberry's followers had voted for it in factious opposition and to make a show of consistency they were likely to do the same again. It would at least be easier than reversing their votes at short notice. This was how they behaved and later they were to represent their tactics quite untruthfully as consistent and far-sighted support for union. Little but personal or sectional interest was involved. A number of cavaliers and country members would support a general proposal for a treaty. A treaty of sorts—there was no agreement as to its nature—was genuinely favoured by a few countrymen as a panacea for all Scotland's ills. But the cavaliers wanted no settlement at all and most countrymen were of the same mind. A vote for a 'treaty' was for both groups merely a device for deflecting the succession or producing deadlock. What Ormiston heard in discussion with Argyll, '. . . that those were for the prince of Wales should go into it without any clog, for 'twas the best handle to hold off the succession . . .'[167] moved him to protest. But a vote for a 'treaty'was an excellent means of avoiding a settlement and for the court a way of staving off open defeat. Nevertheless it involved considerable risk: it was likely to be the end of the road for both succession and treaty. An act for a treaty might well be passed—the proposal was vague enough—but in 1705 it seemed unlikely to lead anywhere. Obstructionists apart, there was no agreement on what a treaty should involve. There was not even an accepted interpretation of the phrase 'communication of trade' which had figured so prominently in the session of 1703.[168] In the union negotiations of 1702–3, for instance, a distinction had been firmly drawn between 'freedom of trade' and access to the plantations.[169] Allowing Scottish merchants into the English colonies was not seen as an essential part of a 'communication of trade'. In fact, by many Scots the navigation acts were looked on as a grievance rather than the plantation trade's appearing desirable.[170] Argyll later said that many who professed to be for a treaty 'were stretching the terms so high that England could not possibly agree to them . . .'[171] An act for a treaty, therefore, might save the court's face but it could have been a defeat in the long term.

But in 1705 saving face was the overriding consideration, especially since Argyll's own position was at stake. He had a parliamentary session to get through without manifest disaster and for this the advice given to him in Edinburgh was good. Argyll had personal difficulties, however. It was initially as a junto agent that he had gone north to settle the succession, and Annandale and Ormiston for their several reasons held out stubbornly for this policy. Ormiston wished to stand well with the junto and made no secret of his alarm at Argyll's dealing with people who seemed to him little better than jacobites.[172] As a tenacious supporter of the junto's line Ormiston could not be ignored. Annandale's motives were not so straightforward. He was determinedly on the make. Whilst vehemently denouncing the grasping propensities of his colleagues the marquess intended to remain a lord of the treasury after being appointed secretary of state, although the two offices were legally incompatible.[173] Seafield reported Annandale's expectation with incredulity. Having been overruled in his campaign against the preferment of Philiphaugh and Loudoun, Annandale had taken a fit of the sulks from which he emerged with the intention of branding all his opponents as jacobites, hoping in the process to acquire merit for his own staunch support of the succession.[175]

This united opposition of Ormiston and Annandale to the treaty policy was awkward for Argyll, preventing him from claiming unanimity of advice. Unable to plead that he was bowing to the collective opinion of the officers of state, he tried to shift responsibility for the decision to Godolphin and the English court. Alternative drafts were drawn up for the queen's letter and the instructions, one set to be used if the succession was to be attempted and one for a treaty. They were sent to London with Argyll's request: '. . . I beg the queen will be pleased to send her positive command which of the two she will have me proceed upon, and I shall dutifully obey . . .'[176] The junto lords who had worked with dedication to circumscribe the court's freedom of action were intensely annoyed at this,[177] but they underestimated the English managers. Neither Godolphin nor Harley had any intention of rescuing Argyll from his predicament by taking responsibility for a decision which would give the junto subsequent scope for manufacturing parliamentary crises. Instead, a conflated version of the two letters and instructions was sent to Scotland, leaving the course to be followed entirely to Argyll's discretion.[178] Later, to avoid blame for some of the humiliations of the session, Queensberry was to assert that all the trouble had stemmed from the English court's insistence on the succession,[179] but in fact the court had gone out of its way to avoid insisting on anything.

Seafield, still lord chancellor despite his earlier deep involvement with the new party scheme, was delicately placed. He was in no danger of losing his post; his usefulness to Godolphin was too great. But he was appalled at Argyll's flagrant breach of all undertakings, completely at variance with Seafield's own convention. On practical grounds he objected to the dismissal of the new party, which, in his opinion, rendered success improbable. He indicated his disapproval to Argyll and declined to take any part in filling vacancies.[180] Contemplation of the future inclined him to deep pessimism. All his calculations led him to conclude that the session would be a failure and that the only realistic aim for Godolphin was to ensure that the blame was put where it belonged. Argyll had been given most of what he asked and so had no genuine cause for complaint.[181] Seafield had earlier told Godolphin: '. . . it is my satisfaction that those in England that supported the old party will have nothing to object against your lordship . . . to necessitate the commissioner to lay down would give still to that party in England their handle to blame the queen's measures . . .'[182] As Seafield knew, there were times when Scotland was wholly subsidiary to English politics.

Everyone would have joined Seafield in expecting failure in 1705 save the junto lords who had been duped by the old party and remained optimistic. The English court's hopes of success had never been extravagant.[183] Argyll was so resigned to failure that he took the precaution of blaming the English ministry at the outset. He complained that he had not been allowed to drop the succession. The court had not given the £10,000–£12,000 necessary to pay arrears of salary, the lack of which cost 'above twenty votes'. He interrupted this display of petulance merely to demand the governorship of Dumbarton castle for his younger brother, lord Archibald Campbell, already appointed to exercise the treasurer's vote in parliament.[184]

Such general pessimism was well grounded. During the session the Scottish ministers lived with a succession of minor failures and the prospect of several major ones.[185] Before Argyll's intentions had become fully apparent, Seafield had appraised with some accuracy the probable intentions of the opposition: to take off the new party into opposition, to pass trade prohibitions to reduce the funds for the civil list and to obstruct both succession and treaty. If necessary they would try to clog a treaty with unacceptable conditions. They would probably resurrect the triennial act and the barons' act from the previous session.[186] '. . . I am sure,' he later reported, 'we have not a majority of our own to carry anything . . .'[187]

The court had nevertheless to try. Anne's English managers, when free of junto pressure, wanted union and the necessary preliminary was an act allowing negotiations for a treaty. Such an act might all too probably lead nowhere but without it no beginning could be made. So behind its apparent abdication of responsibility the English court was secretly exerting itself to obtain a treaty act. Godolphin's steady purpose concerning a treaty was known to Seafield and recognised by him when he afterwards wrote: '. . . I am persuaded that now your lordship may have the honour of completing what you have been sincerely endeavouring these several years past . . .'[188] The initiative, though, had to be seen to rest elsewhere. Argyll, as a junto nominee, was the ideal instrument but some support had to be arranged for him. In the session of 1705 there were three possible contractors: Queensberry, the new party and Hamilton. Godolphin attempted to use all three.

Queensberry's arrears had been paid. Seafield, Annandale and Argyll wanted him in Edinburgh to lead his followers in support of the managers. As an inducement Argyll proposed him for the posts of privy seal and lord of the treasury, appointments which the queen was very reluctant to make. Anne's attitude was seized upon to excuse Queensberry's lack of zeal and his reluctance to leave London.[189] It was no more than an excuse. If Queensberry went to parliament at all he intended to time his arrival for his own benefit and not that of Argyll or anyone else. For him to be there at the defeat of the succession, his followers voting for the opposition, would have been an embarrassment. Alternatively, in the unlikely event of his influence's enabling the court to achieve success from the outset, the credit would have been Argyll's. A late arrival, after the succession had been rejected, and a further delay for Argyll to savour fully the taste of defeat, suited Queensberry very well. This was the timing he eventually adopted, remaining meanwhile in London, despite the pleas of Godolphin and others. Afterwards he was very careful to report that the succession had failed before he reached Edinburgh.[190]

Queensberry was important because without his co-operation success was improbable. Even so his interest still fell short of giving the old party a majority. The vital element in the new situation was the new party, though their opponents firmly refused at any time to admit it. At the start of the session a vote on a disputed election revealed the size of the opposition majority when joined by the new party.[191] As Godolphin noted, Argyll's report omitted any mention of this defeat but the fact was inescapable.[192] After Queensberry's arrival, his great influence and effectiveness lauded by his followers and reported to London, the court still lacked a majority. The balance in parliament depended entirely on either the new party or Hamilton.

8 The squadrone's position in 1705

The new party, or that part of it which followed Tweeddale, nicknamed in 1705 the *squadrone volante*, maintained an ambivalent relationship with the English court. Godolphin kept channels of communication open to them, mostly by way of Johnston and Seafield, and uttered words of encouragement. He spoke of the court's being forced against its will into allowing their dismissal and his understanding of their resentment. Since he could make amends in the future he hoped they would not be too obstructive in parliament.[193]

The squadrone out of office remained undecided what to do. There was no general agreement amongst them. Their policy of 1704 had been the product of circumstances, not conviction, and only the prospect of office had held them together. By 1705, after experience as officers of state, some had come to favour a treaty whilst others thought this would be the ruin of both themselves as a party and of Scotland.[194] Their problem, if they accepted Godolphin's hints as sincere, was how to show resentment without displeasing the English court. Seafield told them, '. . . if they wish to prevail in their court interest, they must serve the queen and endeavour to prevent confusion in this country and to promote a good correspondence between the two kingdoms . . .'[195] Yet, if Godolphin was trying to get something for nothing, they had no wish to forfeit what was left of their country party connections. What emerged as their chief priority was the maintenance of their own position as a separate interest, an aim which dominated all their calculations up to the union. Roxburgh told Baillie before their dismissal, '. . . If *the new party* is laid aside, and *succession* not to be tried, *the new party* will make a sad appearance in the *Scottish parliament*; for to support *Argyll*, or to join with Hamilton, are two bloody pills.'[196] Baillie's thoughts had run on similar lines: '. . . if by our concurrence, Argyll should carry his point, we may both disoblige, and fix that gang over us for ever . . .' In this appears a hint of the dilemma which underlay the new party's actions during the session. They knew that Godolphin wanted an act for a treaty but they had no wish to be told this officially—to know of the court's 'secret', as they put it—for fear of being placed in a position even more embarrassing than they were in already. A choice between succession and treaty was hard enough but a directive from Godolphin in favour of a treaty would be worse.[197] Finally they settled for appearances: to preserve credit by maintaining what purported to be consistency. 'Consistency' was to be the basis of their image in 1705. In order to achieve this they had, according to Baillie, to support the succession, 'for upon what other foot can they set up, unless they'll join as the tail of some other party, which would render them despicable, and must be their last resort; for they had better stick together in a thing indifferent, than join with any in that which is good, in such a manner as . . . would necessarily establish them with whom they joined . . .'[198] Sometimes they proved unable to resist the temptation to show that they held the parliamentary balance, although they were not short of specious excuses for Godolphin's benefit.[199] The English court meanwhile bided its time and Roxburgh

kept in secret contact with Seafield.[200] Only later did Hamilton fit into
the scheme of things.

As the session neared its opening Hamilton had arrived in
Edinburgh with his customary panache, amidst cheering crowds.
Atholl had, as usual, ordered his vassals to accompany him to
parliament.[201] The opposition was obviously determined to make an
impression. Their tactics were designed to block any settlement by
continually deferring such proposals on one patriotic pretext or
another. In the face of this and without a majority all the court could do
was to try to hold on, the summit of their hopes being to secure the
abstention, if no more, of enough members to enable a treaty act to be
passed before the session ended.

9 The parliament of 1705

Opposition tactics and the key position held by the squadrone were
both demonstrated from the beginning of the parliament. On the
insistence of Annandale and Ormiston, the ministry opened with a
proposal aimed at settling the succession. Annandale spoke for the
court. Immediately two opposition motions were moved: one by Mar
proposing a treaty and another by Marischal that parliament should
consider trade. Mar's proposal was ignored and a vote taken on which
of the other motions should have precedence. The succession proposal
was defeated by a majority of fifty-three or fifty-four votes. A growing
tendency to bandy resolutions about alarmed the managers and, on the
ground that it was unwise to bind parliament at such an early stage in
the session, they proposed to regulate procedure so that votes were put
in a less definitive form. Both cavaliers and countrymen vigorously
opposed this but the court won by thirty-three votes.[202] The reason
illustrates the balance of forces within parliament. Annandale's
proposal had been voted out—or postponed, which was technically
what had happened—because Queensberry's men and the squadrone
joined in support of the opposition. On the procedural motion the
squadrone and a few Queensberry men had voted for the court, which
made all the difference.

Marischal's proposal had been no more than a tactical diversion, the
opposition not being prepared to discuss trade just then, so there was a
consequent dearth of proposals. All that could be managed were some
inconclusive proceedings on the relative merits of rival schemes for
expanding Scottish credit[203]—the unlikely occasion of taking Roxburgh

and Fletcher of Saltoun to Leith Sands to fight a duel. George Baillie and lord Charles Ker, as their embarrassed seconds, fortunately effected a last-minute reconciliation and prevented serious trouble. There followed some talk of prohibiting various imports, on which trade seemed to expire as a topic through a lack of ideas.[204]

Nevertheless, such tepid business could have been drawn out to a greater length, and most probably would have been, except that Queensberry was at last on his way north and the opposition expected very soon to lose the support of his group. So to make use of their services whilst they were still available Hamilton again introduced a resolution asserting the need for a treaty. The house split on exactly the same lines as in the previous session. As expected, Queensberry's men, to avoid a sudden *volte-face*, supported the motion whilst the squadrone for the same reason joined the court in opposing it. The resolution was carried by forty-three votes.[205]

To the court this seemed the opportunity they had been waiting for and they argued in favour of considering a treaty with England, whereupon the opposition voted to postpone the treaty until limitations had been debated.[206] When the court expressed willingness to discuss limitations the opposition immediately voted to put trade before limitations. At length parliament agreed to spend four days on trade and four on limitations.[207]

Two acts emerged from proceedings on trade. One, for encouraging the fisheries, was as useless as any other such act, before or since. Its one positive effect was to put Argyll in mind of his grant of the 'assize herrings' caught on the west coast. The grant had still nine years to run but he thought the moment opportune for extending it.[208] The second act set up a council of trade. This involved two issues of significance for gauging what action parliament might later take over a possible nomination of treaty commissioners: whether nomination should be by parliament or by the crown, and whether, if by parliament, the choice should be in full parliament or by each estate separately choosing its own representatives? Nomination by parliament was carried by eleven votes.[209] Had the second question reached a vote it would certainly have been decided in favour of election in full parliament, but the court interposed a legal argument: the proposed council of trade, as other bodies nominated by parliament, was a committee of the house and, by act of parliament, committees were to be chosen by each estate separately. The court in this way could carry the nomination of nobles and burghs, where they had a majority, but not that of the barons, where they were weak.[210] This would provide a court majority on the council as a whole instead of the total exclusion which would have resulted from election in full parliament. The significance of this exercise was not lost upon Hamilton.

Godolphin began to lose patience at this protraction of business and was moved to vague threats. He wrote to Seafield, '. . . it looks to me as if that nation desired to bring things to extremity, in which I am not sure they are very well advised. England is not now in the condition it was when Scotland used to make inroads upon us. We have the power, and you may give us the will to return those visits . . .'[211] The whigs talked in a similar strain but were more positive and vehement. According to Johnston, Godolphin was against war but 'the whigs and Schütz [the Hanoverian representative] are violently and avowedly for; and better now, they say, than after a peace, when France will have her hands free to assist Scotland . . .'[212]

When parliament finally came to debate limitations the voting again made clear the squadrone's importance. Three main proposals were put forward. There were Fletcher's famous twelve limitations, designed to make Scotland a constitutional monarchy or, according to his detractors, a 'republic', and which, to his intense annoyance, failed to find a seconder. Rothes, for the squadrone, reintroduced the limitations offered by the court in 1704 in return for the succession, Baillie indicating the group's willingness to let such an act lie without assent till the successor should be nominated.[213] The cavaliers contributed place and triennial acts intended to take effect during the queen's lifetime. The squadrone's proposal was, in appearance, consistent with their stance in 1704; and since Baillie's offer made the question hypothetical anyway, they felt free to be awkward. On the issue of whether parliament, when choosing officers of state under the limitations, was to select from lists supplied by the court or have a free choice, the squadrone joined the opposition to carry free choice by sixteen votes.[214] Likewise the cavaliers' proposed acts were voted, with squadrone support, by the same majority of sixteen.[215] However, on a vote over whether the triennial act would become operative in one year as the cavaliers wanted, or in three years as the court would have preferred, the squadrone joined the court to give it a majority of thirty-two.[216]

It was plain that, even with Queensberry in Edinburgh and his flock once more in the court fold, the squadrone's switching of sides was decisive. Argyll and Queensberry were at their mercy and did not relish the fact. Argyll refused at any time to admit that he had been rescued by squadrone votes. Queensberry claimed that they had consistently opposed the court in everything.[217] Annandale, on the other hand, to detract from any achievements Argyll and Queensberry might be claiming, stressed the court's entire dependence on the squadrone.[218]

It was through the squadrone that the treaty came to be considered at all. The ministry, despairing of ever bringing the house to debate a treaty, proposed supply. Rothes, whilst supporting a first reading for an act of supply, blocked further progress by proposing that parliament should first debate a treaty, related acts of trade and other acts that were needful. The court welcomed the mention of a treaty but took alarm at the blocking clause. Such other acts as were needful could prove to be a very long course, which was why both Hamilton and Atholl supported the blocking clause with enthusiasm. Then, much to their annoyance and without explanation, Rothes withdrew it. At once, to stop any treaty, Fletcher of Saltoun proposed a similar clause. The squadrone voted with the court to reject Fletcher's clause by a majority of thirty-eight,[219] Argyll claiming it as a court victory.[220]

Thus the way was clear for a treaty act. Now that this had at last been brought to the point of debate there was every reason for it to pass in one form or another.[221] The court's worry was the form the act would eventually take. The act could have been quite preposterous from the point of view of the English managers and a complete bar to any settlement. Godolphin wanted the act to be unconditional, not stipulating, for example, that the alien act should be repealed before negotiations. The junto, he thought, would not care for a clause aimed at their own act and both English parties could make great play with Scottish 'interference' and 'dictation'.[222] The Scottish opposition of course exerted itself to have the act 'clogged' by such conditions, which the court avoided by a mere three or four votes. Marchmont, who had so far been voting with the squadrone, had been persuaded on this issue to join the court and enough of the squadrone abstained to give the court a victory.[223] A cavalier proposal to limit negotiation to a federal union met a similar fate and for the same reason. Then, having in this way allowed the treaty act to pass 'unclogged', the squadrone felt able to indulge in a show of outraged patriotism, joining an opposition protest against the 'unclogged' act.[224]

Once parliament had agreed to negotiate a treaty the next crucial point was the nomination of commissioners. Was parliament to choose them or was nomination to be left to the crown? If the various opposition elements could agree they were quite able to force nomination by parliament; much would then depend on whether the commissioners were chosen in full parliament or by the separate estates. The court had the ruling over the council of trade on its side as a precedent for the latter but the result could still be dangerous. Even though the court dominated the choice of the nobles and the burghs the barons' choice would be firmly opposition, making negotiations difficult. Any dissenting commissioners would be able to sabotage such chance as there was of agreement. But the court was rescued, in an unlikely fashion, from almost certain disaster by Hamilton who emerged briefly from rabid opposition to take the side of the court.

After the lengthy debate about whether or not the treaty act should be 'clogged', a crowd of members, having called out their votes, went off to eat, since business seemed as good as over for the day. Greatly to the surprise of his followers this was the moment Hamilton picked to move that the queen should choose the commissioners. Something like another twelve or fifteen opposition members left the house at once, in disgust but unwisely. In this thin parliament Hamilton then proposed that a vote be taken, a step which the court thankfully supported, and nomination by the crown was carried by a bare eight votes, including Hamilton's own.[225]

This placed the squadrone in a quandary from which they escaped with some ingenuity, arguing that since they had signed a protest against the act anyway there was no point in their voting over the issue of nomination. This meant a sizable squadrone abstention, and once again they managed to adopt a country stance whilst not incurring Godolphin's wrath by blocking the nomination by the crown.[226]

What tipped the balance this time was Hamilton's odd behaviour, for which there is no certain explanation. Both Godolphin and Harley had tried to secure his co-operation in passing a treaty act, using colonel James Graham and Belhaven as intermediaries. Argyll knew about this correspondence and resented it.[227] The negotiation was almost certainly unsuccessful in the wider field. Details might have been agreed, though it is unlikely. Hamilton wanted firm offers whilst the court confined itself to vague assurances about his future.[228] But rumours of his dealings with the court were so widespread that Greg reported him to be suspect even to his own party. Mar was even prepared to discount altogether his effectiveness as an opposition leader in 1705.[229]

However, Hamilton proved to be a very effective opposition leader.

He had done his best to stop and then to postpone the introduction of a treaty act. When it was brought in he had tried to 'clog' it. Through no fault of his own he had failed and it is possible that this changed his personal situation. In the event of an act's being passed he wanted to be a treaty commissioner and he had been taught a lesson over the council of trade. When the court had exerted itself to have trade commissioners nominated by the estates separately, 'one of our reasons for this measure', wrote Seafield, 'was that we thought, if the duke of Hamilton and the duke of Atholl and others of that party had not the interest to be chosen of that committee for trade, they would not insist to have the nomination of commissioners for the treaty named by parliament'.[230] There was no certainty that the court could have excluded Hamilton but neither was his choice a foregone conclusion. So Lockhart's story of a bargain between Argyll and Hamilton with Mar as intermediary might contain some substance although very probably inaccurate in detail. The arrangement, according to Lockhart, was that if Hamilton supported nomination by the crown Argyll would see that Hamilton was appointed as a commissioner. When, despite Hamilton's compliance, he was not appointed, Argyll himself, according to Lockhart, refused nomination. Argyll, it is true, was not a member of the union commission but that was very likely the product of other circumstances.[231]

Hamilton's action was of a piece with the rest of his political career. He had an obligation to his house and following to assert himself, showing that he played second fiddle to nobody. A magnate had either to be dominant within the court or mighty in opposition. Thus far Hamilton had been in opposition although never losing hope of supplanting Queensberry and before every session he half expected the court to turn to him as the solution to all its problems. It never came to this. The court tried to make use of him under cover and offered in return nothing but promises in which he had little faith. Consequently he never received these advances with anything like the glee the court expected but nor was he altogether sure that it was wise to reject them. The court's demand that performance should come before reward left him almost disorientated. If he had no court interest he had to keep a country interest. He would have been a fool to throw away his opposition prestige for the sake of court promises which might never be kept. Yet he had too much at stake to offend the court too violently. This conflict of tensions probably accounts for his sudden shifts and reversals over this period, although inconsistent behaviour was no novelty in his family.

So, by Hamilton's co-operation, the English court obtained its act for a treaty, the nomination of the commissioners being left to the crown. Little credit was due to Argyll, Queensberry or any of the Scottish managers. Even had they been responsible for securing Hamilton's assistance the tactic would still have failed had not a dozen or so members walked out in anger. Nor would the court have got far without the assistance of the squadrone. Seafield's earlier gloomy forecasts for the session had been a realistic appraisal of the court's chances. The Scottish court had not in fact deserved the success it had gained.

Once the treaty was out of the way an address was voted asking for the repeal of the penal clauses of the alien act before negotiations began. Supply was granted with little difficulty and parliament settled down to the congenial task of discussing 'popular' acts: for the prohibition of various kinds of trade with England and for Scotland's separate representation at any peace treaties.[233] Marlborough's caution to Godolphin, 'For God's sake be careful that the queen does not give her consent to any act in Scotland that may give offence to England . . .',[234] came rather late and was anyway superfluous since Godolphin had been extremely cautious. They both had the junto in mind. Assent was given to the fisheries act, the council of trade and the treaty act.[235] The other acts were not touched.[236]

10   The junto and the treaty act

When parliament stood adjourned, the court was left with the outcome they had wanted. If there was to be any settlement with Scotland the opportunity had arrived. But this was not the view of the whigs, who had planned differently for Scotland, and they were galled. When Godolphin received the mail from Edinburgh giving details of the acts passed by parliament and was considering which of them should be given the royal assent, he took the precaution of sending the various papers to Halifax, asking for comments. Halifax replied for himself and Somers, declining any responsibility on the grounds that he had insufficient information. Anything he said purported to be merely his own opinion and that of Somers, and both favoured a wholesale rejection of all the acts of the Scottish parliament. Halifax deplored the proposed council of trade, which was mischievous in intent; he thought the practice of offering cess in return for concessions was the road to ruin; triennial parliaments could not be other than sources of trouble.

The Scottish ministers should be asked to give undertakings for the consequences. He went on, '. . . Perhaps the act for a treaty is not designed to set afoot a union but to affront England. In that case the queen's choice is not difficult to make and the less she has done the better . . . when it is impossible to come to a judgement in any point, all one can do is to suggest what comes to mind, and submit all to your lordship's better judgement. I may be the easier mistaken in this matter, for I never expected any good from this session. I have no hopes of the public good, and, if things are so ordered, that no blame can be laid on the queen's ministers here, 'tis all I can wish. I think the step you have made [of allowing the act of security] cannot be mended, and I hope you will keep your footing . . .'[237]

The junto had been planning for a settlement of the succession to provide minimum security whilst nurturing the other Anglo-Scottish issues over which the court was vulnerable. They had failed and did not at all care for what had happened. The whig lords had become the largest immediate obstacle to the court's hopes for a union.

Notes

[1] *HMCR Laing MSS*, ii, 89–92, [Seafield's] memorial, 6 Aug. 1704.

[2] BL, Add. MSS 34180, 78, Seafield to Godolphin, 27 Aug. 1704; *ib.*, 80, same to same, 29 Aug. 1704.

[3] *Ib.*, 68, same to same, 1 Aug. 1704; SRO, GD 248, Box 2/1, Godolphin's letters, Godolphin to Seafield, 10 Aug. 1704.

[4] NLS, MS 7121, 46, Tweeddale to Godolphin, 21 Aug. 1704; BL, Add. MSS 34180, 76, Seafield to Godolphin, 21 Aug. 1704.

[5] NLS, MS 7121, 48, Tweeddale to same, 29 Aug. 1704.

[6] SRO, GD 205, portfolio 9, Belhaven to Godolphin, 29 Aug. 1704.

[7] *Atholl Chron.*, ii, 36, Atholl to same, Oct. 1704.

[8] BL, Add. MSS 39953, 41, Cromartie to same, 4 Jul. 1704; *ib.*, 49, same to same, 11 Jul. 1704; *ib.*, 53, same to same, 18 Jul. 1704; *ib.*, 61, same to same, 25 Jul. 1704; *ib.*, 63, same to same, 26 Jul. 1704; *ib.*, 28055, 146, Prestonhall to same, [1704].

[9] See above, p. 103.

[10] BL, Add. MSS 28055, 56, Leven to Godolphin, 6 Sep. [1704]; *Seafield Letters*, 155, same to same, 6 Sep. 1704; *Int. Soc. Letters*, i, 44–6, same to same, 26 Sep. 1704; Buccleuch (Drum.), Church and State, Abstract of Letters, [same] to [Queensberry], 8 Aug. [1704].

[11] This Melville–Leven argument appears in various documents, e.g., SRO, GD 26, xiii, 125, [1704]. Parts of it have been incorporated into a revised version devoted entirely to abuse of the new party, lumping them, in company with Seafield, Cromartie, Atholl, Ross and Belhaven, together with the

jacobites: *ib.*, 79, 152, 'Some observations on some of our present ministry', [1704/5]. *Seafield Letters*, 153, Leven to Godolphin, 18 Jul. 1704; *HMCR Portland MSS*, viii, 130, same to Harley, 27 Jul. 1704.

[12] Buccleuch (Drum.), Church and State, Abstracts, M. An[nandale] to [Queensberry], 10 Aug. [1704].

[13] *HMCR Portland MSS*, viii, 150, Carstares to Harley, 20 Sep. 1704.

[14] Buccleuch (Drum.), Church and State, Abstracts, L. Ph[iliphaugh] to [Queensberry], 12 Aug. [1704]; *ib.*, same to [same], 19 Aug. [1704]; *ib.*, Church and State, [   ] to [   ], 2 Sep. [1704].

[15] *Ib.*, [Philiphaugh] to [Queensberry], 9 Aug. [1704]; *HMCR Portland MSS*, viii, Carstares to Harley, 25 Aug. 1704.

[16] BL, Add. MSS 6420, 1, 'The remarks on the proceedings of parliament', [1704. By Mar?]; Buccleuch (Drum.), Church and State, Abstracts, E. M[ar] to [Queensberry], 7 Aug. [1704].

[17] *Ib.*, Church and State, [   ] to [   ], [1704]; *ib.*, 'Memorial concerning the affairs of Scotland', [1704]; *ib.*, Union, i, [draft notes by Queensberry], [1704].

[18] *HMCR Mar and Kellie MSS*, i, 230, Queensberry to Mar, 14 Sep. 1704.

[19] *Ib.*; Buccleuch (Drum.), Queensberry Letters, xvii, [Mar] to [Queensberry], 26 Sep. 1704.

[20] *Ib.*

[21] See above, pp. 71–2.

[22] *Seafield Letters*, 148, Harley to Godolphin, 24 Sep. 1704.

[23] Fraser, *Melvilles*, ii, 188, Godolphin to Leven, 15 Oct. 1704.

[24] SRO, Register of the Privy Council, Acta 52, 17 Oct. 1704; Vernon, iii, 271, Vernon to Shrewsbury, 20 Oct. 1704; SRO, GD 220, S, Seafield to Montrose, 27 Oct. 1704. For the composition of the privy council see SRO, Paper Register of the Great Seal, 15, 156, 17 Nov. 1704.

[25] See above, p. 84.

[26] SRO, GD 220, Copies, Montrose to Tweeddale, 3 Nov. 1704; *Jerviswood*, 32, Roxburgh to Baillie, 9 Jan. 1704/5.

[27] SRO, GD 220, S, Seafield to Montrose, 18 Nov. 1704.

[28] BL, Add. MSS 28055, 136, J. Muirhead to Godolphin, 27 Oct. 1704.

[29] SRO, GD 220, T, Tweeddale to Montrose, 16 Oct. 1704.

[30] *Ib.*, Copies, Montrose to Tweeddale, 3 Nov. 1704.

[31] *Marchmont Papers*, iii, 268 Marchmont to Roxburgh, 4 Nov. 1704.

[32] *Carstares S.P.*, 731, Seafield to Carstares, 21 Nov. 1704.

[33] *Vernon*, iii, 264, Vernon to Shrewsbury, 18 Aug. 1704; *ib.*, 268, same to same, 13 Oct. 1704.

[34] *Great Britain's Union And the Security Of The Hanover Succession Considered* ... (London, 1705).

[35] See above, pp. 57–8, 98–101.

[36] *Jerviswood*, 120, 8 Sep. 1705.

[37] SRO, GD 45, xiv, 336, G. Lockhart to H. Maule, 4 Jun. 1706; Cunningham, *History*, i, 452.

[38] J. Swift, *Memoirs Relating To That Change which happened in the Queen's Ministry in the Year 1710* in *Prose Works*, viii, 114.

[39] See below, p. 170.

[40] *HMCR Ormonde MSS*, viii, 120, Cholmondeley to Ormonde, 28 Nov. 1704; Cunningham, *History*, i, 413–14; Burnet, *History*, v, 182–5, provides a tendentious account of this affair, misrepresenting the relationship between court and junto as also the nature of the alien act.

[41] Burnet, *History*, v, 182, Dartmouth's note, c.

[42] I.e. the new party: *Jerviswood*, 12, Roxburgh to Baillie, 30 Oct. 1704.

[43] Burnet, *History*, v, 182 Dartmouth's note, c.

[44] *Jerviswood*, 12, Roxburgh to Baillie, 30 Nov. 1704. There are other accounts of this debate in *ib.*, 14, Johnston to same, 2 Dec. 1704 and Vernon, iii, 273, Vernon to Shrewsbury, 1 Dec. 1704.

[45] *Jerviswood*, 16, Johnston to Baillie, 7 Dec. 1704.

[46] SRO, GD 205, Letters from Individuals, Jamieson to Bennet, 30 Nov. 1704.

[47] B. C. Brown, ed., *Letters and Diplomatic Instructions of Queen Anne* (London, 1935), 172, queen to Godolphin, 11 Jul. 1705.

[48] Burnet, *History*, v, 225, Dartmouth's note, p.

[49] *Shrewsbury Corresp.*, 646, Somers to Shrewsbury, Dec. 1704.

[50] Vernon, iii, 278, Vernon to same, 8 Dec. 1704; Burnet, *History*, v, 183–4.

[51] E.g. *ib.*, and *Jerviswood*, 46, Johnston to Baillie, 15 Feb. 1705.

[52] 3 and 4 Anne, c. 6.

[53] *Marchmont Papers*, iii, 283, Marchmont to Somers, 3 Mar. 1705.

[54] *HMCR Lords' MSS*, N.S., vi, 230–33; *LJ.*, xvii, 606, 717.

[55] *CJ.*, xiv, 482–3, 477–8, 488, 495–6.

[56] *LJ.*, xvii, 717; Burnet, *History*, v, 183–4.

[57] SRO, GD 205, Letters of Sir W. Bennet, Bennet to Dirleton, 27 Feb. 1705; *HMCR Hamilton MSS*, 200 Lockhart to Hamilton, [Mar.] 1705; *ib.*, Home to same, 3 Mar. 1705.

[58] *Jerviswood*, 12, Roxburgh to Baillie, 30 Nov. 1704.

[59] *Marchmont Papers*, iii, 273, Marchmont to Devonshire, 12 Dec. 1704.

[60] *Jerviswood*, 26, Johnston to Baillie, 21 Dec. 1704.

[61] See below, p. 163.

[62] W. A. Speck, 'The House of Commons, 1702–14: a study in political organisation', unpublished D. Phil. thesis (Oxford, 1965).

[63] See below, p. 129 *et seq.*

[64] *Jerviswood*, 37, 16 Jan. 1704/5.

[65] *HMCR Ormonde MSS*, viii, 121, Miller to Ormonde, 24 Nov. 1704.

[66] *Carstares S.P.*, 731, Seafield to Carstares, 7 Nov. 1704; *ib.*, same to same, 21 Nov. 1704; *ib.*, 735, same to same, 10 Mar. 1705; SRO, GD 26, xiii, 103/10, same to Leven, 13 Feb. 1705.

[67] *Jerviswood*, 38, Baillie to Johnston, 16 Jan. 1705.

[68] See below, pp. 125, 128–9.

[69] *Carstares S.P.*, 729 Ormiston to Carstares, 4 Nov. 1704.

[70] *Ib.*, 729 Ormiston to Carstares, 4 Nov. 1704; *Jerviswood*, 28, Roxburgh to Baillie, 26 Dec. 1704.

[71] *Jerviswood*, 28, Roxburgh to Baillie, 26 Dec. 1704; *ib.*, 32, same to same, 9 Jan. 1704/5.

[72] *Ib.*, 30, same to same, 4 Jan. 1704/5.

[73] Seafield drafted a letter to be sent by Godolphin to pacify Forglen: BL, Add. MSS 28055, 346 Seafield to Godolphin, [Jan. 1705]; *Jerviswood*, 30 Roxburgh to Baillie, 2 Jan. 1704/5; *ib.*, 32, same to same, 9 Jan. 1704/5.

[74] *HMCR Bath MSS*, i, 66, Ormiston to Harley, 3 Feb. 1705.

[75] *Ib.*, 65, 12 Feb. 1704/5.

[76] *Jerviswood*, 29, Baillie to Johnston, 30 Dec. 1704.

[77] *Ib.*, 30, Roxburgh to Baillie, 2 Jan. 1704/5.

[78] See above, pp. 84, 118.

[79] *Jerviswood*, 12, Roxburgh to Baillie, 30 Nov. 1704; *ib.*, 43, same to same, 5 Feb. 1704/5; SRO, GD 205, portfolio 9, Belhaven to Hamilton, 22 Dec. 1704.

[80] *Jerviswood*, 35, 13 Jan. 1705.

[81] *Ib.*, 46, Johnston to Baillie, 15 Feb. 1705.

[82] The responsibility seems to have been his: *ib.*, 74, Baillie to Roxburgh, 11 Apr. 1705.

[83] *Ib.*, 30, Roxburgh to Baillie, 4 Jan. 1704/5.

[84] *Ib.*, 38, Baillie to Johnston, 16 Jan. 1705; *ib.*, 33, Johnston to Baillie, 9 Jan. 1704/5.

[85] *Ib.*, 12, Roxburgh to same, 30 Nov. 1704; *ib.*, 33, Johnston to same, 9 Jan. 1704/5; *ib.*, 35, same to same, 13 Jan. 1705.

[86] *Ib.*, 25, Roxburgh to same, 19 Dec. 1704; *ib.*, 19, same to same, 9 Dec. 1704.

[87] *SHR* (1922), 191, queen to Godolphin, 6 Jun. [1705].

[88] *Ib.*, same to same, 14 Jun. [1705].

[89] *Carstares S.P.*, 732, Seafield to Carstares, 21 Dec. 1704; *ib.*, 733, same to same, 25 Jan. 1705.

[90] Buccleuch (Drum.), Church and State, Abstracts, St[air] to [Queensberry], 31 Aug. [1704]; *ib.*, Church and State, [   ] to [   ], 2 Sep. [1704].

[91] *HMCR Mar and Kellie MSS*, i, 232, Dupplin to Mar, 17 Dec. 1704.

[92] *Jerviswood*, 33, Johnston to Baillie, 9 Jan. 1704/5.

[93] *Ib.*, 40, Roxburgh to same, 30 Jan. 1704/5.

[94] E.g. *ib.*, 45, Baillie to Johnston, 6 Feb. 1705.

[95] NLS, MS 3420, 21–2, Godolphin to [Seafield], 31 Jan. 1704/5.

[96] *Jerviswood*, 42, Roxburgh to Baillie, 1 Feb. 1704/5.

[97] *Ib.*, 47, Baillie to Johnston, 17 Feb. 1705.

[98] BL, Add. MSS 28055, 348, Seafield to Godolphin, 9 Jan. [1705]; SRO, GD 248, Box 2, bundle 38, Queensberry to Seafield, 10 Apr. 1705.

[99] *Jerviswood*, 46, Johnston to Baillie, 15 Feb. 1705; *ib.*, 49, same to same, 22 Feb. 1705; *ib.*, 51, Baillie to Johnston, 1 Mar. 1705.

[100] *Ib.*, 54, Johnston to Baillie, 6 Mar. 1704[/5]; *ib.*, 59, Baillie to Johnston,

17 Mar. 1705; *ib.*, 80, same to same, 28 Apr. 1705; *ib.*, 82, same to same, 1 May 1705. Queensberry was to receive something in the region of £16,400 at a rate of £1,500 per year for eleven years. The sum was in £ sterling and not £ Scots as the editor mistakenly noted. For Queensberry's views on the subject: Buccleuch (Drum.), Church and State, 'Memorial of the duke of Queensberry', [1705].

[101] *Jerviswood*, 49, Roxburgh to Baillie, 27 Feb. 1704/5; *Carstares S.P.*, 735, Seafield to Carstares, 10 Mar. 1705.

[102] Fraser, *Melvilles*, ii, 184, Argyll to Leven, 20 Feb. 1704[/5].

[103] *Jerviswood*, 54, Johnston to Baillie, 6 Mar. 1704[/5].

[104] *Ib.*; *ib.*, 56, same to same, 13 Mar. 1705; *ib.*, 69, same to same, 5 Apr. [1]705.

[105] *Ib.*, 60, Baillie to Johnston, 20 Mar. 1705; BL, Add. MSS 28055, 272, Annandale to Godolphin, 15 Mar. [1705]; *Seafield Letters*, 18, Seafield to same, 24 Mar. 1705.

[106] *Ib.*; *ib.*, 15, same to same, 24 Mar. 1705; *ib.*, same to same, Apr. 1705; *ib.*, 21, same to same, [4 Apr. 1705].

[107] *Jerviswood*, 69, Johnston to Baillie, 5 Apr. [1]705.

[108] *Ib.*, 61, same to same, 22 Mar. 1705; *Int. Soc. Letters*, i, 15–17, Argyll to Godolphin, 13 May 1705.

[109] *Jerviswood*, 40, Baillie to Johnston, 30 Jan. 1705; *ib.*, 51, same to same, 1 Mar. 1705; *ib.*, 64, same to same, 28 Mar. 1705.

[110] *Ib.*, 52, same to same, 6 Mar. 1705.

[111] *Ib.*, 51, same to same, 1 Mar. 1705.

[112] *Ib.*, 40, same to same, 30 Jan. 1705.

[113] *Ib.*, 49, Johnston to Baillie, 22 Feb. 1705.

[114] *Ib.*, 49, Roxburgh to same, 27 Feb. 1704/5.

[115] SRO, GD 220, R, same to Montrose, 1 Mar. 1704/5.

[116] *Ib.*, S, Seafield to same, 3 Mar. 1705; BL, Add. MSS 28055, 140, Roxburgh to Godolphin, 24 Mar. 1704/5.

[117] *Jerviswood*, 54, Johnston to Baillie, 6 Mar. 1704[/5].

[118] *Ib.*, 58, Baillie to Johnston, 13 Mar. 1705.

[119] *Ib.*, 61, Johnston to Baillie, 22 Mar. 1705.

[120] See Sir Richard Temple, *The Tragedy of the Worcester* (London, 1930).

[121] *Seafield Letters*, 29, Seafield to Godolphin, 17 Apr. 1705.

[122] SRO, Privy Council Register, Acta 52, 28 Mar. 1705.

[123] *Jerviswood*, 65, Baillie to Johnston, 31 Mar. 1705.

[124] SRO, Privy Council Register, Acta 52, 3 Apr. 1705; *Jerviswood*, 68, Baillie to Johnston, 5 Apr. 1705.

[125] *HMCR Laing MSS*, ii, 109–10, Roxburgh to [Godolphin?], 31 Mar. 1705; SRO, Privy Council Register, Acta 52, 3 Apr. 1705.

[126] *Seafield Letters*, 21, Seafield to Godolphin, [4 Apr. 1705].

[127] E.g. *Jerviswood*, 64, Baillie to Johnston, 28 Mar. 1705; *Seafield Letters*, 19, Seafield to Godolphin, Apr. 1705.

[128] *Jerviswood*, 74, Baillie to Roxburgh, 11 Apr. 1705.

129 *Seafield Corresp.*, 386, Northesk to Seafield, 2 Apr. 1705; *ib.*, 388, Tweeddale to same, 8 Apr. 1705; *ib.*, 388–9, Ormiston to same, 9 Apr. 1705; *ib.*, 389, Belhaven to same, 9 Apr. 1705; *ib.*, 389–90, Roxburgh to Seafield, 10 Apr. 1705.

130 SRO, Privy Council Register, Acta 52, 10 Apr. 1705; *Jerviswood*, 73, Baillie to Johnston, 10 Apr. 1705. The rest of the crew were later reprieved.

131 *Seafield Letters*, 27, Seafield to Godolphin, 11 Apr. 1705.

132 *Jerviswood*, 70, Johnston to Baillie, 9 Apr. 1705; BL, Add. MSS 28055, 156, Annandale to Godolphin, 12 Apr. 1705; *ib.*, 170, same to same, 26 Apr. 1705. *Cf. Seafield Letters*, 29, Seafield to Godolphin, 17 Apr. 1705. See also *Int. Soc. Letters*, i, 9–12, Argyll to Godolphin, 6 [*sic* for 26] Apr. 1705.

133 *Ib.*; *Seafield Letters*, 178, Glasgow to same, 26 Apr. 1705.

134 Buccleuch (Drum.), Church and State, 'Memorial', [1704].

135 *Int. Soc. Letters*, 9–12, Argyll to Godolphin, 6 [*sic* for 26] Apr. 1705; *Jerviswood*, 96, Baillie to Roxburgh, 26 May 1705.

136 *HMCR Laing MSS*, ii, 7, Argyll to queen, 26 Apr. 1703 [*sic* for 1705].

137 *Seafield Letters*, 32, Seafield to Godolphin, 26 Apr. 1705; *ib.*, 36, same to same, 10 May 1705; *ib.*, 38, same to same, 12 May 1705; *Jerviswood*, 79, Baillie to Johnston, 26 Apr. 1705.

138 Fraser, *Melvilles*, ii, 189, 7 May 1705.

139 BL, Loan 29/12, 6, draft, [May 1705].

140 *Seafield Letters*, 40, Seafield to Godolphin, 13 May 1705; *Int. Soc. Letters*, i, 13–15, Argyll to queen, 13 May 1705.

141 *Ib.*; *ib.*, 15–17, Argyll to Godolphin, 13 May 1705; *ib.*, 18–21, same to same, 26 May 1705.

142 *Ib.*; *Seafield Letters*, 44, Seafield to Godolphin, 24 May 1705; BL, Add. MSS 34180, 84, same to same, 26 May 1705.

143 SRO, GD 220, R, Roxburgh to Montrose, 19 Apr. 1705; *ib.*, same to same, 27 Apr. 1705; *ib.*, A, Argyll to same, 28 Apr. 1705; *Seafield Letters*, 32, Seafield to Godolphin, 26 Apr. 1705.

144 SRO, GD 220, Copies, Montrose to queen, 3 May 1705; *ib.*, W, Wedderburn to [   ], 9 Jun. 1705; *Int. Soc. Letters*, i, 12–13, Argyll to Godolphin, 10 May 1705.

145 *Jerviswood*, 92, Baillie to Roxburgh, 24 May 1705.

146 *Ib.*, 79, Baillie to Johnston, 26 Apr. 1705; *Int. Soc. Letters*, i, 24, Argyll to Godolphin, 12 Jun. 1705.

147 SRO, GD 220, G, Glasgow to Montrose, 31 May 1705; *ib.*, Copies, Montrose to Glasgow, 4 Jun. 1705; *ib.*, same to same, 11 Jun. 1705.

148 Buccleuch (Drum.), Union, ii, [Philiphaugh] to [Queensberry], 25 Apr. 1705; *ib.*, [Stair?] to [Queensberry], 27 May 1705.

149 *Seafield Letters*, 36, Seafield to Godolphin, 10 May 1705; *ib.*, 42, same to same, 17 May 1705.

150 *Jerviswood*, 103, Baillie to Roxburgh, 6 Jun. 1705; *ib.*, 105, Roxburgh to Baillie, 7 Jun. 1705; *ib.*, 106, Baillie to Roxburgh, 7 Jun. 1705; *ib.*, 108, Roxburgh to Baillie, 8 Jun. 1705.

[151] *Seafield Letters*, 52, Seafield to Godolphin, 12 Jun. 1705.

[152] Blenheim Papers, A1/37, queen to Marlborough, 12 Jun. 1705.

[153] Buccleuch (Drum.), Union, ii, [Philiphaugh] to [Queensberry], 3 May 1705.

[154] *Seafield Letters*, 28, Seafield to Godolphin, 14 Apr. 1705.

[155] SRO, GD 26, xiii, 128, Annandale to Leven, 4 May 1705.

[156] *HMCR Laing MSS*, ii, 111–12, Annandale to [   ], 16 May [1705]; *ib.*, 113–14, same to [   ], 27 May [1705]; *Jerviswood*, 92 Baillie to Roxburgh, 24 May 1705.

[157] See below, pp. 173, 255, 327, 332.

[158] *Int. Soc. Letters*, i, 5–8, Ormiston to Godolphin, 7 Apr. 1705; *HMCR Laing MSS*, ii, 112–13, Ormiston to [   ], 22 May 1705.

[159] Blenheim Papers, A1/36, Godolphin to Marlborough, 16 Apr. 1705. In 1705 the junto was actively involved in promoting a scheme for a Dutch guarantee of the protestant succession, so to that extent, at least, they were sincere.

[160] *Jerviswood*, 18, Roxburgh to Baillie, 7 Dec. 1704.

[161] *Ib.*, 102, Baillie to Roxburgh, 5 Jun. 1705; *Seafield Letters*, 50, Seafield to Godolphin, 9 Jun. 1705 (this appears as 29 Jun. in BL, Add. MSS 28055, but on internal evidence must be 9 Jun.).

[162] *Ib.*, 164, Ormiston to Godolphin, 31 May 1705; *HMCR Laing MSS*, ii, 113–14, Annandale to [   ], 27 May [1705]; *Int. Soc. Letters*, i, 5–8, Ormiston to Godolphin, 7 Apr. 1705.

[163] *Ib.*, 25–6, Argyll to same, 29 Jun. 1705; *Jerviswood*, 86, Johnston to Baillie, 8 May [1]705; *ib.*, 87, same to same, 16 May 1705.

[164] Buccleuch (Drum.), Union, ii, [   ] to [Queensberry], 25 May 1705.

[165] *Seafield Letters*, 50, Seafield to Godolphin, 9 Jun. 1705 and see p. 139. See also *ib.*, 44, same to same, 24 May 1705; *ib.*, 46, same to same, 29 May 1705.

[166] *Jerviswood*, 56, Johnston to Baillie, 13 Mar. 1705.

[167] *Seafield Letters*, 166, Ormiston to Godolphin, 1/2 Aug. 1705.

[168] See above, pp. 57–8.

[169] See below, p. 181.

[170] *Jerviswood*, 83, Johnston to Baillie, 3 May [1]705; *Seafield Letters*, 57, Seafield to Godolphin, 14 Jul. 1705; *Volpone: or Remarks On Some Proceedings in Scotland* . . . (1707) made the same distinction at a later date. 'Communication of trade' was used in the sense of normal mainland trade rather than that of access to the plantations. See below, p. 227 *et seq.*

[171] *Int. Soc. Letters*, i, 41–4, Argyll to Godolphin, 6 Nov. 1706.

[172] *HMCR Laing MSS*, ii, 112–13, Ormiston to [   ], 22 May 1705; *Seafield Letters*, 164, same to Godolphin, 31 May 1705.

[173] *Ib.*, 29, Seafield to same, 17 Apr. 1705.

[174] BL, Add. MSS 28085, 225–6, [Argyll's?] Memorial, 21 Sep. 1705.

[175] *HMCR Laing MSS*, ii, 110–11, Annandale to Godolphin, 9 May [1705]; BL, Add. MSS 28055, 210, same to same, 1 Jun. [1705].

[176] *Int. Soc. Letters*, i, 18–21, Argyll to same, 26 May 1705; *ib.*, 21–4, same to same, 7 Jun. 1705.

[177] *Jerviswood*, 99, Roxburgh to Baillie, 30 May 1705.

[178] *APS*, xi, 213–14, gives the final text of the queen's letter. The instructions are in *HMCR Laing MSS*, ii, 113–16, Jun. 1705.

[179] Buccleuch (Drum.), Church and State, [Queensberry] to [   ], draft, [Sep. 1705].

[180] *Seafield Letters*, 41, Seafield to Godolphin, 16 May 1705; *ib.*, 44, same to same, 24 May 1705.

[181] BL, Add. MSS 28055, 228, same to same, 20 Jun. 1705 (printed in *Seafield Letters*, 52 as dated 23 Jun.).

[182] *Seafield Letters*, 46, same to same, 29 May 1705.

[183] *HMCR Bath MSS*, i, 71, Godolphin to Harley, 25 [Jun.] 1705; *Jerviswood*, 62, Johnston to Baillie, 24 Mar. [1]705.

[184] *Int. Soc. Letters*, i, 25–6, Argyll to Godolphin, 29 Jun. 1705.

[185] *Seafield Letters*, 54, Seafield to same, 30 Jun. 1705; *ib.*, 66, same to same, 5 Aug. 1705.

[186] *Ib.*, 15, same to same, 24 Mar. 1705. See above, p. 135.

[187] *Ib.*, 57, same to same, 14 Jul. 1705.

[188] *Ib.*, 83, same to same, 3 Sep. 1705.

[189] Queensberry did have domestic worries and attempts were made to have him excused attendance on those grounds. BL, Add. MSS 28055, 27, Argyll to same, 9 Jun. 1703 [*sic* for 1705]; *ib.*, 34180, 84, Seafield to same, 26 May 1705; Buccleuch (Drum.), Union, ii, [Philiphaugh] to [Queensberry], 25 Apr. 1705.

[190] *Ib.*, Church and State [Queensberry] to [   ], draft, [Sep. 1705].

[191] *HMCR Portland MSS*, iv, 197, [W. Greg] to [Harley], 21 Jun. 1705.

[192] *HMCR Bath MSS*, i, 72, Godolphin to same, 4 Jul. 1705.

[193] *Jerviswood*, 115, Johnston to Baillie, 23 [Aug. 1]705; *ib.*, 118, same to same, 28 Aug. [1]705; NLS, MS 7104, 43, Marlborough to Tweeddale, 9 Mar. 1705; BL, Add. MSS 28055, 286, Johnston to Godolphin, 23 Aug. 1705. See below, p. 260 *et seq.*

[194] *Jerviswood*, 97, Roxburgh to Baillie, 28 May 1705; SRO, GD 205, Letters of Sir W. Bennet, Bennet to Dirleton, 29 Jan. 1705.

[195] *Seafield Letters*, 76, Seafield to Godolphin, 26 Aug. 1705.

[196] *Jerviswood*, 97, Roxburgh to Baillie, 28 May 1705.

[197] *Ib.*, 76–7, Baillie to Johnston, 17 Apr. 1705; *ib.*, 105, Roxburgh to Baillie, 6 Jun. 1705; *ib.*, 108, same to same, 8 Jun. 1705.

[198] *Ib.*, 100, Baillie to Roxburgh, 31 May 1705.

[199] BL, Add. MSS 28055, 286, Johnston to Godolphin, 23 Aug. 1705.

[200] See below, pp. 260–2.

[201] *HMCR Portland MSS*, iv, 197, [W. Greg] to [Harley], 21 Jun. 1705; *Atholl Chron.*, ii, 50–1, 23 Jun. 1705.

[202] *HMCR Portland MSS*, iv, 201, [W. Greg] to [Harley], 5 Jul. 1705; *Seafield Letters*, 54, Seafield to Godolphin, 7 Jul. 1705.

203 The proposals of Chamberlen and Law. *Int. Soc. Letters*, i, 26–8, Argyll to same, 8 Jul. 1705.

204 *HMCR Portland MSS*, iv, 205, [W. Greg] to [Harley], 10 Jul. 1705; *ib.*, 207, [same] to [same], 14 Jul. 1705; *Seafield Letters*, 57, Seafield to Godolphin, 14 Jul. 1705; *HMCR Mar and Kellie MSS*, i, 234, Mar to lady Mar, 16 Jul. 1705.

205 *HMCR Portland MSS*, iv, 208, [Greg] to [Harley], 17 Jul. 1705; BL, Add. MSS 28055, 250, Annandale to Godolphin, [1]8 Jul. 1705; *Seafield Letters*, 58, Seafield to same, 18 Jul. 1705. Selkirk and Belhaven were in the process of leaving the new party and voted against them on this.

206 *Ib.*, 62, same to same, 1 Aug. 1705; BL, Add. MSS 34180, 86, same to same, 21 Jul. 1705; *HMCR Portland MSS*, iv, [Greg] to [Harley], 31 Jul. 1705; *HMCR Laing MSS*, ii, 118–19, Annandale to Godolphin, 1 Aug. [1705].

207 *Seafield Letters*, 166, Ormiston to Godolphin, 1/2 Aug. 1705; *ib.*, 66, Seafield to same, 5 Aug. 1705.

208 *Ib.*, 67, same to same, 8 Aug. 1705; *HMCR Portland MSS*, iv, 218, [Greg] to [Harley], 9 Aug. 1705.

209 *Ib.*

210 *Seafield Letters*, 67, Seafield to Godolphin, 11 Aug. 1705; *APS*, xi, 222, 14 Aug. 1705.

211 *HMCR Seafield MSS*, 207, Godolphin to Seafield, 9 Aug. 1705.

212 *Jerviswood*, 121, Johnston to Baillie, 9 Sep. [1]705.

213 *Ib.*, 116, Baillie to Johnston, 23 Aug. 1705.

214 *Seafield Letters*, 71, Seafield to Godolphin, 18 Aug. 1705.

215 *Ib.*, 77, same to same, 26 Aug. 1705.

216 *Ib.*

217 BL, Add. MSS 6420, 11, [Queensberry's] 'Memorial', 1 Aug. 1705; Buccleuch (Drum.), Church and State, [Queensberry] to [   ], draft, [Sep. 1705].

218 BL, Add. MSS 28055, 288, Annandale to Godolphin, 26 Aug. [1705].

219 *HMCR Mar and Kellie MSS*, i, 234, Mar to lady Mar, 25 Aug. 1705.

220 *Int. Soc. Letters*, i, 33–5, Argyll to Godolphin, 26 Aug. 1705. According to Argyll the clause was rejected by thirty-six votes.

221 See above, pp. 139–40.

222 *HMCR Johnstone MSS*, 122, Godolphin to Annandale, 23 Jul. 1705; BL, Add. MSS 34180, 88, Seafield to Godolphin, 28 Jul. 1705.

223 *Ib.*, 28055, 298, Annandale to Godolphin, 2 Sep. [1705]; *Seafield Letters*, 83, Seafield to same, 3 Sep. 1705.

224 *Jerviswood*, 116, Baillie to Johnston, 23 Aug. 1705; *APS*, xi, 236, 237.

225 *HMCR Portland MSS*, iv, 238, [Greg] to [Harley], 1 Sep. 1705; *Seafield Letters*, 71, Seafield to Godolphin, 18 Aug. 1705.

226 *Ib.*, 83, same to same, 3 Sep. 1705; *HMCR Portland MSS*, iv, 238, [Greg] to [Harley], 1 Sep. 1705.

227 *Ib.*, 171, [col. J. Graham] to Harley, 30 Mar. [1705]; SRO, GD 205, portfolio 9, contains the Belhaven correspondence. *Jerviswood*, 66, Johnston to Baillie, 31 Mar. 1705.

228 SRO, GD 248, Box 5/2, Misc., Hamilton to Seafield, 28 Jan. 1704/5; *ib.*, GD 205, portfolio 9, Hamilton to Godolphin, 30 Mar. 1705; *HMCR Portland MSS*, iv, 171, [Graham] to Harley, 30 Mar. [1705].

229 *Ib.*, 210, [Greg] to [Harley], 19 Jun. 1705; SRO, GD 124, Box 16, MM865/10, Mar to lady Mar, 4 Jul. 1705; *Jerviswood*, 108, Roxburgh to Baillie, 8 Jun. 1705; *ib.*, 114, Johnston to same, 13 Jul. 1705.

230 *Seafield Letters*, 71, Seafield to Godolphin, 18 Aug. 1705.

231 *Lockhart Papers*, i, 132–7.

232 *HMCR Portland MSS*, iv, 243, [Greg] to [Harley], 8 Sep. 1705. Argyll's account of the cess's being carried in the teeth of great opposition seems to have been fictional: *Int. Soc. Letters*, i, 35–9, Argyll to Godolphin, 9 Sep. 1705.

233 *Ib.*; *HMCR Laing MSS*, ii, 119–23, Seafield to same, 9 Sep. 1705.

234 *Blenheim Papers*, A1/37, Marlborough to Godolphin, 24 Sep. 1705.

235 Buccleuch (Drum.), Union, ii, Nairn to [Queensberry], 10 Sep. 1705.

236 *Seafield Letters*, 88, Seafield to Godolphin, [21 Sep. 1705].

237 *Seafield Letters*, 160, Halifax to same, 4 Sep. 1705. See also KCRO, Stanhope MSS, 24/9, same to same, 9 Aug. 1705 (copy).

CHAPTER FIVE
Negotiations

Halifax's ominous letter to Godolphin represented no passing mood and consequently, until the junto underwent a change of heart, the achievement of the court's objective in the Scottish parliament was a dead end. Without junto support the treaty project could go no further and the whigs' disinclination was notorious. The squadrone even had extravagant hopes of turning the whig lords' disappointment to their own advantage—the only party which in 1705 had remained firm to the succession.[1] Discussion was not confined to the squadrone's near-hysterial conjectures. Even confirmed whigs saw that the junto had no desire for a union, since it would change the situation which made them 'necessary to a court that in their hearts hates them'.[2] Lockhart thought the whigs had no wish for Scotland to be a source of strength for the court and he was right. They much preferred it to remain a separate kingdom under English influence.[3]

Godolphin had little idea of whig intentions. Presumably the junto told him only what they wanted him to know. He told Johnston: 'no measures will be taken or resolved on as to *Scotland* till it appear what course matters take in *the English parliament* . . .'[4] When Mar reached London he was doubtful of the treaty's chances.[5] Seafield told Carstares that the obstruction came from the junto. '. . . We have been very doubtful till now of the effect of our act of treaty and address [for the repeal of the alien act clauses]. We have been at great pains to inform the leading men of the whig party, and her majesty's English servants have been very assisting . . .'[6]

If the whigs had remained determined to prevent union they could easily have done it. The obvious course would have been a refusal to repeal the alien act clauses for which the Scots had addressed but, by the beginning of November, the whigs had decided against this.

Seafield wrote to Queensberry: '. . . The difficulty is in repealing the clause declaring us aliens but the queen and the court and the leading men of the whig party are preparing their friends for it . . . I have told that there is no possibility of succeeding in our country but by a treaty and giving us advantageous terms or an union . . .'[7] The affair was cunningly handled.

1   The junto's conversion to union

The queen's speech recommended parliament to consider relations with Scotland but the replies of both lords and commons avoided all reference to the topic,[8] which gave rise to speculation.[9] The tories had calculated, not unreasonably, that the whigs would resist the repeal of clauses in their own act and so, to embarrass both them and the court, decided to make the proposal to repeal. Nottingham spoke first, seconded by Buckingham. But next to speak was Somers, who astonished the tories by a suggestion to take things even further, repealing all the clauses of the alien act save that allowing union commissioners to be appointed. At this the tories took alarm and Rochester tried to hedge, moving that no union should be proceeded with until the Scots had repealed the act of security. This was such a blatant attempt to retract the tories' original proposal that, whatever the party's chagrin, it was not taken further and the lords unanimously accepted Somers's suggestion.[10]

This sudden reversal of the whig position over Scotland led to an outbreak of euphoria about their generous intentions but the junto's decision was not at all due to magnanimity. For the court the elimination of the difficulties of Scottish management provided sufficient reason for a union, but the possibility of strengthening the court's position in both lords and commons was a powerful incentive.[11] These same reasons had led the junto since 1702 to oppose union. They, too, accepted the belief that a parliamentary union with Scotland would increase the power of the court. A very small majority in the lords had enabled the junto since Anne's accession to change drastically the political situation in England. An influx of Scottish peers could remove overnight this leverage against the court. In the commons too the position of the court was critical, as appeared at the beginning of the 1705 session in the contest between Smith and Bromley for the speaker's chair. The court and whigs combined to carry Smith's election by 248 votes to 205. This was in a full house with all the screws

on. After great exertion Harley had been able to bring no more than
twenty-seven tories to support the court candidate, whilst seventeen
tory placemen defected by voting for Bromley.[12] The court had reached
a fork and Godolphin and Marlborough disagreed with Harley about
the way they should take. In the previous session the defeat of the tack
and some consequent blurring of the rigid party division had given
Harley some hopes of increasing the court's freedom of action if a
number of tackers could be eliminated in the 1705 election. Then,
moderate tories, Harleyites and 'sneakers' might collaborate with
moderate whigs to form a larger centre group which could hold the
balance in the commons.[13] Only the remaining tackers and the more
frustrated and rebellious whigs, who had been in tactical collaboration
in the 1704–5 session,[14] would remain in opposition to the court. The
court's grip would have been correspondingly firmer and Harley had
rejoiced at the prospect. He wrote to Marlborough: '. . . the queen hath
wisely and happily delivered herself from a party and I believe she will
not easily put herself again into the power of any party whatsoever
. . .'[15] Marlborough and Godolphin were reaching a different
conclusion. They were concerned above all else with the war and their
own survival. In the knowledge that the whigs were not only the
foremost supporters of the war but dangerous opponents, Marlborough
urged the queen to come to terms with them in the session of 1705–6 to
prevent any obstruction which might unsettle the Dutch.[16] When the
1705 election produced a firm party division in the commons the
differences between the managers became, not acute, but certainly
more pronounced. Harley still urged on Godolphin the desirability of
coming to terms with moderates to avoid junto domination. Godolphin,
having an established whig majority in the lords to contend with, chose
to placate the junto. He interpreted the speaker's division as pointing
inescapably to a whig alliance, however moderately he expressed it.[17]
At the beginning of the session the court was very much concerned
about the voting balance in the commons;[18] and so were the whigs.

    Few politicians were blind to the implications of a union. Later,
when the proposed Scottish representation at Westminster was all but
settled, Francis Annesley wrote to archbishop King of the forty-five
commoners and sixteen peers: '. . . which as so many dead votes one
way will be a great stroke in the legislature . . .'[19]After the union had
been negotiated, the lord advocate, who disapproved of it, hinted at the
same point. If the whigs knew their own interest they '. . . should rather
desire us to continue in the state of a separate kingdom and provide

that we may still remain firm upon the revolution foot . . . As to what may concern the interest of the crown in this affair it is a speculation too delicate to be adventured upon . . .'[20]

The whigs knew as well as the lord advocate the dangers union held for them. After all, as allies of the court in William's reign they had supported union in the hope of improving their own position. At the beginning of Anne's reign they had backtracked for fear union might help the tories. Instead they pressed for the carrying of the succession, leaving the kingdoms separate, with Scotland in the hands of the old party relying heavily on junto support.

But now seemingly the old party had itself produced an act for a treaty with England, asserting that this had been their only feasible course, and by so doing had reduced the possibilities to two: a treaty with Scotland or a complete breakdown in Anglo-Scottish relations. This had presented the junto with a dilemma. It would be easy to sabotage a union treaty but escaping the blame would be less so. Somers seems to have toyed for some time with the idea of a partial union, allowing Scottish representatives at Westminster for the discussion of money bills only—a half-baked proposal which indicates whig desperation.[21] However, the junto finally decided that their only chance of keeping control in the new situation lay in making the policy of union their own, putting the court under enough pressure to ensure whig management of the negotiations, thus giving them an opportunity to extract from the union the utmost party advantage. The old party men were their allies and they too had differences with the court. If the Scottish representatives to a united parliament were all from the old party, then legislative union, despite the accepted opinion, could conceivably benefit the whigs rather than the court. The calculation behind the whigs' *volte-face* did not go unsuspected. George Lockhart thought their intention was merely to use the negotiations to establish a sufficiently close *rapport* with the old party to persuade them to settle the succession and abandon a treaty.[22] Roxburgh came closer. He had no doubts concerning the whigs' conversion to union but wondered whether they were altogether wise. He wrote to Baillie, '. . . The only danger I can perceive to the whigs is, that one day or other Scotland may make an election of cavaliers both for lords and commons, which you know will be no difficult thing when the court has a mind for't . . .'[23] But the main object of the junto was clearly apparent to the duke of Newcastle during the treaty negotiations, when he complained that Scottish representation was too great. Many of the Scots had said 'when they first came to town, they should ask a greater number [of MPs] to exonerate themselves (as they call it); yet did seem as if they would have been content with thirty-six of the lower house. But I suppose our pilots, by the hand they have in the present negotiations, hope afterwards to steer those northern vessels . . .'[24] Somers's correspondence with Leven when the Scottish parliament was debating union shows Newcastle to have been right.[25]

2 *Junto manoeuvres to control negotiations*

So, with their habitual effrontery, the junto decided to face about and support union. It was not their habit to do something for nothing even if that something was for their own benefit, so there had been a further bargain with the court. They needed control of the negotiations and Godolphin seems to have guaranteed that all the junto lords and a substantial number of their allies would be on the union commission. Harley had misgivings over this and wanted to dilute junto influence by having a larger commission but the number in the Scottish commission—thirty-one—could not be exceeded.[26]

This nomination was a junto success but it did not necessarily ensure control of the negotiations. The court's compliance was essential, otherwise the junto could appear to be following the court's lead, which was not their way at all. They were in fact intending to give exactly the opposite impression: that of a court meekly following the junto's initiative to safeguard the protestant succession. This was how Somers represented the situation to the Hanoverian court.[27] To induce in Godolphin the required degree of passivity he had to be kept in a state of continual insecurity, and events played into the junto's hands.

A very devious manoeuvre had its origin with the tories' reaction to the repeal of the alien act clauses in the session of 1705–6. It involved both lords and commons. In the lords the tories sought to regain the initiative by trying to trap Godolphin in a kind of knight's fork. They proposed, in the interests, they said, of safeguarding the protestant succession, to invite to England Sophia, the designated successor to the English throne. This suggestion was notoriously one which the queen found offensive. Any minister who supported it would have lost all Anne's favour. Yet should Godolphin oppose the invitation he could be branded as a jacobite. Indeed, Charles Caesar, in the commons, hinted so strongly and offensively at the lord treasurer's jacobitism that he was sent to the tower.[28] The whigs offered Godolphin a way out—the regency bill, to make provision for governing the country between the death of Anne and the arrival of the successor. Such a bill could be represented as an urgent legal safeguard for the succession, deserving precedence over an invitation to Sophia which was a mere gesture. This would postpone the invitation, perhaps even for the rest of the session. The tories, after professing such zeal for the succession, could hardly take exception to the regency bill. This was the course followed in the lords, where the whigs were seen exerting themselves to extricate Godolphin from this tory ambush.

In the commons the situation was markedly different. There the proposal to invite Sophia was brought in as 'the remedy for the dangers . . . apprehended from Scotland . . .', introduced by the tory leaders despite objections from Packington and some of their wilder and more obdurate followers. The court and the whigs opposed it. If this opposition had remained solid the proposal would have been defeated without difficulty, but a group of whigs in the commons were disinclined to vote out the proposal at once on the ground that it was not safe to do so until the regency bill had passed. James Brydges, in a letter to Marlborough, put a charitable interpretation on this: '. . . The reason of this proceeding, my lord,' he wrote, 'we look upon to have been, that gentlemen might see, that in case the regency should not pass, it would not be impossible for them to go into the other motions, thinking by that means, to make that bill go down the easier in the house of commons.'[29] Harley was closer to the truth. He complained of those who had frustrated the defeat of the invitation proposal. He added: '. . . These are common incidents. We must make the most of everybody even of those who think themselves cunning enough to drive a bargain.'[30] Those responsible were members of the group who later held up the regency bill by insisting on the 'whimsical clause' to keep placemen out of the commons after the queen's death. They have in consequence been taken for a group of 'country whigs',[31] although the 'country' credentials of most of them were more than dubious.[32]

A leading part in keeping open the possibility of Sophia's invitation was played by John Smith, the speaker,[33] who had also been involved in changing substantially the lord's original alien bill.[34] And when the repeal of the alien act's clauses came before the commons, Mar reported to his brother: '. . . the speaker kept it two hours from being approved, still insisting to have their clauses only suspended, but he was forced to yield at last too . . .'[35] This is curious, especially when Smith later appeared as second to none in his enthusiasm for the union.[36] There is a marked pattern here. Burnet hinted that the place clause was a pretext to delay the regency bill.[37] A few of the whig 'rebels' may well have voted for the 'whimsical clause' out of conviction or eccentricity but the probability is that they were being used by others whose sincerity is open to doubt. Suspicion is strengthened when the same names appear in connection with the alien act and the invitation to Sophia. Harley's reference to 'driving a bargain' seems significant. Refusal to reject the invitation outright would not only preserve any credit the whigs might have in Hanover, it would also keep Godolphin under pressure, enabling the whigs to extract their own terms for supporting union, which would account for the bitterness of Harley's reaction to their activities. He, at any rate, did not regard them as merely rogue whigs out of junto control. Not only did he complain to Marlborough,[38] he threatened reprisals. On 5 December 1705 he was quite explicit on the subject to Cowper. Since the whigs had not been co-operative in the commons in the attempt to extricate Godolphin from his Scottish difficulties, then Harley in turn would do what he could to upset the whigs over the report on the Hertford election petition.[39]

The 'whimsical clause' and the Hanoverian invitation apart, the 'country whigs' seem to have been quite orthodox in this session. Other business followed the usual pattern. The alien act clauses were finally repealed and the tories, who had staged a 'church in danger' debate, stressing the fate of the Scottish episcopalians and the dangers from rampant presbyterianism,[40] lost the division 'by above 50 votes'.[41]

3 Whig negotiating tactics

Yet, despite this whig pressure, it was still not at all certain what negotiations would amount to. Even Seafield was vague about what sort of arrangement would prove possible. He told Carstares, '. . . you are perfectly in the right, that there is no other way of taking from the opposing party their pretensions of having a country interest, but by having a treaty . . .' Yet he was not sure whether 'treaty' meant a bargain over the succession or a union.[42]

The English gave no clues until the parliamentary session ended.[43] Up to the beginning of March not even the Scottish ministry had been given any inkling of what was likely to happen,[44] but when it became known that negotiations were to take place it was clear to all that the whigs were in effective control. Such self-abnegation on the part of the

court could have been due only to pressures Godolphin felt to be
irresistible, and later developments show that the court acted from
necessity rather than calculation.[45]

After parliament rose in 1706 the junto lost no time in assuming their
new role—that of the only dedicated supporters of union and a fair deal
for the Scots. Wharton's demeanour was such that he was later
complimented on his part in creating harmonious relations amongst
the union commissioners.[46] The departure of Halifax for Hanover on
official business was represented as a great loss to the negotiations.[47]
Somers's key part in the transaction is well attested.[48] The whig lords'
involvement extended even to administrative details such as pressing
Doddington into service as secretary to the union commissioners.[49] It is
true, as a pamphlet of 1706 declared, that the best way to get business
done is to have the essentials determined by a very few people,[50] but
then the obvious choice was the English court managers. They,
however, remained inactive whilst the whigs conducted the union
negotiations in a way calculated to gain the allegiance of the Scottish
old party, supposing the future representation of Scotland would be
chosen from these carefully nurtured allies. So the junto carried on
private negotiations with some of the Scottish commissioners, reaching
informal agreements ratified later when the official forms of negotiation
had been observed.

Harley was resentful but seemingly powerless, no doubt as a direct
result of Godolphin's agreement with the junto. He complained to
Newcastle, '. . . You need no description of the commissioners north of
Tweed. They are always the same; and for the southern men they
"catched the itch of the others", so that they choose to do that by a
trick which would have passed easier by open dealing. They have only
got this one advantage, that they have forced some of your servants in
the commission to show they are good friends to the union and not
useless members, though they do not treat privately with the "bonny
blewcaps" as the others have been forced to own they do . . .'[51]
Newcastle, also, thought there had been too much double-dealing.[52]

The whig lords even intervened in a dispute amongst the Scottish
commissioners over whether the Scottish church establishment should
be safeguarded by a specific article of union. Such a demand, the whigs
told them, would lead to a clamour in the English parliament for the
toleration of Scottish episcopalians. A far better procedure would be to
exclude church government from the articles and allow each
parliament separately, if it wished, to safeguard its own kingdom's

church establishment.[53] The Scots took this advice.

This junto design of satisfying the Scots to the limit the English parliament would accept had its risks. Their scheme was almost wrecked by the desire of some Scots, in particular Ormiston, to show deference to the whigs by being over-modest, not to say abject, in their bargaining. There was also gossip, which meant that regular accounts of whig intentions were carried to Godolphin, although they could only have confirmed what he already suspected.[54] There were times when the whigs despaired of the whole scheme, but notwithstanding such complications the union proceeded very much as a junto monopoly.[55]

With the junto ostentatiously directing negotiations and the court remaining quiescent, suspicions were bound to arise that the court was not really in favour of union and had opted out,[56] which was, of course, the impression the whigs had aimed at producing. Godolphin was said to lack interest and to be merely tolerating negotiations to avoid the consequences of the act of security.[57] This impression of the respective attitudes of the court and the junto was very marked in the most surprising quarters. William Paterson, after his varied career as a 'projector' in England and Scotland, had been employed as one of the Scottish statisticians to calculate the equivalent and had come to feel that he was again at the centre of affairs. This was greatly to his taste. Being in need of employment, he had offered to go to Scotland to explain the terms of the union.[58] When no immediate appointment was forthcoming he had the temerity to write to Harley threatening him and Godolphin, both, with the junto's displeasure.[59] For the junto to appropriate an idea which, in the teeth of whig opposition, the court had always favoured and to seem to be forcing it upon the queen's reluctant managers was a substantial achievement. There is no reason whatsoever to suppose that Godolphin had become any less attached to union. Doubtless he would have preferred it to have been achieved under different circumstances and other auspices. Possibly, as demands were made on his patience and endurance, he allowed himself in private conversation to appear less than enthusiastic, but this could have been due to no more than weariness and last-minute disenchantment. The problems of Anglo-Scottish relations were still there, with union the only feasible solution. As for the crucial contest over Scottish representation at Westminster which was the pivot of whig policy, the outcome was by no means a foregone conclusion and Godolphin had no intention of letting the point go by default. He could afford to be patient.

The in-fighting between the court and the whigs concerning Scotland had been transformed. It had now to be carried on within the framework of union by which all parties had become trapped: the whigs, who had been averse from union in the first place; the court, which found distasteful the way in which it seemed to be coming about; those Scots whose first priority was the safeguarding of their own position no matter what happened; and others who were prepared to do as they were told. The perennial struggle between court and country in Scotland took on the aspect of a contest over union. As a consequence, the union negotiations and the last session of the Scottish parliament gave rise to some very deep games, most of which proved to be, in the event, too devious by half.

4   The old party and the prospect of union

The Scots had their own problems. The old party leaders had emerged from the session of 1705, greatly to their own surprise, with an act for a treaty. If the English court proved able to carry the policy further, the old party was prepared to follow their initiative for a union, or indeed almost anything else, as long as their jobs were assured. However, they had not survived the 1705 session unscathed. A note of near-hysteria entered into their denials that the new party had had any effect at all in the Scottish parliament, a contention supported by wildly inconsistent arguments. All failures were blamed on the squadrone for what was represented as their constant opposition to the court.[60] This excuse would have been consistent had the old party held to Queensberry's expressed view that the treaty act could be carried if the old party had the support of Marchmont, some north-country presbyterians, Cromartie's followers and the squadrone.[61] But when the treaty act had been carried and disaster seemed no longer imminent the tune changed. The old party claimed to have a majority in parliament. Queensberry represented all the later votes as old party victories against the worst the squadrone, Hamilton and Atholl could do.[62] Godolphin received Sir David Nairn's extravagant claims for the old party with a dryness that was wasted against Nairn's naivety.[63] Godolphin knew very well that the old party had not actually carried anything without squadrone assistance. They were basing their claims on a fiction, as both they and Godolphin were aware.

They had other troubles. In order to obtain some solidarity within the old party promises had been made and it was important that they should be kept, especially since the party was disturbed by renewed schism. A deep rift had appeared between Argyll and Annandale, due largely to incompatibility of ambition and temperament. Argyll had already shown his inability to play second fiddle to anyone, a trait which was to bring him into conflict with every court manager from Marlborough to Walpole. Annandale's ambition was inordinate and far in excess of what anyone else thought his due. He invariably overestimated his indispensability and was frequently thwarted in consequence. He did not take kindly to this and his resentment found release in the fluctuating opinions and erratic behaviour for which he was notorious. In 1705 he had, incredibly, seen himself as the power behind Argyll, who, in Annandale's calculations, was to function as a mere figurehead. Instead, much to Annandale's chagrin, Argyll relied on Stair and Philiphaugh. Annandale made no secret of his resentment and Argyll retaliated by charging him with almost every political crime from intrigue against the queen's commissioner to obstruction in parliament. All the responsibility for the new party dismissals was unloaded on to Annandale, though why, if the squadrone were as steeped in moral and political turpitude as Argyll had maintained, this should have been considered blameworthy is difficult to grasp. He accused Annandale of having tried to sabotage the whole session of 1705, first by introducing the succession proposal at all and then by 'managing the affair most abominably'. No one else seems to have thought that Annandale had bungled the succession or even behaved oddly by proposing what was in the queen's letter. By the end of the parliament Argyll was demanding that Annandale be dismissed or, he conceded under pressure, transferred from the post of secretary to that of president of the privy council.[64] Animosity between the two was so high that it later, in England, brought them to the brink of a duel.[65]

Seafield remained sufficiently detached to give Godolphin realistic advice. He entertained no illusions about the strength of the old party. When Queensberry was with the court the squadrone held the balance in parliament, so their support was essential. But it had become clear that their co-operation would have to be secured on a different basis from that of 1704 because the old party would not tolerate those terms. So Seafield thought the old party should be granted their demands for jobs and pensions as a first step and then, pacified, settled once again in control of the court interest. When it became apparent, as it certainly would, that they were too weak to handle the next parliamentary session, they might the more easily accept the adjustments necessary to gain the squadrone.[66] Without committing himself to the support of Argyll, Seafield did agree that Annandale should revert to his old post as president of the council, where his opportunities for creating trouble would be fewer than if he remained secretary.[67]

The Scottish ministry had thought of giving Annandale's post of secretary to Mar, a Queensberry protégé who had led the Queensberry group in opposition in 1704. The removal of Annandale, whose support for the Hanoverian succession had been consistent and well publicised, in favour of Mar, who had voted against it, could have been made to appear sinister. The queen did think it curious.[68] Had the junto been so minded the move would have been exploited but since their bargain with the court and their conversion to union they had less time for Annandale, so Mar was made secretary almost unremarked. But to Annandale the only way in politics was ascent from promotion to promotion. If he was to leave the post of secretary, then, in his view, it should be as lord chancellor with the title of duke but to suit the new scheme he had to settle for the presidency of the council or nothing. Annandale flatly refused his old job and insisted on seeing the queen.[69] Warnings were sent to London against his being given undue encouragement which would only raise his pretensions higher.[70] The queen, therefore, could offer him no satisfaction. Annandale hung about in London over the winter, attempting to repair his relations with the squadrone, set the whigs against the old party and in general do what he could to stir up further dissension within the court.[71]

There was another and potentially more serious split. To all appearances there had been in 1705 the utmost collaboration between Argyll and Queensberry, but things were not as they seemed. Argyll had come in as an old party magnate to fill the gap created by Queensberry's disgrace. As the price of his support for Argyll in 1705 Queensberry had made a good bargain—his arrears, the posts of privy seal and lord of the treasury—and had, furthermore, timed his arrival in Edinburgh to extract from the situation whatever credit there was likely to be.[72] But he was by no means fully restored to a state of grace. Argyll as commissioner was still nominally his superior and intended, if at all possible, to remain so. He had grown accustomed to the role of major court figure and showed an inclination to eliminate even marginal competition. He had been afraid of Seafield's influence at court and so requested that he be ordered to stay in Scotland after the 1705 session.[73] He was heavily critical of the Scottish secretary-depute, Nairn, a Queensberry man.[74] Before leaving Scotland Argyll seems to have assured Queensberry that after reporting to the queen he would resign, on the strength of which Queensberry fully expected to be reappointed commissioner.[75] But, once in London, Argyll's ambition was undimmed. He was free with his opinions on future arrangements and created a notable disturbance over a delay in passing his patent as earl of Greenwich.[76]

Ultimately there were two impediments to Argyll's attaining his objective. He lacked first of all the qualities necessary for sustained political in-fighting. In misrepresentation, blackmail and character assassination he stood second to none but his temperament was unsuited to a lengthy and devious campaign. But the decisive obstacle was the fact that Queensberry was indispensable in that his opposition could wreck any Scottish policy, and one sure way of bringing this about would be to subordinate him to Argyll. Old party thinking had become dominated by the need to keep Queensberry happy. And not only in the interest of management. Many old party men saw their own fortunes linked with Queensberry's restoration to influence.[77] As Argyll began to encounter the consequent obstacles to his progress he frequently threatened to go to the continent and have no more to do with Scottish affairs, professing to find them intolerable. Even so, he did not carry out his threat until he had lost the contest with Queensberry.[78]

Queensbery's tactics followed his usual style. He stayed away from London, letting the old party's inclinations and Argyll's intolerable personality do his work for him. At quite an early stage he dissociated himself from any complaint against Annandale, implying that if he had to be removed from the secretary's office it was only because Argyll did not get on with him. No love was lost between Queensberry and Annandale but Argyll was dangerous and taking up Annandale's cause was a small price to pay for stopping a Campbell *coup*.[79] In the meantime, as the English managers urged Queensberry to travel to court for consultations, he tried to exact a price for making the journey.

Queensberry claimed justification for delay. One of the private tragedies which haunted his life had struck him. His daughter, lady Mary, was taken ill with smallpox at Durham and died; but this had been in October 1705, too early to serve as an excuse.[80] Queensberry himself was prone to sudden attacks of illness which tended to occur at such opportune times that there was suspicion that they were merely diplomatic indispositions. But some of them, at least, were real enough although they might well have been psychological in origin. He was suffering from such an illness at the beginning of 1706. And, of course, January was not the best time of year for travelling from Scotland to London.[81] But before any of these complications Queensberry had been pleading poverty and the pressing nature of his private affairs as reasons for not going to London.[82] He was also asking for the repayment of yet more expenses.[83]

In London, his supporters did all they could for him. They ensured that Scottish business was delayed until his arrival.[84] Nairn exerted himself over Queensberry's expenses, past and future, deaf as ever to the nuances of Godolphin's reaction and apparently unaware that the lord treasurer was resigned to Queensberry in much the same way as he was to the weather, whilst Anne's loathing for the duke was quite extraordinary. Nairn reported a conversation he had had with Godolphin on Scottish affairs in which the secretary-depute was insistent on Queensberry's merits and indispensability and on the need to reward him handsomely if he were to travel to London, a mere £1,000 precept being neither here nor there. Godolphin gave every appearance of agreeing with all this and then, with what can have been nothing but quiet malice, despatched Nairn to tell the same story to the queen. Nairn went as instructed and the queen told him she would consider what he had said.[85] Nairn added, significantly, to Queensberry '. . . Now I think my lord Hali[fax] or Whar[ton] the best to prosecute what has so far [sic for 'fair' ?] a prospect. Mr. Boyle promised to assist . . .'

Some of Queensberry's friends did occasionally wonder whether financially he was not pushing things too far. They felt he could give the impression that his main concern was self-interest and they advised that if the court wanted him in London he would do better to go with a good grace and hope that money would be forthcoming.[86] In the meantime everything was held up. Even those outside the Queensberry circle were aware that court plans had run into trouble. Baillie told Roxburgh that Queensberry was continually postponing his departure for London and he guessed that the reason was his rivalry with Argyll.[87]

5 The choice of union commissioners

At the core of the problem was the ascendancy of the old party in Scottish politics and, within the old party, the predominance of the duke of Queensberry. Both seemed inescapable, yet the consequences had to be handled. Of crucial importance was the choice of Scottish commissioners to negotiate the union. The opposition expressed a preference for a broadly based commission representing every party so that no one could complain of exclusion, though some undoubtedly had nothing in mind but obstruction. Marchmont had public and private reasons for a broad choice. A representative commission would involve everybody in the project,[88] he said, but to Johnston he confided his fear of Scotland's being under the domination of old party magnates.[89] Otherwise, except for Dupplin, who thought confining the choice to one party a recipe for failure,[90] old party opinion was set out in a joint advice sent from Edinburgh by Queensberry, Glasgow, Stair, Hugh Dalrymple and Philiphaugh, with Sir David Dalrymple concurring. They thought that the union commission should be composed entirely of the old party, for '. . . whatever may be pretended that it is fit for effectuating the design to engage all parties in the treaty, this is certain, that if any is named who are not unite and in good correspondence with the queen's servants, nor will not make application to them to be named, but set up for themselves, independent of the ministry, such persons will never be cordial in advancing the queen's service in this ministry's hands, and if they can have the interest to be named against the ministry's will or without their consent this must infallibly encourage them and others to join with them in opposition to the present ministry . . .'[91] Queensberry himself reiterated this to his supporters in London at the beginning of 1706, asserting that if a mixed ministry were to be forced on them they ought to comply, but remain 'passive'—Queensberry's word.[92]

The English court's attitude had not been made plain, which is why Queensberry was so concerned. If the court should concoct another mixed ministry, Stair wrote to Mar, '. . . I am afraid another step of this kind will render d[uke] Q[ueensberry] so jealous that he will not meddle, and your lordship may consider how the business can succeed without him . . .'[93] But the junto wanted an old party monopoly and the final choice of union commissioners seems in due course to have been arranged between Queensberry and the junto, with Wharton affecting not to know how the nomination came about.[94]

The commission was almost entirely a Queensberry monopoly, even to relatively unimportant men put in at the duke's insistence—John Clerk of Penicuik, for example. As Cromartie complained on being excluded, '. . . There is but one chief on whom they depend, one councillor on whom they rely . . .'[95] But there were occasional inclusions whom Queensberry would not have tolerated without junto pressure: Ormiston, from whom he was very much averse, and George Lockhart of Carnwath, notoriously a jacobite and inexplicably put in at the behest of his uncle, Wharton.[96]

Argyll was left out. He might have declined, as Lockhart said, as a matter of honour, his supposed undertaking to Hamilton having been broken.[97] Or perhaps he was merely in a huff, which would not have been unusual. It is more probable that he was deliberately excluded by Queensberry. Argyll's point of honour would have affected him alone, but the Argyll interest was not at all represented. Neither his brother, lord Archibald, nor his uncle, Lothian, was on the commission. Lothian in particular took this very badly and, claiming to have been 'disgraced', returned his colonel's commission to Argyll.[98] Onlookers interpreted the exclusion of his two relatives as a defeat for Argyll in his struggle to supplant Queensberry. One commented, '. . . Now how the d[uke] of A[rgyll] will behave to see both his brother and his uncle so baulked I can't tell, but I hope he'll do as the latter has done but whatever come on't 'tis plain Queensberry and he can't be at present in good terms . . .'[99] By July 1706, long before parliament met, Queensberry had been appointed commissioner[100] and, since this had been a certainty for some time, by June Argyll had left in disgust to rejoin the army on the continent. Stair's son, lord Dalrymple, thought he would not return unless Marlborough made him a major-general.[101]

When, at last, the commissioners met at the Cockpit to negotiate the union, all the Scots were present save Hugh Montgomery, the member of the Scottish parliament for Glasgow, and lords Arniston and Tillicoultry of the court of session.[102] Of the English commissioners, Newcastle was, and remained, an absentee; Granby called in briefly, 'having declared before he took it he could not attend it by staying in town'.[103]

6 Previous negotiations, 1702–3

Whatever conjectures were in circulation about the possible basis of a treaty between the kingdoms, most of the commissioners in 1706 knew what was practicable and what was not. The ground had been cleared in the abortive negotiations of 1702–3.[104] There was no possibility that union could be based on anything other than a united kingdom and parliament with, for the Scots, freedom of trade with England subject to whatever conditions could be negotiated. The reasons were severely practical. The English would not tolerate an independent Scotland, so some sort of compliance had to be secured from the Scots. The Scottish court, though willing enough to do the bidding of the English, needed something to justify the concessions in sovereignty which Scotland would have to make. Other possibilities much canvassed in Scotland—safeguards for Scottish sovereignty, limitations on the crown or federal union—from the English point of view, merely made the situation worse. The Scottish problem was to be eliminated, not aggravated. But the only concession the English had to offer—or at least the only one which could be expressed in popular terms—was freedom of trade. Such freedom made it imperative for Scotsmen to be brought within the navigation system and subjected to English trade regulation, centrally enforced. Inescapably this pointed to one legislature. The Scottish parliament, which had caused the English court and its Scottish aides so much trouble since 1689, would disappear, together with the power of the Scottish magnates to hold both kingdoms to ransom.

The earlier negotiations which began on 10 November 1702 had proved abortive but, viewed in comparison with those of 1706, were illuminating. There seems to have been no particular reason why they failed.[105] Rather it is surprising that they continued for so long. The negotiations of 1702–3 bear all the marks of having been part of a court plan, rigged beforehand in collusion with leaders of the Scottish old court party, and which broke down as a consequence of the changes on Anne's accession. It is a commentary on the fragile character of Anglo-Scottish politics at this time that, even when the conditions necessary for success had disappeared, as they had before negotiations began, no one in either kingdom was prepared to accept responsibility for abandoning the project. Events were allowed to take their course.

The project was a survival from the end of William's reign when the junto had been clutching at union to strengthen themselves against tory inroads on the ministry. At Anne's accession the whigs found themselves no longer part of the court and since union was not then likely to benefit them they saw no reason to exert themselves to achieve it. Unwilling to execute too blatant a *volte-face*, they gave support to the act for appointing commissioners but then became ostentatiously indifferent to the negotiations. None of the junto lords was nominated to the commission, though some of their associates were. Of those commissioners with whig sympathies only Scarborough recorded a number of attendances approaching anywhere near respectability. The others could barely be said to have attended at all, although, it is fair to note, Newcastle was amongst them, who kept out of it in 1706 too, having at that time nothing against union but a great aversion from staying in London during the good weather.[106] Whig energies were instead devoted to preaching the gospel of a settled succession in Scotland, a view which the duchess of Marlborough urged on the queen together with some mistimed praise of the junto. Anne rejected it outright, noting that a union which the whigs had once favoured would itself solve the problem of succession.[107] The whigs had, of course, glimpsed the prospective dividends in embarrassing Godolphin and Nottingham over the succession and they were to exploit the issue with great success in 1703–4.[108] But there was more to the failure of negotiations than a change in the whigs' outlook.

Professional tory politicians such as Nottingham had considered the possible benefits of union to themselves if they could ensure episcopalian predominance in Scotland. This was an aim the tories had long pursued and one not yet exposed by the Scottish parliament of 1703 for the mirage it was.[109] Others, Normanby for instance, even further removed from reality, supported the union project as expressly designed to re-establish episcopacy in Scotland.[110] But the bulk of the tories—a majority in the commons—wanted no union at all. They saw no advantage to be gained by it and found the prospect of closer connection with a presbyterian kingdom repugnant.

When negotiations were at last discontinued in February 1703 the official reason was quite plausible. It was difficult for English politicians to conduct union negotiations whilst parliament was in session, since they had a continual round of formal engagements to fulfil. As for the Scots in 1703, the queen said, '. . . that by reason of the difficulties some were like to make about paying the taxes and the approaching of the general assembly and parliament, it were fit her servants were in Scotland to attend her service there . . .'[111] But the trouble over payment of the cess was due to its having been voted in the controversial session of 1702 together with the Scottish union commission. Both measures were, therefore, legally open to question.

And the elections of 1702 had greatly changed the situation. Since the commission had begun its work the Scottish ministry, with great acrimony, had undergone some adjustments and more were contemplated.[112] The consequent tensions had intruded themselves into the meetings of the Scottish commissioners. Some antagonism to Queensberry emerged when his right to preside over the commission was challenged, he having no status other than his office as secretary of state. Other, more fundamental, differences emerged. Tarbat, with some confused idea of making the union more palatable to the cavaliers, produced for a future united kingdom a formula for succession which could be taken as ruling out Hanover. On its rejection Tarbat refused to have his proposal formally recorded and the commission's secretary noted it later from memory in his private minutes.

Obviously the winter of 1702–3 was no proper time for union negotiations. The court made a wise decision in adjourning them, hoping to obtain from the next parliament an authority less open to challenge than that of 1702. They were to be disappointed; but one result of these earlier negotiations had been to make the areas of reluctance and even conflict stand out prominently. It seems highly probable that the principles governing the proposed union had been agreed before the commissioners met in 1702. The queen's letter at the outset observed that 'The heads of this treaty are so obvious that her majesty does not think it necessary to mention them but her majesty recommends it to the commisioners to make such proposals initially on this subject as shall occur to them and may be most likely to bring this treaty to an happy and speedy conclusion . . .'[114] Here was an echo of the original plan in which, very likely, a broadly conceived scheme was to be rushed through. But not only had circumstances changed; the negotiations made it clear that not enough thought had been given by either side to the implications of what had been undertaken. Imprecise formulae were tossed about and the consequent bargaining forced both parties to consider what the words were intended to mean.

In 1702–3 the Scots were far less demanding than in 1706 and the explanation would seem to lie in the circumstances in which they were negotiating. The authorisation of 1702 had been pushed through a rump parliament in direct pursuit of an English scheme. The Scottish court, lacking experience of opposition on the scale they had yet to endure, had drifted just so far out of touch with reality. When they asked for exemption from excises already imposed for English pre-union debts or, alternatively, an equivalent money payment, they themselves opened with a proposal for a lump sum of £10,000 which showed their almost complete ignorance.[115] The fact was that they did not know the extent of the clamour they were expected to satisfy until they had met the Scottish parliament of 1703 and lived through three of its sessions.

The English on the other hand were much more intransigent in

1702–3 than in the later negotiations. They were prepared to argue that English debts had been largely incurred in wars which had benefited Scotland. They were very stiff over 'freedom of trade', interpreting it as nothing more than free trade in home produce. Even then they were proposing to exclude wool. Reluctantly, cautiously and then only in principle they conceded to the Scots permission to trade with the colonies, for '. . . the plantations are the property of Englishmen and . . . this trade is of so great a consequence and so beneficial as not to be communicated as is proposed till all other particulars which shall be thought necessary to this union be adjusted'.[116] They then proceeded to festoon the concession with so many qualifications that at one point the Scots resolved to put the direct question: whether the English proposed to accept union in return for freedom of trade with the colonies or whether they did not?[117] The Scots evidently had the impression that the English were going back on some understanding reached before the negotiations. The English commissioners, for their part, saw the plantation trade as the greatest sacrifice they could make and the least acceptable to an English parliament, especially one so completely lacking in enthusiasm for union as that elected in 1702. When the English commissioners were faced with the actual process of negotiation they had become acutely aware of the administrative and parliamentary obstacles to an objective which seemed less than urgent and possibly even undesirable. When the Scots argued that their kingdom was too poor to pay equal duties until the benefits of full union had materialised, the English, who wanted no loopholes in the navigation system, replied that equality of duties was a necessary corollary of freedom of trade.[118]

Although the Scots were less than demanding the English commissioners seem to have been genuinely taken aback by some of the requests made by the Scots as a matter of course. Early in the negotiations the Scottish commissioners had mentioned the need to safeguard the privileges of the companies and manufactures of both kingdoms, which had surprised the English.[119] It ought not to have done. Within a union the Scots would have to respect the privileges of the English chartered companies, so, one of their own assets being a perfectly legal chartered company albeit moribund, they would have been fools to abandon it without question. Quite apart from the loyalties the Africa Company aroused, its very existence was a bargaining point. The Scots did not seriously expect the company to be allowed to continue but they did think the English ought to buy out its rights, thus providing compensation for the shareholders. After all, for many Scotsmen, this was the whole point of a treaty and was to remain so. Argument on this topic filled the last days of negotiation without agreement being reached.[120] For the English the union project had become an unnecessary complication for which it was not worth making sacrifices or taking risks. But by this time everyone was daily expecting an adjournment, which was announced on 3 February 1703, and negotiations lapsed until 1706, when, as a result of the Scottish treaty act, they were reopened by a new set of commissioners.

7 The 1706 negotiations

But to all who dealt in policies rather than oratory some things had become plain. Any union would have to be based on a united kingdom with one legislature—an 'incorporating union' in the jargon of the day—and freedom of trade for the Scots within the structure of the navigation acts. Administrative and political necessity linked the two. The main differences in 1702–3 had appeared over Scottish liability for taxation, particularly taxes appropriated for English debts, and the future status of the Africa Company. These difficulties had still to be surmounted but the meetings of 1702 had defined the areas of disagreement, which were quite clear when final negotiations for union began at the Cockpit on 16 April 1706.

There was this difference between the two sets of negotiations: the earlier session had taken place in an atmosphere removed from reality. On account of the internal politics of the kingdoms the odds against the project's reaching completion had been overwhelming. Nor had the strains of the Anglo-Scottish relationship reached the perilous intensity which had developed by 1705. In 1706 the English court and the junto, for different reasons, were determined to succeed and the Scots were prepared to do as they were told, at least up to a point. The bulk of the Scottish commission was obsessed by the Scottish parliament's reaction to any proposed treaty. As Orkney said, '. . . they will endeavour to get the better terms because they say it will be impossible to succeed [in the Scottish parliament] if they don't bring what is reasonable . . .'[121] If the treaty should ultimately be defeated in Edinburgh it had to be made to appear the fault of a completely intractable opposition. On the other side, the junto, dominating the English commission, were prepared to treat the Scots as generously as they dared, subject to the needs of steering the union through the English parliament. So there were conditions which introduced some of the substance as well as the appearance of bargaining but they were mostly extraneous to the actual union settlement. The commissioners on both sides were looking over their shoulders, their antagonists being respectively the Scottish opposition and the English tories rather than the negotiators across the table. Most were considering their own future rather than that of the two kingdoms.

To ease their task when they eventually faced parliament the Scots' original idea had been to negotiate two agreements: one for a union and another for settling the succession on terms.[122] These alternatives could then be placed before the Scottish parliament, giving the opposition less excuse for ruling out a negotiated agreement on the pretence of favouring something else. The whigs, as Mar told Carstares, were unimpressed, thinking: '. . . all the notions about federal union and forms a mere jest and chimera . . . You see that what we are to treat of is not in our choice . . .'[123] And, whatever their qualms about the reactions of the Edinburgh parliament, those Scots who had been forced to accept union as the only answer to Anglo-Scottish problems also doubted the practicality of a federal settlement. Cromartie, despite his inconsistent behaviour, had a firm theoretical belief in complete union: '. . . Unless we be a part each of other, the union will be as a blood puddin to bind a cat, i.e., till one or the other be hungry, and then the puddin flies . . .'[124] Stair, too, thought an incorporating union necessary, though, with parliamentary difficulties in mind, he had a tentative scheme for implementing a union by stages and hoped that the English would not insist on complete union at once. But the whigs had decided their strategy and had no intention of being deflected. If union was the only way out of the Anglo-Scottish predicament it had to be on terms which preserved the security of the English customs system and gave the whigs a chance of gaining some party advantage from legislative union. Whatever Somers might have told bishop Nicolson,[125] this was the crux of the matter. The junto lords were not negotiating union for the sake of posterity; they were concerned with the political balance at Westminster in the immediate future.[126]

At the Cockpit, after the customary formalities and speech-making, the English and Scottish ministers turned to business. The form of negotiation was that adopted in 1702: all proposals were to be in writing and nothing was to be formally recorded until both sides had agreed.[127] Then very quickly the basic agreement was reached over which the English had been so hesitant before the adjournment of the earlier negotiations. The Scots first of all took out an insurance by proposing a federal union which the English very briskly turned down. The Scottish commission at once capitulated and accepted the English proposal of an 'incorporating union' in return for full freedom of trade and navigation.[128]

Once this basis was settled, formalities created little difficulty: the arrangements for the various seals, the union flag, standard weights, measures and coinage, all went through smoothly.[129] Nor was there any trouble amongst the commissioners over the preservation of Scottish 'private rights'—concessions by grant or charter to individuals or corporations—after the union. A land tax quota for Scotland of £48,000 when the rate in England stood at four shillings in the pound was accepted by the English without any requests for a land reassessment, a proposal which had alarmed the Scots in 1702–3. Argument over Scottish representation in the united kingdom parliament was a sham, the number having been agreed privately beforehand with the junto, though the proper procedures were later observed. The English proposed thirty-eight Scottish members, at which the Scots requested a conference. The final arrangement was initiated by an English proposal: forty-five commoners and sixteen peers.[130] Quibbles about the status and precedence of the Scottish peers were quickly resolved.[131] Few complications emerged over the preservation of the Scottish legal system and those were easily dealt with: the Scottish court of admiralty was to be allowed to function only when private rights were involved; there were to be no appeals from Scottish to English courts. The loophole which was to allow appeals to the house of lords was due to a Scottish proposal and the provision, whatever its motive, was not generally noticed till after the union.[132]

The main arguments were concentrated on equality of taxation. Whilst the English attempted to maintain this principle as nearly as possible in its entirety, the Scots said they could not be expected to pay taxes appropriated for England's pre-union debts, nor could their economy bear the full weight of equal taxes. They asked for tax exemptions or compensation in the form of an 'equivalent' to be paid as a lump sum, or both.[133] The English accepted the idea of an 'equivalent'.

Scottish requests were made in more detail and with far greater precision than in the previous negotiations. They were careful to ensure that Scottish ships owned by Scots before the union should be registered as British ships within the terms of the navigation acts.[134]

Instead of the apparently random sum of £10,000 mentioned as an equivalent in 1702–3 an attempt was made at calculation. Its statistical basis proved to be inadequate but under the circumstances it was probably the best that could be done. The detailed arithmetic was delegated to a working party of three Scots and three Englishmen, all with pretentions to expert knowledge.

This committee attempted to analyse the revenue from English customs and excise according to its appropriation: how much went on current expenditure, the civil list and the payment of English debts. By this means the proportion of the total revenue appropriated for debts could be calculated. The object was to ascertain this same proportion of the estimated yield of Scottish customs and excise after the union when the standard English rates would be payable. This was the calculation which produced the £398,085 10s paid by England as the 'equivalent' in 1707.

Whatever might be said about the method, the information available to the working party was suspect and some of the English commissioners must have known it. English financial statistics were forthcoming, not faultless perhaps, but providing some kind of guide. But the Scots, having admitted that information concerning their own revenue was negligible, nevertheless provided figures. To estimate the produce of Scottish customs and excise under the new rates, import and export statistics were needed for goods subject to duties after the union. For comparison these figures had then to be converted to the standard English weights and measures. Since virtually none of this information was available, guesswork was substituted. Annual Scottish expenditure was estimated very roughly at £160,000 a year. Existing revenue was put, optimistically if not dishonestly, at £109,190 a year. It was conjectured that after the union this already extravagant sum would very likely increase to £160,000, which was convenient. To reach this estimate the Scots claimed to have taken not only the new rates of duty into account but also the probable increase in trade due to union. The number of forecasts the Scots felt able to make inspires awe but no confidence, especially when crown rents were put at 'about £5,500' yearly although it was notorious that the gifts chargeable to them exceeded the total produce. Great attention was focused on England's debts but the English commissioners showed little curiosity concerning Scottish debts, an omission which, after the union when disenchantment had set in, caused unpleasantness.[135] Obviously, in some particulars at least, considerable indulgence was extended to

Scotland.

But once the principle of an 'equivalent' was settled the details of payment and distribution did not seem to worry the Scots overmuch. They were more concerned to secure exemptions from particular duties, at least for a period after the union. Initially the English conceded some small points, agreeing to exemption from short-term excises, due for the most part to expire in 1710: coals and culm, the stamp tax, the window tax and malt. They were prepared to accept a period of relief from the salt tax consumed in Scotland.[136] But to safeguard against such duties being renewed after their expiry in 1710 the Scots pressed for a general exemption.[137] This point and the issue of the salt tax look up a disproportionate amount of time. At length, after much haggling, the English made a series of concessions. They extended the period of exemption from the various named duties and allowed exemption from the salt tax for seven years, subject to satisfactory safeguards for the English salt revenue;[138] in return for these concessions the Scottish parliament was to provide for the kingdom's expenditure for the whole of 1707 and not merely up to the proposed date of union.

How serious this taxation dispute was is uncertain; apart from the official minutes and one or two contradictory private opinions there is little direct evidence. All the official bargaining was recorded in the minutes which John Clerk of Penicuik represented as a true record and the result as a considerable victory for the Scots, won only after a great struggle.[139] Both Clerk and Leven claimed the issue to have been a major obstacle that, had the Scots not been given the concessions they wanted, could have led to the breakdown of negotiations.[140] But Lockhart, hostile yet nonetheless a witness, claimed that all the haggling was a sham: '. . . sometimes they pretended to differ from the English commissioners and reports were industriously noised abroad, that the treaty would break up without concluding on any scheme, particularly when the Scots did insist to obtain a greater abatement of taxes, and the English by piecemeal, and as with reluctancy consented to it . . .'[141] On the face of it this is the word of one commissioner against the rest but, in the light of the general character of the negotiations, Lockhart's version has the ring of truth. He was not even, at this point, ranting about betrayal of Scottish interests; he was merely giving an account of how the Scots obtained concessions. Moreover, the prospect of the Scots withdrawing from the negotiations in 1706 seems hardly worth taking seriously. Since back-room bargains, especially over finance, were common, it does seem likely that rumour and the official record were both part of a propaganda campaign for the benefit of the Scottish parliament.

The Scots made demands for compensation: for losses sustained by private individuals through recoinage, for example, and for Africa Company shareholders.[142] Compensation for the latter was for many Scotsmen the sole purpose of union.[143] The English response to this was a proposal that such compensation should be paid out of the equivalent. [144] The full equivalent was to consist of the original payment together with any sum arising in excess of the calculations should Scottish trade after the union exceed all estimates. This was the so-called 'arising equivalent' which in 1706 seemed to open up the prospect of everlasting bounty. The priorities for claims on this equivalent were listed in the English proposal. First in priority were the debts of Scotland, hitherto ignored, followed by the purchase of the capital stock of the Africa Company, which would cease its existence. Then compensation for coinage losses was to be paid and prescribed sums were to be set aside for the promotion of Scottish fisheries and manufactures. The Scots accepted this English proposal as constructive. [145] Clerk of Penicuik thought it all 'very fair and condescending'.[146] Lockhart's view was, predictably, different and justifiably so. He had continually opposed any equality of taxes which meant that Scotland would pay a share of England's pre-union debts because '. . . 'tis impossible to give an equivalent unless they'll appoint such a sum of money to be put in every man's breeches as their exorbitant taxes will amount to . . .'[147] It is true that Lockhart criticised almost everything, being fundamentally opposed to union and concerned to manufacture as much ammunition as possible against it.[148] Nevertheless on this topic there was substance in his objections.

The equivalent was represented as a great benefit to Scotland. In abstract economic terms it might have been beneficial, as an influx of much-needed capital. But not everybody was going to benefit to the same extent. Debts on the civil and military lists were payable to the nobility, the gentry and their various connections. This was not in itself unjust. Scottish pre-union debts, mainly arrears of salary to officers of state and army officers, were the responsibility of the kingdom of Scotland and had nothing to do with England. Had earlier provision been made for these debts taxation in Scotland before 1707 would have been heavier, so it was reasonable for Scottish debts to be paid out of the expected increase in taxation. It was not, however, reasonable to expect Scotsmen to compensate Africa Company shareholders out of a refund of taxes. The generality of these shareholders thought compensation should come from England, in the belief, for the most part erroneous, that the English were responsible for the company's collapse. The Scottish commissioners had at one stage advanced the sounder argument that the Africa Company legally existed and that if the English wanted it dissolved then they would have to buy it out. Otherwise the logical alternative would have been for the English to tolerate within a united kingdom the embarrassment of a rival to the East India and Africa Companies. This they were determined not to do, so they intended to pay off the shareholders with the equivalent. As Lockhart said, '. . . Scotsmen by this means purchased their own company themselves and made a present of it to the English, since the fund from which this sum had its rise did flow from Scotland'.[149] He looked upon the equivalent as an inducement to the Scottish members of parliament, who in one capacity or another stood to gain from the arrangements.[150] He was probably right. It may also be that the Scottish union commissioners, standing to benefit from the equivalent as did others of their class, either unconsciously or unashamedly identified Scottish interests with their own needs. Later, during the last Scottish parliament, they lent support to this view by helping to vote themselves allowances chargeable on the equivalent for attendance at London.[151] It is arguable that if they were to be paid allowances then these were Scottish pre-union debts which should rightly have been a charge on the equivalent. Nevertheless concern for such niceties was not apparent and the commissioners seemed only to want to dig into the equivalent with both hands. There is the further suspicion that some of the undercover bargains concerned the equivalent and its distribution. Lockhart cannot have been the only commissioner to have seen the catch in paying Africa Company compensation out of the equivalent. The others must have looked the other way just as the English, by intentional oversight, had given Scotland in some respects a better deal than might have been expected. Collusion between the English and Scottish commissioners to concoct an agreement palatable enough for both parliaments is the most likely explanation of such 'blind spots'.

All manner of allegations could be, and were, made against the Scottish commissioners, yet, given the situation, they could hardly have gained more, whatever their apparent lapses. According to one body of opinion the Scots had the better of the bargain.[152] The entire situation had been artificial, the negotiations being real only up to a point. Old party men were involved because the exigencies of politics had brought them to it and at the same time restricted their freedom of action. They had virtually committed themselves to accepting a treaty. Any thoughts of using the open succession as a bargaining point evaporated between 1703 and 1706. Their only real negotiating position was the argument that if a Scottish parliament was to accept union then sufficiently good terms must be forthcoming.

The English, too, were severely circumscribed. Godolphin and the court had always wanted union for administrative and political reasons. The whigs, to improve their own interest, had taken over this policy and elbowed the court into the position of spectators. Yet if the whigs were to gain any advantage the union negotiations had to succeed, and in the process the junto had to secure the firm alliance of the old party men before they joined a united kingdom parliament. Should the negotiations fail, the blame must be clearly seen to lie with the Scots, providing an excuse for future action, possibly military, against Scotland. There would be nothing else to fall back on. All this made necessary the appearance of fairly good terms, but the terms had to be such as the English parliament would accept. So the negotiations were not really all they seemed. All parties to them had in mind ends other than an Anglo-Scottish treaty, which reduced the proceedings at the Cockpit to something not far removed from a conspiracy—but then, as negotiations go, perhaps this ought not to be thought of as too unusual.

The treaty was completed on 11 July, when the proposed date of the commencement of union—1 May 1707—and the provisions for the meeting of the first parliament of Great Britain were added,[153] after which the treaty had to be signed by the commissioners. Lockhart declined to sign it at all. Newcastle, who had not attended the negotiations, saw no reason why the treaty should not be sent up to Welbeck to save him the trouble of going to London. The other commissioners thought Newcastle should be made to travel up for the signing and he was summoned to court.[154] By 22 July the treaty was formally written, signed, sealed and, on the day following, presented to the queen at St James's with the usual formalities.[155] Nevertheless the treaty had to be ratified by both parliaments. There was still a very long way to go.

Notes

[1] *Jerviswood*, 134, Roxburgh to Baillie, 7 Nov. 1705; *ib.*, 129, Baillie to Roxburgh, 9 Oct. 1705.

[2] *HMCR Portland MSS*, iv, 250, maj. Cranstoun to R. Cunningham, 1 Oct. 1705.

[3] *Lockhart Papers*, i, 144–5. A whig-inspired pamphlet represented the maintenance of the *status quo* as the only conceivable course and considered Scottish claims to independence to be quite ludicrous: W. Atwood, *The Scotch Patriot Unmasked* . . . (London, 1705).

[4] *Jerviswood*, 127, Johnston to Baillie, 2 Oct. [1]705.

[5] *HMCR Mar and Kellie MSS*, i, 239, 28 Nov. 1705.

[6] *Carstares S.P.*, 737, 24 Nov. 1705. The whigs had to be convinced for, as Markham wrote to Stanhope, 'The Summerian whigs ride triumphant': KCRO, Stanhope MSS, 34/1, 26 Mar. OS. 1706.

[7] Buccleuch (Drum.), Union, ii, Seafield to [Queensberry], 3 Nov. 1705; *ib.*, Loudoun to [Queensberry], 1 Nov. 1705; *HMCR Mar and Kellie MSS*, i, 238, Mar to J. Erskine, 6 Nov. 1705.

[8] For the queen's speech and replies: *CJ*, xv, 6–7, 13–14; *LJ*, xviii, 11.

[9] *HMCR Hamilton MSS*, Supp., 165, Pencaitland to Hamilton, 10 Nov. 1705; SRO, GD 205, Letters from Individuals, Jamieson to Bennet, 12 Nov. 1705; NLS, MS 3420, 8–9, Carstares to Godolphin, 13 Nov. 1705.

[10] Burnet, v, 246–7; Cowper, *Diary*, 18; SRO, GD 205, Letters from Individuals, Jamieson to Bennett, 1 Dec. 1705; *Carstares S.P.*, 737, Seafield to Carstares, 24 Nov. 1705. Bishop Nicolson had it that Haversham proposed repeal and was seconded by Nottingham: Nicolson, Diary, 23 Nov.1705. After their management of this affair in the lords Cleland agreed with Saltoun's view of the junto as the 'best party men in England': SRO, GD 124, Box 16, 391, W. Cleland to James [Melville], 24 Nov. 1705.

[11] See above, pp. 23 *et seq.*, 123 *et passim*.

[12] W. A. Speck, 'The choice of a Speaker in 1705', *BIHR*, xxxvii (1964), 20–46, and his unpublished D. Phil. thesis, 'The House of Commons, 1702–14: a study in political organisation' (Oxford, 1965).

[13] *Ib.* Harley presumably had in mind the following of such magnates as Newcastle together with whigs who had become disenchanted with the junto, e.g. Robert Molesworth: PRO 30/24/20/137, Molesworth to Shaftesbury, 18 Dec. 1707.

[14] *HMCR Frankland–Russell–Astley MSS*, 176, J. C[utts] to col. Revett, 13 Mar. 1704[/5].

[15] *Blenheim Papers*, A1/25, Harley to Marlborough, 29 Jun./10 Jul. 1705.

[16] *Ib.*, A1/37, Marlborough to queen, copy, 6 Jul. 1705.

[17] *HMCR Portland MSS*, iv, 291 [Godolphin] to [Harley], 22 Mar. 1705/6.

[18] Blenheim Papers, A1/25, Harley to Marlborough, 26 Oct./6 Nov. 1705; *ib.*, same to same, 9/20 Nov. 1705.

[19] *HMCR Archbishop King MSS*, 244, 1706.

²⁰ *HMCR Laing MSS*, ii, 125–35, [*c.* Aug. 1706. Wrongly ascribed by the editor to Seafield].

²¹ Nicolson, Diary, 19 Jan. 1705/6.

²² SRO, GD 45, 14, 336, G. Lockhart to H. Maule, 4 Jun. 1706. This conclusion was shared by the author of *Volpone: Or, Remarks On Some Proceedings in Scotland . . .*(1707).

²³ *Jerviswood*, 137–9, to Baillie, 28 Nov. 1705.

²⁴ *HMCR Portland MSS*, iv, 313, to [Harley], 17 Jun. 1706.

²⁵ Fraser, *Melvilles*, ii, 204, 26 Oct. 1706.

²⁶ *HMCR Bath MSS*, i, 67, Godolphin to Harley, 8 Apr. 1705 [*sic* for 1706]. The general inpression was that the union commission was composed entirely of whigs: KCRO, Stanhope MSS, 24/1, Robert Walpole to Horace Walpole, 13 May 1706.

²⁷ BL, Stowe MSS, 241, 56, Somers to the electoral prince, 12 Apr. [1706]. In French at *ib.*, 222, 383.

²⁸ Blenheim Papers, A1/25, Harley to Marlborough, 21 Dec./1 Jan. 1705/6; R. Sedgwick, ed., *The House of Commons, 1715–1754* (London, 1970), i, 513.

²⁹ *Private Correspondence of Sarah, Duchess of Marlborough . . .*(London, 1838), ii, 233, James Brydges to Marlborough, 4 Dec. 1705.

³⁰ Blenheim Papers, A1/25, Harley to Marlborough, 4/15 Dec. 1705.

³¹ See, e.g., G. S. Holmes, 'The attack on "the influence of the crown", 1702–16', *BIHR*, xxxix (1966) and his *British Politics in the Age of Anne* (London, 1967), 130–34. 'An anonymous parliamentary diary, 1705–6', ed. W. A. Speck in *Camden Miscellany*, xxiii (Royal Historical Society, 1969), 39–43, indicates that it was this same group which wanted to keep open the possibility of an invitation to Sophia.

³² In an unpublished Manchester B.A. dissertation Dr David Hayton argues convincingly that the 'whimsical clause' episode was something much more calculated than a 'country whig' revolt. I am indebted to Dr Hayton for permission to refer to this.

³³ *Private Correspondence of Sarah, Duchess of Marlborough*, ii, 233, Brydges to Marlborough, 4 Dec. 1705.

³⁴ See above, pp. 121–2.

³⁵ *HMCR Mar and Kellie MSS*, i, 241, Mar to J. Erskine, 20 Dec. 1705; SRO, GD 124, Box 16, 391, W. Cleland to James [Melville], 18 Dec. 1705. In this debate Hanmer referred to Scottish policy over the past few years as having been a 'riddle'. Seymour, noting the presence of Wharton in the gallery, said 'there was a noble lord there . . . who could give them the best account of the mystery of proceedings in Scotland if he pleased . . .': *ib.*, same to same, 6 Dec. 1705.

³⁶ Fraser, *Melvilles*, ii, 205–6, Smith to [Leven], 14 Nov. 1706; SRO, GD 45, xiii, 130, Smith to Leven, 30 Jan. 1706[/7].

³⁷ Burnet, v, 239–40. The compromise eventually made between the lords and the whig 'rebels' was looked on as something of a sham: '. . . The lords have got their end, relating to the regency bill—the expedient is a jest as near as

I can take it . . .': T. Heywood, ed., *The Norris Papers* (Chetham Society, ix, 1846), 146–7, T. Johnson to R. Norris, 18 Feb. 1705[/6].

[38] See above, p. 167.

[39] A closely contested election petition for the borough of Hertford, where the whig interest was at stake: *CJ*, xv, 9, 14, 54–5. Cowper, *Diary*, 25. This seems to illustrate Harley's attitude well enough, but cf. SRO, GD 124, Box 16, 391, Cleland to J. [Melville], 18 Dec. 1705.

[40] *Camden Miscellany*, xxiii, 'An anonymous parliamentary diary, 1705–6', 44–9 and App., 'Sir John Packington's speech on "the Church in danger" ', 82–4.

[41] Blenheim Papers, A1/25, Harley to Marlborough, 11/22 Dec. 1705.

[42] *Carstares S.P.*, 737, Seafield to Carstares, 24 Nov. 1705.

[43] Fraser, *Melvilles*, ii, 197–8, Loudoun to Leven, 23 Feb. [1706].

[44] *Ib.*, 198–200, Mar to Leven, 2 Mar. 1705/6.

[45] See below, p. 259 *et seq.*

[46] *HMCR Lonsdale MSS*, 118, Ch. [   ] to [Wharton], 6 May [1706]; *Marchmont Papers*, iii, 311, Marchmont to Wharton, 9 Nov. 1706.

[47] SRO, GD 26, xiii, 136/1, Leven to Melville, 6 Apr. 1706; *Hardwicke State Papers*, ii, 467, Somers to Halifax, 28 May 1706.

[48] W. L. Sachse, *Lord Somers* (Manchester, 1975), p. 243 *et seq.*

[49] *HMCR Lonsdale MSS*, 118, Sunderland to lord [   ], 2 Apr. [1706].

[50] *An Answer To Some Queries, &C, Relative To The Union; In A Conference Betwixt A Coffee Master, And A Country Farmer* (1706).

[51] *HMCR Portland MSS*, ii, 193, 15 Jun. 1706.

[52] *Ib.*, iv, 314, to [Harley], 3 Jul. 1706.

[53] *Carstares S.P.*, 750, Stair to Carstares, 26 Apr. 1706; *ib.*, 751, Leven to same, 27 Apr. [1706]; SRO, GD 18, Box 119, 3131, J. Clerk to his father, 18 Jun. 1706; *ib.*, GD 26, xiii, 136/3, Leven to Melville, 30 Apr. 1706. Concern for episcopalians had only recently been voiced in the commons: see above, p. 168. Something in the nature of a trap had been suspected by Cleland: 'How far then the tories may have forced the ministry here into a dilemma by either going into an incorporating union and so disobliging their best friends the presbyterians in Scotland or a federal one and so losing the whigs in the house of commons . . . a wiser head than mine must determine . . .' (SRO, GD 124, Box 16, 391, W. Cleland to J. [Melville], 18 Dec. 1705).

[54] *Jerviswood*, 156, [Aug. 1706. Undated but endorsed]; *ib.*, 160, Johnston to Baillie, 21 Sep. [1706].

[55] *Seafield Letters*, 93, Seafield to Godolphin, 4 Oct. 1706. See above, pp. 168–9.

[56] *Jerviswood*, 156, Johnston to Baillie, [Aug. 1706].

[57] SRO, GD 45, 14, 336, G. Lockhart to H. Maule, 4 Jun. 1706; Cunningham, *History*, i, 452.

[58] BL, Add. MSS 6420, 22, [Memorial, 1706].

[59] *HMCR Portland MSS*, viii, 243, 25 Aug. 1706. Paterson had also written to Godolphin in less arrogant but fairly specific terms: Paterson, *Works*, iii, 2, 4,

24 Aug. 1706.

⁶⁰ E.g. *Int. Soc. Letters*, i, 29–31, Argyll to Godolphin, 1 Aug. 1705; BL, Add. MSS 6420, 11, [Queensberry's] memorial, 1 Aug. 1705.

⁶¹ Buccleuch (Drum.), Union, ii, [Queensberry] to [   ], [1705].

⁶² *Ib.*, Church and State, [Queensberry] to [   ], draft. [Sep. 1705].

⁶³ *Ib.*, Union, ii, Nairn to [Queensberry], 31 Aug. 1705.

⁶⁴ *Int. Soc. Letters*, 33–5, Argyll to Godolphin, 26 Aug. 1705; *ib.*, 26–8, same to same, 8 Jul. 1705; *ib.*, 35–9, same to same, 9 Sep. 1705; *ib.*, 39–40, same to same, 22 Sep. 1705; BL, Add. MSS 28055, 225, 'Memorial', 21 Sep. 1705.

⁶⁵ Fraser, *Cromartie*, i, 292–3, J. Philp to J. Stewart, 8 Nov. 1705.

⁶⁶ *Seafield Letters*, 88, Seafield to Godolphin, [21 Sep. 1705].

⁶⁷ BL, Add. MSS 34180, 90, same to same, 9 Sep. 1705.

⁶⁸ *SHR* (1922), 193, queen to Godolphin, [?26 Sep. 1705].

⁶⁹ *HMCR Mar and Kellie MSS*, i, 236, Mar to lady Mar, Sep. 1705.

⁷⁰ *Int. Soc. Letters*, i, 40, Argyll to Godolphin, 5 Oct. 1705; *Seafield Letters*, 92, Seafield to same, 6 Oct. 1705; *HMCR Mar and Kellie MSS*, i, 236, same to Mar, 7 Oct. 1705.

⁷¹ *Ib.*, 237, Loudoun to same, 25 Oct. 1705; *Jerviswood*, 132, Annandale to Baillie, 25 Oct. [1705]; *ib.*, 147, same to same, 15 Jan. [1706]; SRO, GD 26, xiii, 129, Annandale to Leven, 20 Dec. [1705].

⁷² See above, p. 143.

⁷³ BL, Add. MSS 28055, 225, 'Memorial', 21 Sep. 1705.

⁷⁴ Buccleuch (Drum.), Union, ii, Nairn to [Queensberry], 22 Sep. 1705.

⁷⁵ *Ib.*, fragment of a memorial in Queensberry's hand, [Sep./Oct. 1705].

⁷⁶ *Ib.*, Loudoun to [Queensberry], 1 Nov. 1705; SRO, GD 205, Letters from Individuals, Jamieson to Bennet, 12 Nov. 1705.

⁷⁷ *HMCR Mar and Kellie MSS*, i, 243, Stair to Mar, 3 Jan. 1706.

⁷⁸ *Ib.*, 247, Northesk to same, 4 Feb. 1706; *Jerviswood*, 147, Annandale to Baillie, 15 Jan. [1706]; SRO, GD 205, Letters from Individuals, Jamieson to Bennet, 30 Mar. 1706; *Stair Annals*, i, 227, lord Dalrymple to Mar, Jun. 1706.

⁷⁹ Buccleuch (Drum.), Church and State, [Queensberry] to [   ], draft, [Sep. 1705]; *Jerviswood*, 148, Baillie to Roxburgh, 24 Jan. 1705/6.

⁸⁰ *HMCR Mar and Kellie MSS*, i, 237, Queensberry to Mar, 8 Oct. 1705.

⁸¹ *Ib.*, 244, duchess of Queensberry to Mar, 4 Jan. 1705/6.

⁸² Buccleuch (Drum), Union, ii, fragment of memorial in Queensberry's hand, [Sep./Oct. 1705]; *ib.*, [Queensberry] to [Godolphin], [5 Oct. 1705], copy.

⁸³ *HMCR Mar and Kellie MSS*. i, 238, Philiphaugh to Mar, 20 Nov. 1705.

⁸⁴ *Ib.*, 246, Mar to J. Erskine, 15 Jan. 1706; *Carstares S.P.*, 738, same to Carstares, 4 Dec. 1704.

⁸⁵ Buccleuch (Drum.), Union, ii, [Nairn] to [Queensberry], 22 Sep. 1705.

⁸⁶ Buccleuch (Drum.), Union, ii, Nairn to [Queensberry] 4 Oct. 1705; *ib.*, [same] to [same], 13 Oct. 1705.

⁸⁷ *Jerviswood*, 143–4, Baillie to Roxburgh, 29 Dec. 1705.

⁸⁸ *Marchmont Papers*, iii, 285, Marchmont to queen, 29 Dec. 1705; *ib.*, 290,

same to Somers, 29 Dec. 1705, and his letters to Wharton, Argyll and Devonshire, *ib.*, 291, 293, 295; *HMCR Marchmont MSS*, 156–7, Somers to Marchmont, 23 Jul. 1706; *ib* Wharton to same, 31 Jul. 1706.

[89] *Marchmont Papers*, iii, 297, Marchmont to Johnston, 29 Dec. 1705.

[90] *HMCR Mar and Kellie MSS*, i, 242, Dupplin to Mar, 29 Dec. 1705.

[91] *Ib.*, 240, Glasgow to Mar, 4 Dec. 1705; BL, Add. MSS 6420, 17, 'Memorial concerning the treaty sent from Edinburgh', 4 Dec. 1705.

[92] *HMCR Mar and Kellie MSS*, i, 244, duchess of Queensberry to Mar, 4 Jan. 1706.

[93] *Ib.*, 243, Stair to Mar, 3 Jan. 1706.

[94] *HMCR Marchmont MSS*, 157–8, Wharton to Marchmont, 31 Jul. 1706.

[95] [Cromartie], *Two Letters Concerning the Present Union From A Peer in Scotland To A Peer in England* (1706).

[96] *Lockhart Papers*, i, 142. The commissions appear in *APS*, xi, 145–7.

[97] See above, p. 150.

[98] *HMCR Mar and Kellie MSS*, i, 254, Lothian to Mar, 14 Mar. 1706.

[99] SRO, GD 205, Letters from Individuals, Jamieson to Bennet, 30 Mar. 1706. In the light of all the other evidence, Clerk's version of the appointments seems either dishonest or exceedingly naive: 'In the naming . . . her majesty had no regard to an equality in our Scots representation as to the numbers of the noblemen, barons and burghs, but made the choice as she herself thought fit, or as the dukes of Queensberry and Argyll did advise her, the chief design being to name persons that would probably stand to that which was called in Scotland, the revolution foot' (SRO GD 18, Box 119, 3132/1,2,3, 'A journal of the proceedings of the Scots and English commissioners in the treaty for a union between the two kingdoms of Scotland and England' [1706]). Clerk's list of commissioners omits Lockhart, who stood on anything but a 'revolution foot'.

[100] Buccleuch (Drum.), Union, ii, 31 Jul. 1706; SRO, GD 220, G, Glasgow to Montrose, 2 Aug. 1706.

[101] *Stair Annals*, i, 227, lord Dalrymple to Mar, Jun. 1706.

[102] SRO, GD 18, Box 119, 3132/1–3, 'A journal of the proceedings . . .' [1706].

[103] *HMCR Rutland MSS*, ii, 184, marchioness of Granby to Rutland, 23 Apr. [1706].

[104] See above, p. 47.

[105] From the start there had, in some circles, been a marked lack of enthusiasm. Thomas Johnson told Norris of the union bill, '. . . I think it will come to nothing at last . . .' (*Norris Papers*, 83, 19 Mar. 1701 [/2]).

[106] Attendances in 1702–03 are recorded in *APS*, xi, 145–61.

[107] *HMCR Marlborough MSS*, 53a, queen to d[uchess] of Marlborough, 11 [Jun. 1703].

[108] See above, pp. 71–2.

[109] See above, chap. ii.

[110] *Jerviswood*, 10, Johnston to Baillie, 13 Feb. 1702/3.

111 So ran Seafield's report to the Scottish commissioners of what the queen had told the privy council of her reasons for adjourning negotiations: Blenheim Papers, Box vii, 15, 'Journal of what passed in the Treatie of Union which commenced at Westminster the 27 October 1702. Containing What was transacted either in the General meetings of both Kingdoms or in the Private Meetings of the Lords Commissioners for Scotland' [probably by Robert Pringle] [referred to as Blenheim Papers, Box vii, 15, 'Journal . . .'], 162–3.

112 See above, p. 39 *et seq.*

113 Blenheim Papers, Box vii, 15, 'Journal . . .', 32–3 *et passim.*

114 *APS*, xi, 148, 18 Nov. 1702.

115 *Ib.*, 156.

116 *Ib.*, 152.

117 Blenheim Papers, Box vii, 15, 'Journal . . .', 65–8.

118 *APS*, xi, 152, 158–60.

119 *Ib.*, 152.

120 *Ib.*, 159–61.

121 NLS, MS 1033, 15–16, Orkney to [Selkirk or Ruglen], 2 Feb. 1706.

122 This thought had occurred to Baillie: *Jerviswood*, 145, to Roxburgh, 3 Jan. 1705/6.

123 *Carstares S.P.*, 743, Mar to Carstares, 9 Mar. 1705/6.

124 Fraser, *Cromartie*, ii, 1–3, Cromartie to Mar, 1 Jan. 1706; *ib.*, 3–4, same to same, 12 Jan. 1706; *ib.*, 4–7, same to same, 15 Jan. 1706; *ib.*, 15–16, same to same, 18 Apr. 1706.

125 See above, p. 165 and n. 21.

126 *HMCR Mar and Kellie MSS*, i, 243, Stair to Mar, 3 Jan. 1706.

127 *APS*, xi, 165.

128 *Ib.*, 165–6; SRO, GD 45, 14, 336, G. Lockhart to H. Maule, 4 Apr. 1706; *ib.*, same to same, 25 Apr. 1706.

129 *APS*, xi, 180–81, 182–3.

130 *Ib.*, 177–80.

131 *Ib.*, 180–4.

132 *Ib.*, 174–5, 176, 178, 179. The motive could have been the preservation of some right of appeal from the court of session where judgements were not always above suspicion.

133 *Ib.*, 168–71.

134 *Ib.*, 181–5.

135 For a fuller account of the equivalent calculation see Riley, *English Ministers*, chap. xiv. The calculations are in PRO, T48/22, *The Minutes of the Proceedings of the Lords Commissioners for the Union of the Kingdoms of England and Scotland.*

136 *APS*, xi, 169–70.

137 *Ib.*, 170–72.

138 *Ib.*, 171–3, 176–8, 179–80, 181–4, 182–5.

139 *SRO*, GD 18, Box 119, 3131, J. Clerk to his father, 23 May 1706.

140 *Ib.*, same to same, 11 May 1706; *ib.*, same to same, 16 Apr. 1706; *ib.*, same

to same, 30 Apr. 1706; *ib.*, GD 26, xiii, 135, Leven to Melville, 9 May 1706.

[141] *Ib.*, GD 45, 14, 336, G. Lockhart to H. Maule, 26 May 1706; *Lockhart Papers*, i, 155–6.

[142] *APS*, xi, 181; Buccleuch (Drum.), Stair, R. Blackwood to [Queensberry], 20 Apr. 1706; SRO, GD 26, xiii, 133, same to Leven, 20 Apr. 1706.

[143] *APS*, xi, 181.

[144] *Ib.*, 183–4.

[145] *Ib.*, 183–8.

[146] SRO, GD 18, Box 119, 3132/1–3, 'A journal of the proceedings . . .'

[147] *Ib.*, GD 45, 14, 336, to H. Maule, 4 Apr. [1706]; *ib.*, to same, 26 May 1706.

[148] *Ib.*, to same, 9 May 1706; *ib.*, to same, 26 May 1706; *ib.*, to same, 4 Jun. 1706.

[149] *Lockhart Papers*, i, 193.

[150] *Ib.*, 157.

[151] See below, pp. 294–5.

[152] SRO, GD 220, N, Nairn to Montrose, 9 Nov. 1706; BL, Add. MSS 40776, 15, Shrewsbury to Vernon, 9 Nov. 1706.

[153] *APS*, xi, 189–90.

[154] *HMCR Portland MSS*, iv, 314, Newcastle to [Harley], 3 Jul. 1706; *ib.*, ii, 194, Godolphin to Newcastle, 9 Jul. 1706; *ib.*, 194, G. Doddington to same, 9 Jul. 1706.

[155] *APS*, xi, 190–91, and above, p. 1.

CHAPTER SIX

Trade and propaganda

The move towards union was the resultant of varied political forces. The attendant discussion about trade, whether in the Scottish parliament or in pamphlets, was little more than a campaign of rationalisation and propaganda. But to emphasise this is not to assert that Scotland lacked economic problems. The kingdom's trading position was assuredly becoming precarious. What has to be doubted is whether, as far as Scotland was concerned, there was much connection between economics and politics during the union of crowns.

1 Scotland's economic condition

The Scottish economy's main problems have been clearly identified.[1] Scottish trade up to the revolution of 1688, the interregnum apart, had increasingly prospered. Had the union proposal of 1689 proved successful the union of the crowns would have been seen as an economic benefit to Scotland, although there remained a great disparity between the trading capacities of the two kingdoms.[2] Despite their denunciation of the English navigation act, Scottish merchants seem generally to have been thriving during the reigns of Charles II and James, his brother.[3] Overseas trade increased and capital was available for investment in the manufacturing enterprises launched between 1663 and 1670. French and English tariffs notwithstanding, Scottish trade continued to expand.[4] The Dutch wars created some disruption but the treaty of Westminster in 1674 was followed by something of a boom, especially in and around Glasgow. There was no decline in Scottish shipping activity until 1681, when at the privy council there was ominous talk of decaying trade. This was to become almost a routine item of business at the council board, though not altogether justified.

On the whole, Scottish merchants were making a living and were quite remote from any prospect of a great crash. And, after all, the merchant community was only a fringe element of the population. They complained, of course, and especially about the navigation act, but their main grievance against it was that in English law Scotland was made a foreign country for purposes of trade. Official exclusion from the plantation trade was legally rather than commercially resented, being seen as a gratuitous slight to the status of Scotsmen. It was not economically serious. Any Scotsman with the capacity to trade with the English colonies continued to do so, the navigation act notwithstanding, greatly to the distraction of the English customs service, whose resources were strained in an attempt to stop this illegal trade.

Scotland's most serious economic troubles came after the revolution of 1688. Few of them were due to the union of the crowns but one which the Scots did not hesitate to blame on the English connection was the state of almost continuous war with France. In the nineteen years prior to the revolution there had been only six years of war. In the nineteen years between the revolution and the union there were a mere five years of peace.[5] Some Scottish merchants suffered great damage through the loss of their French trade and the attacks of French privateers. The inability or, as the Scots saw it, reluctance, of the Royal Navy to give protection to Scottish ships whilst pressing Scottish seamen for naval service, even in Scottish ports despite protests from officers of state, produced an accumulation of spleen.[6] It was not altogether reasonable of the Scots to regard the wars against Louis XIV as being of purely English interest, but feeling in 1701 was strong enough for Philiphaugh to advise Queensberry that Scotland should be kept out of any further Anglo–French conflict.[7] But no matter whose business they were the wars were a disaster for Scottish trade and, in consequence of the reduced customs yield, a blow for the kingdom's revenue which led to demands for the resumption of trade with France, especially since the Dutch had not allowed war to disrupt their own commerce with the French. Scottish ministers urged this course for the sake of the civil list and the upkeep of the forces.[8]

Closer to the mass of the population was the long famine of the 1690s owing to the failure of successive harvests. Crop yields were bad in the four years from 1695. Trade regulations were relaxed to allow grain imports and on two occasions, in 1696 and 1699, for short periods and in the teeth of the mercantilist canon, bounties were paid on imported grain. The harvest of 1699 was normal[9] but the prolonged famine had not only inflicted great hardship on the poorer people but inevitably, in a mainly agrarian country, caused severe damage to the national economy. It created what contemporaries bemoaned as a 'dearth of monies'—a shortage of ready cash. Grain imports had to be paid for in specie, thereby upsetting the trade balance, which exports could not be expanded quickly enough to preserve. Domestic purchasing power was so reduced that merchants were unable to meet even the cost of exporting their goods.[10] Ready money was in such short supply that people were demanding settlement at the most inconvenient times and so involving breaks in the chain of credit. The total result was a severe slump which dramatically diminished the revenue.[11]

It was towards the end of this economic crisis that the kingdom suffered a further blow by the Scottish Africa Company's failure to establish a colony at Darien. Between the sailing of the first expedition in 1698 and the colony's extinction by formal surrender to the Spaniards in 1700, the immediate loss was almost two thousand lives and £153,631 sterling—one quarter of Scotland's entire capital.[12] Quite apart from the sheer human misery—death from disease, starvation and shipwreck—the failure shook the Scottish economy. A large number of influential Scotsmen suffered personal loss, financial or otherwise. This, added to the kingdom's other misfortunes, was a catastrophe.

In economic terms the revolution of 1688, the consequent civil war and the conflict with France combined to produce a slump from which there was little recovery till 1692. Improvement was then steady for a brief period until the onset of famine after the 1695 harvest, when the trade recession worsened. The extra burden of the Darien collapse pushed Scotland deeper into its economic slough. By 1702 investment in new domestic undertakings had virtually stopped.[13] Out of forty-seven Scottish companies known to have been in operation between 1690 and 1695 only twelve seem to have been active in the last years of the seventeenth century and these included the Africa Company and the Bank of Scotland.[14] The nadir of the depression was reached in 1704 when the Bank of Scotland had to suspend payments.[15]

This succession of emergencies focused attention on the kingdom's trade but for the wrong reasons. The crises springing from the French wars, the famine and the Darien expedition were dramatic and could be appreciated. In fact they overlaid Scotland's main problem, which was not so easily discernible, partly because it had been a gradual development and partly because seventeenth-century statistics, even when available, could obscure as much as they clarified. The real trouble was that the country's trading position had become unsound.

The Scots were trying to maintain their traditional channels of trade at a time when the prevailing European fashion of protectionism was blocking them. Nations in the first rank as trading powers were committed to tariff skirmishes if not outright trade war, a situation in which Scotland was extremely vulnerable, since, as a selling country in a buyers' market, she had little scope for successful reprisals.[16] Although her trade as a whole had been expanding during the seventeenth century, her continental trade had declined through war and tariff barriers. Her increased volume of exports was all in some way dependent on England. And even when the dependence was not direct, as in the case of wool, English interest could be sufficiently strong to influence Scottish policy.

There had been an increase in the black cattle trade since 1603 and, despite occasional anguished warnings from English cattle raisers of penury and ruin, the droving business was brisk on account of London's growing demand for meat. Increased impositions had little effect on this trade. Numerous Scottish landowners had committed their estates to cattle production when England was the only market for live cattle.[17] Over the same period linen production had expanded and again, in spite of increasing tariffs, the only feasible market for this was in England.[18] The Scottish coal industry had grown to meet an English and continental demand but by the later seventeenth century the continent was steadily being closed to Scottish coal, leaving as the only outlets England and Ireland.[19] More land had been given over to grain cultivation, in particular that of oats and barley. The main markets for this produce had been the Scandinavian countries and the United Provinces, but just as large landowners were increasing production their export prospects were contracting. The Scandinavian market was unreliable. Because the climate there was similar, when Scotland had a glut so did they. Competition from the Baltic grain areas had seriously damaged Scottish continental trade. At one time England had bought Scottish grain but from 1670 this virtually ceased as England went protectionist against grain imports. By 1700 Scottish landowners were worried about over-production of grain. In 1705 colonel John Buchan of Cairnbulg told Seafield that unless they could find new grain markets landowners would face ruin.[20] Anything which opened the English market to Scottish grain should have been welcome to many

Scottish landowners.

There was a perennial antagonism within Scotland over wool. Growers and cloth manufacturers disputed over whether or not its export should be allowed. When the privy council was inclined to be obsessed with the long-term prospects of Scottish manufacturers, wool export was likely to be prohibited in the interest of ample supply and low prices.[21] Short-term balance of trade crises led to victory for the wool growers and export was allowed in order to bring in specie. English pressure intruded into this conflict. Since Scottish wool had no great reputation for quality the usual practice was to smuggle in English wool for re-export as Scottish wool—a practice which led the English to favour prohibition. English complaints helped to produce the prohibition of 1701. This concern at their wool's being deviously exported to competitors convinced the English that the abandonment of prohibition in 1704 was deliberate Scottish provocation, though it was nothing of the kind. But such reversals of policy, together with the contraction of the continental market, led to stagnation in the Scottish woollen industry by the beginning of the eighteenth century.[22]

Again, as a result of marketing problems, the Scottish fisheries and salt industry were in a parlous state. They too had been virtually squeezed out of the continent and, after the Scots had undersold them during the free trade period of the interregnum, the English had heavily protected themselves against Scottish salt.[23] Yet, if the tariffs could be removed, there was still hope in England for both Scottish salt and fish.

But by the end of the seventeenth century the Scots, tariffs notwithstanding, had drifted into a dangerous dependence on the English market. Even so, a probably substantial amount of smuggling apart, recorded exports to England indicate a marked decline. Between 1698 and 1700 they were reaching an average of £114,000 sterling per year. By 1701 to 1703 the annual average was £74,000 and in the two years before the union it had dropped to £54,000.[24] These figures, though sinking, could have accounted for one half of Scottish exports.[25]

2 The political insignificance of Scotland's economy

In short, Scotland was drifting into serious economic trouble. It was due not to dramatic crises such as Darien but to a persistently adverse trading environment in her traditional markets. Most Scots connected with trade must have had some awareness of this recession, though whether they appreciated its extent, still less its causes, is doubtful.

What had happened was that the English reaction to the Africa Company had impressed on Scotsmen, for the wrong reasons, the significance in their problems of the English connection.[26] Since commercial discontent and protests about English oppression bulked large in opposition campaigns it is easy to assume that economic necessity was a primary Scottish motive and the reason for the Scottish parliament's agreeing to union. It is an unjustified assumption. Indeed, the bulk of the evidence indicates that, from as early as 1603, the part played by national economic interest in Anglo-Scottish relations has been exaggerated and that such influence as it did exert was a discouragement to any closer connection. Hopes of an end to border warfare were entertained, but otherwise economic considerations did not enter into earlier projects for union.[27] Arguments founded on trade emerged from schemes devised for other reasons. Individual interests were suspicious of economic union. 'Whereas,' thought James VI and I on his accession, 'some think this union will bring prejudice to some towns and corporations within England, it may be a merchant or two . . . may have an hundred pounds less in his pack, but if an empire gain and become the greater, it is no matter.'[28] The average merchant, English or Scottish, failed to share the intensity of James's vision and preferred his hundred pounds. Then, from the interregnum onwards, concepts of national interest emerged which put an end to talk of freedom of trade.[29]

The Cromwellian union was a security measure aimed at keeping Scotland and Ireland under control, although economic unity was part of the arrangement. This temporary customs union was unpopular in Scotland, where the wars had damaged productive capacity and merchants were unaccustomed to English patterns of trade.[30] Apart from the salt manufacturers, who had been able to undercut the English, most Scottish producers and merchants welcomed the end of economic union in 1660.

Yet the Scots appeared very much put out by the English navigation act, which was represented as a major national grievance. On the surface the complaint was about economic discrimination against the Scots, who were now to be treated as foreigners, but the issue was not as straightforward as that. The Scots obviously did not want freedom of trade with England. They had just been rid of it, and thankfully, since they wished to be able to protect themselves against English competition. And although the Scots did not care for the English import duties which were on the other side of the coin, Scottish trade to

England expanded in spite of the navigation act.[31] When Lauderdale blamed the act for Scotland's economic backwardness he was introducing a fiction. His request of 1661 that a mere five or six Scottish ships a year should be admitted to the plantations, alarming though it seemed to the English as the thin end of the wedge, would have involved something like the full extent of available Scottish shipping capacity.[32] In fact, blaming the English in sweeping terms was almost a Scottish national pastime. But Scottish objections to the navigation acts, in so far as they were rational, seem to have been based on legal grounds. The status of the Scots in relation to the English was being changed for the worse and, as some were still pointing out in 1706, against a decision of an English court that Scots born after 1603—the *post nati*—were not aliens in England.[33] This was a reasonable complaint. Parliament could undoubtedly change the law but needed to do so specifically. Instead, the legal position had been rendered so vague as to be an irritation. There was a difference between the law as interpreted by the courts and the apparent will of parliament in attempting to regulate trade. Time did little to clarify the confusion. The navigation act had specifically denied that Scotsmen were English subjects. The act of 1696 tightening up the prohibition on Scottish trade to the colonies was even more explicit, forbidding Scots to hold office in England or the plantations. On the strength of this, in 1697, Andrew Hamilton, a Scot and governor of New Jersey, was dismissed. After the attorney and solicitor-general had declared that all Scotsmen 'are qualified to be owners, masters and mariners of ships in these parts' and that the words 'Englishman' or 'native born subjects of England' included the Scots, Hamilton was reinstated. This view was afterwards tacitly accepted by the English parliament in passing the alien act of 1705, there being little point in declaring someone to be an alien who is one already. So the status of the Scots after the navigation acts suffered from a lack of definition which could always be advanced as a grievance.[34] Whenever there was a slump in Scotland the Scots had a permanent scapegoat in the navigation act to which their objections could be multiplied. Their standing claim was that the status of the Scots should be restored to that enjoyed under the first two Stuarts—not aliens—and that English trade should be regulated by the crown, not parliament. It was an argument that some Scots used in 1706 in opposition to union. The Scottish ministry under Lauderdale made full use of this feeling.[35]

But it took a major slump or a national disaster to cause an outcry in

Scotland—famine, French wars or Darien. Agitation, as distinct from mere dissatisfaction, coincided with the acute trading slump consequent on the second Dutch war.[36] This enabled negotiations to be set afoot aimed ostensibly at securing changes in the trade laws. The real aim of the negotiations seems to have been to demonstrate that the only remedy for Scottish complaints was a political union with England with the ulterior motive of strengthening the English crown. The parliamentary opposition in England was to be outvoted by a body of Scottish ministerial dependants.[37] Nevertheless the negotiations were throughout conducted in terms of trade and the man who seemed, on the surface, to be devoted to the idea of improving Scottish trade by negotiation was Tweeddale, for the time being one of Lauderdale's henchmen and later lord chancellor of Scotland. But he was attached to union for its own sake and, all appearances to the contrary, was cunning enough to have been manipulating Lauderdale, ostensibly taking the lead in the project.[38] It was, in fact, Tweeddale who wrote in 1668: 'I am joyed the king and duke [of York] have so good an opinion of Scotland and confidence in it, and hope they shall not be disappointed, for it may be formed into a citadel for his majesty's service in time.'[39]

So, justifiably or not, Scotsmen professed trading grievances. That the ministry took up their cause for anything but political reasons is extremely unlikely. Tweeddale, in 1689, sponsored a movement for union which owed nothing at all to trade, being aimed at preventing an extreme religious settlement in Scotland and gaining for the Scots the benefits of English civil liberties.[40] Was Tweeddale concerned, as he had said earlier, to make Scotland 'a citadel for his majesty's service' or to safeguard the kingdom against arbitrary rule? At one time or another he committed himself to both views. As a very flexible politician his aims varied with circumstances but a constant objective was a political union in which lesser nobility could count for more than in a regional government dominated by magnates, at whose hands Tweeddale had suffered. There was always a strong undercurrent of personal interest in Tweeddale's politics.

Tweeddale's union initiative of 1689 was taken up by other Scots for varied reasons but all deriving from self-interest. The project was disregarded by the English as a political nuisance at a time when they had enough domestic distractions of their own. Most Scots forgot it too save when the opposition for the time being dilated, for tactical reasons, on the wrongs of the kingdom. Then they represented the entire episode of 1689 as a piece of sharp practice whereby the English secured a Scottish settlement on the cheap without concessions. It was convenient to forget that in 1689 the priorities had been different. The fate of the revolution had seemed so precarious in Scotland that it had been politically justifiable for the succession to be put first. However much it might have been afterwards regretted, the responsibility lay with the Scottish convention which gave priority to safeguarding the revolution. Understandably they had not thought of bargains.

In truth economic considerations, before or after the revolution, were not seen by Scottish ministers or their followers as being very important and were always subordinated to politics. Marchmont,[41] as chancellor in 1696, enquired anxiously what the English court desired him to do about the controversial trade act of 1695, setting up the Africa Company.[42] Atholl,[43] secretary of state and commissioner to the 1696 parliament, although raucous on the subject of Scottish interests when in opposition, wrote obsequiously to Portland: '... I shall take all imaginable care ... concerning trade, to pass no act that I can imagine, or any of the officers of state with whom I shall particularly advise with [sic] in that business, do judge can give any just occasion of jealousies in England ... I shall write either to the lord keeper or the duke of Shrewsbury or any the king pleases in this place to know what they think may dissatisfy the English parliament ...'[44] Queensberry could not have made the point more plainly when he wrote in 1697 about the Africa Company agitation: '... I am as deeply engaged in this company as any in the kingdom, yet I am resolved to follow the measures that I think will be best pleasing to the king ...'[45]

When officers of state talked about encouraging trade, as from time to time they did, they usually had in mind not a sleek and contented mercantile community but an increase in customs yield, on which the payment of official salaries depended. This was true of them all. Tweeddale had in 1694 advised William to do without parliament for some time and to concentrate meanwhile on trade for the benefit of the revenue. Seafield in 1705 pressed Godolphin to allow trade with France as the Dutch did, for '... if we have not some connivance for a trade with France there will remain no fund for the support of the civil list ...'[46] Likewise he knew that opposition attempts to prohibit imports were motivated not by concern for the Scottish economy but by a desire to cut down the revenue to coerce the court.[47]

3 *The Darien scheme*

Even when economic forces seem to have been predominant, closer investigation shows them to have been matched by political considerations when not overshadowed by them. Throughout its existence the Africa Company demonstrated this. The years between 1688 and 1692 saw what have been described as the most depressed trading conditions that Scottish merchants had experienced for a generation.[48] Tweeddale, as lord chancellor, and Johnston, as secretary of state, in managing the 1693 parliament, were heavily dependent for support on Hamilton of Whitelaw and his well drilled burghs, and consequently felt the need to act positively to gratify the trading community. What they did was to encourage a lobby of Scottish merchants, supported by money from Scots living in England, in obtaining the trade act of 1693 allowing Scottish companies to be set up with full royal protection and a variety of incentives.[49] After that session of parliament Tweeddale wrote to William urging that something should be done to implement the act.[50] He had more in mind than the well-being of the mercantile interest. There were pronounced splits in the political nation and the ministry was in a state of internal disruption likely to cause trouble in the next parliament. Tweeddale felt the only solution was to postpone the next session and in the meantime hope for an improvement in trade to increase the revenue from customs and excise.[51] The same motives, the extension of political influence and improvement of the revenue, led to Tweeddale's further scheme of setting up a board of admiralty to protect and encourage trade. The new commission was passed in August 1695. It accomplished little but its intention was clear enough.[52]

Tweeddale's hopes for a revival of trade sufficient to extricate the ministry from its political difficulties had never been well founded and the holding of a parliament in 1695 became unavoidable. Predictably the session became the arena in which the issue of dominance was to be decided between the contending parties: the Tweeddale–Johnston group on the one hand and the Dalrymples and their allies on the other, in the contemporary jargon 'presbyterians' and 'episcopalians' respectively.[53] No weapons were left idle. The Glencoe enquiry was used to discredit Dalrymple and old charges were resurrected against Breadalbane. In their turn the 'episcopalians' intrigued to undermine the credit of Tweeddale and Johnston with the king. To keep burgh support the ministry allowed the aims of the trade act of 1693 to be pursued a stage further by the same lobby of merchants. The result was the act of 1695 which set up with extensive privileges the Company of Scotland trading to Africa and the Indies.[54] Obviously underlying the act was economic vision of a kind but the ministry's support was entirely political in motive. The politicians lacked all faith in the project itself, as later appeared.

Similarly the extreme reaction which took place in both English houses of parliament was due to an accumulation of tensions of which few were related to the Scottish Africa Company. Some very dubious measures were contemplated by the commons against the Scottish directors of the new company, over whom the house had no jurisdiction. Nevertheless, Lord Belhaven was one who placed more faith in running for cover to Scotland than in pleas of legal immunity. But, even if the act of 1695 was taken at its face value, both lords and commons would seem to have been over-reacting and on very slender grounds. The main contention was that the Scottish company was about to tread on the toes of the East India Company and the Royal Africa Company. All English subjects were forbidden to infringe the monopolies of the chartered companies, so, as far as Englishmen subscribing to the Scottish company were concerned, and possibly Scots domiciled in England, the position would seem to have been clear.[55] However, to classify Scotsmen living in Scotland as English subjects, presumably as *post nati*, would have been carrying things too far, especially in view of the navigation act's implications. It seems, though, that the commons, in particular, had something of the sort in mind.

Even allowing that Scottish ministers wanted to damp down the fuss they did seem genuinely surprised that anyone should take the trading capacity of the new company seriously. Neither Tweeddale nor Seafield[56] could see that the Scottish company represented any threat to English trade.[57] Since Scottish shipping did not exceed eighty vessels and her customs and foreign excise combined were farmed for a mere £20,300, Tweeddale professed himself unable to understand how Scotland could possibly be looked upon as a trading rival to England.[58]

Of course the Scottish company was not looked upon as a trading rival by anybody. Its inadequacy was fully appreciated by the very interests in England which were vehemently protesting, but for all that the outcry did not subside. The reasons for the uproar were various. As luck would have it the Scottish act had been passed at a critical point in the fortunes of the East India Company. The English company, dominated by Sir Josiah Child, had a strong tory flavour and had come under attack from a determined group of former shareholders, whigs, led by Thomas Papillon. For a combination of reasons, political and financial, the whigs were embarked on a market operation to gain control of the company or, alternatively, to establish a new company which they hoped would absorb the assets of the old one. Their tactics were aimed at destroying confidence in the East India Company. Amongst their weapons were a parliamentary enquiry into the company's affairs and moves designed to bring down the price of Company stock. Both sides indulged in heavy bribery. By 1695 the whigs had not succeeded in gaining control of the company but had lowered the price of stock from an average of 145 in 1692 to 96. It was at this point that news of the Scottish act produced panic in a jumpy market and by October 1695 the company's stock had slumped to 50.[59] Complete collapse suited nobody save interlopers keen to breach the East India Company's monopoly. From the company's point of view anything capable of producing such a panic was bad, and although the threat from Scotland was small it was welcome to neither Child nor Papillon, each concerned to control, not ruin, the company. So a situation developed in which all interested parties saw a chance of using the Scottish act to achieve their own ends. The East India Company and the Royal Africa Company were keen to show that the only solution to the problems surrounding them was the renewal of their charters on favourable terms. To obtain renewal they had in fact for some time been spending a large amount of money, with nothing much to show for it. Papillon's group wanted to steady the market and at the same time show that, as good whigs, they had the interest of trade at heart. Both court and opposition were currently competing in professions of zeal for the mercantile interest. A numerically superior opposition was on the point of defeating the ministry and setting up a council of trade on parliament's authority.[60] All concerned with the security of the plantation trade, particularly Edward Randolph, a zealous customs official with whom illegal Scottish trade to the colonies had become an obsession, prepared to exploit the opportunity to tighten up the navigation system against the Scots. Clauses in the Scottish act allowing the proposed company to establish colonies provided an excuse for raising this subject.[61] The general furore was increased by the presence in London of representatives of the Scottish opposition. With every ounce of purchase gained from the 1695 parliament they were collaborating with English politicians to dislodge

Johnston and Tweeddale. Amongst other pretexts, they were making use of the act of trade, although this meant opposing the act in England and favouring it in Scotland, where it was popular.[62]

Randolph and the customs commissioners may have been indulging their own obsessions over the illegal plantation trade but they were far nearer the heart of the matter than the English East India interest, since, whatever appearances to the contrary, the Scottish act had very little to do with the East India trade. Some very curious circumstances had attended its passing in the Scottish parliament. Every precaution had been taken to keep the act secret from the English, a ruse to which Tweeddale was fully an accessory, making no mention at all of the act in any report he sent to William or his confidants.[63] The reason was that the Scottish company was not a trading venture modelled on the English companies converted only at a later stage by William Paterson into a colonising project. It was a colonising scheme from its inception. Ironically, the reference to Africa and the Indies had been included as camouflage to avoid alarming the English.[64] Once the issue was out in the open Tweeddale admitted this intention to the king, and Johnston, who was in a position to know the truth, did not contest the point. The Scots had been right to assume that an American colony would disturb the English. Had the affairs of the English East India Company not been so politically sensitive at the time, Scottish trade to the Indies would have been thought a much lesser evil than a Scottish colony.

The Scots had not lacked colonising ambitions during the seventeenth century. They had merely had less success than the English. By the late seventeenth century their settlements had been absorbed into the English colonies but, as a consequence of their origins, they were the basis of a Scottish network throughout the West Indies and the mainland colonies. Scottish emigrants retained nostalgic ties with their native kingdom and made it all but impossible for the customs to keep out Scottish traders. Sentiment apart, this trade was very profitable for all concerned. Whilst settlements were being made in Charles II's reign, with the blessing of the crown, within the bounds of the proprietary colonies of New Jersey and Carolina, literature had been published from 1683 stressing the importance of the New Jersey venture as a market for Scottish manufactures, boldly ignoring the fact that the proposed trade was illegal. Nevertheless the chief town of the Scottish part of New Jersey—Perth Amboy—acquired status as a port of entry, was much used by Scottish traders and was a consequent source of distraction to the English customs.[65]

Thus an argument had already been made for a Scottish colony outside, or at least in disregard of, the navigation system to provide a market for any available Scottish goods. Such a colony would be more profitable if the entrepot trade between Europe and the Indies could be seized so that commerce between the English colonies and England's competitors would be in Scottish hands. These were possibilities, striking as they did at the basis of the navigation system, that the English could view only with alarm. Yet, curiously enough, although the Scots realised this and surrounded the passing of the act of trade with such secrecy, their dominant fear in the early stages had been of sabotage by the west-country Scots, already illegally but profitably engaged in the plantation trade and disinclined to share their profits,[66] an attitude which might explain why the member for Glasgow was later to vote against the union.[67]

Since there is no doubt that what the Scots intended from the very beginning was the Darien scheme or something very much like it,[68] there is correspondingly less excuse for the projectors' having misconceived and mismanaged the entire venture. The plan falls firmly into the category of 'clever–stupid'. Whatever the legal rights of Scotland the projectors could not have expected an English welcome for a direct blow at the kingdom's economic system, much less looked forward to official English assistance in carrying out the project. Their secretive behaviour shows they did neither. And if the English interests were directly threatened how could William possibly countenance the Scottish project? Subsequently this was used as an argument against the union of the crowns but only as a direct result of the Darien failure. In 1695 the Scots looked upon themselves as acting within the constitutional framework. Nor can one really defend an attempt to establish a colony in a fever-ridden territory belonging to someone else, especially when the recognised claimants had made plain, as the Spaniards had, their strong objections to intruders. This complicated and aggravated the situation but the position was quite bad enough as it was. What nobody had been expecting, not even the projectors, was the tremendous rush of support for the company after English opposition had become sufficiently notorious. Those detached enough to see the project as the chimera it was had no illusions about the reasons for this enthusiasm. For most it was an expression of resentment at the arrogance of the English towards what the Scots saw as a purely domestic affair. Those who retained sufficient business acumen to judge the project on its merits, feeling under no obligation to

.demonstrate their solidarity with national feeling, held aloof and deplored the stampede as others, blinded by national resentment, or succumbing to gold fever, rushed to subscribe money. Because the act was associated with Tweeddale and Johnston, soon afterwards dismissed, there was strong support for the company from their followers and others, as a means of embarrassing the court. According to Tweeddale the books were opened in Edinburgh on 27 February 1696 and by the following day £80,000 had been subscribed, '. . . so violent are they upon that affair from the ill usage it hath met with in the house of commons . . .' A reasonable subscription for persons of quality seemed to be between £3,000 and £1,000.[69] Queensberry could not for the sake of his reputation afford to stand aside. He put his name down for £3,000, being unable to risk less since the duchess of Hamilton and others had ventured the same amount. Nevertheless, he knew that for most the main drive was defiance of the English parliament.[70] Seafield wrote to Carstares in more specific terms: '. . . I can assure you, this company had been ended before now had it not been for the opposition made by the English which piques them on a point of honour . . .'[71] Marchmont was of the same opinion, writing of 'such an humour of resentments, as, I protest, may make one fear dangerous consequences'.[72]

As the Darien project began to assume the proportions of a catastrophe for a kingdom already sufficiently distressed, investors became worried about their money. Gestures of defiance at the English were one thing; losing money was another. Someone had to be blamed, and since, from the very inception of the project, the English had talked, and seemed to act, like saboteurs it is not surprising that they should have been accepted as such. But whatever steps the English had taken, official or otherwise, were peripheral, as those Scots who retained any sense of detachment saw very well. The cause of the failure lay deeper, in the concept of the project itself, and in the incompetence of the directors.[73] They, having undertaken the scheme despite its manifest impracticability, failed to carry out their basic task of keeping the settlers properly supplied and reinforced. Internal dissension in the company at home and personal jealousy within the expedition at Darien crippled the venture. There were allegations of fraud and embezzlement, charges inseparable from Scottish public affairs and just as likely to be true as not. But even had the financial probity of all involved been established beyond doubt, the project was, quite simply, beyond Scotland's capacity.

Seafield thought that failure was inherent in the plan itself and made no secret of it. As a result although he did all he could to represent to the king the extent of the company's losses and the legal right of Scotland to have a colony he was cast by his fellow countrymen in the role of quisling.[74] There was general rejoicing at the burning down of his Edinburgh house. But this was only one manifestation of popular involvement. The Edinburgh mob abandoned itself to smashing the windows of those unsympathetic to the project and forced the lord advocate to free prisoners from the Tolbooth. Marchmont was alarmed at the generally violent support for the company.[75] Clearly more was involved than economic interest. What was taking place was an anti-English demonstration by the populace, different in manner and degree from that of their betters who had money at stake but the same in kind.

Marchmont was even more worried by the political repercussions of the Caledonia enterprise and how they might be manifested at parliamentary level. A link was being forged between men who had looked upon themselves as risking their substance for the sake of Scotland and others standing ready to use the disaster to strengthen the opposition. He advised the king that all officials of the company should '. . . swear the allegiance and sign assurance and association to your majesty and your government, which would prevent the bad uses, which I indeed suspect many of that company design to make of it, to give disturbance to your majesty's affairs and service . . .'[76] Marchmont's fears were justified. Circumstances had combined to transform the Africa Company into little more than the parliamentary opposition in another guise.

The economic result of the Darien project was that a disastrous loss of capital was added to the kingdom's difficulties. Although it was never more than a fraction of the truth, failure could be blamed entirely on English violations of Scottish sovereignty. This was the oversimplified, emotional version which would attract popular credence. It was a view impossible to combat effectively. English predominance, although only a minor element in the Darien disaster, was at one and the same time vital to the functioning of the united crowns and a basic flaw in the relationship between the two kingdoms. Here was enough for any opposition to turn to good account, and the coalition between committed countrymen and those courtiers embittered by loss of money became a serious problem for Queensberry and the ministry in William's last two parliaments. The Darien episode upset the stability of Scottish politics by threatening the court majority and seriously disrupting Anglo-Scottish relations.

But, apart from the few unusual currents set up by courtiers who had invested unwisely and regretted it, the uproar over New Caledonia was conducted according to the usual conventions of the court and country alignment. It was natural for the country party to dress up mere opposition as solicitude for the national economic interest and the kingdom's rights. After 1698 they adopted a firm pose as defenders of the nation's trade though lacking somewhat in credibility. Queensberry barefacedly used the same technique to justify his followers' behaviour in 1704.[77] Such talk carried no more conviction from Queensberry than from Hamilton or Atholl. The duke had, it is true, declared himself against settling the succession unless the English granted terms freeing Scotland from all interference and obstruction.[78] It was, supposedly, this conviction which led him to abandon the abjuration in 1702 and to conclude the bargain of 1703 with Godolphin whereby the succession was to be avoided. But Queensberry was concerned only with the preservation of his interest in Scotland, where he wished to upset neither his jacobite nor his revolution friends by appearing to be over-enthusiastically pro- or anti-Hanoverian, nor his credit in England, where he wished to stand well with the ministry. This was a precarious balance to maintain, and his position in 1703 was made possible only by Godolphin's willingness to connive at the succession's being left open. Otherwise Queensberry, in order to retain his leadership of the Scottish court, would have undertaken to carry out whatever the English demanded. He did, after all, offer to carry the succession in 1704.[79] Far more important than Scottish interests, economic or other, was the desire to stay in office.

4 The Scottish economy and the court v. country conflict

What emerges is the realisation that, although Scotland, with or without Darien, had economic problems, they made surprisingly little public impact unless deliberately exploited by either court or country for political ends. To be aware of a national *malaise* is one thing but to undertake drastic, or even merely positive, remedies is another. The commonest reaction is to carry on as usual, hoping for the best. Scotsmen, or some of them, did expatiate on trade but for a variety of reasons: private economic interest, concern for public revenue, or merely to justify prejudices and attitudes already well established. Talk of trade became a fashionable and convenient camouflage for less respectable motives. But when the existence of Scotland's economic ailments received even such dubious acknowledgement, no agreement on a remedy was forthcoming, because there was no common interest in finding one. Anyway there were, to many Scots, issues far more important than trade: religion, legalistic quibbles, national pride, public and private resentments and a whole range of individual obsessions of very limited appeal. Some were keenly aware that the existing relationship between Scotland and England was unsatisfactory. Others were less conscious of it. But this situation was related to trade only after Darien. Even then, amongst the wide range of 'solutions' which emerged, there was no distinctively 'Scottish' solution. And if Scotland had any coherent economic interest some such solution should have emerged. Some thought Scotland had to be placed beyond the reach of English interference. Others thought English interference inescapable and better legalised by union. There were those so apprehensive of the jacobite threat that they were inclined to settle the succession on the house of Hanover without further ado in disregard of other considerations. All such views spanned both court and country parties but professed opinions and, more to the point, actions were determined ultimately by political allegiance. It is possible that public stance at variance with private views could cause misgivings, yet political allegiance was almost the sole determinant of conduct. As will later appear, most members of the Scottish parliament voted at the union in accordance with their current political alignment. Either because attitudes to the court were decisive without the need for reflection or, otherwise, lacking any clear idea of the issues involved, members sought security in their normal allegiance.[80] The court, as far as it was able, continued to do what the English managers expected, quite uninfluenced by any thought of Scotland's economic plight. Grievances, real or fancied, against England gave the opposition their platform of national sovereign rights which they could exploit only because they were in opposition. Their demand for 'limitations' was a parliamentary manoeuvre, however worked up they became about it, and talk of 'a previous treaty', when it did not mean specifically compensation for Darien shareholders, was a device to block other proposals. Of those most vociferous about Scottish grievances many wanted no solution at all to Anglo-Scottish problems whilst the remainder had no intention of establishing harmony unless they were paid for it.

So Scotland's economy affected the political situation only by providing an element of the language of conflict. The mercantile community experienced the effects of the war and a slump in some, though not all, areas of trade. The population at large, engaged mostly in subsistence agriculture, was only too well acquainted with famine. But these hardships were not sharply focused grievances until Darien gave rise to a strong anti-English feeling which transformed relations with England into the pivot of the struggle between court and opposition. This Anglo-Scottish issue was political and not economic. Whatever the feelings in the kingdom at large the main target of the opposition was the Scottish court, to harass it and eventually to replace it. Their minds were quite unimpeded by any thoughts of reform; their aim was to gain office, not defend Scottish interests. But the mere fact of opposition generated an intensity of indignation which did crystallise the real issues, although the politicians cared little about them. Successive parliamentary sessions ultimately resolved the tensions between the two kingdoms into two questions: that of Scottish sovereignty and that of compensation for losses incurred through Darien as an infringement of it. The former was a political issue entirely whilst the latter pointed to nothing more than a straightforward money-on-the-table transaction. To express the issue even more starkly, any Anglo-Scottish settlement had to spring from an English initiative and England's requirements were exclusively political. Some of them emerged from domestic politics but to the English court Scotland's grievances were no more than a political nuisance. The Darien crisis and the slump had not in any way changed the character of Scottish management but merely intensified an already established problem. Magnate and jacobite opposition had been presented with an armoury such as they had never before had and which could render the political existence of the Scottish ministry all but intolerable. From the point of view of the English court the Scottish opposition had somehow to be swamped or the Scottish parliament would itself have to go. Such issues represented the reality of the Anglo-Scottish situation. There was a political struggle for the control of Scotland and there were Scottish economic problems; except in so far as the problems made excellent weapons the two were unrelated.

5 *Trade as a tool for propaganda*

Contemporary pamphlets and the less guarded asides of politicians alike point to the trade argument's being a propaganda tool to justify or oppose an essentially political scheme. Few were sufficiently well informed for reasoned debate and those desirous of rational discussion were even fewer. Most pamphleteers were writing propaganda. Age has lent it respectability and posterity given it more serious consideration than it deserves, but it was propaganda nevertheless, and of the most blatant kind. The bulk of pamphleteering did coincide with the economic depression from 1701 to the union but it was unconnected with any search for economic salvation. Coincidentally this was the time when union was an active political issue and most pamphlets were concerned with specific proposals. Pamphleteers, with one possible exception, did not attempt to analyse Scotland's economic plight and then seek solutions. Had they been driven to publish by the approach of economic disaster this is the pattern one would expect to find. Instead they started from the issue of union and argued for or against it. Apart from the Darien agitation, which was a separate opposition campaign, pamphlets and published speeches coincided not with trade recession but with attempts at political union.

Trade arguments were used to justify political intentions, which could be taken to indicate the importance attached to trade as an issue and therefore as a means of persuasion. It would be unwise to make this assumption. Economic arguments did not significantly affect the situation.[81] Roxburgh's often quoted statement, in apparent contradiction to this view, seems to carry the more weight for having been written in a private letter to Baillie. '. . . That a union will do in the Scottish parliament I think very probable, reckoning the old party, Marchmont, the burghs, Cromartie, the president of the session, Aberdeen and Murray-men all for it. The motives will be, trade with most, Hanover with some, ease and security with others, together with a general aversion at civil discords, intolerable poverty, and the constant oppression of a bad ministry, from generation to generation, without the least regard to the good of the country . . .'[82] This seems a sufficiently comprehensive utterance but it has to be read with caution. Roxburgh was far from presenting Baillie with an objective assessment; he was rather trying to convert him to an acceptance of union. Since Baillie's main concern was whether union was likely to be successful, Roxburgh was trying to convince him that it was a winning cause which they ought to back. Despite the importance given to trade in Roxburgh's catalogue his conjectures on the subject proved excessively optimistic. The earl of Aberdeen was one of the very few to espouse union on what he took to be its merits, but the claims of his political allegiance—he was a jacobite—were so strong that rather than vote against his party he stayed away from parliament. Nor did all the burghs support union.[83] In fact, but for Roxburgh, Baillie and their squadrone allies, whose votes were due entirely to political calculation, the division in parliament would have been much the same as in 1703 and the union would not have passed at all.

Stair, too, attached undue importance to trade. He stressed the need to gratify 'the northern squadron' of members, especially Hugh Rose of Kilravock, 'for he manages the rest', together with Grant and George Brodie, '. . . For though that corner who [sic] has many representatives are the most disaffected to the present establishment or the succession, yet the matter of trade is more in their heads than any others in the nation; which may make them easy in parliament to ratify these good terms that may be obtained in the treaty . . .'[84] Grant the younger, having received Mar's regiment as an inducement, did vote for union but his father stayed away; Brodie was mostly in opposition; Rose's record was most notable for abstention.[85] None of them seems to have been moved by trade considerations. In the same letter Stair remarked on '. . . those who would not enter into a treaty because they pretended no good would be got by it, and others who were so fond as to have rendered [sic] without any terms, to which it was impossible to have brought our nation or parliament . . .'[86] The entire union transaction was to show that what 'the nation' thought was immaterial whilst the possibility of making converts from the opposition on trade or any other grounds was virtually non-existent.[87] One can take Stair to have meant only that the appearance of a sell-out had to be avoided for fear of a court revolt such as that over Darien.

Seafield, writing to Montrose, made one of his rare references to trade, which seems otherwise not to have entered into his calculations. '. . . The poverty in our country will probably increase unless we can promote trade and this does very much depend upon what we shall obtain by the treaty . . .'[88] This was a very cautious statement. More rashly, James Erskine of Grange reported opinion on the union to his brother, Mar. '. . . The most part of the trading people talk pretty favourably of it . . .'[89] an impression not borne out by the event.[90]

Johnston made a show of representing the issue in one of the aphoristic statements he liked so much. Conversing with Marlborough about Scottish sovereignty, he argued that '. . . the true state of the matter was, whether *Scotland* should *continue subject* to an *English ministry without trade* or *be subject to an English parliament* with *trade*'.[91]But

Scotland's subjection to an English ministry was little more than
negative. The English court, if it chose to accept the consequences,
could impose a veto but its capacity to promote positive measures was
limited. It had to work through a Scottish ministry which, in the face of
magnate-inspired opposition, too frequently proved unable to carry out
directives. The history of Anne's reign to 1707 showed the impossibility
of consistent management in Scotland within the union of the crowns.
This was the problem that the union treaty, in so far as it involved
public policy, was designed to solve. One pro-unionist writer put in
print, probably to the managers' alarm, what nobody else had dared to
say publicly—that within a union England would find the task of
managing Scotland much easier and that everyone would be the better
for it.[92] Other such references were more veiled as, since the topic was a
sensitive one, they needed to be.

But amongst politicians privately, references to trade were rare.
Most of the talk other than self-interested calculation was of preserving
peace between the kingdoms, keeping out popery and preventing
confusion on the death of the queen.[93] The need to keep to generalities
only tenuously connected with the real issues was a considerable
limitation. It was dificult to think of reasons for union which could be
fully ventilated and almost as difficult for many to find excuses for
accepting it. Some were driven to seek justification within an already
well established Scottish tradition of national self-denigration,
sombrely indicating what they took to be serious defects in the Scottish
character. According to Baillie, '. . . considering the temper of this
people, how unfit to govern ourselves, how likely to weary of
limitations, were they got . . . I must be convinced that union is our
only game . . .'[94] The earl of Orkney professed to share these
sentiments, lamenting '. . . we have not virtue enough . . .'[95] This bleak
opinion can be found also in the pamphlet literature of the time. There
is much to be said for this appraisal of early eighteenth-century
Scotland, though those who made it did not necessarily believe it.

Apart from the cranks who emerged briefly to utter warnings or
propose eccentric remedies, most pamphlets indicated political
alignment rather than personal opinion. A strong connection appeared,
naturally, between opposition to union or even a belief in separation
from England and the view that Scotland's problems were capable of a
domestic solution. Views changed, moreover, with political loyalties. In
1701 there was advanced one of the most ambitious schemes to be
contrived for Scotland. It was based on the premise that Scotland's

ailments were internally generated and would be responsive to self-medication. Its author was William Paterson, hoping at the time for advancement through the goodwill of the then Scottish ministry. In his *Proposals and Reasons for Constituting a Council of Trade*[96] he declared Scotland to be suffering from a long period of national negligence. For especial condemnation he singled out 'avaricious hucksters and monopolists'. His proposals were breathtaking: a completely planned economy, no less, to transform Scotland into a vast commercial enterprise financed by taxation and run by a council of trade with full responsibility for developing the resources of the kingdom to their utmost extent. Paterson had incorrectly assessed the outlook of the Scottish officers of state. He was thought at the time to have had a bee in his bonnet about economic problems, exaggerating them out of all proportion. Most found his scheme alarming, impracticable or both.[97] Paterson's ostensible aim was to produce a flourishing, independent, Scotland. However, by 1706 his hopes of employment were centred on the junto and the English court, converting him into a devout supporter of union and a government propagandist. William Seton, younger, of Pitmedden underwent a not dissimilar change, supporting union, in 1700, for sound country party reasons but by 1706 using the court arguments, having in the meantime secured official employment.[98] Some authors, too, changed their views from one pamphlet to the next according to the readership aimed at, involving themselves in enough discrepancies and contradictions to destroy any faith in their professed convictions.

If the state of the Scottish economy had been consciously the central issue of the union, then discussion of trade prospects ought to have dominated the dispute. In fact economic controversy was far from monopolising the pamphlet war. Trade was overshadowed by religion and at least rivalled by talk of sovereignty. The reason was that trade had importance only in unionist propaganda strategy as distinct from the real motives for union, into which trade hardly entered. It was therefore vital for the anti-unionists to diminish its significance, which they did with fair success, partly by a cold douche of scepticism and then by concentrating on other topics seemingly of more interest to the political nation. When they mentioned trade as a grievance it was merely to reduce it to the status of a minor topic, an irrelevance or, in over-reaction to unionist pamphlets, as a condition that union would aggravate. Even then they did little more than hark back to the Darien episode, inseparable from the idea of English oppression and a more emotive topic by far than commerce. Unionist writers lost the initiative and instead of finding themselves driving home the trade advantages to be gained they were merely reacting to a flood of criticism unrelated for the most part to the economy. The unionists' trade argument has in retrospect taken on great significance because it was sound. That it was seen to be so at the time, even by those who made use of it, is difficult to believe.

6 Arguments against union

A typical anti-unionist argument issued from a self-styled 'member of the country party' to whom the problems of Scotland were far wider-ranging than the state of the economy. They included the maladministration of justice, a surfeit of nobles and the spread of atheism. In so far as he had any economic complaint it was levelled at English interference. He wanted the crowns separated '. . . if England shall go on to oppress us in our trade, oppose our foreign settlements, and appear against our innocent endeavours for advancing the wealth of our poor country with both their houses of parliament . . .'[99] These were old grudges relating to Darien and exhumed to support the argument for an independent Scotland.

Sovereignty was a topic which frequently emerged. The old medieval dispute concerning England's claim to suzerainty over Scotland had always been dear to the hearts of lawyers with antiquarian interests. Proposals for a union treaty restored the controversy to vigorous life, though the state of Anglo-Scottish relations at the time had placed it several removes from reality. Pamphleteers assailed each other with great verve, but inconclusively, with legal and antiquarian hairs finely split.[100] There was debate over whether, within the proposed union, any appeal was allowable from Scottish courts to the British parliament.[101] Sir George Mackenzie's objection to an earlier union project was resurrected: that parliament had no right to vote a union, since to do so would break a fundamental law changeable only by reference to the electors. To this was opposed assertions, Burkeian in principle rather than style, of parliamentary sovereignty and the right of members to exercise their judgement.[102] But the latter argument had less immediate appeal, and the notion that parliament had no power to contract a union 'over the belly of the nation' gained wide popular acceptance. This opinion took on a more serious aspect when the south-western presbyterians, for example, acted upon it, burning the articles of union at Dumfries, declaring they would not consider themselves bound by the treaty even if it were passed.[103]

A steady flow of pamphlets advanced variations of the main country argument that if only Scottish sovereignty were safeguarded against English encroachments all would be well. To ensure this some favoured complete separation, others limitations on the power of the crown. Whichever method was favoured heavy criticism had to be levelled against any 'incorporating union'. *A Copie of a Letter from some of the Nobility of Scotland, To King James the 6th, of Ever Blessed Memory, Concerning the Union*[104] was reprinted in which the king had been asked to content himself with a union of crowns and a declaration that the people of both kingdoms were equal subjects. One writer was bold enough to reject union because it involved the Hanoverian succession, his contention being that the Scottish throne passed by proximity of blood and no man could be debarred from his rights on account of his religion, a view which called into question not a few Scottish laws.[105] Loss of sovereignty and imperial dignity, with lamentation for the end of the Edinburgh parliament, were recurring themes in opposition writing. There was alarm at the alleged inevitability of Scotland's being overrun and oppressed by English magistrates and garrisons. Other prophecies had an even more cataclysmic flavour: 'We shall lose the light of the Gospel, and shall be burdened with the superstitions and idolatries of England . . . Our names shall be extinct as a nation, and like the Jews, we shall be vagabonds over the whole earth . . .', this clearly from a man not much given to worries about the economy,[106] but not in any way singular in that. The author of *Some Queries Proposed to Consideration, Relative to the Union now intended* (1706) had a similar order of priorities. He, too, questioned parliament's competence to pass a union and especially one involving a breach of the covenants and the claim of right. He dwelt on the English test act and feared for the security of the church. Only then did he wonder whether the loss of the Scottish parliament would harm Edinburgh merchants or the kingdom would be reduced to poverty and desolation by the imposition of the salt tax. For the rest he felt that the existence of the Africa Company was worth more to Scotland than a union and that one year's trade with the countries at war with Scotland would exceed the profit to be made in seven years under the treaty. Such economic conjectures were neither profound nor well-informed and, to their authors, were obviously minor considerations.

The reverend William Wright of Kilmarnock affected a whimsical style of propaganda, using the analogy of a marriage negotiation, in his *Comical History of the Marriage Betwixt Fergusia and Heptarchus* (1706). Wright was aware of some of the economic issues but was obliged by the country propaganda line to contend that Scotland's commercial salvation must begin at home. To him trade with the plantations was a dangerous delusion. Colonial trade could serve no purpose but that of draining away Scotland's population. He professed to be disturbed by incompatibilities between the interests of England and Scotland—over the wool trade, for instance. So any union which brought Scotland under the rule of an English majority at Westminster could not be other than ruinous. Yet even as these disadvantages occurred to him his main concerns were the retention of the 'honours' of Scotland and to urge upon his readers the benefit of fasting, meditation and reflection.

Wright was a typical opposition propagandist whose expressed views were wholly characteristic of the main anti-union campaign. If such writers affected to favour a 'treaty' they meant that Scotland should force the best possible bargain out of England whilst remaining separate. Such a bargain was to contain safeguards for Scottish sovereignty, favourable terms for direct trade with England and freedom to embark on national trade projects.[107] Alleged benefits from trade with the colonies had to be disparaged because this was the unionists' biggest inducement. No better solution for Scotland's predicament could be proposed, according to one pamphleteer, than the act of security itself, which '. . . will set us upon such an equal foot with the English that they will be obliged to grant us concessions, tending to the honour and advantage of our nation which may render us equally incapable of their influence, and harm by any manner of way . . .'[108] Serious country argument always returned to the question of sovereignty; but, in failing to appreciate Scotland's dependence on the English market, they overestimated her bargaining power and were too optimistic, even deluded, over her capacity to rejuvenate her economy by drastic prohibitive legislation.

There were other writings which made no pretence of reasonableness. Outraged nationalism and hatred of the English abounded. The author of *A Pill For Pork-Eaters; Or, A Scots Lancet For An English Swelling* (1705) was incensed at, amongst other things, English objections to the execution of captain Green and two of his crew. He threatened more violence and threw in, for old times' sake, a reference to Bannockburn. As for the union:

> . . . 'Tis nothing but a treacherous decoy,
> To bring us to their measure, then destroy
> The rights and just pretences of our crown,
> And jeer and laugh at us when they have done . . .

Not so crude in presentation but capable of creating as much mischief was one of George Ridpath's pamphlets of 1705: *The Reducing of Scotland by Arms And Annexing it to England as A Province, Considered* . . . Ridpath was employed by the country party, having special connections with the Tweeddale group, but after the latter's conversion to union he remained with the opposition. The bulk of this pamphlet, for which he was prosecuted, was a recital of the wrongs allegedly inflicted on Scotland by the English since 1603. Though he denied there was reason to think England intended an invasion of Scotland, he nevertheless considered the prospect at length, concluding that the English would not find conquest easy. Ridpath was not engaged in conjecture because invasion had been thought of, as he no doubt knew, but the subject would have been better not publicised.

An English answer to this demonstrated only that national prejudice was not a monopoly of the Scots. The anonymous author listed the injuries which Scotland had inflicted on England, his catalogue extending to the injustices to which the Scots had subjected James VI and his mother. He accused the Scots of dangerous designs, the arming clause of the act of security being a threat to England. Indeed, there was no one else it could be aimed at: '. . . all the maritime powers in Europe are engaged in a war already, except the Turk, Danes and Venetians, who will scarce put themselves to the trouble of fetching oatmeal and thistles so far . . .' He asserted Scotland's legal dependence on England and attacked presbyterianism as not only anti-monarchical but barbarous. Reflecting, finally, on England's conduct in the face of such unpleasantness, he stood amazed at her moderation.[109] He was matched by Patrick Abercromby, for the Scots, who fancied complete separation from England, the result of which, according to him, would be complete freedom of trade for Scottish merchants with the whole of Europe and a revival of the 'old alliance'. He did not much care whether it led to war with England or not.[110] It is difficult to say from which century he was a refugee but he was out of place in 1706.

The objection to union which occupied the most shelf space was fear for Scotland's religious settlement. This may have been due to no more than the church's capacity for organising a propaganda campaign through its network of ministers, a literate and verbose group of men. It is possible, too, that with religion people felt on firmer ground than with trade. Nevertheless, if sheer bulk of publication counts for anything, religion was the most important cause of opposition to the union. The staple argument was that the mere acceptance of a united kingdom parliament involved the recognition of episcopacy, there being bishops in the lords. This was thought not only bad in itself but a breach of the covenants in that some connivance at churchmen's intervention in matters of state was involved. No certain safeguard for true religion was possible against a parliament dominated by enemies of presbyterianism. Protests were continuous and loud. The commission of the general assembly petitioned against union, setting out the major religious objections.[111] Inevitably this led to considerable trafficking in past controversies. The early 1640s were much brooded upon and one of Calamy's sermons of 1645 on the sinfulness of covenant-breaking was reprinted.[112] One writer thought the religious relations of England and Scotland should be resumed from where they stood in 1643.[113] Members of the Scottish parliament were exhorted from the pulpit to reflect on what was of value in a true church and on the dangers to which it was being exposed. To reach a wider and possibly more responsive audience the sermon was printed.[114] The opinion of the redoubtable James Hodges that Scotland's misfortunes were due to sin was repeated and embellished. Atonement for the nation's sinfulness would, it was asserted, be more efficacious than union. England was given the same neighbourly advice.[115] Addresses to parliament from assorted presbyteries represented the union as destructive of true religion.[116] Religious tension reached such heights, especially in the south-west, that the commission of the general assembly felt called on to advise the presbytery of Hamilton to avoid tumults.[117] Even after the union was ratified the flood of warnings of its dire religious consequences did not abate. William Wisheart, preaching in 1707 before the earl of Glasgow, commissioner to the general assembly, cautioned Scotsmen to be on their guard against corruption in worship and manners.[118] The author of *Smoaking Flax Unquenchable* . . . had no confidence in the Scottish church establishment's ability to protect itself, since, according to him, it had been unfaithful to the covenants for eighteen years.[119] A 'considerable body of people in the south and western shires' denounced the proposed union as a religious abomination and in a 'humble address' declared their intention of defying parliament if the treaty was put into effect.[120]

A key point in this religious dispute was the sanctity or otherwise of

the covenants. The hard-line presbyterians made great play with the
covenants in their opposition to union.[121] A pamphlet controversy
developed between James Webster, maintaining the sanctity of the
covenants as interpreted by himself and other sympathisers, and the
reverend William Adams, who thought the covenants in no way
sacrosanct and that more attention was being paid to them than they
deserved.[122] But Webster viewed the probable fate of true religion
within a union with something like despair. No help was to be expected
from English presbyterians. Webster even denied them the name
'presbyterian' because they had in the past negotiated with an
episcopal church, an argument which Defoe thought it worthwhile to
dispute.[123]

Amongst all this religious apprehension one pamphleteer was bold
enough to point out that the English dared not endanger peace by
interfering with the Scottish religious settlement and that to suppose
otherwise was ridiculous. In his view presbyterians, cameronians in
particular, were allowing themselves to be used by the jacobites; nor
was he far from the truth.[124] Yet, from the strict presbyterian point of
view, there was cause for fear. Webster[125] thought union would bring
toleration for episcopalians, pernicious in its effects and corrupting to
true doctrine. Some English tories had aroused this suspicion. An
occasional extremist English pamphlet increased apprehension. *The
Restoration of Episcopacy in Scotland, The only sure Foundation for a lasting
Union with England In a Letter to Sir J[ohn] P[ackington?] Bar.*,[126] proposed
that Scotland should adopt episcopacy before union and that
membership of the Westminster parliament should be confined to
episcopalians. This was blunt enough, and answering voices were
raised in Scotland. From an episcopalian hand came a long-winded
piece of doggerel favouring a secret referendum on religion to justify the
re-establishment of episcopacy in Scotland,[127] the author having no
doubt that the majority was episcopalian.

Schemes involving comprehension were no less threatening. If one
queen and one parliament could be accepted, why not variants of one
religion? Bishops could be regarded as directly in the apostolic
succession or merely superintendents, according to taste,[128] talk which
scared such men as Webster who reacted noisily. Whether the noise
was a quite spontaneous reaction or whether known fears were being
exploited by propagandists is impossible to say. But undeniably
religion was a vital element in the anti-union campaign. It is significant
that, apart from the Edinburgh crowd's addiction to smashing glass

and crackling flames, the main threats of force against the union came from jacobites, whose reactions were predictable, and extreme presbyterians.

Although the dispute was less extensive than that over religion there was inevitably, since the court had decided to make trade benefits the central argument for union, a substantial interchange on the trade issue. This was not because clear-sighted men had identified it as the most important topic. In England security for the revolution and the protestant succession was a sufficient argument. It was far from being so in Scotland, where many had no desire to see a Hanoverian succession and amongst those who had were some who claimed an open succession as Scotland's only weapon for extracting 'terms' from the English. That union would make Scotland easier to manage could hardly be avowed in public. There seemed only one safe argument for selling union to the Scots: the increase in trade and wealth it would supposedly generate.[129] Few would declare themselves averse from prosperity. Even those who preached hardship as an answer to Scotland's problems did so in the name of a healthy trade balance. But at whom was this campaign directed? A block of members would support the union anyway as courtiers, just as others would oppose, either as countrymen or as jacobites or merely because they had been disobliged. There was little, if any, scope for persuasion. Nevertheless those reponsible for seeing union through the Scottish parliament could not afford to leave it at that. The anti-unionists would obviously attack the treaty to make it unpopular in the country, frightening the generality of the people and branding unionists as unpatriotic. So a case for union had to be argued at least as strongly as that against to preserve solidarity in the court party, to combat the charge of treachery and to quieten popular opposition. A stray or indecisive member might even abandon his normal party allegiance. It was unlikely but court managers had to hope.

The significance for the country at large of the debate on trade is even harder to assess than that over danger to the church. Questions concerning the church establishment were well defined even though the publicity given them might have been in part intended to generate, rather than express, alarm. With trade the issues were shadowy, the evidence confusing and, save for one or two people who held strong individual opinions about Scotland's economy, the bulk of writing was mere contrived propaganda for or against union. The anti-unionists had either to refute this central point of the unionists' official argument:

that union would promote wealth, or greatly reduce its importance. Contentions on both sides almost always lacked substantiation. It could hardly have been otherwise, the available information being meagre and its significance doubtful. Opposition writers were either sceptical of, or rejected outright, the assumption that union would lead to increased wealth. Ostensibly this led them to the conclusion that Scotland could best resolve her problems by independence. In fact they were justifying separation, which had been their original aim.

The onus was on them to show how Scotland could remain separate and flourishing, so an entire school of writers emerged, dedicated to the condemnation of what they claimed to be Scotland's extravagant standard of living, the origin of the country's misfortunes. Their proposed remedies were no novelty although none could have had much appeal save amongst those who could not afford luxuries and those who could but who disapproved of other people's extravagances. They preached the utmost frugality of life. There would have to be strict control or even prohibition of imports—foreign wines, tobacco and East India goods—to restore the trade balance.[130] Such national austerity was recommended as Scotland's only way to salvation.[131]

Yet many anti-unionist writers felt their assertion that Scottish problems could be solved independently of England to be unconvincing, so they advanced the apparently feasible alternative of a federal solution, one of whose chief attractions to many was that the English would never accept it, especially on the terms demanded. Some countrymen acknowledged the importance for the Scottish economy of exports to England and wanted freedom of trade for their merchants exporting to England. They were not necessarily prepared to grant the same freedom to English merchants in the Scottish trade and they were rejecting the more speculative advantages of the English colonial trade. Andrew Fletcher of Saltoun expressed the common opposition sentiment: 'For my own part I cannot see what advantages a free trade to the English plantations would bring us, except a further exhausting of our people, and the utter ruin of all our merchants, who should vainly pretend to carry that trade from the English . . .'[132]

William Black, as an anti-unionist, shared this opinion. Writing as a group of Scottish merchants,[133] he gave coherent expression to justifiable fears. Only long-term experience of union could prove how soundly based they were. He made detailed criticism of certain articles of the treaty, showing that he had at least read it, which not all opposition writers seem to have done. His professed conviction was that

Scotland would reap no benefit from union, rather the reverse, its being more than doubtful whether she could profitably share in the colonial trade. Like Fletcher and the rest who voiced this doubt he found it convenient to ignore the Scots already illegally engaged in this trade, but they were few and their existence did not really dispose of the argument that Scotland was giving up her continental trade for dubious advantages, there being no certainty that her merchants would be able to withstand English competition when legally within the navigation system.

Black was against equal taxation. All heavy taxes were harmful to trade; they had done the English no good and would do the Scots no good either. This was not an unreasonable argument, but then he undermined his credibility by advancing a curious proposition. Since the French wars, he said, the English had increased their taxes until they could not afford to pay them, thus producing a vast debt and a welter of bankruptcies amongst merchants. Obviously he did not understand the national debt. Scotland's taxes, about a quarter of those of England, were already so burdensome that she could hardly keep her head above water. Yet he subscribed to the common anti-unionist creed that things were getting better in Scotland. Indeed he discounted the need for a union at all, asserting, quite unjustifiably, that the country's adverse trade balance had begun reacting to careful regulation. A very little more control, especially of luxury imports, would make Scotland as prosperous as she had ever been. So, he complained, just when the country was entering a period of prosperity the parliament was going to hand over control to England, 'which . . . may in [the] end make us glad to transport ourselves and families to the plantations as the last refuge for our subsistence'. 'We presently enjoy a free trade to all the known world except the plantations. We can as freely trade to the East Indies, to the Levant, to Russia, and all over the Baltic as any company in England; and after the union we are restricted in most of these . . .'[134] In fact, the right to trade to these places and the establishment of profitable links with them were two quite different things, as Black must have known. But it all helped to support the contention that an English connection was unneccessary—the point he was trying to establish.

However, he hedged. He claimed to support the principle of union although reiterating his particular objections, affecting not to care whether they made him an opponent of the treaty or not.[135] They certainly made him hostile to any union within the scope of practical politics. He seemed instead to favour some kind of trade agreement but tried to establish a distinction between trade which affected both countries, in which an English demand for uniform trade regulations was justified, and purely Scottish trade, to Germany and the United Provinces, for instance, which was no business of the English.[136] By venturing so far he was really conceding the need for a link between the kingdoms and trying to define its extent. Throughout his writings Black swung between whole-hogging separatism and visions of a federal arrangement. Both ruled out the union as negotiated.[137] When a man is resolutely opposed to one course for constantly varying reasons it is fair to assume that his opposition is more significant than the arguments.

Since the motives of both court and opposition were, with few exceptions, highly suspect, though for different reasons, there is little ground to suppose that writers on either side were any more devoted to principle than their masters. Yet, because the countrymen were free to abandon themselves entirely to opposition, their attack on the union, for all its scaremongering and dishonesty, contained some sound criticism. Despite the wildness of their assertions, their attitude of consistent scepticism is even now quite impressive. Both Fletcher and Hodges exposed some of the weaknesses of the unionist argument. Fletcher was a political original and idealist in permanent opposition and therefore in alliance with whoever formed the country party for the time being. Conventional terminology apart, he was one of the very few real countrymen. Notwithstanding his prophecies about the probably dire effects of Scottish access to the colonies, he had some insight into the weaknesses of the Scottish economy. He expressed starkly enough the crux of the argument for rejecting union: the case for the treaty was not proven and so the risks were too great for Scotland to take. Union would doubtless increase the power and wealth of a united kingdom but where would the wealth go? It would not, thought Fletcher, find its way to Scotland: '. . . our trade . . . will be only an inconsiderable retail, in a poor, remote and barren country, where the richest of our nobility and gentry will no longer reside . . .' This was a fair conjecture, but Fletcher, like the rest, was unable to propose any convincing alternative to union. He could think only of taking Scotland right out of the English orbit.[138] In 1706 he was still arguing that only a Scottish parliament could guarantee Scottish interests; a union would merely subordinate them to an English majority and the country would be worse off than before.[139] This was reasonable comment but it solved none of the problems of Scottish government, which were what most concerned the court. But then if the debate was to be carried on in spurious terms it was hardly to be expected that the opposition would solve the court's problem for it.

James Hodges was also of Fletcher's mind. He found ludicrous the professed unionist faith that although England and Scotland as separate kingdoms had incompatible interests, yet once united they would have one indistinguishable interest. Hodges would have none of it. The prospect of an incorporating union filled him with undiluted pessimism. England would be dominant and would never allow Scotland to grow wealthy. Even if the union should create opportunities for Scottish trade the kingdom had too few natural advantages to seize them. Again, such statements were not based on evidence but felt in the bones and others accepted or rejected them according to political ties. Hodges's other objections to an incorporating union were many: legal, constitutional and religious. His rational discourse pointed to a federal union as the only safe arrangement, but his deeper conviction was that Scotland's ills sprang from the wrath of God, whose favour needed to be supplicated as an essential preliminary to whatever was attempted.[140] Indeed, his forebodings about divine wrath proved by far the most popular part of his work, the relevant section being reprinted as a separate pamphlet, with or without his permission.[141] But, Divine displeasure apart, the contention that Scotland should retain parliament, since its abolition would deprive her of all security, became the standard anti-unionist argument, backed sometimes by fears for Scottish trade but more often by the alleged threat to religion and the mere dislike of seeing any vestige of national independence surrendered.[142] On a much lower level it was propagated by a cruder strain of literature typified by *A Copy of a Letter From a Country Farmer to His Laird, a Member of Parliament*,[143] written in bogus vernacular, nauseous with homespun philosophy and farmyard imagery. The author aimed at activating the most deep-rooted Scottish phobias: the folly of trusting England, the profound enmity of the English to the Scots and their Church, the likelihood of dragoons being quartered on the population and the country filled with English garrisons.

Even the convention of royal burghs officially opposed the treaty. At a curious meeting the convention approved an address, a majority of smaller burghs outvoting a minority of the wealthier burghs, with twenty-four out of sixty-seven representatives either absent or abstaining. The address as voted professed agreement with the principle of union but asserted that Scottish interests, religious, civil and economic, could not be secured unless the Scottish parliament were retained. If Scotland had suffered through English interference when she had her own parliament she was more, rather than less, likely to suffer if her representatives were outnumbered in a united kingdom parliament.[144]

The lord advocate, an opponent of union, spoke of the expected growth of trade with pessimism, especially in the plantation trade, which he thought would prejudice Scotland rather than otherwise, 'For it has always been my thought that the concessions as to trade, and this entire union may indeed enrich and be the advantage of Scotsmen, but that it will enrich the part of Britain now called Scotland is that which I still doubt . . .'[145] Some courtiers suspected that the Dutch had bribed him to oppose union. They might well have been right, Stewart having no conscientious objection to that sort of thing, but nonetheless the doubts he expressed could have been well founded.

But all critics of the union were better at exposing its weaknesses than at making constructive suggestions. The feasibility of separation was ingeniously argued but it remained a dubious remedy and politically impossible. Some commentators, of course, had ideas of feasibility that were bizarre. One took the view that Scotland should unite with the Dutch if with anybody, since they at least were prosperous, whilst the English were near to ruin.[146] No one seems to have consulted the Dutch. The federal unions favoured by Hodges, the royal burghs and others required trading concessions from England whilst allowing no security for the enforcement of trade regulations in Scotland.[147] Such an arrangement would have been ideally suited to Scottish traders on the fringe of the law or beyond it. But federal union, apart from such economic objections, had no bearing on England's political problems and she had no intention of tolerating any such arrangement.

Amongst the numerous and for the most part ill-qualified commentators on the Scottish economy one man stood at this time in a class by himself, not because his conclusions were sounder but because he took pains to investigate. This was John Spreull, a Glasgow merchant, who when he wrote was not concerned with union, although what he had to say became relevant to it. His significance lies in that, writing during 1705 with Scotland threatened by the alien act, he attempted a detailed and reasonably dispassionate appraisal of Scotland's economic position. He concerned himself particularly with her English trade to discover whether the kingdom could withstand such sanctions as might be imposed. His conclusions were largely erroneous, but his detachment and industry were remarkable. Naturally he had to rely on such figures as were available and for the rest, like everyone else, he ventured on speculation. But, having embarked on a method he thought correct, he did not shrink if it led to a conclusion not generally .accepted at the time. For instance, his calculations led him to believe that Scotland's trade balance with England was unfavourable, a conclusion which even most anti-unionists could not bring themselves to accept although proof would have delighted them. It was certainly incorrect. Instead of merely concluding on this basis that Scotland would therefore be better off without the English trade, *quod erat demonstrandum*, he set himself to work out carefully how Scotland could produce a favourable trade balance if she should be forced out of the English market. No novel solutions were forthcoming, which is not remarkable, since there were none. Spreull's remedies were the usual ones of exploiting Scottish produce for export and avoiding certain imports. Unlike most such suggestions his were precise, detailed and, not infrequently, quaint: nobles raising horses instead of importing them and the development of the wig trade so that the finished product could be exported instead of human hair. He analysed Scottish produce in relation to imports from various countries. The resulting tables led him to suggest how these products could be employed to create a favourable trade balance with each trading area. His eventual conclusion was that Scotland could remain excluded from English trade and enjoy a favourable balance—an extremely over optimistic appraisal which assumed more regulation and self-restraint than was possible. Spreull was honest in acknowledging the extent of Scottish trade to areas within the navigation system, which must have been unwelcome to anti-unionists. The shifts to which he was driven in suggesting how to counterbalance this trade indicate in themselves how damaging to Scotland the alien act would have been. So, ironically, his work, as distinct from his conclusions, tended to support the unionist rather than the anti-unionist case, though no one seemed to realise it.[148] Much of Spreull's importance lies in his value as a yardstick against which to measure all other contributions, both unionist and opposition, on the subject. As a merchant who had taken the trouble to analyse the information available to him, he represented the best informed opinion of the time. It led him into some gross errors and a few unpalatable truths, but by comparison other writers appear even more clearly as the mere traders in guesswork and wishful thinking that they were.

From such literature two points seem to emerge. First of all, although most of the writing was propaganda it gives some guide to Scottish priorities: religion, sovereignty and trade in that order. Secondly, the economic objections were only a part of the case against union and for the most part cursory and even vague. Scepticism about future prosperity within a union was amply justified but elaborations of the theme veered between speculative fancy and brusque assertion, though the substance was much the same. The debate was comparable with a wrangle in a public bar, owing less to informed argument than to *a priori* commitment.

7 *Unionist propaganda*

What of the propaganda arguments for the union as distinct from the real reasons? Since trade was one of the few ostensible motives which could be openly avowed by the English and Scottish courts it was more prominent than in anti-unionist writing, where it seemed to be introduced merely to undermine the official argument. But nevertheless, significant emphasis was laid, particularly by Scotsmen outside Queensberry's orbit, on some of the political benefits to be expected from union. Just as anti-unionists sensed the fears latent amongst Scotsmen and blatantly appealed to them, some unionists perceived grievances for which the treaty could be represented as a remedy.

Though not a member of the Scottish parliament in 1700, William Seton was going through his country party phase, emerging only when made collector of the bishops' rents in 1705. In 1700 he published anonymously a work intended to be of some significance: *The Interest of Scotland In Three Essays* ... Notwithstanding its pretentious and philosophical tone it was a work of propaganda. In the third essay, 'Of the present state of Scotland', he took up a firm country position, denouncing the entire religious and political structure and representing union as a remedy for Scotland's political grievances. Presbyterian clergy were mean of birth and opinionated, disputing endlessly over trivialities. The court comprised for the most part time-servers and such as were consumed by greed. He did concede that some countrymen, too, were selfishly motivated but they nevertheless served a good purpose as watchdogs of rights and liberties. According to Seton, the rottenness in the state sprang from 'this loose and irregular tie of crowns'. An end could be put to the power of Scottish courtiers

only by a union which would be a blow struck for the Scottish
opposition. By 1706, having meanwhile become a courtier, Seton was
steering clear of the political aspects of union and making trade benefits
the central plank of his unionist argument. But his earlier theme of the
evils arising from the separate parliaments still ran strongly throughout
one, perhaps subterranean, stream of unionist propaganda emanating
from anti-Queensberry elements of the court party. During the 1702
negotiations the point was made by Fairfax. A union, in his opinion,
would greatly reduce the power of the Scottish nobility, which would be
no loss and entirely for the good of the kingdom.[149]

The political benefits of union were one of Cromartie's favourite
themes. He was a strong theoretical supporter of union and also in
practice to an extent which did him credit, his flesh being weak. His
support was restricted to an incorporating union; he had no use for
federal schemes, as politically impracticable. In so far as he attached
importance to trade it was not necessarily Scottish trade he had in
mind but that of the whole united kingdom, which he visualised as a
concentration of power and wealth large enough to excite wonder and
admiration. On the threshold of the 1702 negotiations he had
supported union in his anonymous *Parainesis Pacifica; Or, A Persuasive To
The Union Of Britain.*[150] At the time he was engaged in his struggle with
Queensberry over the composition of the Scottish ministry[151] and in his
pamphlet he stressed the probability that union would end internal
strife and prevent factions in each kingdom interacting with each other
to debilitate the power of the monarchy, so liberating the energies of a
united kingdom. When the final union was negotiated he again took up
the theme of factions, particularly those in Scotland joining with
English parties to gain advantage over their rivals, a danger which only
union could prevent.[152] Both in 1702 and 1706 he was really criticising
Queensberry's hold on Scottish politics but perhaps it was too much to
expect him to say so. At least it was as specific as Cromartie ever
allowed himself to be. And he was, of course, overlooking his own
considerable part in such faction struggles. He was right nevertheless
and coming as close as he dared to the real reasons for union.
Spottiswoode agreed. A separate parliament led to the dominant
faction's monopolising office, which a union would prevent.[153] As yet
another author put it, 'Great men, then, dare not oppress mean men,
nor one faction oppress another'.[154] Thomas Spence advocated holding
up the treaty, if necessary, until various wrongs were remedied.
Whatever ulterior motive he might have had the wrongs are significant:

the power of the Scottish secretaries, their tendency to curry favour with the English and the appointment of lords of session on political recommendation, which inevitably bore out the old Scottish maxim: 'Show me the man, I'll show you the law . . .'[155]

Such echoes of protest against what Roxburgh called the 'constant oppression of a bad ministry, from generation to generation . . .'[156] were appeals to a sense of grievance within the political nation and aimed most probably at countrymen impervious to other arguments but who might respond to the prospect of toppling Queensberry. They did not respond, as it happened, but the attempt was worth making. The same theme was evident in pro-Hanoverian writings opposed to separation or limitations. According to one pamphleteer, limitations could do nothing but harm, since '. . . seven or eight great families will not only appropriate to themselves the council of state, but direct also the parliament as they ever did, when the king was a minor, or facile, or not seconded by a competent number of the great families . . .'[157] Such comment, though probably relished in the deeper recesses of the English court, was not likely to receive a welcome from Queensberry and the Dalrymples.

Queensberry and most of the Scottish court party were accepting their task by virtue of an English initiative, following the axiom that, whether the task allotted was congenial or not, it was better to undertake it and remain in office than to go out. In general they proceeded on lines decreed in London, planning meanwhile for the future and hoping to snatch as much as they could out of passing the union. In these circumstances the only two propaganda themes on which the Scottish court party could agree were ridicule of anti-unionist fears and an emphasis on the trade benefits union would allegedly bring.

It was in ridicule that Defoe purported to sum up mercantile opposition to the union:

> . . . The merchants are the next on the stage,
> The enchantment has circled them in;
> For fear they in wealth should engage,
> They resolve they'll never begin;
> The burghs are afraid
> They shall have too much trade,
> And the Nation to plenty be safely betrayed,
> So they gravely address, that to keep them secure,
> As you find them, you leave them, both foolish and poor . . .[158]

Defoe also administered rough treatment to particular individuals, as Annandale, who found his real motive for opposing union more starkly exposed than he could have cared for.[159]

The official union argument was presented by Arbuthnot, pamphleteering in the style of a sermon on the text 'Better is he that laboureth and aboundeth in all things, than he that boasteth himself and wanteth bread' (Eccles. x, 27). The importance of the trade concessions was brought squarely into the debate. He dismissed opposition to union as being compounded of pride, poverty and idleness. Nor had he any time for talk of federal unions, which, as far as he could see, seemed to mean that the English should give away trading concessions to the Scots if they settled the succession. Such an agreement was not only unreasonable but many of those who claimed to support it neither wanted nor expected it. They were merely being obstructive.[160]

But when the unionist argument became specific most of its propagandists proved to be no better informed than the opposition, their writing tinged by wild, speculative optimism. Living in a century exposed to 'hard selling' techniques it is difficult for us not to applaud the sales resistance of those who regarded as suspect the economic claims for union, however impracticable their own suggestions. But trying to overcome this scepticism was seen by unionist writers as one of their main tasks. A favourite tactic was a call to abandon selfish interests for the greater good of the whole island, which would derive immeasurable economic benefits from union. Such views were usually advanced in the guise of concern for Scottish welfare. It was of course true that a union would, in the absence of complete disaster, almost certainly save some branches of Scottish trade from ruin. But there was nothing in union to prevent Scotland's becoming even less flourishing as part of a greater unit than as an independent kingdom, a possibility overlooked by unionists presumably as salesman's licence. The intent to sell regardless of quality is clear from the change of direction in unionist propaganda between 1702 and 1706. Arguments in 1702 were largely aimed at the English merchant community, the most probable field of resistance to a union whose advantages were political. Cromartie, although insisting, for the benefit of countrymen and cavaliers, that union would break the hold of a single court interest, went out of his way to assure English merchants that they could not suffer through concessions to Scottish traders.[161] Others emphasised, fairly blatantly, how the incorporation of Scotland would benefit, as they put it, the whole island: providing England with a working population—the term 'sweated labour' was not then current—whilst Scottish fisheries would be a nursery of seamen for the Royal Navy. Inconsequential references to a possible rise in Scottish land values were made and to the profitability of Scottish fisheries after union, but the main argument was undoubtedly based on Scotland's potential contribution to the economy of a united kingdom.[162] And it is clear that 'united kingdom' was by some identified with England.

The shape of the problem was modified by the Scottish parliaments of 1703 and 1704, in consequence of which unionist propaganda began to be directed at Scottish rather than English opinion. The boldest statements aimed at Scotland were made by Seton of Pitmedden, who continued in favour of union although changing his reasons. Writing anonymously and unashamedly as one who had no part in public affairs, he stated in its extreme form the case for equating union with prosperity. If the whole united kingdom benefited, the argument ran, so must all the parts, and Scotland would necessarily have her share. The alternative did not bear contemplation: '. . . either union with peace and plenty, or disunion with slavery and poverty . . .' [163]

Speaking as a courtier on the first article of the treaty in the union parliament he was rather more effective.[164] To have envisaged some kind of Eldorado in the parliament house would have exposed him to ridicule. He chose instead to match against the anti-unionists' pessimism over the treaty his own despondency over Scotland's fate in separation. Prosperity, he said, required, in the first place, money to set up trade and then force to protect it. Scotland had neither. Nor could this situation be remedied unless she joined with a more powerful nation able to give her both a share of its own trade and the necessary protection. As a separate kingdom Scotland could expect no help in a competitive world and her trade would be inconsiderable. This was true. Most historians would unhesitatingly endorse such a statement and perhaps for this reason it has come to be taken as evidence that its truth was apparent at the time. But many Scots declined to accept its validity. It is not necessary to suppose that Seton was more clear-sighted than anyone else. For him, as for others, the problems had been political until his appointment as collector of the bishops' rents. He was engaged in a debating tactic rather than an economic analysis.

There was more than a little for unionists to explain away. It was apparent that some Scotsmen would lose by the union, either through strong English competition or through increased taxation.

Pamphleteers had to accept that some of their readers would be at least as perceptive, so some admissions had to be made. Techniques differed. Some writers conceded that whole trades might suffer, others reduced it to a merchant or two, but all resorted to appeals in the name of the general good against mere individual interest[165] and consequently unionist writers seemed oddly defensive. They had frequently to abandon their intended priority of trade to combat arguments arising from religion, law or minor details of taxation. There was a big difference between Seton's vision and the tax on twopenny ale which became a major issue. Paterson, having settled down as a court agent and propagandist, tried to refute criticism of the treaty. He deplored the outcry from selfish vested interests and the narrow vision of individual merchants who were, according to him, the greatest obstacle to national prosperity. His propaganda tactic was to regard union as not only a self-evident blessing but as the norm, properly achieved under the interregnum although defeated in 1603, 1667–1670 and in 1689 by scheming courtiers and vested interests. From this position he could concentrate on explaining away possible difficulties: heavier taxation, the draining away of specie to England and the like. He clearly regarded the good of the whole island as his trump card but he, like other unionists, found himself driven to concentrate on those topics which seemed to obsess the opposition: '. . . nothing less than a complete union can effectually secure the religion, laws, liberties, trade, and in a word the peace and happiness of this island . . .'[166] Significantly he had to turn away from the merchants to those whose interests were other than commercial.

Particular criticisms of the treaty had to be refuted. Scots were alarmed at the prospect of having to pay taxes at the English rate. At some point most anti-unionist writers professed themselves apprehensive of the crushing weight of taxation about to descend on Scotland. Court pamphleteers tried to play down this aspect of the treaty. James Donaldson thought the probable size of the increase had been greatly exaggerated. Much of the Scots' pre-union taxation arose from trade with England, on which duties would cease to be paid. For the rest, he claimed, any increase could be controlled by the discouragement, or even prohibition, of foreign imports.[167] Others were confident that the extra taxes would be spent in Scotland for the upkeep of forts and garrisons, thereby reducing the cess.[168] Both arguments were misleading if not dishonest. After the union, trade regulation was to rest with a British parliament, quite beyond unilateral action by

Scotland. The cess was fixed by the treaty itself, being related to the English land tax. Money spent on forts and garrisons was irrelevant.

No financial provision of the treaty attracted more criticism than the equivalent arrangements,[169] especially the priorities of its distribution. Critics usually agreed with Lockhart:[170] the equivalent was a confidence trick by which England gave Scotland back her own money as a gift to incline people towards union. The priorities, it was fully appreciated, were intended to satisfy the political nation: the men who wanted their salary arrears, the Africa Company shareholders, in fact 'to stop the mouths of those of considerable substance who are more particularly concerned there and generally to amuse the whole nation in removing the national prejudice on that account'. Instead, it was argued, compensation for recoinage should have a higher priority as affecting more and poorer people.[171] One cynic even made the bald statement that the equivalent was not even a bribe but merely the offer of one which the English had no need to pay once the union had been accepted.[172]

An attempt at an answer was made by John Clerk of Penicuik, well enough informed on the mechanics of the calculation, for which he was partly responsible. But he was unable to refute the criticisms altogether. Instead he attempted to undermine the whole basis on which the criticisms rested. He welcomed the increase in Scottish taxation, without which there would have been no claim to an equivalent at all, 'by which means we should want a fund or stock to trade with, and a communication of trade, in that case, would be like giving a man the property of a rich mine, who wants the materials and ability to dig it, for without a stock of money put in our hands, a communication of trade can be of very little use to us . . . If we had entered into an union with England at the late revolution, we could have had no pretence to entitle us to a sum of money per advance and so would have wanted means to carry on any valuable trade'.[173] This meant, presumably, that Scotland needed enough liquid capital to trade successfully and was borrowing from England a sum of money repayable in instalments through increased taxation. From this it followed that channelling the equivalent into the pockets of the political nation was highly desirable, these being the people most likely, as was Clerk himself, to invest in trade and industrial enterprise. To people liable for taxation and too poor to invest the proposition was not attractive. Compensation to Africa Company shareholders went unexplained and unjustified.[174] The topic was embarrassing and had to be avoided. Many of the issues raised were on delicate ground and union pamphleteers come often under suspicion of not being wholly convinced by their own arguments. On the whole it was easier not to argue at all but to rely on highly generalised and dubious assertions incapable of proof. For the rest, abusing the opposition seemed an effective way out and some pamphleteers manufactured abuse with relish and even dedication.[175]

Most aspects of the pro-union campaign are epitomised in the work of Defoe, the most prolific writer on the court side. His anonymous output was prodigious, especially if one takes into account his secret reports to Harley and the private business ventures which engaged his attention at the same time. There was one difference between Defoe and most others. Defoe could generalise as sweepingly as anyone but he was skilled at using the apparently precise and convincing detail which ultimately proves to be either untrue or so out of context as to be misleading. This created at the time exactly the impression he wanted. He liked to appear knowledgeable, some would say cocksure, on the subject of trade, although his apparent grasp of technicalities failed to protect him from his several business failures. Nevertheless these attributes have given Defoe's views on the union an undeserved authority. In 1706 he was a government agent, employed specifically to support the union in any way he could. He carried out the task zealously, but as merely another job, in the hope of immediate reward and a lucrative future in the Scottish customs. However, on the evidence of his writings, Defoe had as little idea as anyone else of the probable effects of union. It is possible that he did not greatly care either one way or the other. He directed his arguments to whatever group seemed in need of persuasion, dismissively countering any criticisms as they appeared. As a result his inconsistencies were frequent, which did not seem in the least to trouble him.

The first two parts of his *Essay At Removing National Prejudice Against A Union With Scotland*[176] were written in England, directed at an English readership and aiming to spread the belief that England would have the better of any bargain. Scotland could provide the 'inexhaustible treasure of men' England needed to man her fleets, handle her manufactures and inhabit her colonies.[177] There was no concept here of British as distinct from English interests. Some Englishmen feared that to give the Scots freedom of trade would reduce England's profits but Defoe reassured them: 'I make it appear that a freedom of trade is our advantage more than the Scots'. . .'[178] In woollen manufactures, for instance, the English could undersell the Scots any time they liked.[179] London would remain unchangeably the trading centre of the united kingdom. For the encouragement of high Church of England men who lacked enthusiasm for union he held out the hope of toleration for Scottish episcopalians.[180]

Once Harley had dispatched him to Scotland his arguments, being then directed at the Scots, had to be modified. He discounted any danger of Scotland's becoming depopulated. With the increase in the value of Scottish estates as a result of union—he gave no reason for this—it would be Scotland's own fault if people did not stay at home.[181] He referred to presbyterian fears, caused mostly by the machinations of English high churchmen who opposed union, yet presbyterianism would, he thought, be more secure after the union than before,[182] and he was firmly against giving episcopalians any more toleration than they already had.[183] To Scottish merchants afraid of English competition he offered comfort, assuring them that in many commodities the Scots could undersell the English. As an example he cited woollen manufactures. He conceded that England might have an advantage in fine woollen goods but this would change as soon as the Scots could import English wool.[184] Not, as he later told the Scots, that their wool was naturally coarse; bad husbandry was to blame. The Scots ruined the wool by treating it with grease and tar whilst it was on the sheep.[185] Subsequently his views on wool remained very flexible. Acknowledging at last that all Scottish woollens were dearer than those of English make and were likely to remain so, he drew the remarkable conclusion that since what they sold would be dearer than what they bought Scotland could only gain by this disparity.[186] Clearly anyone who relied on Defoe for guidance on the future of the Scottish woollen industry was being misled some, if not all, of the time.

On the whole it was less perilous for Defoe, as for everyone else, to concentrate on ridicule of the opposition. In his attack on Hodges's proposals for a federal union he turned the opposition's weapon of scepticism against one of their own writers. Hodges, he wrote, 'pretends in some places of his book, that by the providence of God, he has found out some wonderful expedient to make us happy, even though an union should not take: 'tis spoke very like a quack doctor on a stage, and for that reason will be much alike believed . . .'[187] When discovering an inconsistency or a factual error on the part of the opposition, Defoe was at his journalistic best. He laughed at talk of the sanctity of 'fundamental law' in relation to Scotland, where such laws

had been changed before without hesitation.[188] The unfortunate
Hodges was caught out asserting that members of the English
parliament had to take the test, an inaccuracy which gave Defoe some
enjoyment.[189] With criticisms of the equivalent he was unjustifiably
dismissive,[190] realising perhaps that it was ground not easily defended,
but his exposition of the law relating to twopenny ale after the union
was formidable,[191] so much so that he confused the issue with
technicalities. He was weighty in speculation—for it was no more—on
the burden of Scottish taxes after the union. If Scotland's trade
remained unchanged she would pay less rather than more, he
concluded, but if her trade increased then any resulting extra taxation
could hardly be looked upon as an imposition.[192]

Defoe had boundless energy and optimism, qualities at the disposal
of almost anyone who chose to employ him. It was not that he
completely lacked scruples, but he was able to control them if there was
even half a chance of showing a profit. But even Defoe, however
expansive he seemed in Edinburgh taverns and when acting as adviser
to the Scottish parliament's trade committee,[193] had spasms of caution
when called upon to be specific about the benefits of union. In fact,
despite all his apparent assurance, he, like other unionist writers, lost
the initiative, being driven to correcting what he claimed to be
misapprehensions about the union and doing little more than take up
points raised by opposition writers. Notably, for a man who claimed a
speciality in trading questions and whose original exposition of union
was almost entirely economic in character, much of his energy had
increasingly to be expended on other topics: fear about the safety of the
church, the loss of parliament, the alleged smallness of Scottish
representation at Westminster and the surrender of Scottish
sovereignty.[194] These objections were being raised in opposition
pamphlets but Defoe's concern indicates that they were also being
voiced in the Edinburgh streets. In his pamphlet of 1706, *The Rabbler
Convicted: Or A Friendly Advice to all Turbulent and Factious Persons, From one
of their own Number*, he affected to write as a reformed street
demonstrator who in the past had rampaged against union in the name
of 'Crown, sovereignty and independency'. Defoe had had plenty of
opportunity to know what Scottish crowds were shouting about and he
was writing for people who also knew. Trade was scarcely mentioned.

Under pressure of opposition propaganda, Defoe was much exercised
over whether parliament had the right to pass a union in the teeth of
national opposition. He moved through a whole spectrum of

inconsistencies. Perhaps they amounted to no more than one would expect from a journalist trying to cope at speed from day to day with other people's quibbles about which he had no strong feelings. And he was writing anonymously, which must have made a difference. Nevertheless they were inconsistencies, reinforcing the idea of Defoe as a mere hack writer, better than most but not different in kind. Parliament could not, he said, override the rights of the people, although it could determine how those rights should be exercised.[195] But in relation to the Glasgow riots the wishes of the majority assumed more importance. He told the demonstrators they had no right to act against the government unless they comprised a majority of the kingdom,[196] as distinct, presumably, from parliament and with some ingenuity attempted to prove that a majority in the nation was unionist, despite appearances to the contrary. This arithmetical rather than statistical exercise involved comparing the number of people who signed anti-union addresses with the number of freeholders who voted for unionist members of parliament.[197] The fact was that Defoe did not care whether there was a majority in the country for union or not. When Belhaven suggested that Queensberry was acting in defiance of the national will, his retort was that if this were so the duke was doing Scotland a good service by making her rich despite herself.[198] And although earlier he had taken the addresses seriously enough to count the signatures he deplored the outcry by 'poor ignorant people' against union and supposed that '. . . if they have but patience, I doubt not, but like some of their brethren in England, they will be made happy against their wills'.[199]

Defoe's general attitude was one of incredulity that anyone should doubt the benefits of union to Scottish trade, although his arguments were at least as conjectural as those of the opposition. Like other unionists he encouraged illusions of the potential wealth of the Scottish fisheries; he tried to induce visions of a massive boom in Scottish shipbuilding and his opinions on the Scottish woollen industry, although flexible, were always authoritative.[200] However, a curious restraint characterised his estimate of the prospects of the plantation trade. In his *Fourth Essay* he maintained that England had no closed trades, since the Scots could buy East India or any other stock just as well as the English, but later he qualified this. The Scots, he came to assert, could hardly expect to share the profits of the English joint stock companies on equal terms, since this would give them the fruits of English blood and treasure. Perhaps he had to take into account that the East India trade was still a sensitive topic in English politics. There remained the Baltic trade to be exploited, and as the best field of Scottish expansion he fanced the West Indies but neglected to explain why.[201]

Assuming the identity of a group of imaginery Scottish merchants living in England, he found much of a general character to say in favour of union.[202] The English court and the junto had agreed to the Scottish parliament's demand for broader concessions on certain articles of union—the 'explanations', as they were euphemistically called.[203] Consequently Defoe supported the 'explanations' in principle but had no patience with the general clamour against higher taxes. He castigated the Scottish trading community: '. . . you will not have the trade for fear of the customs; you will not catch fish for fear you wet your feet . . .' He dispensed the usual advice for limiting the customs burden which previously he had denied would exist:[204] '. . . use only things of necessity and things for encouraging manufactures and get drawbacks for your tobacco, your fish, your corn, and your sugar, etc. . . .' Having ridiculed the opposition and warned them of the consequences of rejecting union he then held out the usual inducements, though, in view of the reservations he had expressed elsewhere, somewhat indiscriminately: the plantations, the Guinea trade, encouragement for manufactures and exports to England herself.[205]

Defoe's best-founded argument was the importance of the English trade to Scotland, though he overstated even this. Any question of separation was academic, he said, since Scotland could not do without English trade. Where else would she dispose of her cattle and linen?[206] He drew up a conjectural and highly inflated post-union trade balance between England and Scotland and concluded that if Scotland did not achieve a favourable balance of over £300,000 per annum it would be her own fault. Nor would this mean, he hastened to add for the sake of his own countrymen, that England would lose, since the whole island would be gaining.[207]

Defoe's contribution to the union debate can be summed up in only one way: he was an English agent saying what he was paid to say. He brought to the controversy little or no relevant specialised knowledge, merely energy and the illusory impression that the bulk of trading opinion favoured union. At the same time he made what profit he could on the side by publishing fulsome praise of Scotland and its government, disclaiming, as a private visitor, all knowledge of the dispute about union. However, this professed ignorance did not hinder his writing verse panegyrics on the subject.[208] Finally, in 1709, his work of 'instant history' appeared, the *History of the Union of Great Britain*, which has probably misled as many readers as Bismarck's *Reflections and Reminiscences*.[209]

But the whole debate was really no more than a propaganda duel which was not going to settle anything. In the last resort the fate of the union would not be decided by the literature, but by votes in the Scottish parliament, and of these the majority was predictable.

Notes

[1] Most of the following account of Scotland's economic condition is based on Smout, *Scottish Trade*.

[2] *Ib.*, 244. See also Sir Robert Sibbald's unfinished 'Discourses Anent the improvements may be made in Scotland for advancing the wealth of the kingdom' (NLS, MSS 33. 5. 16)

[3] Smout, *Scottish Trade*, chap. xi. Ferguson, *Scotland's Relations*, 152–7, contends that the effect of the navigation act on the Scottish economy was greater than Smout allows. He adds another Scottish grievance, viz., that after the restoration English trade regulation was in the hands of parliament and not within the royal prerogative. This must have created tensions, though not necessarily economic ones. There were certainly complaints of economic decline but much depends on the significance one chooses to attach to them. Professor Smout has found no evidence of economic hardship sustained by merchants, though obviously there is such a thing as relative hardship—they could have been prosperous though not as prosperous as they had been. However, the Scots had no desire for free trade and it is quite possible to conclude that they were merely setting up a wail to gain advantages in the English trade, e.g. free trade in salt, whilst protecting Scotland against imports. What can be interpreted as evidence for the resilience of Scottish trade appears in Donald Woodward, 'Anglo-Scottish trade and English commercial policy during the 1660s', *SHR*, lvi (1977) and in the same writer's 'A comparative study of the Irish and Scottish livestock trades in the seventeenth century' in L. M. Cullen and T. C. Smout, eds., *Comparative Aspects of Scottish and Irish Social History, 1600–1900* (Edinburgh, 1977).

[4] Scott, *Joint-Stock Companies*, i, 282.

[5] Smout, *Scottish Trade*, 244.

[6] *Ib.*, 245.

[7] See above, p. 32.

[8] See above, pp. 59, 205.

[9] Smout, *Scottish Trade*, 244–8.

[10] *Ib.*, 125–8, 248–9.

[11] See, e.g., *Marchmont Papers*, iii, Polwarth to Tullibardine, 4 Mar. 1697.

[12] Smout, *Scottish Trade*, 250–3; Scott, *Joint-Stock Companies*, i, 371; T. C. Smout, ed., Sir John Clerk's 'Observations on the present circumstances of Scotland, 1730,' in *Miscellany of the Scottish History Society*, x (1965), 190–1 and n. 1; F. R. Hart, *The Disaster of Darien* (London, 1930); G. P. Insh, *The Company of Scotland trading to Africa and the Indies* (London, 1932); John Prebble, *The Darien Disaster* (London, 1968).

[13] Scott, *Joint-Stock Companies*, i, 361.

[14] *Ib.*, 356.

[15] Smout, *Scottish Trade*, 254–5.

[16] *Ib.*, 249–50; Scott, *Joint-Stock Companies*, i, 372–3.

[17] Smout, *Scottish Trade*, 212–15.

[18] *Ib.*, 232–4.

[19] *Ib.*, 225–9.

[20] *Seafield Corresp.*, 414–16, 25 Jun. 1705.

[21] For the measures proposed for the protection of wool growers such as Queensberry, see Buccleuch (Drum.), Union, i, [pres. Dalrymple] to [Queensberry], 13 May [1699]; *ib.*, Queensberry Letters, xiv, [same] to [same], 25 May 1699. See also Smout, *Scottish Trade*, 215–17.

[22] *Ib.*, 234–6.

[23] *Ib.*, 219–24, 229–31.

[24] *Ib.*, 255 and n. 67.

[25] *Ib.*, 238.

[26] See below, p. 206 *et seq.*

[27] See above, pp. 3–4.

[28] Quoted, Lythe, 206.

[29] *Ib.*, 200–10.

[30] Keith, *Commercial Relations*, chap. iii.

[31] See above, pp. 197–8, and Keith, *Commercial Relations*, 89–91.

[32] Lee, *Cabal*, 44.

[33] See, e.g., *Essay Upon the Union Showing, That the Subjects Of Both Nations Have been, by the Union of the Two Crowns, justly Intitled to all manner of Privileges ...* (Edinburgh, 1706) and [Ridpath], *The case of Scotsmen residing in England ...* (Edinburgh, 1703).

[34] Paterson's statement that the judgement in Colvill's case was intended to apply only to Scots resident or owning land in England seems dubious: Paterson, *Works*, iii, 7. One of Atholl's complaints in the parliament of 1704 was of the injuries done to the Scots as *post nati*: SRO, GD 124, Box 16, 'An Account of what past in the Parliament of Scotland, 1704', 5, 17 Jul. [1704]. Keith, *Commercial Relations*, 138–40.

[35] See below, p. 204.

[36] Keith, *Cromartie Relations*, 91, 156–7.

[37] Lee, *Cabal*, 44 *et seq.*

[38] *Ib.*, 50.

[39] Quoted *ib.*, 51. The previous year Tweeddale had told Lauderdale: '... This business of trade betwixt the kingdoms will, I hope, fairly introduce the consideration of an union ...' (BL, Add. MSS 23128, 56, 21 Sep. [16]67. *Ib.*,

76, 28 Sep. [16]67, gives a similar impression).

40 Burnet, *History*, i, 512–13. See *ib.*, Dartmouth's note for the political motive. See Riley, *King William and the Scottish Politicians,* chap. 3.

41 Then Polwarth.

42 *Marchmont Papers*, iii, to Ogilvy, 27 May 1696.

43 Then lord James Murray.

44 NUL, Portland collection, PwA 956a, 21 Jul. 1696.

45 *Carstares S.P.*, 312–13, to Carstares, 29 Jun. 1697.

46 Ib., 344–6, Ogilvy to Carstares, 21 Sep. 1697; *ib.*, 347–9, same to same, 28 Sep. 1697; *ib.*, 356–8, same to same, 19 Oct. 1697; *ib.*, 616, same to same, 14 Aug. 1700; *ib.*, 699, same to same, 22 Jul. 1701; *ib.*, 705, same to same, 31 Jul. 1701; *ib.*, 709, A. Cunningham to same, 22 Aug. 1701; *ib.*, 710, same to same, 26 Aug. 1701; NLS, MS 7028, 13, Tweeddale to Johnston, 1 Feb. 1694; *ib.*, 7104, H[amilton] to [Tweeddale], 22 [Sep.] 1701; Buccleuch (Drum.), Queensberry Letters, xvi, Seafield to [Queensberry], 30 Aug. 1701; *HMCR Laing MSS*, ii, 119–23, same to Godolphin, 9 Sep. 1705.

47 See above, p. 142, for example.

48 Smout, *Scottish Trade*, 253.

49 See Riley, *King William and the Scottish Politicians*, chap. 4.

50 NLS, MS 7027, 49, [1693].

51 *Ib.*, 7028, 13, Tweeddale to Johnston, 1 Feb. 1694.

52 The saga of the new admiralty board can be followed in *ib.*, 7028, 33v., 67, 76v., 80v., 82, 94, 104v., 115v., 137, 144; *ib.*, 7029, 15, 64v.; Fraser, *Cromartie*, i, Lennox to Cromartie, 1 Jun. 1694.

53 See above, pp. 8–10.

54 See Riley, *op. cit.*, chap. 4.

55 Scott, *Joint-Stock Companies*, ii, 209.

56 Then Sir James Ogilvy.

57 NLS MS 7029, Tweeddale's letters at 112, 92v., 95, 121, 132v., 143v., 147 and 7030, 2, 6v.; *Carstares S.P.*, 270, Ogilvy to Carstares, 10 Dec. 1695.

58 NLS, MS 7030, 20, [Tweeddale] to Johnston, 18 Jan. 1696.

59 Scott, *Joint-Stock Companies*, ii, 213, 321–5. For the struggle between the English companies: *ib.*, ii, 128–79. For the 'new company': *ib.*, 179–206. For the Darien Company: *ib.*, 207–27.

60 R. M. Lees, 'Parliament and the proposal for a Council of Trade, 1695–6', *EHR*, liv (1939), 38–66; I. F. Burton *et al.*, 'Political parties in the reigns of William III and Anne: the evidence of division lists', *BIHR*, Special Supplement No. 7 (1968), 4–7; BL, Add. MSS 17677PP, 463 and v., L'Hermitage to the States General, 13/23 Dec. 1695.

61 Keith, *Commercial Relations*, 117–28, 172–4; Smout, *Scottish Trade*, 249–50; see also Jacob M. Price, 'The rise of Glasgow in the Chesapeake tobacco trade, 1707–1775', in *Studies in Scottish Business History*, ed. Peter L. Payne (London, 1967), 302 n. 17 (314).

62 See Riley, *op. cit.*, chap. 4.

63 NLS, MS 7029, 123v., [Tweeddale] to king, 28 Nov. 1695; *ib.*, 7018, 36, A.

Johnston to [Tweeddale], 12 Sep. [16]95; *The Darien Papers: Being A Selection Of Original Letters and Official Documents Relating To The Establishment Of A Colony At Darien* . . . ed. J. H. Burton (Bannatyne Club, 1849), 1, Paterson to Chiesly, 4 Jul. 1695; *ib*., 2–3, same to same, 9 Jul. 1695; *ib*., 6, same to same, 3 Sep. 1695.

⁶⁴ NLS, MS 7029, 139, [Tweeddale] to Johnston, 19 Dec. 1695; *ib*., 140v., [same] to king, 20 Dec. 1695. Oddly enough, the intention had been openly expressed to the Scottish parliament by Tweeddale in his address (*APS*, ix, App., 95, 9 May 1695). Perhaps the need for secrecy arose only when the general statement had become more specific in an act of parliament.

⁶⁵ Keith, *Commercial Relations*, 128–38.

⁶⁶ NLS, MS 7029, 121, [Tweeddale] to Johnston, 27 Nov. 1695.

⁶⁷ See below, p. 278.

⁶⁸ NLS, MS 7030, 12v., [Tweeddale] to Yester, 9 Jan. 1696.

⁶⁹ *Ib*., 68v., [same] to same, 28 Feb. 1696.

⁷⁰ *Carstares S.P.*, 312–13, Queensberry to Carstares, 29 Jun. 1697.

⁷¹ *Ib*., 314–15, Ogilvy to Carstares, 1 Jul. 1697.

⁷² *Ib*., 511, Marchmont to Carstares, 25 Nov. 1699; *Marchmont Papers*, iii, 148, Marchmont to Tullibardine, 8 Jan. 1698; *ib*., 189, same to Seafield, 11 Nov. 1699.

⁷³ See above, p. 210.

⁷⁴ E.g. *Marchmont Papers*, iii, 184, Marchmont to Seafield, 24 Oct. 1699.

⁷⁵ *Carstares S.P.*, 511, same to Carstares, 25 Nov. 1699.

⁷⁶ *Marchmont Papers*, iii, 181, same to king, 24 Oct. 1699.

⁷⁷ Buccleuch (Drum.), Church and State, [Queensberry] to [   ], copy, [Sep. 1705].

⁷⁸ Buccleuch (Drum.), Seven Letters, [Philiphaugh] to [Queensberry], 5 Aug. 1701. See above, p. 37.

⁷⁹ See above, p. 73 *et seq*.

⁸⁰ See below, p. 273 *et seq*.

⁸¹ See below, chap. vii, *passim*.

⁸² *Jerviswood*, 137, Roxburgh to Baillie, 28 Nov. 1705.

⁸³ See below, App. A.

⁸⁴ *HMCR Mar and Kellie MSS*, i, 243, Stair to Mar, 3 Jan. 1706.

⁸⁵ See below, chap. vii and App. A for the divisions on the union.

⁸⁶ *HMCR Mar and Kellie MSS*, i, 243, Stair to Mar, 3 Jan. 1706.

⁸⁷ See below, p. 273 *et seq*.

⁸⁸ SRO, GD 220, S, 9 Mar. 1706.

⁸⁹ *HMCR Mar and Kellie MSS*, i, 267, 22 Jun. 1706.

⁹⁰ See below, chap. vii and App. A.

⁹¹ *Jerviswood*, 176, Johnston to Baillie, 14 Dec. 1706.

⁹² *An Answer To Some Queries, &C, Relative To The Union In A Conference Betwixt A Coffee-Master And A Country Farmer* (1706).

⁹³ Fraser, *Melvilles*, ii, 194–7, Mar to Leven, 22 Feb. 1705/6; SRO, GD 18, Box 119, 3131, J. Clerk to his father, 14 Dec. [1705]; *Marchmont Papers*, III, 291, Marchmont to Wharton, 29 Dec. 1705; *Carstares S.P.*, 740, Nairn to Carstares,

[Nov./Dec. 1705].

94 *Jerviswood*, 145, Baillie to Roxburgh, 3 Jan. 1705/6.

95 NLS, MS 1033, 12, Orkney to [Selkirk or Ruglen], 11 Jan. 1705/6.

96 Printed in Paterson, *Works*, i. Cf. the mss. in Buccleuch (Drum.), Church and State, 'Heads of things fit to be granted and done in the ensuing session of parliament' [1700].

97 *Carstares S.P.*, 655, J. Stewart to Carstares, 21 Sep. 1700; *ib.*, 584, Queensberry to same, Aug. 1700. See also *ib.*, 633, 3 Sep. 1700; *ib.*, 645, 14 Sep. 1700.

98 See below, pp. 233–4, 237.

99 *A Letter From One Of The Country Party To His Friend Of The Court Party* (Mar. 1704).

100 The whole question is discussed in W. Ferguson, 'Imperial crowns: a neglected facet of the background to the Treaty of Union of 1707', *SHR*, liii (1975). See also W. S. Mackechnie, 'The constitutional necessity for the union of 1707', *ib.*, v (1908); W. Atwood, *The Superiority and Direct Dominion of the Imperial Crown and Kingdom of England over the Crown and Kingdom of Scotland* (London, 1704); J. Anderson, *An Historical Essay showing that the Crown and Kingdom of Scotland is Imperial and Independent Wherein the Gross Mistakes of a late book . . . are exposed* (Edinburgh, 1705).

101 [Cromartie], *A Letter to a Member of Parliament Upon the 19th Article of the Treaty of Union between the two kingdoms of Scotland and England* (4 Dec. 1706).

102 *Sir George M'Kenzie's Arguments Against An incorporating Union Particularly Considered As they are in his Observations upon James vi Parl. 17* (Edinburgh, 1706).

103 *An Account of the Burning of the Articles of the Union at Dumfries* (20 Nov. 1706); *The Scotch Echo to the English Legion: Or the Union in Danger . . .* (1707), printed in *Somers Tracts*, xii.

104 3 Mar. 1607. Reprinted 1706 (?).

105 [A. Bruce], *A Discourse of a Cavalier Gentleman On The Divine and Humane Laws; with respect to the Succession. By Don A.B.* (1706).

106 *To the Loyal and Religious Hearts in Parliament . . .* (1706).

107 *Several Reasons Why the Succession Ought not to be Declared by This Parliament, And All Objections to the contrary answered . . .* (1704).

108 *The Act of Security is the only Rational Method of procuring Scotland a happy Constitution, free from the Illegal Invasion of its Liberties.*

109 *Remarks upon a late Dangerous Pamphlet Intitled The Reducing of Scotland by Arms . . .* (London, 1705).

110 [P. Abercromby], *The Advantages of the Act of Security . . .* (1706) and *A Reply To the Authors of the Advantages of Scotland By An Incorporate Union And Of The Fifth Essay . . .* (1707).

111 *The Humble Representation and Petition of the Commission of the General Assembly of this National Church* [1706].

112 E. Calamy, *The Great Danger of Covenant-Breaking &C Being The Substance of a Sermon Preached January 14, 1645 . . .* (reprinted 1706).

113 *Queries To the Presbyterian Noblemen and Gentlemen, Barons, Burgesses and*

Commoners in Scotland, who are for the Scheme of an Incorporating Union with England . . . [1706].

¹¹⁴ *A sermon preached before his Grace James Duke of Queensberry, Her Majesty's high Commissioner . . . upon the 27 October 1706. By Mr John Logan Minster of the Gospel at Alloa* (1706).

¹¹⁵ *That Part of a late Book Which Relates to a General Fast and Humiliation* [?1706].

¹¹⁶ E.g. *The Humble Address of the Presbytery of Lanark* [1706], and the like from the presbyteries of Dumblane and Hamilton.

¹¹⁷ *A Letter From The Commission of the General Assembly To The Presbytery of Hamilton* . . . [1706].

¹¹⁸ *A Sermon Preached before his Grace, David, Earl of Glasgow, Her Majesty's High Commissioner, and the General Assembly . . . on the 8th day of April 1707* (1707).

¹¹⁹ *Smoaking Flax Unquenchable; Where the Union Betwixt the two Kingdoms is Dissected, Anatomised, Confuted and Annuled* [sic] . . . (1706).

¹²⁰ *The Humble Address of a Considerable Body of People in the South and Western Shires* (12 Nov. 1706).

¹²¹ E.g. *The Grounds of the Present Danger of the Church of Scotland* (Jan. 1707) and *A Phenix or The Solemn League and Covenant* . . . (reprinted, 1707).

¹²² [J. Webster], *Lawful Prejudices against an Incorporating Union with England* . . . (Edinburgh, 1707), *The Author of the Lawful Prejudices . . . Defended* (Edinburgh, 1707), and *A Second Defence of the Lawful Prejudices* . . . (1707); [Rev. W. Adams], *A Letter From The Country Containing Some Remarks Concerning the National Covenant* . . . (Edinburgh, 1707) and *A Second Letter From The Country In Vindication Of the former* . . . (10 Apr. 1707).

¹²³ [D. Defoe], *The Dissenters in England vindicated from some Reflections in a late Pamphlet* . . . [1707].

¹²⁴ *Counter Queries to the Queries burnt at the Cross of Edinburgh December 17, 1706* . . . (1706).

¹²⁵ *Lawful Prejudices* . . .

¹²⁶ London, 1705.

¹²⁷ *Unio Politico-Poetico-Joco-Seria . . . By the author of Tripatriarchicon* (revised, Edinburgh, 1706).

¹²⁸ *A Draught For A National Church Accommodation* . . . (London, 1705).

¹²⁹ See below, p. 215 *et seq.*

¹³⁰ E.g. *The Circumstances of Scotland Considered, With Respect to the present Scarcity of Money* . . . [1705].

¹³¹ E.g. [D. Black], *Essay Upon Industry and Trade* . . . (Edinburgh, 1706).

¹³² *An Account of a Conversation Concerning a Right Regulation of Governments For the Common Good of Mankind* . . . (Edinburgh, 1704), printed in *The Political Works of Andrew Fletcher* (London, 1732), 401–2.

¹³³ *Answer To A Letter concerning Trade, sent from several Scots Gentlemen that are Merchants in England* . . . (7 Dec. 1706).

¹³⁴ [W. Black], *Remarks Upon a Pamphlet, Intitled The considerations in relation to Trade Considered* . . . (18 Dec. 1706). See also his *Letter Concerning the Remarks upon the Consideration of Trade, by the Author of the 4th Essay at removing National Prejudices*

(1706).

135 [W. Black], *Some Overtures And Cautions In Relation to Trade and Taxes, Humbly Offered* . . . (1707).

136 [W. Black], *Some Considerations In relation to Trade Humbly Offered* . . . (1706).

137 [W. Black], *A Short View of our present Trade and Taxes* . . . [1706. Originally published 1705].

138 *The Political Works of Andrew Fletcher,* 400–1.

139 [A. Fletcher], *State of the Controversy Betwixt United and Separate Parliaments* (1706).

140 [J. Hodges], *The Rights and Interests of the Two British Monarchies* . . . *Treatise III* . . . (London, 1706).

141 *Faithful Advice from England By an Honest Scotsman* (1706).

142 See, e.g., *Unto His Grace, Her Majesty's High Commissioner, And the Right Honourable Estate of Parliament, the Humble Address of the Barons and Freeholders within the Stewartry of Kirkcudbright* (1706); *HMCR Portland MSS,* iv, 282, J. Cranstoun to [   ], 27 Jan. 1705/6; Wodrow, *Early Letters,* 289, Wodrow to G. Serle, 30 May 1706. *Dr Davenant's Opinion Anent the Salt and Malt Taxes In England* (23 Dec. 1706); *Some Few Remarks Upon The State of Excise after the Union, compar'd with what it now is* [?1706].

143 [1706].

144 *The Address of the Commissioners to the General Convention of the Royal Burrows* . . . [1706].

145 *HMCR Laing MSS,* ii, 125–35, *c.* Aug. 1706. The editor wrongly attributed this memorial to Seafield. It is unsigned but almost certainly by the lord advocate.

146 *A Letter Concerning the Consequence Of An Incorporating Union In Relation To Trade* (1706).

147 [J. Hodges], *War Betwixt the Two British Kingdoms Considered* . . . (London, 1705); *An Essay Upon The Union of the Kingdoms of England and Scotland* (1705).

148 [J. Spreull], *An Accompt Current Betwixt Scotland and England* . . . *By J. S.* . . . (Edinburgh, 1705).

149 [B. Fairfax], *A Discourse upon the Uniting Scotland with England* (London, 1702).

150 Edinburgh, 1702.

151 See above, p. 40 *et seq.*

152 *Two Letters Concerning the Present Union From A Peer in Scotland To A Peer in England* (1706).

153 [Sir J. Spottiswoode], *The Trimmer: Or, Some necessary Cautions, concerning the Union* . . . (1706).

154 *An Information to all True Scotsmen, who are misinformed of the union* [1706 or 1707].

155 [T. Spence], *The Testamentary Duty Of The Parliament of Scotland* . . . (1707). See also *A Letter From One Of The Country Party To His Friend Of The Court Party* (Mar. 1704).

156 See above, p. 216.

[157] *The Right of Succession to the Crown and Sovereignty of Scotland Argued* (London, 1705).

[158] *The Vision, A Poem* (1706).

[159] *A Scots Poem . . .* (Edinburgh, 1706).

[160] [J. Arbuthnot], *A Sermon Preach'd to the People, At The Mercat Cross of Edinburgh; On the Subject of the Union* [?1707].

[161] *Parainesis Pacifica . . .* (Edinburgh, 1702).

[162] [J.B.], *A Memorial Briefly pointing at some Advantages of the Union . . .* (London, 1702).

[163] [W. Seton], *Scotland's Great Advantages By An Union with England . . .* (1706).

[164] Quoted Smout, *Scottish Trade* , 274.

[165] E.g. P[eter] Paxton, *A Scheme of Union Between England and Scotland, With Advantages to both Kingdoms* (Edinburgh, 1705).

[166] [W. Paterson], *An Inquiry into the Reasonableness and Consequences of An Union with Scotland . . .* (London, 1706), printed in Paterson, *Works*, i.

[167] [J. Donaldson], *Considerations In Relation to Trade considered . . .* (1706).

[168] E.g. *The State of the Excise &C Vindicated . . .* [1706]. See also *The State Of The Excise After the Union . . .* (1706).

[169] See above, pp. 180, 185–6.

[170] See above, pp. 187–8.

[171] *A Letter To A Member of Parliament Anent the Application of the . . . Equivalent . . .* (20 Dec. 1706). See also *An Enquiry into the Disposal of the Equivalent* [?1707].

[172] *The Anatomy of an Equivalent By the Marquess of Halifax Adapted to the Equivalent in the present Articles* (1706).

[173] [J. Clerk], *An Essay Upon the xv Article Of The Treaty of Union . . .* (1706). This argument was supported by Defoe who regarded the equivalent as a mere loan to be paid off by merchants through increased customs: *A Letter To A Friend Giving an Account how the Treaty of Union Has Been Received here . . .* (Edinburgh, 6 Nov. 1706).

[174] See above, pp. 187–8.

[175] E.g. [Defoe], *A Seasonable Warning or The Pope and King of France Unmasked* (1706).

[176] London, 1706.

[177] *An Essay At Removing National Prejudice Against A Union . . . Parts* I and II.

[178] *Ib.*, Part I.

[179] *Ib.*, Part II.

[180] *Ib.*, Parts I and II. He also defended toleration in *An Answer To My Lord Belhaven's Speech* (1706).

[181] *An Essay At Removing National Prejudice . . .* Part III; *A Letter To A Friend Giving An Account how the Treaty of Union Has been Received here . . .*

[182] *An Essay . . .* Part III.

[183] *Presbyterian Persecution Examined . . .* (Edinburgh, 1707).

[184] *A Letter from Mr Reason, To The High and Mighty Prince the Mob* [1706].

[185] *A Fifth Essay At Removing National Prejudices . . .* (1707).

[186] *Considerations In Relation to Trade Considered . . .* (1706).

[187] *A Letter To A Friend Giving an Account how the Treaty of Union Has been Received here* . . .

[188] *Ib.*

[189] *A Fourth Essay* . . . (1706).

[190] *An Enquiry into the Disposal of the Equivalent* (1706); *Observations on the Fifth Article of the Treaty of Union* . . . (1706).

[191] E.g. *A Fourth Essay.* . .; *The State Of The Excise After the Union* . . .

[192] *Ib.*; *Considerations In Relation to Trade Considered* . . .; *The State of the Excise &C Vindicated* . . .

[193] Defoe, *Letters*, 144, [Defoe] to Harley, 9 Nov. 1706; *ib.*, 158–60, 168–70.

[194] E.g. *A Letter To A Friend Giving An Account how the Treaty of Union Has been Received here*; *A Fourth Essay* . . .; *A Seasonable Warning* . . .; *Two Great Questions Considered* . . . *Being A Sixth Essay* . . . (1707); *Passion and Prejudice* (Edinburgh, 1707). In his *Review Of The State Of The English Nation*, vi–ix, *passim*, he concentrated on questions related to the law, the constitution and the church.

[195] *A Fourth Essay* . . .

[196] *A Short Letter to the Glasgow-Men* (1706).

[197] *A Fifth Essay* . . .

[198] *An Answer To My Lord Belhaven's Speech.*

[199] *A Fourth Essay* . . .

[200] E.g. *A Letter from Mr Reason* . . ., and above, p. 241.

[201] *A Fourth Essay* . . .; *An Answer To My Lord Belhaven's Speech.*

[202] *A Fifth Essay* . . .; *A Letter Concerning Trade, From several Scots Gentlemen that are Merchants in England* . . . [1706].

[203] See below, pp. 290 *et seq.*

[204] *A Letter Concerning Trade* . . .

[205] *Ib.*

[206] *A Fifth Essay* . . .

[207] *A Fourth Essay* . . .

[208] *Caledonia, &C. A Poem In Honour of Scotland* . . . (Edinburgh, 1706); *The Fifteen Comforts Of A Scotchman* (London, 1707).

[209] Ferguson, *Scotland's Relations*, 307–8, has justifiably urged caution in using Defoe's *History*. The book is more interesting for the light it sheds on Defoe than for what it has to say about the union.

CHAPTER SEVEN

Ratification

The negotiation of the treaty was in itself no great triumph. Both parliaments had to ratify the agreement and since the Scottish parliament was expected to be the more troublesome the reaction was to be tested first of all in Edinburgh. The difficulty was that the party situation there was still unchanged.

As Seafield had warned, the claims made by the old party after the 1705 session were far removed from reality. Not since 1702, and then in peculiar circumstances, had the old party unaided carried anything in parliament. They had subsisted on temporary alliances and fortuitous combinations leading to occasional success, though they steadfastly refused to acknowledge their indebtedness. But now, however much they had boasted of their achievements in the 1705 session, they were faced with carrying an entire legislative programme. Since they had no majority in parliament their prospects were poor.

1   The position of the old party consolidated

No new ideas emanated from Queensberry and his advisers save recipes from William's reign: bribery, patronage and pressure on individuals. But the situation had been different then. The court's task had been merely to recapture the support of its own wayward members, not to make inroads into the opposition, which was now the problem. Queensberry's policy had not been feasible since the 1702 election and nothing had happened to make it so in 1706. Yet, as the 1705 session had ended, this was the scheme put into effect, though it produced internal dissension within the old party, many of whose members were seized with the conviction that it was every man for himself. Ramsay, the commander-in-chief, Scotland, and

Queensberry's brother, March, had both died suddenly in a prolonged drinking bout. Leven was the favourite candidate for appointment as commander-in-chief and his ambition was to combine it with his existing posts, Edinburgh Castle and the master-generalship of ordnance. Queensberry thought the last two should be used to oblige others, particularly Galloway, if Leven should be made commander-in-chief,[1] but Leven had received court promises that he would enjoy all the posts. He got his own way by threatening to boycott the union negotiations unless the promises were kept.[2] Leven's *coup* reduced the available places. Galloway had to be made a lord of the treasury to keep him from opposition, thus annoying Buchan, who had fully expected to be in the treasury, and disappointment drove him to oppose the union.[3] Rosebery, in the interests of something regular to keep the wolf from the door, always did as the court told him and went to London without demur, though hinting strongly at his great poverty and hardships in the queen's service.[4] Grant, younger, was given Mar's regiment to predispose him in the court's favour.[5] Since Annandale had rejected the post of president of the council, and with it both court and union, Montrose was persuaded to accept, though not without the hair-splitting qualifications to which he was prone.[6] Wemyss was appointed lord high admiral.[7] To extend the available patronage, additions were made to the privy council and exchequer.[8] Stair had to be gratified. His son, lord Dalrymple, was made a brigadier and given lord John Hay's regiment on the latter's death.[9] Lord Rankeillour died and his places were divided. The lord of session's gown went to James Erskine of Grange to please his brother, Mar, and Tillicoultry, one of Queensberry's men, was given the place in the justice court.[10] The position of the old court party was being consolidated as far as possible, in accordance with Seafield's advice. But Seafield had an ulterior motive: the old party was to be fully satisfied to make them more inclined to take others into alliance when they finally had to admit that they could not carry the union without assistance.[11] It is doubtful whether Queensberry saw so far. Despite 1703 he was still hinting that the cavaliers would support the court in return for the toleration of episcopalians.[12] In fact, in so far as the old party men thought at all, it was of their own profit, which they conveniently linked with the management of the next parliament.

The English court, to avoid blame for failure, was ostensibly doing what the old party asked. The whigs and the old party, in alliance, had set out to make the union their affair, so Godolphin was determined that any miscarriage was to be seen as their responsibility.[13] But gratifying even some of the old party could be a strain. The English court could not have evaded the appointment of Queensberry as commissioner though they found the prospect distasteful. With him commissioner ratification was by no means assured; without him failure was certain. Queensberry would ensure that. This decided the outcome of the rivalry between the two dukes, although the uncertainties of co-operating with one of Argyll's temperament must have had some weight. Argyll left for Flanders in a temper and was reluctant to return whatever the fate of the union. His ultimatum to the court was plain, summing up Argyll's attitude to politics. 'My lord', he wrote to Mar, 'when I have justice done me here and am told what to expect for going to Scotland, I shall be ready to obey my lord treasurer's commands . . .'[14] On an unfounded rumour that lord Cutts was dead Argyll pestered Marlborough for his post.[15] At length, Marlborough agreed to promote him to major-general and give him the premier English regiment, whereupon Argyll not only consented to support the union but became enthusiastic. He even wanted parliament to be adjourned till his arrival. If this could be done '. . . to [allow him to] show his inclinations and use his interest for so good a cause under the care of his best friends, it will be most acceptable'.[16] But there were more requests to follow. His brother, lord Archibald Campbell, felt neglected and was in no very good mood.[17] Both brothers pressed for an earldom for lord Archibald, a demand which had to be met because his support was needed. His intention was to take the title of Dundee, which Montrose thought calculatedly offensive. Finally, with a show of Campbell displeasure at Montrose, lord Archibald made do with the earldom of Islay as long as it was interpreted not as a concession but merely a change of mind.[18]

2   Distribution of the £20,000 arrears

The Campbell brothers could be a burden but were not unique in that. Queensberry, too, tried to squeeze all he could from his position in 1706. Johnston reported to Baillie: '. . . *Queensberry*, till two days before he left this, railed at *the lord treasurer*; said he was not for *the union* & C., but at last a sum of money quieted him. I believe *the sum of money* is *ten thousand pounds*; the thing itself is no secret . . .'[19] The sum in fact was £20,000, and from this sum, paid by the English court to ease the passage of the union, Queensberry deducted £12,325 as a first instalment of his own arrears before anyone else could be paid. But there was pressure, too, from others who sensed a favourable opportunity of recovering back pay. Queensberry asked for speedy payment '. . . in regard that many of our nobility who are come to parliament, that want their bygone pensions, are calling for some money, and that it is for her majesty's service that they have a part at this juncture . . .' With some insignificant exceptions the money was distributed amongst political interests able to exert pressure.[20] Seafield could fend for himself, tapping the fund on his own and his father's behalf. Ormiston could make trouble and was placated by the payment of some arrears. A whole group of court peers received something. For the rest, money went to members of the Argyll interest, to Cromartie and two of his relatives, to the squadrone and their allies, as part of their bargain with the court,[21] and, surprisingly, it has seemed, to two country peers, Atholl and Elibank.

A remarkable thing about these payments is the relatively modest nature of most of the sums involved. Even Queensberry's £12,325 was less than half his recorded arrears. Most received only token payments from their arrears of salary although there is some doubt about whether money was due to everyone who received it. The official statement of arrears has no record of money due, for instance, to Balcarres, Dunmore or Fraser, but this is not necessarily conclusive. No arrears were stated as due to Roxburgh for that matter but it is possible that money was outstanding from his period as a secretary of state. Lord Banff, a recent convert from catholicism to the presbyterian church, greatly to the surprise, even bewilderment, of his local minister, asked for what he called 'encouragement' to attend parliament. He received £11 2s, presumably as a contribution to his expenses.[22] The only persons, apart from Queensberry, to receive really substantial sums were former lord high commissioners: Tweeddale, Marchmont and Atholl, though this might have been coincidence. Their arrears were considerable though less than those of others who received much lower amounts.[23] The money was distributed in great secrecy, whether for reasons of discretion or because the court did not want recipients comparing their payments. But charges of bribery cannot be completely ruled out. No one can be blamed for accepting arrears of salary, or even pressing for payment, but more was involved than that. Payment was selective. Not all who were owed money received any, so the intentions of the court were not altogether pure although perhaps grounded in political common sense. There was another aspect to the

payments. Lockhart alleged, on the strength of the accounts
commissioner's investigations of 1711, that the £20,000, having been
paid secretly, was not officially accounted for and so the sums paid
were not deducted from recorded arrears. As a result, he claimed, some
persons were paid twice. This could have been true. In the last resort
the only safeguard lay in the scruples of the persons concerned.
Queensberry was one of those alleged to have been paid twice, although
he is said to have offered to pay back his original instalment.[24]
Queensberry's arrears consisted of amounts owing to him as a former
lord commissioner. Subsequently there would have been arrears from
his appointment as privy seal and lord of the treasury in 1705, his grant
for equipage as lord commissioner on his appointment in July 1706 and
his daily allowance as commissioner from that date. For the earlier
sums he had received the contentious 'appropriation'.[25] It would be
interesting to know whether until the union he continued to receive
half-yearly payments from the customs in addition to the sum he took
out of the £20,000.[26] But such a degree of secrecy and—probably
intentional—confusion surrounds this transaction as to render it
virtually impenetrable. Ultimately Lockhart's testimony has to be
taken or left alone; there is no other conclusive evidence. But in their
investigations of 1711 the accounts commissioners were faced with
some very shifty answers and notable lapses of memory. One has the
feeling that at another time and in another country some of the
witnesses would have invoked the fifth amendment.[27]

Bribery, of course, must involve the intention of influencing
behaviour and the recipient must know what is expected of him. Many
of those who received money in 1706 would have supported the union
anyway—possibly even the squadrone.[28] In fact the only man to receive
money and subsequently vote against his former political allegiance
was Elibank, whose payment was £50. Whether this sum affected his
behaviour is doubtful but it seems a modest price. And since Elibank's
vote was not vital it seems curious that the court should have paid him
at all unless he had already changed sides.

A more important peer recorded as having received money was
Atholl. The circumstances were not quite as straightforward as they
seem, although his appearance in the list has been welcome to those
anxious to show that payment was not restricted to union supporters.
As early as July 1706 Atholl had been offered payment of arrears if he
would stay away from the next session of parliament, the approach
being made indirectly through his brother, Dunmore, a former cavalier

who had joined Queensberry. The duchess of Atholl declined on her husband's instructions. However, the offer was not unequivocally rejected. The duke was in debt to Dunmore and offered to transfer his arrears to him, leaving him to make the best bargain he could with the court.[29] It is possible that Dunmore received Atholl's £1,000 in addition to the £200 listed in his own name. Dunmore supported the union and Atholl could have benefited indirectly from it, whilst himself opposing the court though abstaining or absent on the ratification vote.[30]

Indeed, the closer one looks at the payments the more mysterious they seem. Argyll had complained in 1705 that he lost votes because no money was available to pay arrears, an assertion which seems to have been merely another of his attempts to blame the English court for his own failures. The voting pattern in 1705 was entirely as expected and would doubtless have been the same had money been paid. It is difficult to imagine that the situation was much different in 1706, so one wonders why money was paid at all. The probability is that the payments of 1706 were due entirely to Queensberry. He used his strong bargaining position to extract money for himself, the surplus being merely to placate those able to criticise his gains, their payments being limited on the excuse that there was not enough to go round. Exceptions to this were the members of the squadrone, who have to be considered rather differently.[31]

However, these payments must have reinforced the impression that henceforth Queensberry was to be the sole source of largesse, a conviction which the duke fervently desired the Scots to retain. A majority of the old party, after a time of insecurity, was once more consolidated under his leadership.

The English whigs favoured this policy of keeping the old party happy. Since 1704 their strategy had been aimed at transforming the old party into effective junto allies. As they wanted the union to be carried by these collaborators alone the prospect of the court's enlisting other support alarmed them lest their calculations should be upset. Should reinforcements prove necessary the whigs themselves wanted to do the recruiting in the hope of strengthening even more their post-union position.

3   Schemes to thwart the junto

The lines of whig strategy were apparent to the English ministry. Both Godolphin and Harley knew of the transactions between the

Scottish commissioners and the junto lords. Harley had very sensitive political antennae and was well served by his intelligence service. He was acutely conscious of the dangers of allowing the whigs to become the dominant figures in the union project and of their Scottish allies' claiming the entire credit for ratification.

There was an obvious counter-strategy. Support for union in the Scottish parliament had to be broadened by the court itself. After the union the court might then escape being overwhelmed at Westminster by a block of Scottish members committed to the whigs. In retrospect this court fear seems to have been unfounded but some insurance was necessary. If any group outside the old party could be induced to support union, then Scottish representation in a British parliament would be fragmented and some support for the English ministry would be almost certainly forthcoming to preserve the balance. Both Godolphin and Harley were involved in schemes to this end.

i The squadrone and the court

Godolphin's scheme was directed at the squadrone. By this time, Belhaven, Selkirk and other marginal supporters having reverted to the main body of the country party, the group had been reduced to little more than the Tweeddale interest, but it was a bigger group than when newly emerged from opposition. Marchmont and his family, for instance, had been totally absorbed.[32] Furthermore the group had taken on a special character. The events of 1704 and 1705 had transformed the squadrone into a quasi-court party, a status which Godolphin reinforced by maintaining a special relationship with them. This had continued even after their precipitate dismissal on Argyll's appointment as lord commissioner,[33] so that although the squadrone were not in office they were not wholly in opposition. By 1705 they were, understandably, not on very good terms with any other Scottish group. The old party regarded them as elbowing upstarts, to be discredited lest there should be any repetition of the deplorable happenings of 1704. To the country party and the cavaliers they were deserters. Their dismissal led the opposition to see them as returned prodigals but worthy of scorn rather than forgiveness. Mistrust was justifiable. The squadrone had developed ideas above their station, hankering after an influence they could not sustain. They were really an unemployed court interest waiting for something to turn up, their only hope of regaining influence depending on cohesion as a separate

party to improve their bargaining power and perhaps being able to
hold the balance. One thing was obvious: whatever benefits came their
way would come from the English court. No Scottish group would
willingly do anything for them.

In the 1705 parliament they had attempted a high-wire performance.
They wanted to be accepted as good countrymen. In alliance with the
country party they could savage Argyll, since the old party was
outnumbered, yet they had no wish to destroy all credit with the
English court by outright opposition. After some dithering they decided
that the key to their conduct would be 'consistency'. In opposition they
would support the policy of succession with limitations that, as court
managers, they had had thrust upon them, a stance which allowed
them to oppose Argyll with some show of principle. Items of other
business they claimed to assess on their merits, an astute tactical
decision which, since they held the balance in parliament, left Argyll at
their mercy from vote to vote.[34] Johnston represented them to
Godolphin as men doing their best to be consistent though led into an
occasional mischievous vote in resentment at the way Argyll had
treated them.[35] So, during the 1705 session, whilst they struck country
party attitudes and made a noise, there was in it all a theatrical
element. Although ostensibly opposing Argyll they were in contact with
Godolphin by way of Johnston in London, through Seafield in
Edinburgh and by a secret arrangement between Roxburgh and
Godolphin.[36] These exchanges were kept from Argyll and the old party.
Baillie did wonder at one stage whether Queensberry had some inkling
of an arrangement between the lord treasurer and Roxburgh. Johnston
thought it inconceivable, the whole point being to keep the old party in
ignorance.[37] Seafield provided corroboration of the strict secrecy
maintained. He reported to Godolphin a conversation with Roxburgh
as the latter was leaving for Bath with a game leg before the end of the
session. '. . . He satisfied me that he had done all he could in his present
circumstances with regard to the treaty, for some of the party did not
vote, and E[arl] of Marchmont and some others joined with us, whom
he thought he could have influenced. However, he did not allow me so
much as to write this to your lordship . . . He pretends to have a desire
to be employed, but parted very friendly with me. I desired he might
stay till the supplies were granted. He said he believed that would be
carried, and he hoped the new party would assist us. I desired he might
recommend it to them. He said he would. If your lordship take any
notice of this, let it be by a separate letter, for I own no correspondence

with any of the new party . . .'[38] And of the act for a treaty Seafield was
able to write: 'I know that the new party are well enough satisfied with
it for I have seen some of them since who have said so to me'.[39] So the
squadrone leaders, at least, had known of the court's intention to have
an act for a treaty passed but had no wish to be told officially, which
would involve obedience to or defiance of the court.[40]

This intrigue was more than an attempt to secure the squadrone's
support for the session of 1705. Even before their dismissal Johnston
had suggested to Godolphin that the squadrone be kept 'on ice' until
they were needed again.[41] Throughout the session of 1705 and after, the
undercover message emanating from Godolphin was that the
squadrone should keep themselves as a separate group, to 'shun
concerts' and keep distinct from both the old party and Hamilton.[42]
Baillie wrote to Roxburgh: '. . . I design to write to Rothes tomorrow,
in such terms as he may understand that the court design not the new
party should come to an understanding with the old . . .',[43] a constant
theme in squadrone correspondence right up to the preparations for the
1706 parliament.[44]

Keeping the squadrone 'on ice', separate from other interests, suited
Godolphin admirably. It also accorded with the inclinations of the
squadrone leaders, giving them the illusion of a special status. But their
position had its problems. What was to be their attitude to the treaty
negotiations? And was it desirable that any of them should be union
commissioners? The crucial point for them, as their correspondence
makes plain, was not whether union was going to benefit Scotland but
whether it was going to pass. Unable to foresee the outcome of the
negotiations and the ultimate fate of a possible treaty, the squadrone
leaders vacillated. In a letter to Roxburgh Baillie summed up the
squadrone attitude precisely: 'if . . . [the commission] fail, it's best they
bear the burden who were the occasion of it; but if good were like to be
done by it, it will be necessary that interests be made that the new party
be of it, that the old party may not have the sole praise . . .'[45] Later he
remarked, '. . . To oppose good things or to set up our enemies are
equally hard. One of them will be our case; but what remedy? . . .'[46]
Each whisp of rumour had its effect on squadrone calculations. When
Baillie discovered that Marchmont had all the time been writing to the
whigs and others recommending a fully representative union
commission there was alarm and exasperation.[47] In fact the
squadrone's main concern in any development was, like that of most
Scottish politicians, with its effect on their own position.[48] In the event

their worries were needless, for the old party and the whigs had decided
that the Scottish union commission was to be 'all of a piece', the
squadrone having no opportunity of being involved in negotiations.[49]

This still left them with the problem of how to react if union
negotiations were successful. Since the end of the 1705 session Baillie
had exerted himself to keep the party's options open. He was alarmed
lest Roxburgh compromise both himself and the squadrone whilst he
was in England. His fears were justified. Roxburgh began negotiations
for his marriage to Nottingham's daughter and decided to stay in
England for the winter,[50] during which period he became a full convert
to union. He had long been aware that union was the court's policy.
Whilst still in office he had reached the conclusion that limitations were
a lost cause since even if they should be passed England would never
allow them to take effect.[51] So any concern he showed for limitations in
the 1705 parliament was camouflage. From England, in the winter of
1705–6, before negotiations had even started, Roxburgh set out to
convert Baillie, bombarding him with arguments in favour of union,
listing reasons for its necessity.[52] Baillie responded by emphasising the
disadvantages of union for their own party though he gradually came to
accept, even whilst protesting, the inevitability of their supporting it.
Initially he thought a federal union might be tolerable but felt sure that
England would insist on an 'incorporating union'. Yet the latter
contained so many pitfalls that he could not see where the greatest
advantage for the squadrone lay.[53] The union, he wrote, '. . . would not
be my choice, and what sticks most with me is, that it will render the
[court of] session disposers of our estates at pleasure, when there shall
be no appeal from their sentence but to the house of peers. For the
appeal that now lies to the Scots parliament is the only thing that keeps
them within bounds . . . Nevertheless, the union is certainly preferable
to our present condition, and of two evils the least is to be chosen . . .'[54]
Such calculations were the stuff of politics at the time, and Baillie was
of a brooding and pessimistic cast of mind. But Roxburgh was 'selling'
the union and could permit himself to be more expansive and
optimistic. He thought a union the only security Scotland had against a
jacobite restoration, since, once a union had passed, English troops
would be able to move freely in Scotland. Whatever the significance for
party advantage, Roxburgh thought that the Scottish parliament
would probably accept union, but his opinions cannot be taken at their
face value, since he was trying at the time to convince Baillie, by the
only arguments to which he seemed responsive, that union would

succeed.[55] The previous voting record in the Scottish parliament was evidence that Roxburgh's conjectures bore no relation to reality, divisions in the union parliament merely confirming their inaccuracy. In face of the squadrone's opposition the union treaty could not have passed but then they, rather than the country and cavalier parties, would have carried the blame for failure, which would have damaged Roxburgh's prospects. He was trying to convince Baillie that union was the policy most likely to succeed whilst obscuring the fact that its success could be ensured only by the squadrone's co-operation. And in the event of Baillie's seeing through this Roxburgh claimed that by supporting union the squadrone would enjoy the fruits of the old party's labours.[56]

Baillie did not swallow Roxburgh's arguments uncritically, seeing that some wishful thinking was involved; but after a period of indecision he seemed inclined to agree with Roxburgh. He accepted the political and military arguments for union but remained unconvinced by any mention of trade. Nevertheless the former arguments seemed to him decisive: '. . . were we as certain of riches by the union as of security from foreign and domestic oppression, all other difficulties might be either adjusted, or easily passed from. But many are of opinion it will rather impoverish us . . .' [57]

Although Baillie could envisage many undesirable consequences, circumstances were compelling him to agree with Roxburgh. He doubted and qualified but none of it did more than prolong a debate that was deciding itself.[58] For one reason or another there was a move in squadrone opinion towards union. William Jamieson, in London with Roxburgh, did his best to propagate his master's views.[59] Bennet was professing a belief that union was the only solution, laying 'our little skirmishing aside'. He had abstained on the treaty vote in 1705, having, alone of the squadrone, been kept in office in 1705 as mustermaster, and wanted to stay there.[60] The views of others were changing. By January 1706 Tweeddale seemed to favour union. Rothes was not sure but was prepared to go along with whatever the rest decided.[61] By April Baillie confessed that most of the squadrone he spoke to favoured union yet, he himself though resigned to it, was still prepared to jump either way.[62] Some tactical advantages were to be gained by reserving the squadrone's position but, if the leaders waited too long before declaring themselves, some of their support would undoubtedly evaporate. Individual members of the squadrone were no more immune from court pressures than anyone else and the group had nothing to bargain with but solidarity. The leaders had been counting on the increased strength which the allegiance of Montrose would bring, but Montrose accepted the presidency of the council as Baillie had feared he might.[63] Bennet, again for fear of losing his job, was sedulously cultivating both Queensberry and Argyll as a precaution. Such developments could not be other than a threat to party solidarity.[64] Cockburn of Ormiston, in so far as he was possible to classify, was still with the old party and a union commissioner. Through his son, John Cockburn, and his two former wards, Haddington and Rothes, he had squadrone connections. He had a tendency to boast of his influence over the two last and, although it was not as great as he claimed, Baillie was apprehensive,[65] especially since Haddington had drifted into support of Argyll in 1705.

There was only one way the decision could go and Baillie realised it. He told Johnston: '. . . the new party would lessen themselves more by opposing than by going into it; for by the former they would divide, and Roxburgh and one or two more be left to themselves . . . In short, the new party must keep together though in things that would not be their choice . . .'[66] Typically, despite his early inclination towards union, Tweeddale seems to have been the last man to come into line with his own party. '. . . Tweeddale,' Roxburgh told Baillie, 'is far from being at a point so it will be necessary for us to be at Edinburgh two or three days before the parliament sit down . . .'[67] But the other squadrone leaders were used to dragging Tweeddale behind them and there was no doubt over which way they would vote. Before Tweeddale had made up his mind the question was no longer whether they would support union, but on what terms, and a preoccupation developed with how the union settlement itself could be turned to squadrone advantage.

As far as terms went, one obvious basis for negotiation was the payment of salary arrears due to the squadrone. Tweeddale had earlier been pressing unsuccessfully for his payment[68] and negotiations reached a critical point just before the 1706 parliament. Mar reported to Godolphin: '. . . my lord Montrose has now fully declared himself . . . My lord Tweeddale and most of his people appear very reasonable, and I hope will join with us in carrying it through. I told his lordship that you had been pleased particularly to recommend to me to do what I could for getting him payment of what is owing him by the queen when he was in her service, and I assured him of all the assistance in my power, and that I believed much would depend on himself to make it in my power or not . . .'[69] Conceivably this question had been

Tweeddale's sticking point, Mar's strong hint being intended as a final push to bring him into line with the rest of his party. Subsequently some of the larger payments out of the £20,000 went to the squadrone.[70]

Other conciliatory steps had been taken by the court. As early as March 1706 Marlborough was raising a regiment for lord Mark Ker in the hope that it would have some effect on the Scottish political situation.[71] Subsequent promotions and appointments indicate other aspects of the bargain.[72] When the squadrone had given evidence of their commitment in the 1706 parliament, Marlborough was concerned to do what he could for their connections through military patronage. A regiment was proposed for lord William Hay, and lord Polwarth, Marchmont's son, was later given the 7th dragoons.[73] Lockhart, quick to catch the scent of such things, claimed that the duchess of Marlborough had written to Roxburgh promising rewards to the squadrone if they supported union.[74] And Alexander Cunningham, who seems to have known everybody and was well disposed to the squadrone, had no illusions about their primary motive. 'The marquesses of Tweeddale and Montrose, the earls of Roxburgh, Rothes and Haddington, Mr John Cockburn and Mr Haldane, and others, were also for the union, who, though they made a specious pretence of the public good, yet had an eye, in the midst of the public affairs, to their private interest.'[75]

Another possible source of advantage had been borne in mind by some of the squadrone: the compensation to the Africa Company shareholders. Although the treaty provided for compensation out of the equivalent, no machinery of distribution had been set up. The strong connection between the Tweeddale interest and the Africa Company had resulted in their exercising strong influence in the governing body. Some of them had been hoping that the directors would be allowed to distribute compensation, since the disposal of money meant power. This consideration had not passed unnoticed by the squadrone's political rivals. According to Mar, such an arrangement would have given the squadrone 'more influence than all the queen's government here'. Consequently, at the end of the union parliament, an alliance of the squadrone's ill-wishers squashed their hopes of wielding such influence, though it is fair to note that two of the squadrone, one of whom was Tweeddale, opposed their own party on this issue.[76]

But aside from the prospect of immediate rewards some of the squadrone were making long-term calculations. A few of them supported the union only with reluctance, fearing to help the old party achieve the success it badly needed, thus making its position virtually unchallengeable. After all, they had been squeezed out and treated with contumely by the old party. However, the situation could be appraised in other ways. Should the old party receive the credit for carrying the union, then within the confines of Scottish politics they would undoubtedly be dominant yet their success in carrying the union might drastically change the situation, shifting the focus of affairs to Westminster. In Scottish politics, as a group aspiring to the status of court party, the squadrone's outlook was bleak; within a union which might lead to the abolition of the separate Scottish ministry their prospects could be improved. Some of the leaders were greatly exercised by this possibility. One of Roxburgh's reasons for claiming union would succeed was 'the constant oppression of a bad ministry . . .'[77] Arguments used in private to convince sceptical members of the party concentrated not on economic benefits but on this point.[78] Baillie indicated their hopes to Johnston during the union parliament: '. . . There is now a vacancy in the session. The new party have agreed to use their interest for a delay till the parliament is over and that it be not filled by the present ministry . . .'[79]

So, although in the last resort prepared to vote for union, they were determined to do so as an independent group, as much for their own tactical reasons as in response to Godolphin's request. The squadrone's '. . . actings will be without concert with the present ministry . . .', Baillie told Johnston.[80] Their trust in Godolphin was far from boundless but for the time being his wish that they should remain a separate group served to make their own manoeuvre respectable. They were waiting, as was Godolphin, to see how affairs developed after the union.

What the squadrone had in mind was none other than an alliance with the junto. On the evidence of their past relations this might have seemed a vain hope, but the squadrone sensed that the whigs were the rising power. They were aware too of the tensions existing between the junto and the court. A constant theme in their correspondence was the need to cultivate the good will of the whigs. There was frequent speculation over whether the time was yet ripe for overtures.[81] When the squadrone, with Ridpath's assistance, were planning a propaganda campaign to discredit the old party as lukewarm towards the succession, they decided to spare the junto in case they ever needed them as allies.[82] And when, in the face of Montrose's disturbingly non-committal attitude and Ormiston's grandiose talk, Roxburgh had an

attack of nerves and suspected them of plotting to seize the credit for
the squadrone's support for union he was prepared to write to Wharton
at once and offer the whigs an alliance. Only the thought that this
would commit the squadrone too far to be able to withdraw gave him
pause.[83] Obviously the squadrone and Godolphin viewed each other as
expendable. Godolphin showed no qualms over jettisoning the
squadrone in due course, nor did they show any at leaving him.

But for the time being the whigs were too involved with their old
party scheme to have any time for the squadrone.[84] Nevertheless it was
the squadrone's intention to make their debut in British politics
uncommitted, hoping that the right alliance at Westminster would
make them the dominant interest in Scottish politics. When, at the
beginning of 1707, Johnston told them that, after the union, the whigs
would ally themselves with anyone who could give them a
parliamentary majority it began to seem as though squadrone
calculations might not be too wide of the mark.[85]

However, this was a very distant prospect. For the time being
Godolphin's relations with the squadrone had to be governed by the
possibility that the old party could arrive in force at Westminster fully
committed to the whigs. The squadrone had therefore to be held in
support of union as a separate interest obliged only to the English
court.

ii   Hamilton and the court

The lord treasurer was not alone in preparing such insurance
schemes. Robert Harley, at the time secretary of state, probably had
more to fear from the junto in the short term than had Godolphin.
Already he was out of sympathy with Godolphin and Marlborough's
conviction that it was necessary to placate the whigs. In fact the
managers' dedication to a whig alliance was anything but fervent but
they thought it in the long run inescapable. All they were hoping for
was to gain time, which was the point of keeping the squadrone in
reserve in case they might prove useful in a united Kingdom
parliament. Harley, though, saw no need at all to appease the whigs.[86]
All attempts to reconcile him with the junto by convivialities came, in
political terms, to nothing,[87] the junto having identified him as one of
their chief enemies whilst Harley, whatever public face he was forced to
wear, resented whig control of the union negotiations. Being sucked
into the wake of the junto was not a fate he relished.[88]

Harley's public pose was that of one who declined to meddle at all with Scottish affairs. Once he claimed in the commons that 'he knew no more of Scotch business than of Japan, and that he avoided even the conversation of those of that country . . .'[89] In fact, he was frequently consulted on Scottish affairs and was sometimes active in them although deviously and often with more than one purpose. In 1704 he seems to have embarked on a tactic of his own to upset junto priorities in Scotland despite the fact that it ran counter to Godolphin's policy for that session.[90] Again in 1705 he and Godolphin in collaboration played a double game aimed at trapping Argyll into the treaty policy.[91]

After the Scottish parliament of 1705 Harley's field of manoeuvre, like that of everyone else, was circumscribed by union. To represent union as a constraint, with managers on the brink of attaining one of their long-standing objectives, may seem curious, but Harley, in particular, felt the junto's appropriation of union to be a direct threat to the court. He resorted to techniques of sapping and mining. His tactics, like those of Godolphin, were dictated partly by the situation; both aimed at broadening support for union in the Scottish parliament to achieve some balance in Scottish representation at Westminster. Whilst Godolphin concentrated on the squadrone Harley resumed the negotiations with Hamilton which he and Godolphin had pursued in 1704 and 1705.[92] Hamilton might in theory have seemed a good choice to counterbalance the old party—a magnate, irreconcilable to Queensberry and certain to be as opposed to him after the union as before, an important consideration for the ministry. So the summer of 1706 found Harley angling for Hamilton's support for union, though as a personal bargain, something in the nature of Harley's earlier agreement with the duke of Newcastle, rather than an official court agreement. Nevertheless, he had his colleagues' connivance. Marlborough certainly knew what Harley was attempting. Such a personal approach was possibly thought to be less vulnerable to junto interference. Harley chose to approach Hamilton with hints that the duke could be in a position to wield the power in Scotland to which his status entitled him.[93] But plans involving Hamilton did not usually survive exposure to the peculiarities of his personality and position. The duke was vulnerable in so many ways that he could seldom commit himself wholeheartedly to anything. However, the prospect of a bargain was distant. What Hamilton wanted from the court was a precise offer, not hints of what might conceivably come his way if he did what was expected of him. As for the offer, he had visions of a handsome down payment to settle his debts and a share in Scottish management and patronage initially at least equal to Queensberry's but with prospects of further expansion. Failing this he preferred to retain his standing as an opposition magnate, which was not surprising. Much of his support was jacobite, dependent on his opposing union. Only a promise to transform him into a court magnate could have compensated him for the loss of this following and even then a change of sides would so reduce his power as to make him less valuable to the court. The negotiations of course came to nothing, at least on the surface. What they may have achieved was a significant increase in the pressures on Hamilton as an opposition leader which could have contributed to his odd behaviour during the union parliament. This might indeed have been all that Harley was hoping to achieve. Anyone driven to dependence on Hamilton was very hard-pressed and to bring him into the court would have caused more disruption than it was worth. Harley was enough of a realist to be aware of this. However, it suited him to talk like a man who was trapped. He reported to Marlborough the apparent failure of the negotiations, blaming it on the junto, who were, he said, 'pursuing their old maxim, to make as many people as they can desperate',[94] which was less of an appraisal than an attempt to damage the junto's credit with Marlborough and Godolphin.

4   Whig precautions

The whigs, for their part, knew the courses of action open to the court and the threats these could pose to their scheme, so their constant aim was to limit wherever possible the options open to the queen's managers. Their attitude was so hard and suspicious that Marlborough became apprehensive, hoping they would not oppose attempts to broaden support for the union.[95] More votes were needed in the Edinburgh parliament and there was a danger that the junto's concentration on their own objectives might lead to the union's being defeated. For the junto, like the court, were so fearful of the possible consequences of union for English politics that they too were in the shadows, warding off imaginary demons. One of their convictions was that the squadrone, as lackeys of the court, represented the greatest threat to their plans, and although the whigs did appreciate, in due course, the need for more Scottish support they wanted the squadrone kept out of it.[96] Such extra voting power they preferred to acquire for themselves on their own, rather than court, terms. This attitude led them into an indiscriminate search for alliances. They opened negotiations not only with Hamilton but with Atholl. The junto wanted one or both of the dukes to support union as whig allies ensuring, if possible, that any additional union supporters would vote with the junto at Westminster.[97] This policy, if it can be called that, contained too many internal contradictions to be feasible. Neither Hamilton nor Atholl would ever have supported Queensberry, nor would they for very long have remained in alliance with each other. But this element of unreality had been present in most English appraisals of Scotland since 1688 and the junto remained a prey to such delusions longer than most.

One of the whig fears was that after the union the court would distribute English peerages to the squadrone leaders, so eliminating the whig majority in the lords. Later developments proved this to have been nothing more than a private nightmare but the junto did what they could from the start to stifle any such project[98] They praised the union but denigrated the Scottish nobility, implying that as a body they were unfit to be sitting peers. '. . . *The whig lords* run you all down,' wrote Johnston to Baillie, 'particularly your nobility, who they declare, might have had better terms if they had pressed for them, and therefore they must take care of promotions, for what are not such men, say they, capable of, who parted with, & C . . .'[99] The squadrone tried to turn this to their own advantage. The squadrone pamphlet *Vulpone* . . .[100] seems to have been contrived especially to make the junto's flesh creep at the thought of Scottish representatives at Westminster proving all to be court men who had shown no scruples about the constitution of their own kingdom.

Nevertheless, apart from Godolphin's flirtation with the squadrone and Harley's slender link with Hamilton, the union progressed very much under junto direction. Whilst the Scottish parliament discussed the treaty, officers of state and the inevitable busybodies were writing to the junto lords rather than the queen's managers asking for advice. The whigs found this gratifying and dispensed guidance liberally enough. Much of the correspondence dealt with concessions to Scotland beyond those already negotiated. The junto's advice, determined by what could be pushed through the English parliament, was sound.[101] After all, this was a field in which they were extremely competent.

5   *Squadrone support decisive for the union*

Yet, without Godolphin's arrangement with the squadrone, to whom the junto continued hostile, the union could not have succeeded. Their votes and the assistance of Marchmont, by this time almost fully identified with them, tipped the balance in the Scottish parliament.[102] Godolphin's dealings with the squadrone's leaders by way of Roxburgh and Seafield, together with the squadrone's own calculations, had ensured that they would vote for union. His ulterior motive would emerge only if later events made it necessary. For the time being it was enough that, when the Scottish parliament met, the court could be sure that the squadrone would support union despite the official squadrone attitude of refusing to announce their intentions until the opening of the session. Baillie's reference to the squadrone's 'declaring' themselves on a vote of 15 October 1706 has to be taken less than seriously.[103] So many channels of communication existed between the court and the squadrone that it is hardly credible that the court was unaware of their intentions, apart, possibly, from Tweeddale's own final resolution, since he himself was not sure. Nor had the squadrone rushed headlong into support of the union without assurances of reward. Bargains had been made which rendered any statement of intent superfluous.[104] In August Seafield knew that Marchmont and Nisbet of Dirleton would both support union.[105] At quite an early stage Godolphin had had talks with Roxburgh which Ormiston took as a key to the squadrone's decision.[106] Before the vote of 15 October neither Seafield nor Mar doubted that the squadrone would vote for the court.[107] But if all the squadrone's show of secrecy followed by a dramatic 'declaration' was a pantomime, as it undoubtedly was, perhaps it was a necessary pantomime. They were indicating that they were a separate interest, supporting the union, as they would have liked people to believe, on its merits. They did not wish to appear as the 'tail' of the old party. If any mystification at all was created by this public reticence it was strictly amongst the rank and file. No one who mattered was in the least misled.

The squadrone's support for the union was decisive. What had been engineered was the alliance Seafield had envisaged in the winter of 1703–4 as the *sine qua non* of any Scottish settlement, but with this difference: in 1706 the old party was in control, with the squadrone as seasonal labour. Between the two groups there was little amity or goodwill.

6 Party voting in the Scottish parliament

The assertion that squadrone support was decisive in giving the court a majority involves a big assumption, namely that votes on the union were almost entirely party votes, cast for political reasons and therefore predictable.[108] Nevertheless this is the only hypothesis which explains the ratification of the union in Scotland. A man's vote depended on whether he was old party and tied to the court or whether he was a cavalier or countryman and so against the court. It depended on whether an habitual courtier had been 'disobliged,' deciding consequently to be a nuisance. The blend of calculation and deviousness from which the squadrone's final decision emerged might well have accounted for other deviations from the norm, usually through absence or abstention, but generally obscured by the lack of evidence. Failure to cast a vote does not fall as easily into a pattern as a clear voice on one side or the other. However, a distinct alignment appears in the voting of the union parliament: votes were cast for or against the court rather than for or against union. And this is exactly what the political structure in Scotland would have led one to expect.

Of course members were aware of the existence of other issues. They had ties and loyalties other than court or country. When an occasional member diverged from his normal behaviour by abstaining or staying away from the house, other considerations must have come to the surface, but on the whole votes were dictated by party allegiance. The very uncertainty of many members over such a crucial decision must have reinforced their urge to huddle together in accustomed corners. Comparatively few were utterly confident in their attitude to union. Seafield was secure enough, wanting an end to the complications of managing a separate kingdom and, anyway, carrying out orders as he always did. Queensberry was doing what the English wanted as the best way of preserving or advancing his interest. Officers of state were doing what was expected of them as courtiers. The cavaliers were determined in opposing a further obstacle to a jacobite restoration and Fletcher of Saltoun, always very positive in his opinions, regarded union as an abomination. For the rest there was incessant talk and speculation, creating the illusion of an issue hanging in the balance: '. . . people's minds have been so changeable that it was hard to make any tolerable judgement till now . . .', Dupplin wrote to the lord treasurer.[109] Erskine of Grange told his brother: '. . . I think there seems to be very many who are neither much for the union nor against it, but are in a kind of suspense about it and know not what to think . . .' [110]

Opinions did fluctuate but that does not imply any purposeful debate. Issues were too involved for most members to be capable of making up their minds in any rational way, especially when subjected, as they were, to the utmost political pressure. The economic pros and cons were too complicated, statistics too meagre and attempts to supply them too conjectural or confusing for the commercial merits or otherwise of union to be soundly appraised. Even those, such as the unionist pamphleteers, who affected cocksureness relied on guesswork and most of them were wrong. Scotland was not enveloped in affluence even in the not-so-near future. Such prosperity as developed sprang from circumstances that no one could have foreseen. What hope, then, was there for the ordinary members in the parliament house? Those with convictions about union—nurtured in their bones rather than through cerebration—did not allow them to affect their conduct if doing so would have violated their party allegiance. Practically all voted their normal party line to an extent that is quite beyond coincidence. There were a few strong-minded but rare exceptions: Hugh Montgomery, member for Glasgow, a court man nominated for the union commission, who stayed away from the negotiations then voted against the union in parliament; or Walter Stewart of Pardovan, a courtier, who sat for Linlithgow and resolutely opposed union. The remainder voted in parties or were absent.

The likelihood of party voting had been foreseen. Indeed, it could hardly have been otherwise, although contemporaries fell victim to the sports commentator's urge to inject uncertainty and excitement into a foregone conclusion. Orkney, in early 1706, had written to his brother: '. . . I believe you are all got in so violent into parties [sic] that if really they should get reasonable concessions from England yet, because they are the doers of it, it would be objected against by the others . . .' [111] Stair accorded party much the same importance. He told Mar: '. . . There's indeed a charm in being engaged into a party. For common cants take men off from their own reason . . .' [112] He was right, up to a point. Some acted on the principle of solidarity whatever the issue, but others, confused and undecided, were left with no security but party allegiance. One has to accept, however, that there are limits beyond which motives cannot be assessed. The individual views of most members of the Scottish parliament are, and perhaps were, obscure. How they acted appears in the voting lists and mostly we have no way of telling whether or not they voted with clear consciences. A few took refuge in abstention or absenteeism. Sir James Stewart, the lord advocate, pronounced himself against union although, scepticism about its alleged beneficial effects apart, he provided no very cogent reasons and detractors were not slow to hint at unworthy motives.[113] He was allowed to stay in office on condition that he abstained and gave no trouble. He seemed pleased to oblige. The earl of Bute was a Queensberry man and a jacobite opposed to union who escaped his dilemma by staying away. The earl of Aberdeen was an active member of the cavalier party who had come reluctantly to the conclusion that union was the only feasible course for Scotland to take and avoided embarrassment only by being absent from parliament.[114] Sir John Anstruther, although a squadrone man, disapproved strongly of union and refused to change his mind. Rothes with difficulty persuaded him to abstain on the crucial divisions for the sake of the party's interests although he was present in parliament and voted on particular articles.[115] All these were men for whom the obstacles to toeing their party line were so considerable that they either chose or were persuaded to remain inactive. There is no method of discovering how many court men voted for union with misgivings merely because they were expected to or feared the consequences of doing otherwise. Allegations were circulated that some courtiers lacked enthusiasm.[116] Nor can we know how many voted ostentatiously against union, secure in the knowledge that its ratification was certain whatever they did. Hamilton, for instance, with large debts, an income from the export of black cattle to England and considerable estates at risk in Lancashire, stood to be ruined if the union failed. Yet, after a fashion, he led the compaign against it, though the character of his leadership provoked speculation about which side he was on.[117]

Contemporary generalisation can be misleading. Paterson was a shade too concerned to deny that support for union was based on party interest. According to him, support for the union was based on principle whilst opposition 'proceeded rather from party humours and passions than any settled design'.[118] It would be unwise to assess motives on an observation of this kind. For conclusions which within their limits are more objective one is driven back to the evidence of division lists. These, by reason of the voting system in the Scottish parliament, may be taken as accurate, especially since feeling was such as to ensure thorough scrutiny. So in them we have authenticated evidence of how members behaved rather than the impression they might have conveyed of either their thoughts or intentions. The result indicates a sharp distinction between pro and con which does scant justice to any nail-biting indecision, but clerks of parliament were counting votes, not divining sympathies or diagnosing anxiety states.

Amongst the listed votes on particular articles and questions of procedure were two key divisions on the principle of union: that of 4 November 1706 on the first article of the treaty providing for a united parliament[119] and that of 16 January 1707 ratifying the entire treaty.[120] If members are classified into parties on the basis of their previous record, their probable behaviour over the union forecast on that basis, and the prediction compared with the actual divisions, the result is a convincing demonstration that voting was determined largely by political allegiance. For the former division such a prediction is 92·9 per cent accurate, and for the latter 91·6 per cent. Its accuracy for the divisions combined is 92·3 per cent. This calculation disregards a number of otherwise predictable members unavoidably absent for reasons ranging from terminal illness to imprisonment for debt. The list of pro-union voters is for the most part a register of the old party interests as they had been since Atholl's departure for opposition in 1698 and Hamilton's emergence into open politics shortly afterwards: Queensberry and Stair with their following, the Campbell interest, Seafield's small group and those who passed as 'old revolution men'. Added to these, for the union parliament, were the squadrone. Against union were the Hamilton and Atholl interests together with the cavaliers, the bulk of whom had first entered parliament in 1703. The amount of cross-voting was small and most of it readily explicable in political terms, leaving very little to account for otherwise.[121]

The voting lists dispel some of the conjectures one might otherwise be tempted to make. They show, for instance, no general correlation between a member's voting record and his ostensible economic interest. Although a large proportion of the trading and industrial enterprise in the kingdom was due to the nobility, the majority of whom voted for union, the two circumstances seem to have been unrelated.[122] Since the country party had always been a minority amongst the peers no further explanation seems called for. There were no variations directly attributable to obvious economic interests: grain production, coal, salt, the raising of black cattle and wool growing. Theoretically, interests involving the first four of these would have found union a good prospect, rendering the English market more accessible, but wool growers would expect to suffer from the strict English prohibition on wool exports which was likely to depress their prices. This division of interest finds no clear expression in the voting record, both sides being involved in all these enterprises. The north-country nobility—Sutherland, Seafield, Banff and Cromartie, for example—were all heavily committed to the grain trade and all supported union but were all court men anyway. Cromartie's following, though presumably sharing his economic interest, were of jacobite inclination, anti-unionist in sympathy and difficult to manage, although in the last resort, it is true, they voted for union or stayed away. There is perhaps no need to look further than political pressure for an explanation of this behaviour. Stair raised black cattle and voted for union but he, too, was a courtier. Galloway, in the same business, gave one single pro-union vote on the first article and afterwards consistently opposed the treaty. Wigtown opposed union. He was a wool grower, but also a cavalier opposed to union on political grounds. And one of the largest wool growers in Scotland was Queensberry—the 'union duke' himself. Amongst Queensberry's following was the earl of Wemyss, who, as a courtier, supported union, though his industrial interests lay in coal, exported mainly to the United Provinces, involving him in the importation of Dutch goods. Union was likely to disrupt his trading pattern but that did not affect his political allegiance. Nor, apparently, did economic considerations influence the policy of Hamilton, whose interests should have led him to support union but who, in parliamentary terms, led the opposition to it.[123] That, of course, might not have been the whole story. Perhaps in this context Hamilton was in a category by himself.

The bulk of opposition to union came from the estate of barons, but a majority of them had always been country or cavalier and unaccountable deviations from their normal allegiance were negligible. Nor do the burghs offer much support for the idea of commercial influence as a determinant, despite reports of dissatisfaction amongst merchants. The convention of royal burghs had addressed against union but the significance of the address was dubious.[124] Though Dupplin told Godolphin, '. . . the merchants, who everybody thought would have been the first that would have grasped at the union are afraid that the little trade they have will suffer by it . . .',[125] merchants could not be categorised as a group in this way. They shared the urge to make money but their profits were so diverse in origin that they could hardly be united either for or against union. Moreover it was not ordinarily the merchants who dictated a burgh's vote in parliament, a burgh member's own political allegiance deciding in most instances whether he voted for or against the court. Amongst the sixty-seven burgh representatives there were few exceptions. Some departed from their usual pattern for identifiable political reasons: the Johnstons, for example, for Annan and Dumfries, followed Annandale in opposing the court. Others are not so easily accounted for. Hugh Montgomery, a court man, the member for Glasgow, voted consistently against the union whilst still sufficiently a courtier to be elected to the first United Kingdom parliament. Possibly his vote expressed some view of Glasgow's economic interest, though it is not easy to see what it was, unless Glasgow merchants doing very nicely out of the illegal trade to the colonies feared that union would bring competition and severely damage their role as middlemen in the trade between the Dutch and the English colonies. William Cultrane, who sat for Wigtown, had received for no ascertainable reason £25 out of Queensberry's union fund; he voted for the first article but, although usually a Queensberry man, opposed all the treaty's economic provisions. His voting pattern followed almost exactly that of the earl of Galloway, his burgh's patron, who was also, normally, one of Queensberry's following. The only difference between them was that Galloway went a step further and opposed ratification whilst Cultrane abstained. Jedburgh's representative, William Scott, was another court man who opposed union, conceivably reflecting his burgh's fears for the wool trade or for its status as a border customs post after a union, but this is mere conjecture. William Sutherland, for Elgin, ordinarily a countryman, voted against the first article but by the ratification vote was supporting union. He could have been opposing the first article on procedural grounds or, more probably, signifying a preference for a federal union whilst being prepared to settle for the treaty as negotiated. On the other hand his voting might have been the result of quite other pressures which have left no evidence.

For the motivation of Walter Stewart of Pardovan, for Linlithgow, there are rather more clues, although not necessarily leading to a complete explanation of his behaviour. He was a courtier whose opposition to union came close to being obsessive. He was a hard-line presbyterian, probably opposing the treaty for mainly religious reasons whilst prepared to make use of any other objections that occurred to him. The convention of royal burghs nominated him as one of their representatives to present their anti-union address to the parliament.[126] On parliament's third sitting he proposed a fast to be observed in Edinburgh, an observance unwelcome to the court but zealously supported by opponents of the union, some of them people whose zeal for mortification lacks credibility.[127] He wanted the church question settled before any article of union was debated, whilst on the act for the security of the church he abstained in conformity with the policy of the commission of the general assembly, which petitioned against it. All this seems to indicate a certain single-mindedness. But he also protested against the arrangements for Scottish representation.[128] and, oddly for a burgh member, he opposed confirmation of the privileges of the royal burghs as prejudical to trade, so his stance seems unlikely to have been taken up in deference to his constituents. It appears that as long as the treaty was resisted all the way he barred no weapons.[129] But there remains little firm evidence concerning these cross-votes and it might well remain impossible to penetrate further the motives of such members.

However, such cross-voting as did take place, as also the peculiarity of certain divisions, have to be viewed in the light of the new balance in the parliament. Once the squadrone decided to support union the outcome in the house was a foregone conclusion and everybody knew it. This gave rise to a highly artificial parliamentary conflict in which members who chose could indulge their idiosyncracies and strike all manner of poses in the knowledge that they were not affecting the final result. Ratification of the treaty was so certain that the fact dominated the tactics of the opposition. Countrymen and cavaliers, certain of parliamentary defeat, set out to use the proceedings for other purposes. They used speeches, votes and protests to intensify and mobilise the feeling against union apparent amongst the vocal part of the nation and to create in England as much uncertainty as possible over the security of a union which roused such opposition. They aimed too at delaying the business of the house as much as possible in the hope that something might turn up.

The fact that opposition members were playing in parliament a role designed to produce an effect elsewhere would explain the peculiar voting on certain articles. On the communication of trade clause the opposition vote was the lowest recorded: nineteen votes against one hundred and fifty-six.[130] Twenty-six consistent opponents of union voted in favour of the communication of trade, whilst opposing the other economic clauses.[131] The rest of the opposition abstained. Any explanation of these figures must be conjectural. It seems likely that some were unwilling to be seen opposing a concession. They might well have been indicating, sincerely or not, that in their opinion better terms could have been wrested from England—federal union, freedom of trade and no uniformity of customs and excise—being amongst those mentioned by Argyll in 1705 as professing support for union but only on terms that were unobtainable. Rather than opposing the treaty because of its shortcomings they were establishing a reason for opposition.

A further attempt to inflame feeling outside parliament was made in proceedings on the act for the security of the church. An address from the commission of the general assembly was taken as the opportunity to introduce an act safeguarding the presbyterian church settlement as earlier agreed between some of the union commissioners and the junto.[132] Opposition attempts were made, sincerely by some but by others as a wrecking tactic, to insert clauses of an extreme presbyterian character: that a future united kingdom parliament should for all time be debarred from granting toleration to episcopalians[133] and that Scots should be allowed to hold office in England without taking the test.[134] The intention was to excite Scottish presbyterian opinion whilst possibly disrupting ratification proceedings in the English parliament by such signs of Scottish religious intransigence. The court fended off these extreme amendments. In consequence the act was still altogether repugnant to some and not rigorous enough for others. An address against the act by the commission of the general assembly caused some odd behaviour. A majority of seventy rejected the address but twenty-four members went to the length of protesting against its rejection. Defoe entertainingly asserted that all twenty-four last-ditch defenders of the church settlement were episcopalians. He was, of course, exaggerating, but numbered amongst them were some episcopalians, including the earl of Kincardine, who, as Sir Alexander Bruce, had in 1702 been expelled from parliament for saying that presbytery was inconsistent with monarchy.[135] On the act itself a large number of the opposition abstained, allowing it to pass by one hundred and twelve to thirty-eight.[136] The minority, regardless of religious affiliations, were all hard-core opposition. Thus Atholl, Hamilton and Annandale, each in his own way professing a relatively faded presbyterianism, were fighting shoulder-to-shoulder with episcopalians such as Balmerino and Blantyre, some to indicate support for presbytery in an extreme form, others to oppose it.

Apart from such attempts to turn sensitive issues to propaganda use there seems to be no general pattern to such specific cross-voting as took place. Of those who supported union a very few voted against individual articles. No particular article was singled out for opposition;

nor were economic articles exclusively involved. Furthermore these dissentient voters were rare and evenly spread over all three estates.

Failures to record votes are plentiful and not easy to interpret. For the most part it is impossible to say whether the members were *non liquet*[137] or absent. Sometimes it seems obvious that no significance should be attached to a failure to vote. When a zealous anti-unionist such as Lockhart of Carnwath did not bother to declare himself, or when a secretary of state, Loudoun, has no vote recorded it is doubtful whether anything was involved other than a need for fresh air. As the session advanced the opposition's strength declined, a development reflected in the ratification vote. We have Lockhart's testimony that by the time the twenty-second article was reached not many of the opposition were present,[138] through despair, he said, although there are other possibilities. Altogether the division lists for the union parliament lend little support to the view that independent judgement was exercised.

This conclusion applies also to obvious economic interest. Economic affairs were, of course, much talked about. Union had to be debated in respectable though fictitious terms, so many issues being too delicate to raise. But contrary to an apparently reasonable hypothesis, trade considerations seem to have exerted no influence worth speaking of if economic interest is defined solely in terms of enterprises such as coal mining, salt panning and cattle raising. Perhaps such a view is unduly restrictive. Courtiers had an obvious interest in the income from office, a clear economic motive for them, however they exploited their estates or whatever they felt about union, to execute court policy laid down in London. Some did feel that union might lead to some contraction in official employment so that by supporting it they would be cutting their own throats, but nevertheless they thought it better to vote for the court in hope rather than oppose and suffer prematurely.

But this does no more than shed light on the structure of politics in Scotland or anywhere else where a spoils system operates. It explains the cohesion of a court party on almost any issue but not support for union in particular. Union was merely another question over which the Scottish parliament divided on court and opposition lines and it needs to be explained in no other terms.

7 *Popular anti-unionist feeling*

There being no doubt that parliament would ratify the treaty, court fears were concentrated on what might happen in the kingdom at large. Every sign pointed to the union's unpopularity and the opposition's parliamentary tactics were aimed at stimulating these anti-union sentiments. The full extent of this feeling is impossible to estimate. It was noisy enough in expression. One reason was the clamour set up by presbyterian ministers, some of whom saw union as equivalent to damnation, maintaining that the presence of twenty-six bishops in the house of lords was a violation of the covenants.[139] Their continual preaching on the subject was widely looked upon as a cause of rioting.[140] Carstares recommended the presbytery of Hamilton to discourage tumults, which produced the somewhat equivocal reply that they were as quiet there as anywhere else. 'As to the disposition of the people, the plain truth is that they are generally most averse from the union and many have expressed themselves broadly enough against it . . .'[141] This presbyterian opposition was diligently exploited inside and outside parliament by people completely lacking in concern for either the covenants or the established church.

Numerous addresses against union were presented to parliament but their significance was in dispute. Argyll declared them fit only to make kites of. Lockhart was to represent them as the true voice of the people, silenced only where the court was powerful, as in Argyll's own territory.[142] Defoe attempted to explain them away by devious and involved arithmetic.[143] Others argued that the opinion of parliament, not the voice of the mob, was the sense of the nation[144] but there was a tacit unionist admission that something had to be explained away. Normally the only significance attaching to an address was that it reaffirmed the allegiance of the organiser and demonstrated his local influence. Pressures were certainly applied. Atholl commanded his vassals to sign an anti-union address and others doubtless did the same.[145] Also, with very few exceptions, the addresses came from shires represented predominantly by opposition members of parliament, but some burghs with court members also produced addresses.[146] Montrose, suffering from an anti-unionist address in his own territory, alleged that many addresses were signed by people who had refused the oaths,[147] thus equating them with disaffection. But the addressing campaign did deviate from the usual pattern in two ways. Since addresses were usually produced under pressure from local nobles or gentry, it is remarkable that there was no comparable influx of unionist addresses from areas under court influence. Then, there was much more behind some of the anti-union addresses than noble coercion. In Glasgow rioting broke out when the provost and council refused to sign the burgh address against the union. The provost's house was attacked, his windows smashed and, with some of the councillors, he had to leave town until troops restored order.[148] Outside Edinburgh, most of the trouble on this scale occurred in the western shires, led, if not fomented by, cameronian preachers with a tradition of resisting authority in the name of religion. Crowds from surrounding districts beset the Glasgow magistrates demanding money and arms. The magistrates of Dumfries had to meet a force estimated at over four hundred foot and more than one hundred horse. It was commanded by one Herries who first read and then burned the articles of union. Such incidents led to a proclamation forbidding armed assemblies, and suspension of the arming clause of the act of security.[149]

Unionist members were greatly alarmed by the violence in Edinburgh. Mar thought the population's fears of higher taxation were being exploited,[150] but whatever the reason Edinburgh, always excitable, was never free from the threat of violence during this session of parliament. Tension built up amongst apprentices and others looking for trouble or excitement. Disturbances began with the cheering which greeted Hamilton on his contrived progresses round the town and the corresponding abuse shouted at Queensberry. Stones were thrown at the commissioner as he went to the parliament house, under heavy guard, his coach horses galloping as a security measure. The crowds which congregated near the parliament house were a permanent menace to order. Rioting and disorganised brawling were followed by an attack on the house of Sir Patrick Johnston, the lord provost, a courtier. The streets were taken over by the mob—'a company of rude, ignorant and desperate fellows, mad women and boys, with huzzas in the streets till they plunder the houses of honest people . . .'[151] This was the night when Defoe thought of De Witt and took refuge in his lodgings.[152] Only the use of regular troops subdued the rioting. Once in Edinburgh, the troops remained, despite opposition protests that force was being used to overawe parliament.[153] Nevertheless, violence was intermittent and never far below the surface. Leven reported to Godolphin: '. . . there are a great many people coming every day to town who have no business in it and whom we know are disaffected to the queen and government and who declare

themselves enemies to the union . . .'[154] Queensberry continued to be
pelted with stones as he passed between the abbey and the parliament
house and his servants 'beat, wounded and robbed'.[155]Courtiers were
alarmed by the mob outbreaks and their possible intensification by the
opposition's policy. Seafield wrote to Godolphin of the efforts of: '. . .
the opposers to incense the gentry, towns and common people against
us, and in places disaffected . . .' He thought Belhaven's famous 'vision'
speech, which parliament took as something of a joke, 'contrived to
incense the common people'.[156] Both Baillie and Roxburgh, not
without malice, thought that violence and the threat of it were having
an effect on the old party, weakening their resolution, though the voting
figures do not bear this out. Baillie gave his opinion that '. . . this nation
will run into blood, whether the union or succession be settled . . .'[157]
He was habitually pessimistic but others shared his fears. The general
attribution of violence to the influence of the disaffected, together with
the fact that in Scotland no one was sure how much disaffection there
was, might account for the curious lack of pro-union addresses. In
1706–7 any attempt to organise them might have had undesirable
repercussions. Much of the trouble in the south-west, for instance, was
virtually on Queensberry's own doorstep. The court was
understandably anxious to keep business to essentials and have the
union ratified before even more serious trouble broke out. So the
absence of pro-union addresses, which some at least of the court
nobility could have organised, may well have resulted from a deliberate
and organised act of self-denial, even self-preservation, by the court.
Appeals in parliament for proceedings to be slowed down or even
postponed lest more violence be provoked make this explanation seem
likely. Naturally, some of these requests came from opposition men as
an obvious delaying tactic. Other appeals were made by men
committed to union: Stair and Cromartie,[158] who were taking very
seriously the possibility of open rebellion, which no one in the court was
anxious to provoke.

8   Court fears of insurrection

Godolphin was not impressed. In his opinion if opposition to union
got out of hand it would be because business was not pushed fast
enough through parliament.[159] He was inclined to think that much of
the talk of violence was bluff. If it were not, then the anti-unionists were
'. . . the first people that ever I knew in a fixed intention of going into

open rebellion who thought fit to make so public a declaration of it beforehand . . .'[160] Queensberry was too close to take such a detached view. He asked for troops to be sent to the border. First he wrote to Godolphin and, when this produced no immediate effect, to Marlborough. '. . . It's easier,' he wrote, 'to discourage the taking up of arms than to reduce men once gone into rebellion in popular cause . . .'[161] The security measures he requested were almost beyond English military capacity, on account of the continental war and the consequent manpower crisis, but in spite of the difficulties Marlborough managed to produce some semblance of support. Troops were moved up to the border and the issue of arms and ammunition from Berwick authorised in case of emergency. English troops were to enter Scotland only at Queensberry's request.[162] As a further precaution troops were sent to the north of Ireland[163] to discourage any sympathetic demonstrations there which its proximity to the west of Scotland would have made uncomfortable.

If Lockhart is to be believed various plans for revolt existed. Some people in the western shires had decided that union could be stopped only by armed uprising to end the parliamentary session. Cameronians led by their preachers were to form the bulk of this projected movement. Tentative plans were made to co-ordinate this rising with another in the highlands—an odd combination. Both Hamilton and Atholl were sounded about their attitudes. Hamilton, predictably, was reluctant to commit himself but at length seemed to acquiesce. Atholl showed more enthusiasm, offering to ensure a passage to the south for highland troops. A force of between seven and eight thousand men were counted on for a march on Edinburgh. None of this materialised. Lockhart blamed Hamilton, who, he claimed, at the last minute, privately and on his own initiative, cancelled the assembling of forces. This would certainly have accorded well with Hamilton's usual conduct. But Hamilton apart, it was a curious conspiracy in which so many of the leaders seemed to be government agents bent on stopping the rising. According to Lockhart, one Hepburn, a cameronian minister and an accepted leader of the conspiracy, was exposed as a government agent by major Cunningham of Aiket. At the same time, Cunningham, quite unsuspected by Lockhart, was running a security operation to stop a western rising. At the union he was paid £100 for himself but in 1715 was still trying to secure payment for his agents.[164] In addition, Queensberry was employing another cameronian leader, Ker of Kersland, for the same purpose whilst Harley and Defoe had various agents on west country security.[165] Infiltration on this scale indicates that perhaps the projected rising was not so much of a threat as Lockhart had hoped. But even if the plan amounted to no more than inflated talk and imagination the extent of security measures shows serious concern on the part of the court.

The planned rising, if Lockhart is to be believed, was not the only project rendered abortive by Hamilton. The jacobites had thought of trying to block union by resuscitating the policy of succession with limitations[166] but then abandoned it in favour of a scheme for a country-wide representation from the barons to parliament for rejection of the union treaty. Hamilton professed hearty support but at the last moment refused to be associated with the representation unless it asked for the succession to be settled on Hanover, otherwise, he argued, the English tories preparing to oppose union would have the ground cut from under their feet, the anti-union campaign in Scotland being too easily equated with disaffection. By this time the jacobites were refusing to risk the taint of the Hanoverian succession even for tactical purposes and the project collapsed. Later, being unable to conceive of anything better, they again came to think that the tactic of the Hanoverian succession might have something to be said for it. A proposal was to be made that Sophia should be declared the successor. When this was rejected in parliament, as they confidently expected it would be, they intended to register a formal protest and then secede in a body. The opposition was hoping to reduce the authority of parliament, as in 1702, to the extent that union would not be feasible. At the least this would have been a great embarrassment to the court and it could have been an effective weapon.

It had been generally but unwisely assumed that Hamilton was to lead this demonstration. On the appointed day he was absent, complaining of toothache. Emissaries were sent to persuade him to attend the house, which he finally did, though refusing flatly either to make the proposal or lead the protest. Rumour had it that he had been threatened by the commissioner although it was not very clear how.[167] Certainly Hamilton was open to pressure, but whether his erratic behaviour was due to threats from Queensberry, whispers from Harley, a financial position which meant he could not risk the union's failing or a combination of all of these is impossible to divine. His dilemma was that he could not afford to wreck the union but equally did not dare to say so, the outcome being such conduct that it is surprising he retained any credit at all in Scotland, as he did even after the union when his unreliability had been amply demonstrated. Perhaps it is necessary to make a distinction between his personal credit and his position as the leader of a magnate interest. As a person no one took him as seriously as he took himself. His position as leader of an interest was quite different. A magnate interest had its own momentum. Those who had invested their career prospects in it could not afford to admit any lack of faith in its leader, so however much the duke himself wavered the pretence had to be maintained that he was effective.

9   The union parliament

When the parliamentary session opened the court's first task was to demonstrate its majority. At the beginning of a session there was always a test vote, the court managers taking the first chance that presented itself. In 1706 the opportunity came on a vote over whether Sir Alexander Bruce should be admitted to parliament as the earl of Kincardine, his inherited title, which was being disputed. The issue was neither here nor there. Sooner or later he would have to be admitted and would vote against the union, but the court, to show they could exert power over one of the opposition, forced a vote.[168]

This court victory made the position plain to the few who had not expected it and the opposition embarked on its campaign of obstruction and intensified propaganda. There was a superabundance of florid oratory and a proliferation of appeals to the memory of Scotland's independent past. All were addressed to an audience beyond the parliament house. Some of the anti-unionists had euphoric visions of obstructing the treaty until it was too late for ratification by the English parliament.[169] The court managers were not at all worried by this but they did fear the possible effects of opposition tactics outside parliament, whether in the form of violent popular resistance to union or of a jacobite rising with union as its pretext.

The major business of the treaty gave rise to a series of opposition delaying tactics. A few sittings were taken up by the formality of having the treaty read out with an explanation of each article.[170] Hamilton then proposed a recess until the queen could be told of the kingdom's great aversion for union.[171] He complained incessantly of the speed at which business was conducted, making adequate consideration impossible.[172] Belhaven proposed a week's delay for thought and, although opposed by some of his own allies, insisted on its being put to a vote. He was defeated by a majority of sixty-six.[173] An attempt was made to enforce a referendum of sorts by obliging members to consult their constituents.[174] Frequent recourse was had to filibusters: '. . . when we offered to state the question', Seafield wrote, 'they had always some of their side offered to speak . . .'[175] Every opportunity was taken to confuse proceedings as the opposition played for time day by day. The voting of the second article, establishing the Hanoverian succession for the united kingdom, was reached, according to Philiphaugh, 'with great struggle, after much debate and wrangling, and even scandalous disorder in the house'. The struggle was not over whether the court would have a majority but over how long the vote would take. Murray described the proceedings when, as an alternative to voting the second article, Hamilton proposed a recess. There was a lengthy wrangle over the precise wording of the question to be put, the court at length managing by a preliminary vote to pin it to whether the second article should be approved or not. 'Then my lord chancellor ordered the clerks to call the rolls upon that question. The duke of Hamilton and Saltoun interrupted and pretended they should be heard further against the article before the vote. This was complained of as an unprecedented novelty and a breach of all order, to interrupt the calling of the rolls upon a question that was fixed and agreed to by a vote of the house; and upon this the house was in great disorder for a long time. Many members from all corners cried, "Call the rolls, call the rolls!" The duke of Hamilton and two or three others cried, "No! No! Till the members be heard speak." In short I never heard more confused noise at any mob or tumult . . .' The row appears to have subsided, only to be renewed when Balmerino, supported by Kilsyth, proposed that the acts relating to the English succession might be read, whilst Hamilton continually protested it was no good reading acts unless they could be debated. Finally the court succeeded in having the question put and the succession was voted.[176]

Saltoun had, from the beginning, been anxious to sink his teeth into the fourth article—that granting freedom of trade—and had pressed for it to be debated immediately after the first article.[177] When the trade clause was at last reached his motive became evident. A communication of trade with England had disadvantages, he said, and claimed to have elicited from this one article twenty different items for discussion. He wanted each one separately dealt with, according to Hume of Crossrig 'an evident design to protract and delay business'.[178] Saltoun's tactic was circumvented by referring the fourth article to a committee.

Unionist pamphleteers tried to discredit the opposition's parliamentary behaviour. Defoe wrote, not unfairly, in *A Seasonable Warning or The Pope and King of France Unmasked*, '. . . Though I have not the honour to vote in parliament, yet I have been admitted sometimes into the house, where I admired to hear so much huffing and bawling, so much noise, and so little reason against the articles than in debate; to hear one in a vision or rhapsody of nonsense, talking of Hannibal, Caesar and the ancient heroes, of whom he knows little but the names; another transported with a degree of passion, inconsistent with good manners and unbecoming a reasonable man; others pleading much for security of religion and presbyterian government who by their practice seem to have little regard to either: which indeed might give one a just prejudice against their arguments, as not sufficient to convince reasonable men, but calculated for the mob, who have nothing to say but *our crown, our sovereignty and ancient kingdom* . . .' If things had come to this it was because argument had ceased to matter.

Other motions were put forward for the sake of popular appeal. Hamilton, for example, proposed that Scottish members in the united kingdom parliament should have a veto on all questions pertaining to union. Atholl suggested that the united kingdom parliament should meet in Scotland once every three years.[179] Rabble-rousing statements fuelled popular indignation. Saltoun announced that, in his opinion, the union commissioners had betrayed their trust. This led to a demand that he should go to the bar of the house and consequently, in the ensuing debate, he withdrew his statement,[180] but the idea had been put into circulation. The argument was advanced that to negotiate for union was necessarily treason, as being against the claim of right[181]—not a very soundly based contention since the commissioners had had parliamentary authority. Such quibbles could be fairly easily disposed of in parliament but not in the kingdom outside for which they were designed.

Despite all this the union was pushed steadily forward by the court–squadrone majority. The first article, conceding the whole principle of union, was carried at the start on the understanding that it was not to become operative until the entire treaty was ratified.[182] Some curious priorities appeared. The house voted, for example, to consider the twenty-third article, concerning the privileges of the sixteen elective peers, immediately after the second.[183] But throughout the proceedings the court vote remained steady within very narrow limits whilst on especially sensitive questions the opposition vote occasionally slumped, as on the act to safeguard the security of the church and the freedom of trade article. The court group was, of course, under tighter control than the opposition, who were not subjected to the same pressure to attend and vote. Nevertheless the serious drops in the opposition vote would seem to have been significant.

10 The 'explanations'

Trouble for the court developed over the so-called 'explanations'. The committee appointed to examine the financial and trade articles detected what they thought were disadvantageous provisions relating to trade and taxation. As a remedy they proposed amendments which, for the sake of appearances, since the treaty was already negotiated and published, it became customary to call the 'explanations'. Some of these concerned questions of minor principle whilst others involved wording rather than substance. Marchmont thought, justifiably, that most of them would have no material effect.[184] Defoe, masquerading as a disinterested Englishman with some knowledge of trade who merely happened to be in Edinburgh, was virtually co-opted on to the committee and helped to draft the 'explanations'. He, too, thought them insignificant.[185] But insignificant or not, great importance began to attach to them in the Scottish parliament. A sufficient number of courtiers favoured them to allow ministers to argue that they were necessary for the passing of the union. Seafield, for instance, claimed that 'without these alterations nothing can be done that will please the trading people'[186] although the 'trading people' had not hitherto been much in evidence or greatly considered. It is not at all clear, either, why the 'explanations' caused such a stir. The changes were in practice quite as insignificant as Marchmont and Defoe had thought them, so that the question does arise of what all the fuss was about: a lot of noise generated in the excitement of the moment, a final gesture of independence by some members of the Scottish parliament or, more probably, a political tactic on the part of the court to indicate that they were not as dependent on the English as they might have appeared?

One 'explanation' was an amendment to the provisions under which Scottish ships were to be accepted as British within the meaning of the navigation acts. All ships in which Scotsmen had a share were to count as British if within twelve months of union the Scots bought out any foreign interests. In the original articles ships owned partly by foreigners at the union were to have been excluded. Apart from the principle involved the effect of this change would seem to have been minimal.[187] The same was true of the demand for drawbacks on the export of salted beef and pork, in which Scotland's trade was inconsiderable anyway, but this was carried by one vote to give Scottish merchants, on paper, the same rights as the English.[188] Premiums on the export of meal were adjusted and the linen duty was more closely defined.[189] More emotional appeal lay in the question of the excise on Scottish 'twopenny ale'. A proposal that it should not be taxed any higher than the current rate was carried with some enthusiasm.[190] The twentieth article was 'explained' in the sense that superiorities were to be treated as private rights and safeguarded as such.[191] Really serious breaches in the negotiated treaty were avoided, though sometimes narrowly. Demands for a more rigorous exemption from malt duty and Saltoun's motion that the exemption should be perpetual were defeated in favour of exemption for the duration of the war, but only as a result of Seafield's casting vote.[192] Obviously there were limits beyond which the court could not go in demonstrating that they were not English lackeys if such was their intention. The usual sequence was that the court put forward an 'explanation' in response to some criticism of the treaty only to find it challenged by a more radical proposal which had then to be put to a vote. Proposals for reducing taxation were bound to be popular. In this situation the court was probably hard put to it to restrain some of their own supporters, over reducing the malt tax, for example. Courtiers could easily have found themselves carried away when amendments were being accepted and changes seemed not only allowable but officially approved. The Scottish managers seemed to be agreed on the policy of allowing 'explanations' though Argyll tried to claim some sly credit by representing himself as the only man true to the original treaty.[193] However, some 'explanations' were obviously more significant than others and the court knew where to draw the line.

The 'explanations' led to some harassed correspondence with the English court and also the junto, the Scottish managers being apprehensive of criticism from that quarter. The English did disapprove because every amendment was likely to make their task more difficult when the revised treaty came before the English parliament. The junto and Godolphin did their utmost in urging the Scots to avoid changes in the original articles, suggesting that the required alterations should instead be put into an address to the queen. The Scots were assured they could depend on a British parliament taking note of this, it being unthinkable that any region should be treated too harshly.[194]

But as it appeared that the Scots were already voting amendments the English tone changed and they were prepared to accept minor changes which did not affect the calculation of the equivalent.[195] Reopening that topic was out of the question. It would lead to delay and actively invite trouble in Scotland, where the opposition had already challenged not only the equivalent appropriations but the whole basis of the calculation. Early in the session Atholl had moved that no union should be agreed to unless England refunded the losses of the Africa Company before February 1707, presumably as a direct payment in addition to the equivalent. That proposal was shelved.[196] Saltoun later put forward a motion that Scotland should not be committed at all to repayment of any English debts. As with many of Saltoun's statements of principle it is difficult to detect exactly what he had in mind, but his motion seems to have been taken as an attack on the basis of the equivalent. The Scottish managers fully accepted the English view that the Scottish parliament was no place for a detailed reappraisal of the equivalent and were able to remain firm over this. A number of the opposition, too, preferred not to vote against the prospect of ready money from which some of them stood to gain and this proved to be another occasion when the strength of the opposition dropped.[197]

11   Last-minute manoeuvres in the Scottish parliament

The full treaty of union with 'explanations' and the act of church security tacked on to it was finally voted and touched with the sceptre on 16 January 1707.[198] From this point differences began to emerge between the unionists in parliament as the prospect of changes loosened discipline. Friction appeared between the estates. Disagreements and accusations of broken faith occurred amongst the old party as different elements sought their own advantage. Nor was the squadrone immune from internal recrimination. More dramatically co-operation between the old party and the squadrone began to break down, relations between them, never very cordial, taking a bad turn for the worse. This antagonism between the court and the squadrone was in fact only one aspect of the disruption in the parliament but because each party tried to use any dispute to discredit its opponents the issues were so misrepresented that the party split appears to predominate.

Nevertheless the differences became public, and were fought out at the end of the session in a thin house. So ill-attended was parliament by then that the election of the thirty shire representatives to the United Kingdom parliament was arranged by only thirty-five barons.[199]

The apportionment of the forty-five representatives between shires and burghs brought to the surface the latent antagonism between barons and nobility. The barons wanted to exclude from commons representation the eldest sons of peers, an attitude greatly resented by the peerage. When the allocation of seats was being decided the barons tried to gain their point by means of a bargain with the burghs. They agreed to the burghs' taking fifteen out of forty-five seats—seen as a generous if not excessive share—in return for the burghs' support against the eligibility of peers' eldest sons. Some of the burghs then defaulted, helping the peers to avoid a definite prohibition of their eldest sons. It was left to the house of commons to declare them ineligible as an outcome of election petitions in 1708.[200]

There were strong disagreements, too, about how and when the first Scottish election for the British parliament should take place. Some of the opposition favoured a general election for the Scottish commons' representatives. Both the old party and the squadrone shied away from this as likely, in the then state of the country, to produce an anti-unionist or even jacobite majority. In an attempt to ensure that all members returned to Westminster were supporters of union Marchmont proposed that election should take place in the existing parliament and be confined to its members. There was not much dispute over this, the proposal being carried by twenty votes.[201] But the crucial point was the timing of this election. It was over this that differences of opinion began to create what seemed like an alignment of the squadrone against the old party. Some of the old party wanted an election later in the year in a special session of parliament when the dust had settled on the union debate. It was the squadrone's suspicion that this timing was designed to arrange their exclusion from any share in representation in favour of some of Queensberry's cavalier friends who had opposed the union. If this was intended it was a difficult scheme to press in the face of the squadrone's pleas of urgency and talk of security for the union, so the decision was taken to hold an immediate election. The squadrone claimed the credit, using the old party's desire for delay in an attempt to discredit them with the junto. They hinted that the old party's ambivalent attitude to the election sprang from uncertainty about what the English court expected from them, a rumour, well founded or not, precisely calculated to undermine the whigs' faith in their strategy of an old party alliance. It was true that the old party lacked enthusiasm for an immediate election, some being either absent or abstaining when the issue was decided. Animosity towards the squadrone accounted for this in part but it might even have been true that some were unwilling to risk offending if the English court's wishes were in doubt. Reluctance was shown not only by Queensberry men but also by Leven, who passed for a dedicated supporter of the Hanoverian succession.[202] The squadrone made much of this. Baillie was fully aware of the significance of the Scottish elections in the whig scheme. He reported to Johnston that the proposed deferment 'might defeat the design of a whig election . . .' Without squadrone support '. . . the union could not have been done, nor this last job [of having an immediate choice of Scottish representatives from the existing parliament], the failing whereof might have ruined the whig lords . . .'[203] The squadrone were making the first positive moves to convince the junto that support for them might prove a better investment than the old party alliance they had in mind. Some benefit might be extracted from the junto's disillusionment if they could be convinced that not even Leven was to be relied upon.

After the election had produced some curious alignments, especially over the peers' voting lists, the shape of the squadrone plan became even more definite. They turned, much less tentatively than hitherto, to the idea of a whig alliance. Baillie made the most of what ammunition was provided for him. '. . . Since concluding the union,' he told Johnston, 'the ministry have not dealt by the new party as formerly . . .'[204] '. . . The ministry are our masters and overawed by Argyll, who pretends not only to a good share but to exclude others . . .'[205] Then, when Hamilton and some of the jacobites were found voting for old party men who reciprocated by voting for them in preference to the squadrone, Baillie wrote, 'The court's having been for any who voted for tories, and that the tories should have voted for the ministry, may be easily understood unless the whigs be blind.'[206]

Squadrone attempts to influence the whigs were accompanied by their efforts to pose as champions of the popular interest. A dispute arose between them and the old party over payment to the union commissioners of 1702 and 1706. Payments to courtiers, when publicised, were always unpopular, and the squadrone tried to take advantage of the fact. It seemed a promising move, since payment involved the equivalent in which so many Scots had an interest. Nor had the squadrone anything to lose, none of them having sat on either commission. Their views on what they claimed were extravagant payments to union commissioners were well known to the old party, though that did not deter Argyll from proposing £1,000 for noblemen and £500 for others who served on the commission of 1706. Baillie's counter-proposal of a more modest sum was defeated. Then, without previous warning to the squadrone, the court moved similar payments to the commissioners of 1702 which were also carried. The allowances were accorded a priority on the equivalent immediately following compensation to Africa Company shareholders.[207] At this the squadrone spoke out strongly against priorities, demanding proportionate payments across the board to all classes according to the money available. Courtiers resented the publicity given to such payments and blamed squadrone malice. John Clerk was outraged at opposition to what he saw as his just payment but once the allowances were safely voted he reflected upon his financial prospects with his habitual complacency. His father was not sure that he was right to do so. He did not object to payment for the commissioners but thought it monstrous that the money should be a charge on the equivalent.[208] Technically there was nowhere else the money could have come from. Yet in his objections Sir John Clerk's instinct was right. The equivalent was already being looked upon, and by people who should have known better, as a cornucopia which would supply all the financial requirements of the kingdom. There is no doubt that the mere idea of such a sum went to the heads of a large number of Scotsmen. They were later to discover that £400,000 or thereabouts did not go as far as they expected.

The squadrone also had internal squabbles. Some annoyance was aroused by Roxburgh and Montrose, who began to show symptoms of the complacency and inertia which explain much of their subsequent ineffectiveness. In addition to other rewards these two peers had had their elections virtually guaranteed by the court and, content with that, made no attempt to push on their colleagues' behalf.[209] According to Baillie, had they done so, Rothes, Haddington and Marchmont would also have been elected, but Roxburgh and Montrose remained passive. In all this it is possible to detect the tensions arising from their forthcoming entry into united kingdom politics. The squadrone leaders were agreed that their options had to be kept open and the possibility of a whig alliance borne in mind.[210] Beyond that, varying degrees of purposefulness were manifested. During the passage of union the party's only guarantee for the future lay in their special relationship with Godolphin and such rare whiffs of goodwill as emanated from the old party. Roxburgh and Montrose, lulled by the promise of further reward, were reluctant to antagonise the English court, placing excessive trust in Godolphin's gratitude. Others, uneasily aware that their hold on the court had evaporated with the passing of union, were intensifying their search for an alternative form of insurance. Baillie, for one, had no illusions about Godolphin's position. The lord treasurer would do whatever seemed best for the management of the British parliament, so much depended on the future relationship between the Scottish old party and the English court. One thing was certain: no generosity was to be expected from the old party leaders. During the union parliament Seafield, in his reports to Godolphin, was invariably scrupulous over giving the squadrone full credit for their exertions[211] In this he was quite alone. The leading figures of the old party denied any obligation to the squadrone even when acknowledging their existence, which was seldom. The malice shown towards the squadrone is remarkable by most standards. The explanation of some of it lies in Queensberry's character. Apart from his desire to damage possible competitors he could neither accept blame nor tolerate the thought of credit being due to others. The mere rumour that Montrose, then lately appointed president of the council, was not in favour of union produced on Queensberry's instructions a hasty letter from Sir David Nairn to Mar. Should Montrose 'be indifferent in the matter, it will be a reflection on all of you who concurred in recommending him . . .'[212] Not, seemingly, a reflection on Queensberry, who had not only concurred but persistently attempted to secure Montrose's alliance. Initially he had claimed he could pass union solely on his own interest. Closer to the event he was sure he could do it with help from numerous others,[213] a dependence which filled him with chagrin and aroused him to obsessive self-justification. In consequence he arrogated to himself the credit for all the court's successes.[214] Seafield, who carried the burden of the session, was still *persona non grata* to Queensberry and received scant acknowledgement. At Godolphin's suggestion that the union was not proceeding quickly enough Queensberry denounced the squadrone for insisting on frequent adjournments.[215] Hamilton, meanwhile, was blaming the squadrone for pushing on business too frenziedly and too fast.[216] Johnston told Baillie, '*Queensberry* seems to be much in earnest but cannot bear, in case matters do, that others should bear the name'.[217]

Other members of the old party did everything they could to deny the squadrone any credit. Montrose was represented as the man who had converted them to union and so, by implication, their support was due to the courtiers who had brought in Montrose.[218] Leven's attempts to belittle the squadrone were incessant and tortuous. Early in the parliament he claimed that the majority of sixty-six against Belhaven's demand for a week's adjournment demonstrated the old party's supremacy, showing they could manage comfortably without assistance[219] whereas part of this majority was due to the squadrone and to opposition members anxious to show zeal for business. Even Hamilton had voted with the court.[220] Leven subsequently went out of his way to deny that the squadrone were in any way necessary to the court, which was the lie direct, its being by that time obvious that the court depended on squadrone votes. He estimated their strength at no more than fifteen votes or so. Lest there should still be doubt at the English court as to his meaning, he claimed that the court had already taken off most of the squadrone so that the leaders, Tweeddale, Roxburgh, Rothes and Haddington, had had to follow or lose their interest.[221] It was perfectly true that the squadrone leaders had been under pressure but Leven's version of events was brazen. His malice against Rothes, his family's rival in Fife, and all his connections, had bitten so deeply into him that on the subject of the squadrone he was quite unbalanced. Since Godolphin was in a position to evaluate all this misinformation perhaps the English had some excuse for habitually treating many Scottish politicians with contempt.

There was, naturally, more to all this than malice although that was plentiful. Calculation had its part. The Scots were enveloped in uncertainty over what was to happen after the union. Everyone knew that the political balance at Westminster was precarious. The whigs had managed the union and were apparently in the ascendant yet an outright alliance with them still seemed a gamble. Whatever bargains the Scots had made during the negotiations they did not intend keeping if they became disadvantageous. And all were agonising over how best to conduct themselves, leaving open the way for an alliance with either court or junto according to developments. Even Seafield was worried. His acknowledged allegiance was to Godolphin and the court but he knew that others were writing continually to the whig lords. Uneasy at the prospect of losing valuable ground with men who might shortly constitute the court and have his future at their disposal, he pleaded with Godolphin to be allowed at least to establish communication with

the junto: '. . . I believe it will not be unfit that some who treated with
us also know what is my part in all this matter, and, if your lordship
approve of it, I will write to my lord Sunderland or my lord Somers
. . .[222]

12   *English reappraisals of the effects of union*

Such fears were understandable. The union could make a big impact
on the political situation at Westminster. Interested parties in England
found their enthusiasm for union fluctuating in accordance with their
latest appraisal of the possible results. All had contingency plans
against one eventuality or another. Even whilst the treaty was before
the Scottish parliament it was not easy from outside to establish quite
clearly what anyone thought about the union now that its completion
was in sight, much less what any group proposed to do about it.
Johnston was as close to the English court as most interested onlookers
and, although over-prone to alarms, excursions and deep suspicion, he
was puzzled. About one thing only was he clear: '. . . None [connected
with the court] are so *against the union* as to be willing to take *the load* of
the *miscarriage upon them* . . .[223] That was not to say there would be no
attempt at quiet sabotage if it proved feasible and served a purpose. But
both the court and the junto were in the same predicament, committed
to support of the union, had in the junto's case claimed credit for it, and
now, unless it could be sabotaged indirectly, they had to see it through.
As Johnston told Baillie, there was disquiet under the surface. 'The
court is mighty uneasy: they do not dissemble that the union confounds
them by disjointing all their measures . . .[224] The junto had had
misgivings for some time. Johnston tried to fathom their real feelings
but without success. '. . . *The whig lords* see enough and apprehend the
worse, but they distrust one another and indeed there is so much
artifice at present that nobody knows whom to trust in . . .[225]
Marlborough started to murmur that the junto were turning against
the union 'and indeed some of them have talked very oddly', Johnston
thought.[226]

As the date of union approached there were enough portents to make
them at the very least talk oddly. Their original scheme of an old party
alliance seemed increasingly unrealistic. Such hesitation as they
showed gave the court opportunity for a campaign to recover the
initiative by reasserting their position as the constant union interest
whilst representing the junto as the jibbers and shufflers.

Marlborough's reported comments seem to have been part of this move. Once again the court set out to placate the old party who were to form the majority of Scottish representatives at Westminster. Malborough assured Leven that the court would take their advice in all things.[227] A squadrone observer in London reported, '. . . The duke of Queensberry manages all. The squadrone is not so much as minded . . .'[228] With some satisfaction Clerk of Penicuik remarked on the same development: '. . . The squadrone behaves very discreetly for they never make a complaint, nor are they in any capacity to wrong anybody for they have not the queen's ear but by the duke of Queensberry . . .'[229] According to Clerk, so great was the court's appreciation of Queensberry's services that they would do nothing without his advice, so that the squadrone's attempts to 'stand upon their own legs, without owing their preferment to the duke of Queensberry . . .' were doomed to failure.[230] This sudden court zeal to gratify Queensberry beyond the mere granting of routine honours meant one of two things: either they were making a strong effort to recover the allegiance of the old party or they had already been assured of it and were paying the price. The latter appears the more likely.

It is clear what Godolphin was playing at, and who could blame him? As the parties stood in the Scottish parliament the squadone had been vital to the passing of the union. Had the whigs' original gamble succeeded the squadrone would have been extremely useful in the Westminster parliament, which had been the point of Godolphin's earlier plan. But after the elections it was obvious that, in British politics, they were going to be numerically insignificant. If the old party, as the bulk of the Scottish representation, reverted to type, as courtiers, Godolphin had no need of the squadrone. Some semblance of gratification could be given them by elevating Roxburgh and Montrose to Scottish dukedoms and distributing amongst the remainder such places on the exchequer, privy council and commission of the equivalent as their numbers seemed to warrant.[231] If this retained their allegiance in addition to that of the old party so much the better, otherwise the court would make do with such reinforcement as the old party brought.

Developments during and after the last session of the Scottish parliament disturbed the whigs. Their original gamble had failed and now the situation had continually to be reappraised and all eventualities taken into account. For the junto, as for everyone else, the key question was which English group now seemed most likely to benefit from union. Each interest had the problem of minimising any advantage to their rivals whilst doing the best they could for themselves. At first the whigs had clung to their original scheme, opposing any development which seemed to endanger it. But those days were over. The Scottish court party was not to be relied upon and consequently the future had come to seem hazardous. For the time being the junto resorted to paring down the advantages that seemed likely to fall to the court. They had resisted the proposal that Scottish peers should be chosen in rotation as too much of a lucky dip threatening the junto's position in the upper house.[232] They became preoccupied with the possibility of Scottish peers' being given English peerages and being allowed to sit by right. Originally they had thought the squadrone the most probable candidates for promotion but this was no longer true. The whigs had begun to fear the old party. There were precedents for elevating Scotsmen to the English peerage and no shortage of candidates. Argyll had squeezed an English peerage out of the court in 1705. Queensberry was made duke of Dover as part of his reward for the union. Stair had died of a stroke in the last days of the Scottish parliament and his eldest son was already asking for an English peerage in recognition of his father's services.[233] There was talk of twelve creations in addition to the sixteen elective peers provided for in the treaty.[234] The addition to the lords of twenty-eight extra peers would certainly have been aimed at destroying the whig majority there. Whatever allegiance the sixteen elective peers might profess the court would make sure that any new creations were courtiers. Such rumours and possibilities inclined the five lords to pessimism. Nottingham said that by the terms of the union he thought the queen could not make any more Scots sitting peers, at which 'my lord Halifax answered that he wished it were so . . .'[235] and the whigs used all the leverage they could muster against such new creations. They succeeded in starting such a rumble of discontent that assurances were squeezed from the court to the effect that there would be no new creations for at least two years. Nevertheless the junto did not relax the pressure. When the Scots, particularly the peers, were stigmatised as corrupt by the tories in the English union debates in the commons, the whigs seemed disposed to agree with them. The Scots were to be discredited as unfit for permanent seats in the lords.[236]

So the junto's private attitude to union fluctuated, as did that of everyone else, in accordance with their current estimate of its effect on their own position.[237] They placed no reliance on the old party whilst still experiencing the occasional resurgence of hope. They were quite prepared to claim credit for union where they thought it would do them some good, in Hanover for instance,[238] where they represented the union as part of a sweeping international scheme to ensure the safety of the Hanoverian succession.[239] Somers implied that the queen herself was but a recent convert to union, owing her final persuasion to the whigs, than which nothing could have been further from the truth.[240]

At the same time and nearer home they hinted that the union project bristled with insuperable difficulties.[241] Somers was reaching the conclusion that it would damage the whigs' prospects in England.[242] Significantly, when, in December 1706, after a long struggle with the queen, they secured a real foothold in the administration with the appointment of Sunderland as secretary of state, their interest in the union noticeably waned.[243] Such an advance in influence seemed to show that their attitude to union in the early years of the reign had been the right one. Pressure on Godolphin paid off. They would have been better without union, which was bringing too many complications to the political scene. Even so, they could not be seen to withdraw their support mid-stride. After all that had been said they had to allow the union to take its course however half-heartedly.

When the treaty had been ratified in Edinburgh the next step was to push it through the English parliament, which only close collaboration between the English court and the junto could guarantee. The whigs were briefly perked up by this spell of acting as almost a part of the court. '*The lord treasurer* and *the whig lords* having concerted matters as to their own parliament, seem more one than ever . . .' wrote Johnston. But at least one piece of grit ensured that the machinery was not completely smooth-running. Johnston continued: '. . . I told you that *Harley* is certainly *against the union*. I cannot be deceived in that . . .'[244] Politicians underestimated Robert Harley at their peril and there was no perfidy of which the whigs did not profess to believe him capable. He constituted an obstacle to their advancement, and with him in the court they could never be wholly certain of its attitude. So they bore in mind the need for insurance against the old party's treachery, since by this time it was obvious that the court and Queensberry had reached some agreement. Johnston reported to Baillie '. . . *The whig lords* begin to talk very favourably of *the new party*, and affect to do it of Roxburgh. Somers & C are now convinced of what *Johnston* has often said, that without *the new party the whigs* will not be gainers by *the union* . . .'.[245] Shortly afterwards Somers wrote to Marchmont hinting that they were open to proposals and asserting that everyone concerned in passing the union should be given credit.[246] Johnston, who believed in clinching advantageous bargains as soon as they became possible, urged the squadrone leaders to travel to London as soon as the Scottish parliament was over; '. . . if nobody come, *Queensberry* & C will get all that is to be given and do what they please whereas *the whig lords*, now that the great job is done, will yield to what is reasonable if they be well informed, particularly for gaining a majority to their own side . . .'[247]

13 Ratification in England

But in the meantime, whatever doubts stirred under the surface, once the Scots had ratified the treaty the English had to do likewise. Nobody, as Johnston said, was anxious to take publicly upon himself the onus of wrecking the union. On 28 January 1707 the queen spoke to both houses to tell them that the Scots had ratified the treaty and she recommended them to do the same.[248] Immediately afterwards the commons began proceedings and the treaty was ratified there by a combination of court, junto and Harleyite votes to an accompaniment of tory dissent and abuse but little effective action. There was, perhaps, by this stage, little the tories could have done but their tactics resembled those of the Scottish opposition: attempts to complicate and delay proceedings by such expedients as trying, but unsuccessfully, to force a debate on the minutes of the abortive negotiations of 1702.[249] The union treaty was considered by a committee of the whole house with Compton in the chair. Charles Caesar opened for the opposition 'and raised, though modestly, some scruples against the union'. He was seconded by Packington, who was anything but modest. He gave one of his most intemperate performances. The union, he said, 'was like the marrying a woman against her consent: a union that was carried on by corruption and bribery within doors and by force and violence without . . .' It was unpopular in Scotland and opposition had been restrained only by force and the threat of it. The Scottish unionists '. . . in thus basely giving up their independent constitution had actually betrayed the trust reposed in them and therefore he could leave it to the judgement of the house to consider whether or no men of such principles were fit to be admitted to sit amongst them?' He then emphasised the impossibility of the queen's being sworn to maintain the Church of England in one half of a united kingdom and presbyterianism in the other half.[250] After this general dununciation of union and all it stood for, the opposition proposed deferring the first article until the rest of the treaty had been debated. They were defeated, which led some to secede, so enabling the treaty to be pushed through with even more expedition.[251] On 4 February the committee approved articles one to five and on the 8th the rest of the treaty. There were protests that they were going post-haste on a question of the greatest importance. Sir Thomas Littleton, for the court, answered: 'That deliberation always supposes doubts and difficulties, but no material objections being offered against any of the articles there was no room for delays.' Some members at this began to shout 'Post-haste! Post-haste!' to which Littleton replied: 'They did not ride post-haste but a good easy trot and for his part, as long as the weather was fair, the roads good, and their horses in heart, he was of opinion they ought to jog on and not to be up till it was night.'[252] The committee took in its stride the lords' bill for the security of the Church of England, added to the treaty to balance the act for the security of the Scottish church establishment.[253] At the report stage some opposition amendments with a high church flavour were voted out.[254] Amendments extending to English traders any extra benefits the Scots had obtained by the 'explanations' were accepted.[255] The union passed the commons on 1 March by 274 votes to 116, which seems to indicate the extent of tory secession or abstention and possibly some cross-voting by tories prepared to accept union whether they relished it or not for the sake of the Hanoverian succession.[256]

In the lords the hard-line opposition to union stood no chance in the face of the combined court and junto vote. Perhaps because of this the tory peers seemed to take a perverse pleasure in beating their fists against a solid union vote and shouting about it. Nottingham,[257] backed by Rochester and Buckingham, had earlier tried to create entanglements by proposing to debate the union before the Scottish parliament had ratified it but Godolphin, with support from Wharton, Somers and Halifax, had put a stop to this proposal.[258] When the lords finally came to debate union it was in a committee of the whole house. Objections varied from the procedural to issues of principle. With few exceptions the ground taken by the opposition was that of favouring union whilst doubting the wisdom and equity of some of the provisions. They professed fears for the constitution and the safety of the Church of England. The usual demand was made for discussion of the first article to be postponed until the rest had been considered. Nottingham took exception to the title 'Great Britain', claiming that its use would totally

invalidate all existing English laws though with complete unanimity
the judges pronounced him to be in error on this point. The heavy work
was left to Haversham, who relished it. His preference, so he said, was
for a federal union with the same succession in both the kingdoms.
Indeed, as he pointed out, such offers had been made in the Scottish
parliament—by jacobites for the most part but he omitted to mention
this even if aware of it—so that he felt the proposed union to be
completely unnecessary. Furthermore: '. . . though the articles of union
are ratified by the Scotch parliament, yet the bulk and body of that
nation seem to be against them. Have not the murmurs of the people
there been so loud as to fill the whole nation? And so bold too, as to
reach even to the doors of the parliament? . . . my lords, I think an
incorporating union one of the most dangerous experiments to both
nations, in which, if we happen to be mistaken, however we may think
of curing things hereafter, the error is irretrievable . . .'[259] Scarborough,
oddly enough for a whiggishly inclined peer, made a speech of dubious
relevance ranging over Scotland's ills from Glencoe to Darien, laying
them all at the door of the unfortunate Tweeddale, having confused
him with his father, dead for ten long years.[260]

Apart from such general denunciations, every article seems to have
been opposed. At the end of the committee stage, on 24 February 1707,
Nottingham apologised for having troubled their lordships in almost
every article, but he saw cause. The end of the laws and constitution of
England was imminent and he prayed that God might 'avert the dire
effects which might probably ensue from such an incorporating
union'.[261] All this came strangely from a man who had been in favour of
such a union in 1702. Three days later the bishop of Salisbury reported
from the committee and the union was voted in the house.[262]

The lords divided on the articles with regularity. The court and whig
majority remained steady at about seventy, with the opposition vote
fluctuating slightly between nineteen and twenty-three.[263] This points
to a fairly normal attendance in the lords, with the kind of division to be
expected when the whigs and some of the moderate tories voted with
the court.[264]

When ratification was completed the queen spoke to both houses in
terms proper to the occasion: '. . . I desire and expect from all my
subjects of both nations, that so it may appear to all the world, they
have hearts disposed to become one people. . .'[265]

Soon afterwards the commons tidied up various financial loose ends
by voting the equivalent and compensating Carlisle and various

individuals for the loss of tolls due to the abolition of the border.[266] This virtually concluded official business save for the many necessary administrative provisions, for the most part the task of the treasury. The mere thought of them led Godolphin to write gloomily to Harley: 'I foresee a thousand difficulties and inconveniences during this whole summer, and perhaps longer, of making the management of the revenues of that kingdom but tolerably practicable . . .'[267] The state of Scottish revenue was to be quite intolerable for most of the eighteenth century but it was perhaps as well for Godolphin's peace of mind that he could not foresee that.

14 Harley and the union

The political repercussions were not mentioned quite so openly but they occupied a dominant position in everyone's mind. It was widely known that there was no sympathy between Harley and his new colleague, Sunderland. Harley had watched with increasing disquiet the junto's steady encroachment on the court throughout the union proceedings. Defoe, in Edinburgh, had been asked for information by both Halifax and Somers but knowing Harley's feelings he had felt obliged to ask how much it was proper to tell them.[268] Shrewsbury had decided, on the strength of Vernon's reports, that there was little hope of harmony at court, given Harley's views on the junto.[269] He was not mistaken. During the previous November whilst the treaty was still before the Scottish parliament Harley had given Godolphin a solemn warning against junto pressures, to back up his earlier complaints about the whig attitude.[270] No matter what had been done for them, he argued, they felt under no obligation to the court, as their future conduct would increasingly show. They had begun to concentrate their attacks on the 'sneakers', or moderate tories, without whose assistance they would not have done so well in the 1705 election. It was for these moderates, some of them his own followers, that Harley was appealing. 'I hope your lordship will rescue us from the violence of either party . . . There is a disposition to do everything that is reasonable without any previous engagement . . .',[271] a different attitude, he might have added, from that of the junto. Into this situation an uncertain Scottish element was to intrude. Harley was worried about its likely effect and was thought to be trying to sniff out the squadrone's intentions.[272] As a court manager, Harley had favoured union from an early date. Later, when the union took on more and more the appearance of a junto scheme and Godolphin seemed to be binding himself to the whigs more closely than Harley thought desirable, his attitude to the union became equivocal. Sunderland's appointment in December 1706 seems to have placed Harley in a dilemma over his priorities. To solve the Scottish problem and strengthen the court, if that was to be its effect, Harley wanted union. If, however, it settled Scotland but led to junto domination at Westminster, it would mean the end of all his hopes for moderate government and the extreme likelihood of his dismissal. He might well have been unwilling to make such sacrifices for the sake of union.

But Harley, like the junto, could not risk being branded as its public executioner. Appearances had to be preserved whatever his ultimate decision. Harley preserved them to the extent that he is frequently regarded as the English minister who contributed most to the union's success. This reputation rests on letters in which he commended union to his various Scottish acquaintances[273] and his employment of agents, notably Defoe, to assist the cause of union in Scotland. But this task was Harley's as secretary of state. To have shirked it would have meant abandoning everything to the junto. Yet there is little evidence of any zeal in 'working' his agents, even allowing for the importance of maintaining secrecy. He did not answer Defoe's letters. This could have been due to caution but Defoe, no stranger to this kind of activity, thought it sufficiently odd to complain frequently.[274] More singular was the fact that Harley did not see Defoe before he left for Scotland, nor did he give him any instructions. Initially, Defoe drafted his own.[275] Defoe professed himself '. . . unhappy only in wanting your letter, instructions, & C . . . Methinks I look very simple when to myself I reflect how I am your messenger without an errand, your ambassador without instructions, your servant without orders . . . Sir, you know without a strict correspondence it will be impossible for me to act by your measures or to know what course to steer . . .'[276] Some rather belated and sketchy instructions seem to have been sent, probably some time in October.[277] There is no sign here of unusual zeal for the union. Johnston sent in October the latest gossip from London, where Harley's intentions were a subject of continual speculation, about the secretary's attitude to the union. Johnston's views were based partly on general talk and in part on an appraisal of Harley's position if the union were passed. He thought Harley was for union merely for the sake of appearances, having no desire to be blamed should anything go wrong.[278] Later, in the following month, Johnston was more positive:

'You may depend on this, and that Harley is against the union . . .'[279]

So much is conjecture. It is difficult to say what Harley was up to, not merely in 1706–7 but for much of the time. However, circumstances provide one glimpse into the way his mind was working. There proved to be a loophole in the union's trade provisions. On 1 May 1707, when the union was officially to begin, trade restrictions between Scotland and England were to cease, the border customs posts were to close and goods could then be freely transported within the United Kingdom. Until that date the Scots were to operate their own customs and excise system with substantially lower duties than those in England. Some merchants, English for the most part but including some Scots—and, according to Harley, 'Dutch, Jews, Swedes, Danes, & C . . .'[280]—had seen the possibility of making a 'killing' out of this technicality. Goods, wine especially, could be imported from Holland to Scotland before the union, at the lower duties. After 1 May they could be sold in England to the great advantage of all concerned. How great an advantage is indicated by the fact that Samuel Shepheard, who did not involve himself with trifling profits, was in the scheme up to his neck. The project was London-based and members of parliament representing outports, such as Peter Shakerley for Chester, were worried on their constituents' account.[281] The affair was brought officially to the commons' notice by a petition from merchants importing wines and brandy from Spain, Portugal and Italy and various goods from Holland.[282] This was backed by strong protests from others calling themselves 'fair traders', fearing the damage they might suffer at the hands of the less scrupulous or at least those who had been quicker off the mark. The political significance of the issue was that almost overnight the junto lords had become unusually vulnerable. Clerk of Penicuik told his father that the fault lay with the whigs, who had failed to see this loophole when negotiating the union.[283] Now the junto had their own dilemma. They were anxious to retain merit in the eyes of the Scots for the sake of any support it might attract but at the same time they wished to retain the goodwill of the English merchant community. In the circumstances it was going to be difficult to succeed in both. Because of this dilemma the whig lords proved completely unable to deal with the problem.[284] Harley knew this quite well and seized the opportunity of increasing the junto's embarrassment and of inflicting on them, if possible, the utmost political damage regardless of any wider consequences. He is unlikely to have had any intention of sabotaging the union even had it been possible at that stage. More probably he aimed at discrediting the junto in both kingdoms, taking what advantage of their predicament he could.

In an attempt to close the loophole the treasury sponsored a bill, introduced by Lowndes in a depleted end-of-session commons.[285] The scheme provided for the compilation of a list of all ships importing goods to Scotland before the union. On 1 May the owners of such ships would then be liable for the normal English duties should the cargoes be transported from Scotland to England. Two difficult questions were involved. From when would this restriction operate? And was such a measure, applied to Scottish merchants, an infringement of the union? The proposal was from the start unpopular amongst merchants as an interference with normal trade. The decision to make it operate from 1 February was particularly opposed.[286] Ostensibly to meet the objection that the proposal infringed the union Harley brought in a clause exempting Scottish merchants resident in Scotland who could prove that their goods were imported on their own account, not by partnerships or rings including foreigners. To English merchants this was favouritism towards the Scots. The Scots in the partnerships against which the bill discriminated were ready to scream that there had been a breach of the union,[287] a cry likely to be widely echoed in Scotland regardless of the circumstances. Harley's proposal created a serious crisis. Edward Ashe told Townshend: ' 'Tis certain the method our very good friend the secretary got to pass the commons was not approved by the lords . . .'[288] It was not approved because Harley had neatly trapped the junto. They had negotiated the union and claimed the credit. Now Harley was trying to nudge them off the pedestal they had chosen for themselves. One of the union's more embarrassing defects was to be placed before them on the pretext of an honest attempt's being made to help them solve a problem. There seemed no action the whig lords could take which would not bring them into disfavour with one or other of the groups they had so assiduously cultivated. If they deleted the concession to Scotsmen living in Scotland there would without doubt have been a breach of the union. Letting it stand would arouse strong feelings in England. Harley's motive was fairly clear and the junto lords were enraged. An embarrassed Godolphin told Marlborough that much of the trouble was due to private animosities.[289] Shrewsbury thought that the bill might break up the court coalition.[290] Cunningham, an observer of the scene though writing a considerable time afterwards, attributed responsibility for the commons' measure to Harley. In fact he dated the estrangement between Godolphin and Harley from this episode.[291] It was left to Rochester, of all people, to propose an expedient, albeit an unsuccessful one: the prorogation of parliament for a day or so to allow the commons' bill to lapse and give them time to think of some other solution. The court adopted this course but when parliament reconvened the commons passed the same bill. There seemed to be only one way out—to bring the session to an end, leave things as they were and ignore the problem.[292] This is what Godolphin did, not wishing to see the junto gratuitously offended. Harley's account to Marlborough of the incident was written with every appearance of innocence. The commons, thought Harley, had shown great moderation, although some had thought the proposals too lenient to the Scots.[293] Sunderland was beside himself with rage at what he represented to Marlborough and Godolphin as Harley's treachery. '. . . I believe you will be surprised at this short prorogation,' he wrote to Marlborough. 'It is entirely occasioned by him who was the author of all the tricks played here. I need not name him having done it in my last letter to you. I will only say no man in the service of the government ever did act such a part. I wish those to whom he has acted it were ever capable of thinking him in the wrong for I fear it may be some time or other too late . . .'[294]

Harley attracted some blame from the Scots which he was anxious to shift elsewhere. He told Defoe: '. . . I am very sorry that you or your humble servant should bear reproach for doing what others could not or would not do, but it has been often so . . . the house of commons would have rescued us from the scandal and obliged Scotland; they had contrived to make the cheats do justice, and at the same time indulged the Scots with an opportunity of getting clear and honestly £150,000 to speak with the least— but Satan hindered . . . this is certain, if our Scots friends knew what a sweet morsel these people have taken out of their mouths, they would turn their rage the right way.'[295] Godolphin wrote to Harley in terms of mild remonstrance. He affected to believe that all the trouble had emanated from the Scots and their interpretation of the treaty. 'You were right,' he wrote, 'certainly not to be at the head of this thing, and perhaps your appearing in it before has been the occasion of all this broil . . .[296]

As far as the politicians were concerned this sort of episode had little to do with Scotland but a great deal to do with British politics after the union, a topic on which Harley's views and those shared by Godolphin and Marlborough were on divergent courses. None of them relished the prospect of being under the junto's thumb. However, Godolphin and

Marlborough, although prepared to evade this outcome as long as possible, were not prepared to issue open challenges and, in the last resort, were resigned to coming to terms with the whigs. Harley was not resigned to anything of the kind, thought his colleagues too easily alarmed by what to him was junto bluff which he was fully prepared to call. For Godolphin this was a dangerous rocking of the boat, hence his decision to prorogue parliament in 1707 before the affair got out of hand.

Similar considerations were involved in an apparently technical disagreement over the legal status of the first British parliament. This was due to meet in the autumn of 1707. Marlborough envisaged it as a completely new parliament with a full three years of life although there had been no election. Harley's view was that it should be treated as the English parliament elected in 1705 with only one year to go before the next election. Harley was undoubtedly right and his opinion prevailed. Onslow later saw this as a concern for legality on Harley's part which wholly became him as a former speaker of the commons.[297] Nevertheless, each man was taking the view which better suited him politically. Already a national war-weariness was apparent which Marlborough found alarming. For this reason he preferred to postpone an election until 1710, buying support for the war in the meantime by gratifying the junto. But an election in 1708, with the nation probably even more weary of the war and no collaboration as in 1705 between 'sneakers' and whigs, would certainly have damaged the junto's prospects. It could, though, have made the court stronger and more able to carry on government in accordance with Harley's ideas. It might at the same time have strengthened the wilder as well as the more moderate tories but this was a price Harley might have been prepared to pay in the hope that the court might hold the balance. The calculations of both Marlborough and Harley had a certain validity at the time. But the election was preceded by the ministerial crisis of 1708, Harley's dismissal and the attempted jacobite invasion. The jacobite attempt of 1708 produced a temporary swing of opinion in favour of war sufficient to return a whig majority to the commons for the first time in Anne's reign.[298] So Marlborough, in spite of having been worsted in the political skirmish, got in due course rather more than he had wanted.

15 *The measure of union*

By the side of more grandiose concepts of union such concerns seem petty. However, people exerted themselves to keep such sordid manoeuvres out of sight, successfully on the whole. When the Scots were welcomed to the first British parliament in October 1707 it was the sense of involvement in the creation of a new political entity which was formally dwelt upon. Seafield's uncle, Francis Montgomery of Giffen, in an atmosphere of great cordiality seconded the nomination of the speaker and helped to lead him to the chair. Yet these Scottish members, whether before the union or after, never ceased to be involved almost exclusively in competitive and opportunist manoeuvres. For the union was far from being the outcome of sweeping vision. What mattered to contemporaries were its more mundane and even sordid by-products. In so far as any single wider motive produced the union of 1707 it was that the two kingdoms, from the English point of view at least, were linked indissolubly, not only by historical accident but for practical reasons of security. The English and Scots had to make the best or worst of it and the worst could have been very bad. Looked at in these terms union was the best way of forging a manageable, though not necessarily a satisfactory, relationship. Some of the men of 1707 might have seen themselves as state-builders unleashing the tremendous potentialities of a united kingdom. Apart from Cromartie, whose name springs to mind and inspires no confidence, it is more than doubtful. When a change is proposed too radical or too complex in its ramifications to be understood by most, the politics of it, when not reduced to trivialities, are translated into other terms. The issue becomes a vehicle for consolidating alignments, crystallising existing differences or promoting sectional interest. So it was with union. If one persists in thinking in terms of foresight, vision and statesmanship, little praise is due to most of the architects of union. Some mention, up to a point honourable, may go to such as Godolphin and Seafield, whose realisation of what the worst could be led them to fear it. But the achievement of union was due more to shifty devices for achieving predominance in Scotland or to the calculations concerning Scottish representation at Westminster which so exercised the junto and the court. The court hoped that union would bring it an accession of strength as conventional political wisdom had always held it would. The junto had been driven to gamble on the Scots' tipping a finely balanced parliament in the whigs' favour although aware that the conventional view might well prove correct. Busily scavenging what they could on the fringes of this rivalry were the main Scottish interests. In terms of immediate practical politics this is what the union of 1707 was about.

Yet most of the short-term plotting proved to have been misdirected, creating results quite at variance with its aims. The old party, chased by the whigs as prospective allies in the British parliament, succumbed rapidly to the pull of the court and Godolphin's willingness to hand over to them, as a 'subaltern ministry', the management of Scotland.[299] After the union they remained courtiers and Godolphin accepted them as such. The squadrone, groomed for the status of court party to support Godolphin should the old party go astray, found themselves jettisoned when he was assured of the old party's continued co-operation. So the winter of 1707–8 found the squadrone and the junto in active alliance against the courtiers of both North and South Britain. Only with the whig victory in the election of 1708 and Godolphin's almost complete identification with the junto did the old party and squadrone find themselves, in spite of everything, temporarily on the same side. Notwithstanding their variegated past the old party, or most of them, achieved recognition as 'Scottish whigs' whilst the squadrone, perched on the junto's shoulder like a sailor's parrot, preened itself on being a rival whig interest.

Henceforward, although knives were frequently out in local rivalries, Scottish politics became little more than a reflection of divisions at Westminster. The old rule still remained valid: whenever the central government was stable and spoke with one voice the Scots did as they were told. Dissident whispers at the centre made Scottish management immediately less effective. This remained the pattern from the election of 1708, when the authentic voice of the court was in doubt and the Scots were undecided which group to support, to the ineffective handling of Scottish affairs after the fall of Walpole.

The union of itself did not bring immediate prosperity to Scotland, but then, although debated in those terms, it had not been designed for that purpose. Economic conditions after the union support the view that what pamphleteers, of either side, had written bore little relation to the Scottish economy and its prospects. If the absence of immediate prosperity fulfilled some of the anti-unionist predictions this was merely a particular instance of the general law that optimism is more often than not unjustified. The immediate economic effect of union was neither prosperity nor ruin. For long enough there were no consequences worth speaking of. The Scots were incensed by higher rates of taxation, discrimination against Scottish linen and the imposition of the malt tax in 1713, as they claimed, illegally. But these complaints merely focused sentiments that already existed. Scottish respect for the law was not great enough to make these grievances too burdensome in practice. The truth of the matter was that the Scots did not deserve to be taken quite as seriously as a trading and manufacturing nation as the union controversy suggested. Trade and manufacture were fringe activities in an agricultural economy rather than central features. Ultimately the well established Scottish enterprises—the grain trade, black cattle and the tobacco trade from the plantations to Glasgow, hitherto illegal—were provided with conditions enabling them to flourish quietly until the growth of Scottish capital and an influx of English capital permitted the exploitation of Scotland's resources during the industrial revolution. Scotland's economy was not suddenly energised by the union but, at least in the lowlands, underwent an almost imperceptible improvement in circulation which in time had a beneficial effect.

The long-term effects of the union, on the cultures of both nations, on British imperial expansion and on nineteenth- and twentieth-century politics have been incalculable but in the short term, which is what most were thinking of in 1707, the union made little noticeable difference. There was one big exception. The court, the chief motivating force behind the union, achieved its main objectives. Its aim had been the solution, or perhaps abolition, of serious political and administrative problems: the increasing difficulty of managing the Scottish parliament, the impossibility of containing the ambitions of Scottish magnates, tending as they did to anarchy, and the divisive effects of the religious settlement which identified episcopalianism with opposition or even disaffection. The Scottish parliament disappeared at the union and the power of the magnates did not for long survive exposure to British politics. When Archibald, the third duke of Argyll, died in 1761 he had for some time been an anachronism, although several administrations found him no less of an embarrassment for that. With his passing one of the main objectives of the union had been achieved. The incorporation of Scotland into a larger entity made it possible for episcopalians to be tolerated as they could not have been within the narrower confines of the Scottish kingdom. All these vital changes lifted a great burden from the court. Apart from the emergencies of the Fifteen and the Forty-five, never again until very modern times would the Scots be able to exert such pressures on the government in London as they had under William and Anne. The Scottish habit of supporting the court when its voice was unmistakable, and the absorption of Scotland into the English patronage system, transformed the ancient kingdom from a disruptive force into one which considerably strengthened the power of the central government. Scotland thus became an additional buttress of court dominance, helping to preserve the smooth working of the constitution and administration. If this is political stability then the union helped to establish it. In this sense the development of the British constitution owes more to the dead weight of the eighteenth-century Scottish members and the scandal of faggot voting than to the bill of rights.[300] When Seafield, as chancellor of Scotland, signed in 1707 the engrossed act of union and handed it to one of the clerks of parliament with the undeservedly notorious words 'Now there's an end of an old song',[301] he was signifying the end of a system which had no future but anarchy, civil war and English conquest with, most probably, an era of Scottish 'troubles' to follow in the nineteenth or twentieth century. For him good government was efficient management—the removal of friction between interests and of obstacles to the court's will. He was helping to inaugurate a period of fairly calm management and frictionless administration of a kind he must have dreamed of during the Darien crisis and the parliament of 1703. If there was any vision at all in the union it was that of Seafield and others like him with first-hand experience of the two kingdoms under the union of crowns. We may not find the vision an inspiring one but there are worse things than an obvious political solution to an otherwise intractable and dangerous problem, especially since in this instance the result was succcess. Other effects of union, whether viewed as a cultural and economic monument or as a disaster, are irrelevant to any judgement of the men who made it. Even a passionate belief that the United Kingdom has proved a blessing to both England and Scotland cannot transform Queensberry, Argyll or the five lords of the junto into far-sighted statesmen. But those who condemn what happened in 1707 as an act of violence against Scotland should reflect on the dire alternative, rapidly emerging after 1688, and say whether they find it acceptable.

Notes

¹ Buccleuch (Drum.), Union, ii, [Nairn] to [Queensberry], 13 Oct. 1705.

² Fraser, *Melvilles*, ii, 191–2, Marlborough to Leven, 15 Jan. 1705/6; *ib.*, 200–1, Leven to Mar, 7 Mar. 1706; *ib.*, 202–3, same to same, 14 Mar. 1706.

³ *Carstares S.P.*, 746, Mar to Carstares, 25 Mar. 1706; *HMCR Mar and Kellie MSS*, i, 256, Carstares to Mar, 2 Apr. 1706.

⁴ *Ib.*, 254, Rosebery to same, 11 Mar. 1706.

⁵ *Seafield Letters*, 92, Seafield to Godolphin, 6 Oct. 1705.

⁶ BM, Add. MSS 28055, 344, same to same, [Mar. 1706]; Fraser, *Melvilles*, 198–200, Mar to Leven, 2 Mar. 1705/6; SRO, GD 220, G, Glasgow to Montrose, 18 Jul. 1706.

⁷ *Ib.*, L, Loudoun to Montrose, 2 Mar. 1706.

⁸ *Ib.*, same to same, 9 Mar. 1706; *ib.*, N, Nairn to same, 25 Mar. 1706; *ib.*, L, Loudoun to same, 16 Jul. 1706.

⁹ *HMCR Mar and Kellie MSS*, i, 279, Nairn to Mar, 17 Sep. 1706; Blenheim Papers, A1/46, Queensberry to Marlborough, 28 Sep. 1706.

¹⁰ *Seafield Letters*, 171, Loudoun to Godolphin, 14 Oct. [1706].

¹¹ See above, p. 145 *et seq*.

¹² Buccleuch (Drum.), Union, ii, [Private instructions to Queensberry], 31 Jul. 1706.

¹³ *Stair Annals*, i, 228, lord Dalrymple to Mar, 9 Sep. 1706.

¹⁴ *HMCR Mar and Kellie MSS*, i, 270, Argyll to Mar, 18 Jul. 1706.

¹⁵ *Marlborough Dispatches*, iii, 17, Marlborough to Argyll, 23 Jul. 1706.

¹⁶ *Stair Annals*, i, 228, lord Dalrymple to Mar, 9 Sep. 1706; *HMCR Mar and Kellie MSS*, i, 279, Nairn to Mar, 17 Sep. 1706; *ib.*, 282, D. Campbell to same, 28 Sep. 1706.

¹⁷ *Ib.*, 286, Mar to Godolphin, 8 Oct. 1706; *ib.*, 288–9, same to Nairn, 8 Oct. 1706.

¹⁸ *Seafield Letters*, 94, Seafield to Godolphin, 14 Oct. 1706; *ib.*, 171, Loudoun to same, 14 Oct. [1706]; *HMCR Mar and Kellie MSS*, i, 295, Godolphin to Mar, 19 Oct. 1706; *ib.*, 303–4, Mar to Nairn, 29 Oct. 1706.

¹⁹ *Jerviswood*, 160, Johnston to Baillie, 21 Sep. [1706].

²⁰ *Seafield Letters*, 182, Glasgow to Godolphin, 4 Oct. 1706. For the distribution of the money see App. B.

²¹ See below, pp. 265–6.

²² As Dr Ferguson points out (*Scotland's Relations*, 249), such sums were more substantial in Scottish terms, though, one would have thought, still not over-impressive to Scottish peers. If £11 12*s* mattered then no wonder Scottish politicians were so venal.

²³ Compare Glencairn with Marchmont, for instance (App. B).

²⁴ *Lockhart Papers*, i, 271.

²⁵ See above, p. 90.

²⁶ Queensberry's arrears as stated at the union were made up as follows: £22,986 12*s* 2$\frac{7}{6}$*d* as lord commissioner, £1,500 as lord privy seal and £769 16*s* 9$\frac{5}{6}$ *d* as a lord of the treasury (BL, Add. MSS 35904).

[27] Cobbett, vi, 1110 *et seq.*

[28] See below, p. 260 *et seq.*

[29] *Atholl Chron.*, ii, 57, Scott to Atholl, 5 Jul. 1706; *ib.*, 58, duchess of Atholl to Scott, 13 Jul. 1706.

[30] Ferguson, *Scotland's Relations*, 247, 300 n. 49, discounts this possibility since there is no record of Dunmore's having received the £1,000. However, had the bargain been made as seems to have been intended, the money would not have appeared against Dunmore's name. They were Atholl's arrears and he did abstain or absent himself over ratification.

[31] See below, p. 260 *et seq.*

[32] See above, p. 118, and App. A.

[33] See above, p. 129 *et seq.*

[34] See above, p. 145 *et seq.*

[35] BL, Add. MSS 28055, 286, Johnston to Godolphin, 25 Aug. 1705.

[36] SRO, GD 248, Box 2/1, Letters from Godolphin, Godolphin to [Seafield], 1 Sep. 1705: '. . . give my humble service to my lord Roxburgh and acquaint him from me that the queen depends upon his assistance in everything extremely essential for her service and therefore hopes he will endeavour so to moderate the act for a treaty that she may be capable of giving her royal assent to it which in her majesty's opinion is the only way possible to avoid confusion in her kingdoms . . .' See also *Seafield Letters*, 76, Seafield to Godolphin, 26 Aug. 1705; *HMCR Laing MSS*, ii, 119–23, same to same, 9 Sep. 1705.

[37] *Jerviswood*, 119, Johnston to Baillie, 1 Sep. 1705.

[38] *Seafield Letters*, 82, Seafield to Godolphin, 2 Sep. 1705.

[39] *Ib.*, 83, same to same, 3 Sep. 1705.

[40] *Jerviswood*, 105, Roxburgh to Baillie, 6 Jun. 1705.

[41] BL, Add. MSS 28055, 188, 5 May 1705.

[42] *Jerviswood*, 111, Johnston to Baillie, 27 Jun. 1705; *ib.*, 119, same to same, 1 Sep. 1705.

[43] *Ib.*, 103, 6 Jun. 1705.

[44] *Ib.*, 103–74, *passim*; *ib.*, 155, 1 Jun. 1706.

[45] *Ib.*, 135–6, 13 Nov. 1705.

[46] *Ib.*, 139–40, Baillie to Roxburgh, 3 Dec. 1705.

[47] *Ib.*, 127, Johnston to Baillie, 2 Oct. [1]705; *ib.*, Baillie to Roxburgh, 10 Jan. 1705/6.

[48] *Ib.*, 148, same to same, 19 Feb. 1705/6.

[49] see above, p. 175 *et seq.*

[50] *Jerviswood*, 130, Baillie to Roxburgh, 15 Oct. 1705; *ib.*, 134, same to Annandale, 12 Nov. 1705; *ib.*, same to Roxburgh, 3 Dec. 1705; *ib.*, 146, same to Annandale, 8 Jan. 1705/6; *ib.*, 126, Roxburgh to Baillie, 29 Sep. 1705; *ib.*, 133, same to same, 29 Oct. 1705.

[51] *Ib.*, 21, same to same, 12 Dec. 1704; *ib.*, 28, same to same, 26 Dec. 1704.

[52] See above, p. 216.

[53] *Jerviswood*, 142, Baillie to Roxburgh, 15 Dec. 1705.

[54] *Ib.*, 143–4, same to same, 29 Dec. 1705.

⁵⁵ *Ib.*, 137–9, Roxburgh to Baillie, 28 Nov. 1705, quoted above, p. 216.

⁵⁶ E.g. *ib.*, 141, same to same, 15 Dec. 1705; *ib.*, 143, same to same, 22 Dec. 1705.

⁵⁷ *Ib.*, 145, Baillie to Roxburgh, 3 Jan. 1705/6.

⁵⁸ E.g. *ib.*, 150, same to same, 1 Apr. 1706.

⁵⁹ SRO, GD 205, Letters from Individuals, Jamieson to Bennett, 9 Jan. 1704/5; *ib.*, same to same, 20 Feb. 1704/5; *ib.*, same to same, 12 Nov. 1705; *ib.*, same to same, 1 Dec. 1705.

⁶⁰ *Ib.*, Letters of Sir W. Bennet, Bennet to Dirleton, 29 Jan. 1705; *ib.*, same to same, 5 Nov. 1705; *ib.*, same to same, 23 [Nov. or Dec. 1705]; *ib.*, same to same, 13 Apr. 1706.

⁶¹ *Jerviswood*, 145, Baillie to Roxburgh, 3 Jan. 1705/6.

⁶² *Ib.*, 152, same to same, 13 Apr. 1706.

⁶³ *Ib.*, 135–6, same to same, 13 Nov. 1705; SRO, GD 220, S, Seafield to Montrose, 1 Mar. 1706.

⁶⁴ SRO, GD 205, Letters of Sir W. Bennet, Bennet to Dirleton, 16 Oct. 1705; *ib.*, same to same, 2 Jan. 1706; *ib.*, same to same, 6 Jan. 1706; *ib.*, same to same, 27 Feb. 1706; *ib.*, Letters from Individuals, D. Hay to [Bennet], [31 Dec.] 1705; Buccleuch (Drum.), Stair, Bennet to [Queensberry] 12 Apr. 1706.

⁶⁵ *Jerviswood*, 159–60, Roxburgh to Baillie, 19 Sep. 1706.

⁶⁶ *Ib.*, 163, Baillie to Johnston, 8 Oct. 1706.

⁶⁷ *Ib.*, 159–60, Roxburgh to Baillie, 19 Sep. 1706.

⁶⁸ Blenheim Papers, A1/46, Tweeddale to Marlborough, 5 Jan. 1706; *HMCR Laing MSS*, ii, 124–5, same to Godolphin, 5 Jan. 1706.

⁶⁹ *HMCR Mar and Kellie MSS*, i, 286, 8 Oct. 1706.

⁷⁰ See App. B.

⁷¹ Fraser, *Melvilles*, ii, 203, Marlborough to Leven, 26 Mar. 1706.

⁷² See below, p. 295, and Riley, *English Ministers*, chap. 2.

⁷³ *Marlborough Dispatches*, iii, 239, Marlborough to Argyll, 29 Nov. 1706; Fraser, *Melvilles*, ii, 211, same to Leven, 4 Jan. 1706/7; *ib.*, 212, same to same, 13 Jan. 1706/7; *Marchmont Papers*, iii, 319, Marchmont to queen, 1 Feb. 1707.

⁷⁴ *Lockhart Papers*, i, 159.

⁷⁵ Cunningham, *History*, ii, 60.

⁷⁶ *HMCR Mar and Kellie MSS*, i, 379, Mar to Nairn, 27 Feb. 1706/7; *APS*, xi, 439–40. It was a very low vote: seventy-six to twenty-six.

⁷⁷ *Jerviswood*, 137–9, Roxburgh to Baillie, 28 Nov. 1705.

⁷⁸ SRO, GD 220, A, lord Anstruther to Montrose, 23 Dec. 1707.

⁷⁹ *Jerviswood*, 164, 15 Oct. 1706.

⁸⁰ *Ib.*, 163, 8 Oct. 1706.

⁸¹ E.g. *ib.*, 120, Roxburgh to Baillie, 8 Sep. 1705; *ib.*, 154, Baillie to Roxburgh, 14 May 1706 and *ib.*, 151–83, *passim*.

⁸² *Ib.*, 151, Johnston to Baillie, 6 Apr. [1]706; *ib.*, 153, Baillie to Roxburgh, 19 Apr. 1706; *ib.*, 154, same to same, 14 May 1706. The pamphlet *Vulpone: Or, Remarks On Some Proceedings in Scotland* ... (1707) bears the stamp of this strategy.

[83] *Jerviswood*, 159–60, Roxburgh to Baillie, 19 Sep. 1706.

[84] *Ib.*, 161, Johnston to Baillie, 5 Oct. [1706]; *ib.*, 162, same to same, 7 Oct. [1706].

[85] *Ib.*, 180, same to same, 17 Jan. 1706/7.

[86] See above, pp. 163–4, 168–9, 270.

[87] Cowper, *Diary*, 33, 6 Jan. 1705.

[88] See above, pp. 168–9.

[89] *Jerviswood*, 26, Johnston to Baillie, 21 Dec. 1704.

[90] E.g. BL, Add. MSS 28055, 5, [Harley] to [Godolphin], [1703]; Longleat, Portland MSS, 'Miscell. MSS' (a volume of Godolphin–Harley correspondence uncalendared by the HMC), 27, 130, 162–3, 166–7, 204: all undated letters; Blenheim Papers, B2/33, Harley to Godolphin, 20 Sep. 1703; BL, Loan 29/12, Harley's draft of a letter from the queen to Argyll, 6 [May 1705]. See above, p. 91, and BL, Add. MSS 28055, 103, Johnston to Godolphin, 19 Jun. 1704. Defoe, as Harley's mouthpiece, was a lone voice in defending Scottish proceedings over captain Green of the *Worcester* when the junto and the old party were condemning the new party to secure their dismissal: *Review*, 26 Apr. 1705.

[91] See chap. iv.

[92] See above, pp. 88–9, 149, *Jerviswood*, 35, Johnston to Baillie, 13 Jan. 1705; *ib.*, 102, Roxburgh to same, 3 Jun. 1705.

[93] BL, Loan 29/127, 7(8), W. Brenand to Harley, 22 Jul. and 18 Aug. 1706; *HMCR Portland MSS*, iv, 318, Harley to Brenand, 23 Jul. 1706; *ib.*, 324, Brenand to Harley, 24 Aug. 1706.

[94] Coxe, *Marlborough*, ii, 162, Harley to Marlborough, 6 Sep. 1706.

[95] *Ib.*, 177, Marlborough to Godolphin, 9 Aug. 1706.

[96] *Jerviswood*, 164, Johnston to Baillie, 19 Oct. [1706].

[97] *Ib.*; *ib.*, 162, same to same, 7 Oct. [1706].

[98] *Ib.*, 171, same to same, 28 Nov. [1706]; *ib.*, 189, same to same, 25 Feb. 1706/7.

[99] *Ib.*, 190, same to same, 4 Mar. [1707].

[100] See above, p. 267.

[101] Fraser, *Melvilles*, ii, 204, Somers to [Leven], 26 Oct. 1706; *ib.*, 206–8, same to [same], 15 Nov. 1706; *ib.*, 209–10, Halifax to [same], 23 Nov. 1706; *ib.*, 210–11, Somers to [same], 26 Nov. 1706; *Marchmont Papers*, iii, 303, Marchmont to Somers, 9 Nov. 1706; *ib.*, 311, same to Wharton, 9 Nov. 1706; *ib.*, 312, same to Somers, 17 Jan. 1707; *Hardwicke State Papers*, ii, 465–6, ii, Argyll to same, 1706. The junto's fears for the union's parliamentary prospects, derived apparently from Sunderland, are reflected in PRO 30/24/20/117, 121, Shaftesbury to B. Furley, 11/12 Oct. and 2 Dec. 1706.

[102] *Marchmont Papers*, iii, 303, Marchmont to Somers, 9 Nov. 1706; *ib.*, 319, same to queen, 1 Feb. 1707.

[103] *Jerviswood*, 164, Baillie to Johnston, 15 Oct. 1706.

[104] See above, p. 265–6, and below, p. 295. The only evidence which apparently conflicts with this interpretation appears in the letters of Godolphin and

Johnston to Marlborough (Blenheim Papers, A1/36, 18 and 22 Oct. 1706, and A2/2, 29 Oct. [1]706. Since the letters are somewhat ambiguous the conflict is arguable.

105 *HMCR Mar and Kellie MSS*, i, 273, Seafield to Mar, 20 Aug. 1706.

106 *HMCR Laing MSS*, ii, 139–40, Ormiston to [Godolphin], 16 Nov. 1706.

107 *HMCR Mar and Kellie MSS*, i, 286, Mar to Godolphin, 8 Oct. 1706; *Seafield Letters*, 94, Seafield to same, 14 Oct. 1706.

108 It will be clear that 'party' is not used in relation to Scotland as it would be possible to use it in an English context. The Scottish 'parties' were organised patronage groups operating within a spoils system—i.e. 'court' and 'country'.

109 *Ib.*, 173, 25 Oct. 1706.

110 *HMCR Mar and Kellie MSS*, i, 267, 22 Jun. 1706.

111 NLS, MS 1033, 15–16, Orkney to [Selkirk or Ruglen], 2 Feb. 1706.

112 *HMCR Mar and Kellie MSS*, i, 243, Stair to Mar, 3 Jan. 1706.

113 It was alleged, for instance, that he had taken Dutch money: BL, Add. MSS 28055, 388, Mar to Godolphin, 21 [printed as 22 in *Seafield Letters*] Sep. 1706; *Jerviswood*, 176, Johnston to Baillie, 14 Dec. [1706]; *ib.*, 165, same to same, 22 Oct. [1706]; *ib.*, 169, same to same, 12 Nov. [1706].

114 *Lockhart Papers*, i, 130

115 SRO, GD 220, R, Rothes to Montrose, 21 Dec. 1714.

116 E.g. *Jerviswood*, 164, Baillie to Johnston, 15 Oct. 1706.

117 See below, pp. 285–7.

118 'An Inquiry into the State of the Union of Great Britain . . .' (London, 1717), printed in Paterson, *Works*, ii, 27, 32.

119 *APS*, xi, 314–15.

120 *Ib.*, 404–6.

121 See App. A.

122 Smout, *Scottish Trade*, 272–3.

123 See below, p. 287 *et seq.*

124 *Lockhart Papers*, i, 171–3; Hume, *Diary*, 179–80. *RCRB*, i, 399–402, gives a list of burgh representatives present and notes that twenty-one burghs were not represented. Of the representatives of these twenty-one in parliament, thirteen were for union, six against, one abstained and one was absent. Of those at the convention, if one discounts Edinburgh, which had two representatives, one voting for union and one against, and the members for Wigtown and Kilrenie, who changed their minds between the first article and ratification, the burghs divided twenty-one against union and eighteen for it, with three abstentions. If the vote in the convention on the anti-union address followed the same pattern it must have been very close.

125 *Seafield Letters*, 173, Dupplin to Godolphin, 25 Oct. 1706.

126 *RCRB*, 399–402.

127 Hume, *Diary*, 173, 12 Oct. 1706; *ib.*, 173–4.

128 *Ib.*, 194.

129 *Ib.*, 194.

130 *Ib.*, 185.

[131] Discounting the four members who merely voted against the first article (App. A).

[132] Hume, *Diary*, 180–81, and see above, pp. 169–70.

[133] *Seafield Letters*, 102, Seafield to Godolphin, 11 Nov. 1706.

[134] *Ib.*, 104, same to same, 13 Nov. 1706.

[135] Defoe, *Letters*, 148–9, Defoe to Harley, 14 Nov. 1706, had it that twenty-five signed the protest. The list of protestors included Annandale, who, whatever his faults, was hardly one of the 'known enemies of the Church': *APS*, xi, 320.

[136] Hume, *Diary*, 181–2.

[137] I.e. abstaining.

[138] *Lockhart Papers*, i, 214–15. The number of votes cast on the twenty-second article was 147 but this increased in later divisions, so some, at least, of the despair must have been of a transitory nature.

[139] *Seafield Letters*, 101, Seafield to Godolphin, 7 Nov. 1706; *Jerviswood*, 166, Baillie to Johnston, 29 Oct. 1706; Defoe, *Letters*, 139–41, Defoe to Harley, 2 Nov. 1706.

[140] *Seafield Letters*, 176, Mar to Godolphin, 26 Oct. 1706.

[141] *A Letter From The Commission of the General Assembly To The Presbytery of Hamilton with The Presbytery's Answer* [1706] (17 Dec. 1706).

[142] *Lockhart Papers*, i, 168–71.

[143] See above, p. 243.

[144] *Remarks Upon the Lord Haversham's Speech in the House of Peers, Feb. 15 1707* (1707).

[145] *Atholl Chron.*, ii, 67, Atholl to the Atholl lairds, 24 Oct. 1706.

[146] E.g. Ayr, Burntisland, Culross, Dunfermline, Inverkeithing, New Galloway and Stirling. Most Scottish shires returned four M.P.s, so it is possible to write 'preponderantly'.

[147] SRO, GD 220, N, Nairn to Montrose, 14 Nov. 1706.

[148] *Seafield Letters*, 105, Seafield to Godolphin, 16 Nov. 1706.

[149] Hume, *Diary*, 187–8; *Carstares S.P.*, 755, J. Sh[   ] to Carstares, 17 Dec. 1706.

[150] *Seafield Letters*, 176, Mar to Godolphin, 26 Oct. 1706.

[151] *A Seasonable Warning . . .*

[152] Defoe, *Letters*, 132–6, Defoe to Harley, 24 Oct. 1706.

[153] *Int. Soc. Letters*, i, 49–53, Leven to Godolphin, 26 Oct. 1706; *ib.*, 53–7, same to same, 26 Oct. 1706; *Lockhart Papers*, i, 163; Hume, *Diary*, 176–7, 25 Oct. 1706.

[154] *Int. Soc. Letters*, i, 57–8, Leven to Godolphin, 5 Nov. [1706].

[155] Hume, *Diary*, 184.

[156] *Seafield Letters*, 98 Seafield to Godolphin, 3 Nov. 1706. The speech was printed.

[157] *Jerviswood*, 167, Baillie to Johnston, 5 Nov. 1706; BL, Add. MSS 28055, 400, Roxburgh to Godolphin, 5 Nov. 1706.

[158] *Marchmont Papers*, iii, 422, Hamilton to [Godolphin], 14 Nov. 1706; *ib.*, 431, Cromartie to [same], 18 Nov. 1706; *ib.*, 435, Belhaven to same, 30 Nov.

1706; *HMCR Portland MSS*, iv, 359, Stair to [Harley], 26 Nov. 1706.

159 BL, Add. MSS 6420, 70, Godolphin to Queensberry, 31 Apr. [*sic* for Oct.] 1706.

160 *Ib.*, 72, same to [same], 14 Nov. 1706.

161 Blenheim Papers, A1/46, Queensberry to Marlborough, 27 Nov. 1706.

162 *Marlborough Dispatches*, iii, 246, Marlborough to Leven, 7 Dec. 1706; *ib.*, 247, same to Queensberry, 7 Dec. 1706; Buccleuch (Drum.), Union, ii, W. Dobyus to [Queensberry], 9 Dec. 1706; Blenheim Papers, A1/46, Queensberry to Marlborough, 17 Dec. 1706.

163 *HMCR Ormonde MSS*, viii, 262, Lord Cutts to Ormonde, 16 Nov. 1706; *ib.*, 265, same to same, 5 Dec. 1706.

164 App. B; SRO, GD 220, C, Cunningham to Montrose, 26 Feb. 1715.

165 Defoe, *Letters*, 163, n. 3; *ib.*, 180–82, Defoe to Harley, 26 Dec. 1706; John Ker of Kersland, *The Memoirs of J[ohn] K [er] containing his secret transactions and negotiations in Scotland, England, the Courts of Vienna, Hanover and other foreign parts* ... (London, 1726–7), i, 27–36.

166 *Jerviswood*, 166, Baillie to Johnston, 29 Oct. 1706.

167 *Lockhart Papers*, i, 193–214.

168 *Seafield Letters*, 93, Seafield to Godolphin, 4 Oct. 1706.

169 *Marchmont Papers*, iii, 312, Marchmont to Somers, 17 Jan. 1707; SRO, GD 220, N, Nairn to Montrose, 4 Jan. 1706/7.

170 Hume, *Diary*, 174–8.

171 *Ib.*, 182–3; *Marchmont Papers*, iii, 427, Philiphaugh to [Godolphin?], 16 Nov. 1706.

172 *HMCR Portland MSS*, viii, 248, [Hamilton] to [G. Mason], 15 Oct. 1706; *ib.*, 248, [same] to [same], 17 Oct. 1706. Mason was not a code name for Harley as the editor conjectured (cf. *Jerviswood*, 162, 7 Oct. 1706).

173 Hume, *Diary*, 174, 15 Oct. 1706.

174 *Ib.*, 178; *Seafield Letters*, 96, Seafield to Godolphin, 16 Oct. 1706.

175 *Seafield Letters*, 98, Seafield to Godolphin, 3 Nov. 1706.

176 *Marchmont Papers*, iii, 427, Philiphaugh to [Godolphin?], 16 Nov. 1706.

177 Hume, *Diary*, 182.

178 *Ib.*, 184–5.

179 *Ib.*, 183–4.

180 *Ib.*, 177.

181 *Marchmont Papers*, iii, 303, Marchmont to Somers, 9 Nov. 1706.

182 *Ib.*; Hume, *Diary*, 179.

183 *Ib.*, 183.

184 *Marchmont Papers*, iii, 438 [Marchmont?] to [Godolphin?], 10 Dec. 1706.

185 Defoe, *Letters*, 144–5, Defoe to Harley, 9 Nov. 1706; *ib.*, 145–7, same to same, [13?] Nov. 1706.

186 *Seafield Letters*, 101, Seafield to Godolphin, 7 Nov. 1706.

187 The proposed 'explanations' are set out in *HMCR Laing MSS*, ii, 135–9, 'Memorial with regard to the obviating of difficulties against the union', Oct. 1706. Hume, *Diary*, 185.

[188] *Ib.*, 193.

[189] *Ib.*, 190–2.

[190] *Ib.*, 186–7.

[191] *Ib.*, 194.

[192] *Ib.*, 189.

[193] *Marchmont Papers*, iii, 433, Argyll to [Godolphin?], 22 Nov. 1706; *Hardwicke State Papers*, ii, 465–6, Argyll to Somers, 1706.

[194] BL, Add. MSS 6420, 72, Godolphin to [Queensberry], 14 Nov. 1706; *ib.*, same to [same], 26 Nov. 1706; Fraser, *Melvilles*, ii, 206–8, Somers to [Leven], 15 Nov. 1706; *ib.*, 209–10, Halifax to [same], 23 Nov. 1706; *ib.*, 210–11, Somers to [same], 26 Nov. 1706.

[195] SRO, GD 220, N, Nairn to Montrose, 4 Dec. 1706; *ib.*, same to same, 7 Dec. 1706; *ib.*, same to same, 2 Jan. 1706/7; BL, Add. MSS 6420, 76, Godolphin to [Queensberry], 4 Dec. 1706.

[196] Hume, *Diary*, 175.

[197] *Ib.*, 190.

[198] *Ib.*, 196. The Scottish parliament had to be kept in existence by a series of short adjournments in case the English parliament made any amendments which would need ratification: BL, Add. MSS 6420, 98, Godolphin to [Queensberry], 11 Jan. 1706/7. The act as passed (5 and 6 Anne, c. 11) appears in *APS*, xi, 406 *et seq.*, *Statutes of the Realm*, viii, 566 *et seq.*, and G. S. Pryde, *The Treaty of Union of Scotland and England, 1707* (London, 1950).

[199] SRO, GD 18, Box 119, 3135, J. Clerk to his father, 17 Feb. 1707.

[200] *Marchmont Papers*, iii, 444, Seafield to [Godolphin?], 28 Jan. 1707; *CJ*, xvi, 27.

[201] Hume, *Diary*, 196–7.

[202] *Jerviswood*, 181, Baillie to Johnston, 21 Jan. 1706/7.

[203] *Ib.*, 186, 6 Feb. 1707.

[204] *Ib.*, 183, l Feb. 1707.

[205] *Ib.*, 186, 6 Feb. 1707.

[206] *Ib.*, 188, Baillie to Johnston, 13 Feb. 1707.

[207] Hume, *Diary*, 198–9; *Jerviswood*, 183, Baillie to Johnston, 1 Feb. 1707.

[208] SRO, GD 18, Box 119, 3135, J. Clerk to his father, with endorsement by Sir John, [25 Jan. 1707]; *ib.*, same to same, 2 Feb. 1707.

[209] *Jerviswood*, 183, Baillie to Johnston, 1 Feb. 1707.

[210] See above, pp. 266–8.

[211] BL, Add. MSS 28055, 314, Seafield to Godolphin, 2 [*sic* for 21, under which date it appears in *Seafield Letters*] Oct. 1706; *Seafield Letters*, 98, same to same, 3 Nov. 1706.

[212] *HMCR Mar and Kellie MSS*, i, 273, Nairn to Mar, 24 Aug. 1706.

[213] See above, p. 171 *et seq.*

[214] *Jerviswood*, 165, Johnston to Baillie, 22 Oct. [1706].

[215] *Ib.*, 171, same to same, 26 Nov. [1706].

[216] *Ib.*; *ib.*, 171, same to same, 28 Nov. [1706].

[217] *Ib.*

218 SRO, GD 220, N, Nairn to Montrose, 23 Oct. 1706.

219 *Int. Soc. Letters*, i, 48–9, Leven to Godolphin, 16 Oct. 1706.

220 Hume, *Diary*, 174.

221 *Int. Soc. Letters*, i, 53–7, Leven to Godolphin, 26 Oct. 1706.

222 *Seafield Letters*, 102, Seafield to same, 11 Nov. 1706, See also *ib.*, 93, same to same, 4 Oct. 1706 and *ib.*, 107, same to same, 16 Nov. 1706.

223 *Jerviswood*, 172, Johnston to Baillie, 5 Dec. 1706.

224 *Ib.*, 190, same to same, 4 Mar. [1707].

225 *Ib.*, 178, same to same, 24 Dec. [1706].

226 *Ib.*, 179, same to same, 4 Jan. [1707].

227 Fraser, *Melvilles*, ii, 212–13, 4 Mar. 1706/7.

228 SRO, GD 205, Letters from Individuals, Jamieson to Bennet, 24 Apr. 1707.

229 *Ib.*, GD 18, Box 119, 3135, J. Clerk to his father, 24 Apr. 1707.

230 *Ib.*, 3134, 'Memoirs of the affairs of Scotland after the adjournment of the parliament anno 1707'.

231 For the disposal of places after the union see Riley, *English Ministers . . . ,* chap. ii.

232 SRO, GD 220, N, Nairn to Montrose, 18 Jan. 1706/7.

233 *Marchmont Papers*, iii, 447, Stair to [Godolphin], 22 Feb. [1707]. The first earl had died during the union parliament.

234 *Jerviswood*, 187, Johnston to Baillie, 8 Feb. [1707].

235 *Ib.*, 189, same to same, 25 Feb. 1706/7.

236 *Ib.*, 187, same to same, 8 Feb. [1707]; *ib.*, 189, same to same, 25 Feb. 1706/7; *ib.*, 190, same to same, 4 Mar. [1707].

237 *Ib.*, 162, same to same, 7 Oct. [1706].

238 BL, Stowe MSS 222, 497, Halifax to Sophia, 15/26 Oct. 1706.

239 *Ib.*, 463, [Somers] to [electoral prince], 23 Aug. 1706; *ib.*, 499, Halifax to [same],18/29 Oct. 1706.

240 Fraser, *Melvilles*, ii, 206–8, Somers to [Leven], 15 Nov. 1706.

241 *Jerviswood*, 170, Johnston to Baillie 23 Nov. [1706].

242 *Ib.*, 171, same to same, 28 Nov. [1706].

243 *Ib.*

244 *Ib.*, 169, same to same, 12 Nov. [1706].

245 *Ib.*, 180, same to same, 17 Jan. 1706/7.

246 *HMCR Marchmont MSS*, 158–9, 11 Feb. 1706/7.

247 *Jerviswood*, 183, Johnston to Baillie, 25 Jan. 1706/7.

248 Chandler, iv, 53.

249 *Ib.*, 53–4.

250 *Ib.*, 54

251 *Ib.*, and Bruce, *Report . . .* , i, 372–3.

252 Chandler, iv, 55–6.

253 5 and 6 Anne, c. 8.

254 Chandler, 56. Coxe, *Walpole*, ii, 6, R. Walpole to H. Walpole, 12 Feb. 1706/7.

[255] Chandler, iv. 57–8.

[256] *Ib.*

[257] Drafts of Nottingham's various speeches on this topic are in Leicestershire County Record Office, Finch MSS, Political Papers, 128, *passim.*

[258] Timberland, ii, 167–8.

[259] *Ib.*, 168–73. The speech was printed as a pamphlet.

[260] *Jerviswood*, 186, Johnston to Baillie, 4 Feb. [1707].

[261] Timberland, ii, 174–6.

[262] *Ib.*

[263] The core of tory opposition can be identified by references to speakers in the debates and the names of those dissenting from the various articles. They number twenty-six in all. *Ib.* 176–8.

[264] Scarborough's outburst (n. 260 above) might have been designed to discredit the squadrone.

[265] Chandler, iv, 59.

[266] *Ib.*, 60.

[267] *HMCR Bath MSS*, i, 170, Godolphin to Harley, 22 Apr. 1707.

[268] Defoe, *Letters*, Defoe to Harley, [13?] Nov. 1706; *ib* 200–2, same to same, [13 Feb. 1706/7].

[269] BL, Add. MSS 40776, 55, Shrewsbury to Vernon, 7 Apr. 1707.

[270] See above, e.g., p. 168.

[271] *Blenheim Papers*, B2/33, Harley to Godolphin, 16 Nov. 1706.

[272] *Jerviswood*, 174, Johnston to Baillie, 10 Dec. 1706.

[273] E.g. Fraser, *Melvilles*, ii, 203–4, Harley to Leven, 7 Oct. 1706; *ib.*, 208–9, same to same, 21 Nov. 1706.

[274] See, e.g., Defoe, *Letters*, 125, 130, 132, 152–5, 180–2.

[275] *Ib.*, 125–8, Defoe to Harley, 13 Sept. 1706.

[276] *Ib.*, 130–31, same to same, 30 Sept. 1706.

[277] *Ib.*, 132 and n. 4; *ib.*, 132, Defoe to Harley, 24 Oct. 1706.

[278] *Jerviswood*, 165, Johnston to Baillie, 22 Oct. [1706].

[279] *Ib.*, 171, same to same, 28 Nov. [1706]. See also *ib.*, 169, same to same, 12 Nov. [1706].

[280] Defoe, *Letters*, 227–9, Harley to Defoe, 12 Jun. 1707.

[281] SRO, GD 18, Box 119, 3135, J. Clerk to his father, [1707]; *HMCR Chester MSS*, 394a, P. Shakerley to the Chester merchants, 18 Feb., 20 Feb., 6 Mar. 1706/7.

[282] Chandler, iv. 68.

[283] SRO, GD 18, Box 119, 3135, J. Clerk to his father, 13 Apr. [1707].

[284] *HMCR Chester MSS*, 395a, P. Shakerley to the Chester merchants, 24 Apr. 1707.

[285] *Ib.*, 394a, same to same, 15 Mar., 18 Mar. 1706/7; *HMCR Bath MSS*, i, 166, [Godolphin] to [Harley], [19 Mar. 1707].

[286] *HMCR Chester MSS*, 394a, P. Shakerley to the Chester merchants, 11 Mar., 20 Mar. 1706/7 and 25 Mar. 1707.

[287] *Ib.*, 395a, same to same, 9 Apr. 1707; Defoe, *Letters*, 127–9, Harley to

Defoe, 12 Jun. 1707.

288 *HMCR Townshend MSS*, 331, 10 Apr. 1707.

289 Coxe, *Marlborough*, ii, 180, Godolphin to Marlborough, [1707].

290 BL, Add. MSS 40776, 57, Shrewsbury to Vernon, 12 Apr. 1707.

291 *History*, ii, 69–70.

292 See Boyer, *Annals*, v. 480–2; N. Luttrell, *A Brief Historical Relation of State Affairs* . . . (Oxford, 1857), vi, 157–63; Defoe, *Review*, 20 May 1707; D. Defoe, *History of the Union between England and Scotland* (1786), 567–74; Burnet, v, 298–9; Coxe, *Walpole*, ii, 8; *CJ*, xv, 377–89, *passim*.

293 Blenheim Papers, A2/24, 8/18 Apr. 1707.

294 *Ib.*, 11 Apr. 1707.

295 Defoe, *Letters*, 127–9, Harley to Defoe, 12 Jun. 1707.

296 *HMCR Bath MSS*, i, 169, 17 Apr. 1707.

297 Burnet, v, 341–2, and Onslow's note (a).

298 W. A. Speck, *Tory and Whig* (London, 1970), 123. Some had hoped for a dissolution at the union but whig opinion was, understandably, very much opposed to that: KCRO, Stanhope MSS., 34/12, Somerset to Stanhope, 12 Feb. OS. 1706/7.

299 BL, Add. MSS 9102, 72–3, Montrose to Sunderland, 22 Jun. 1708.

300 For general accounts of the post-union history of Scotland see, e.g., W. Ferguson, *Scotland 1689 to the present* (Edinburgh, 1968), R. Mitchison, *A History of Scotland* (London, 1970), R. Campbell, *Scotland since 1707: The Rise of an Industrial Society* (Oxford, 1965), J. H. Plumb, *The Growth of Political Stability in England, 1675–1725* (London, 1967), chap. vi, P. W. J. Riley, *The English Ministers and Scotland, 1707–1727* (London, 1964); see also R. Mitchison and N. Phillipson, ed., *Scotland in the Age of Improvement* (Edinburgh, 1970) and T. I. Rae, ed., *The Union of 1707: its Impact on Scotland* (Glasgow, 1974).

301 *Lockhart Papers*, i, 222–3.

APPENDIX A

An analysis of the voting patterns on the first article of union (4 November 1706) and on the ratification of the treaty (16 January 1707)[1]

An attempt to analyse the composition of the Scottish parliament at one or, in this instance, two particular divisions presents difficulties. The chances of overcoming them in a fashion universally acceptable are slight. It might aid clarification if the main problems are listed at the outset together with the solutions adopted and the reasons for choosing them.

1 Total membership of the Scottish parliament

The Scottish parliament was a single chamber legislature, comprising the three estates of nobles, barons (or shire representatives) and burgesses. The representation of the two last was fixed by law and, vacancies caused by death or other misfortune excepted, remained stable. Membership of the estate of nobles varied according to the eligibility of the peers. The full membership of parliament in 1706 has here been calculated by accepting the list of elected shire and burgh representatives and adding those peers who had taken the oaths at any time since the last election and were still alive. If Queensberry, as lord high commissioner in 1706, and Seafield, who as lord chancellor did not normally have a vote, are excluded, we have a total of 247.

2 Classification according to parties

Evidence concerning each member's political connections and his previous political behaviour makes possible such an analysis. The documentation involved is too extensive to be printed but leaves small margin for doubt. Problems of classification have not been due so much to lack of information as to last-minute or temporary changes of allegiance. Earlier[2] the principle of classifying members according to their long-standing allegiance was adopted. There were instances in which this merely confused the pattern of voting at the union. Since one of the main contentions of this work is that votes for or against union were really votes for or against the court, it has seemed more sensible to classify members according to their known relationship with the court at the time of the union parliament. Annandale and his dependants, for example, and Buchan, who had been courtiers before the parliament and were to be so again, had been disobliged in 1706[3] and joined the country party in opposition to union. They have for this reason been classified as opposition members. Dickson of Inveresk, Scott of Logie, Seton of Pitmedden and Alexander Grant of Grant, all formerly country party men, had permanently changed their allegiance on receiving places or promises.[4] Grant's father, on the other hand, who showed no positive change of allegiance and merely stayed away, has been treated as an opposition absentee. Even so, some marginal cases remain. Reay had a court history but at the time of the union was estranged from the ministry. Whether union was the cause of his alienation is not clear but he did not attend parliament and for want of other evidence has been treated as a court absentee. Teviot had been a placeman as a former commander-in-chief, Scotland. Nominally he remained a courtier but he had a feud of long standing with Queensberry and, even more notoriously, with Archibald, the first duke of Argyll. His sympathies seem to have been with the country party and if voting for the court meant supporting Queensberry his habit was to stay away so he was absent for much of the time. He has been classified as a country absentee. Sir John Swinton of that ilk was a courtier up to the 1703 parliament, when he began to act with the opposition. At the union he voted with the court and from that time remained a courtier. Though he, like Elibank, seems to have been making a permanent change of allegiance in 1706, both have been counted as opposition cross-voters failing evidence of an earlier change.

Marchmont and his family had become squadrone allies to the extent of being indistinguishable from them. Montrose is more open to doubt. In 1706 his allegiance was publicly claimed by both the court and the squadrone though both groups had private doubts and some courtiers regarded him as squadrone. Immediately after the union he was quite definitely squadrone whilst during the parliament his voting pattern was the same as theirs. His lieutenant, Graham of Gorthie, behaved in the same way. All have been classified as squadrone allies.

Adam Cockburn of Ormiston needs to be mentioned, having been reclassified since the last attempt at analysis.[5] He was listed previously as a squadrone ally in view of his connections with them[6] and his voting as they did in the union parliament even opposing his own financial interest as a union commissioner. However, it is clear that he was acting either in his usual fashion as a rogue courtier or, conceivably, throwing out a line to the junto in case a junto–squadrone alliance became a reality and, more to the point, a success. He appears amongst the courtiers.

3 Voting pattern

The calculation of the percentage of voting consistency may be open to question in that it takes into account only the relationship of cross-votes to the number of votes cast. It could be argued that absence or abstention are equally signs of dissatisfaction with the party line and should therefore be treated as dissident behaviour. This view has not been adopted here in the belief that taking refuge in absenteeism or abstention rather than voting cross is in itself an indication of the strength of political allegiance. Since the intended significance of the calculation is to indicate the percentage of predictable votes it has seemed logical to include the squadrone as registering 'party' votes although some might question this.

4 The divisions

The analysis has been confined to the two divisions directly involving the principle of union. On other divisions there was more cross-voting and abstention and non-attendance were more frequent.[7] For the most part this failure to vote seems to have had little significance but some members voted so rarely that the explanation must lie either in a lack of enthusiasm or even interest or in an excess of caution. Members voting in half or fewer of the union divisions have their names italicised in the lists below.

General totals

Composition of the 1706 parliament

	Present and active	Abstainers / temporary absentees	Absentees	Total
Court	99	5	8	112
Opposition	87	5	14	106
Squadrone	24	3	2	29
	210	13	24	247

Division on the first article of union (4 November 1706)

For			Against
Court	86	Opposition	74
Squadrone	24	Court cross-votes	9
Opposition cross-votes	5		83
Seafield	1		
	116		

Division on the ratification of the treaty (16 January 1707)

	For		Against
Court	79	Opposition	61
Squadrone	23	Court cross votes	8
Opposition cross votes	7		—
Seafield	1		69
	—		
	110		

Lists of members

Absent

Court:
  Bute[8]
  Dunbar[9]
  Gray[10]
  Kellie[8]
  Melville[11]
  Reay[12]
  Sir Archiband Stewart of
    Burray
  David Sutherland, younger,
    of Kinnald[13]

Squadrone:
  James Brodie of Brodie[14]
  Robert Douglas of Strahendrie[15]

Abstainers or temporary absentees

Court:
  Cranston[19]
  Bellenden[20]
  Sir James Stewart, lord
    advocate[21]
  James Campbell, senior, of
    Ardkinglas
  Colin Campbell (Renfrew)[19]

Squadrone:
  Robert Dundas of Arniston[19]
  Sir John Anstruther
    (Anstruther-Easter)[21]
  Sir Robert Anstruther
    (Anstruther-Wester)[19]

Opposition:
  Aberdeen[16]
  Burleigh
  Home
  Lindores
  Pitsligo
  Ruglen
  Teviot
  Robert Dunbar of Grangehill[9]
  Alexander Gordon of Garthie
  Ludovic Grant of Grant[17]
  Kenneth Mackenzie of
    Gairloch[9]
  Kenneth Mackenzie of Scatwall
  John Stewart, younger,
    of Blackhall[18]
  George Moncrieff (Craill)

Opposition:
  Alexander Abercromby of
    Tullibody[19]
  Hugh Rose of Kilravock[19]
  John Stewart of Kinwhinlick[22]
  John Udny of Udny[19]
  John Allardice[19]

Voting record

Courtiers

	First article	Ratification
Queensberry	–	–
Seafield	*pro*[23]	*pro*
Abercorn	–	*pro*
Argyll	*pro*	*pro*
Balcarres	*pro*	*pro*
Banff	*pro*	*pro*
Crawford	*pro*	–
Cromartie	*pro*	*pro*
Dalhousie	*pro*	*pro*
Deloraine	*pro*	*pro*
Duffus	*pro*	*pro*
Dunmore	*pro*	–
Dupplin	*pro*	*pro*
Eglinton	*pro*	–
Elphinstone	*pro*	*pro*
Findlater	–	*pro*
Forbes	*pro*	*pro*
Forfar	*pro*	*pro*
Fraser	*pro*	*pro*
Garnock	*pro*	–
Glasgow	*pro*	*pro*
Hopetoun	*pro*	*pro*
Hyndford	*pro*	–
Islay	*pro*	*pro*
Kilmarnock	*pro*	*pro*
Kintore	*pro*	*pro*
Lauderdale	–	*pro*
Leven	*pro*	*pro*
Lothian	*pro*	*pro*
Loudoun	*pro*	–
Mar	*pro*	*pro*
Morton	*pro*	*pro*
Northesk	*pro*	*pro*
Rollo	*pro*	*pro*
Rosebery	*pro*	*pro*
Ross	*pro*	*pro*
Stair	*pro*	–
Sutherland	*pro*	*pro*
Wemyss	*pro*	*pro*
Adam Cockburn of Ormiston, lord justice clerk	*pro*	*pro*
Sir James Murray of Philiphaugh, lord clerk register	*pro*	*pro*

Alexander Abercromby of Glassaugh	*pro*	*pro*
Sir James Campbell of Auchinbreck	*pro*	*pro*
James Campbell, younger, of Ardkinglas	*pro*	*pro*
John Campbell of Mamore	*pro*	*pro*
William Dalrymple of Glenmuir	*pro*	*pro*
Sir Robert Dickson of Inveresk	*pro*	*pro*
Archibald Douglas of Cavers	*pro*	*pro*
William Douglas of Dornoch	*pro*	*pro*
James Dunbar, younger, of Hempriggs	*pro*	*pro*
Alexander Grant, younger, of Grant	*pro*	*pro*
Alexander Horsbrugh of Horsbrugh	–	*pro*
Sir John Johnstone of Westerhall	*pro*	*pro*
Francis Montgomerie of Giffen	*pro*	*pro*
John Montgomerie of Wrae	*pro*	*pro*
William Morison of Prestongrange	*pro*	*pro*
John Murray of Bowhill	*pro*	*pro*
Sir Robert Pollock of Pollock	*pro*	*pro*
John Pringle of Haining	*pro*	*pro*
William Seton, younger, of Pitmedden	*pro*	*pro*
John Stewart of Sorbie	*pro*	*pro*
Robert Stewart of Tillicoultry	*pro*	*pro*
William Stewart of Castle Stewart	*pro*	*pro*
George Allardice (Kintore)	*pro*	*pro*
William Alves (Sanquhar)	*pro*	*pro*
Charles Campbell (Campbeltown)	*pro*	*pro*
Daniel Campbell (Inveraray)	*pro*	*pro*
William Carmichael (Lanark)	*pro*	*pro*
John Clerk (Whithorn)	*pro*	*pro*
William Cultrane (Wigtown)	*pro*	–
Sir David Dalrymple (Culross)	*pro*	*pro*
George Dalrymple (Stranraer)	*pro*	*pro*
Sir Hugh Dalrymple (North Berwick)	*pro*	*pro*
Robert Douglas (Kirkwall)	*pro*	*pro*
Lieut-col John Erskine (Stirling)	*pro*	*pro*
Sir Robert Forbes (Inverurie)	*pro*	*pro*
Sir Patrick Johnston (Edinburgh)	*pro*	–
Capt. Daniel MacLeod (Tain)	*pro*	*pro*
Alexander Maitland (Inverbervie)	*pro*	*pro*
Patrick Moncrieff (Kinghorn)	*pro*	*pro*
John Muir (Ayr)	*pro*	*pro*
George Munro (Irvine)	*pro*	–
Sir Alexander Ogilvy (Banff)	*pro*	*pro*
Patrick Ogilvy (Cullen)	*pro*	*pro*
John Rose (Nairn)	*pro*	*pro*
James Scott (Montrose)	*pro*	*pro*

John Scrymgeour (Dundee)	pro	pro
Sir James Smollett (Dunbarton)	pro	pro
James Stewart (Queensferry)	pro	–
John Urquhart (Dornoch)	pro	pro

Court cross-voters

Galloway	pro	con
Glencairn	con	pro
Alexander Douglas of Egilshay	con	pro
Sir Gilbert Elliot of Minto	con	con
William Maxwell of Cardoness	pro	con
John Sharp of Hoddam	con	–
Robert Inglis (Edinburgh)	con	con
Hugh Montgomery (Glasgow)	con	con
Walter Scott (Jedburgh)	con	con
George Spens (Rutherglen)	con	con
Walter Stewart (Linlithgow)	con	con

Opposition (countrymen and cavaliers)

Annandale	con	con
Atholl	con	–
Balmerino	con	con
Bargany	con	con
Belhaven	con	con
Blantyre	con	con
Buchan	con	con
Caithness	–	con
Colville	con	con
Erroll	con	con
Hamilton	con	con
Kilsyth	con	con
Kincardine	con	–
Kinnaird	con	con
Marischal	con	con
Oliphant	con	con
Saltoun	–	con
Selkirk	con	–
Sempill	con	con
Stormont	con	con
Strathmore	con	–
Wigtown	con	con
William Baillie of Lamington	con	con
Maj. Henry Balfour of Dunboug	–	con
David Bethune of Balfour	con	con

John Brisbane, younger, of Bishoptoun	*con*	*con*
James Carnegie of Phinhaven	*con*	*con*
Sir Hugh Cathcart of Carleton	–	*con*
William Cochrane of Kilmaronock	*con*	*con*
Sir Humphrey Colquhoun of Luss	*con*	*con*
Alexander Ferguson of Isle	*con*	*con*
Andrew Fletcher of Saltoun	*con*	*con*
John Forbes of Culloden	*con*	*con*
Sir James Foulis of Colinton	*con*	–
Alexander Gordon of Pitlurg	*con*	*con*
David Graham, younger, of Fintry	*con*	*con*
James Graham of Buchlivie	*con*	–
John Graham of Killearn	*con*	–
James Hamilton of Aikinhead	–	*con*
Sir Patrick Home of Renton	*con*	*con*
Thomas Hope oi Rankeillour	*con*	*con*
Sir John Houston of Houston	*con*	*con*
Sir Henry Innes, younger, of Innes	*con*	*con*
Sir John Lauder of Fountainhall	–	*con*
George Lockhart of Carnwath	*con*	–
Patrick Lyon of Auchterhouse	*con*	*con*
George Mackenzie of Inchculter	*con*	*con*
Alexander McKie of Palgown	*con*	*con*
James Moir of Stonywood	*con*	–
John Murray of Stowan	*con*	*con*
Sir Patrick Murray of Ochtertyre	*con*	–
James Ogilvy, younger, of Boyne	*con*	–
Sir David Ramsay of Balmain	*con*	–
Robert Rollo of Powhouse	–	*con*
Thomas Sharp of Houston	*con*	*con*
James Sinclair of Stemster	–	*con*
John Sinclair, younger, of Stevenson	*con*	*con*
Sir Robert Sinclair of Longformacus	*con*	*con*
John Bayne (Dingwall)	*con*	*con*
John Black (Dysart)	*con*	–
George Brodie (Forres)	*con*	*con*
John Carruthers (Lochmaben)	*con*	*con*
Sir David Cunningham (Lauder)	*con*	*con*
Alexander Duff (Inverness)	*con*	*con*
Alexander Edgar (Haddington)	*con*	*con*
Robert Frazer (Wick)	*con*	*con*
George Hume (New Galloway)	*con*	*con*
John Hutcheson (Aberbrothock [Arbroath])	*con*	*con*
Robert Johnston (Dumfries)	*con*	–
William Johnston (Annan)	*con*	–

Robert Kellie (Dunbar)	*con*	*con*
John Lyon (Forfar)	*con*	*con*
Francis Molison (Brechin)	*con*	*con*
James Oswald (Kirkcaldy)	*con*	—
Alexander Robertson (Perth)	*con*	*con*
Robert Scott (Selkirk)	*con*	*con*
Archibald Shiells (Peebles)	*con*	*con*
George Smith (Pitttenweem)	*con*	—
Dougal Stewart (Rothesay)	*con*	—
Alexander Watson (St Andrews)	*con*	—

Opposition cross-voters

Elibank[24]	*pro*	*pro*
Sir Kenneth Mackenzie of Cromartie	*pro*	*pro*
Aeneas MacLeod of Cadboll	*pro*	*pro*
Sir John Swinton of Swinton	*pro*	*pro*
James Bethune (Kilrenny)	*con*	*pro*
Roderick Mackenzie (Fortrose)	*pro*	*pro*
William Sutherland (Elgin)	*con*	*pro*

Squadrone and allies

Haddington	*pro*	*pro*
Marchmont	*pro*	*pro*
Montrose	*pro*	*pro*
Rothes	*pro*	*pro*
Roxburgh	*pro*	*pro*
Torphichen	*pro*	*pro*
Tweeddale	*pro*	*pro*
Sir William Anstruther of Anstruther	*pro*	*pro*
George Baillie of Jerviswood	*pro*	*pro*
William Bennet of Grubbet	*pro*	*pro*
John Bruce of Kinross	*pro*	*pro*
Sir Thomas Burnett of Leys	*pro*	*pro*
Sir Alexander Campbell of Cessnock	*pro*	*pro*
John Cockburn of Ormiston	*pro*	*pro*
Mungo Graham of Gorthie	*pro*	*pro*
John Haldane of Gleneagles	*pro*	*pro*
James Halyburton of Pitcur	*pro*	*pro*
Sir William Ker of Greenhead	*pro*	*pro*
William Nisbet of Dirleton	*pro*	*pro*
Patrick Bruce (Coupar)	*pro*	—
Sir John Erskine (Burntisland)	*pro*	*pro*
Sir Peter Halkett (Dunfermline)	*pro*	*pro*
Sir Andrew Hume (Kirkcudbright)	*pro*	*pro*
James Spittal (Inverkeithing)	*pro*	*pro*

Notes

[1] This is a slightly revised and more detailed version of the analysis in P. W. J. Riley, 'The union of 1707 as an episode in English politics', Appendix A, *EHR*, 1xxxiv (1969), pp. 522–5

[2] *Ib.*

[3] See above, pp. 173, 255.

[4] Dickson was made a customs commissioner after the union, Scott was master of works, Seton collector of the bishops' rents and Grant had been given Mar's regiment.

[5] Riley, *art. cit.*

[6] *Ib.*, App. A.

[7] See above, pp. 279–80, 289–90.

[8] Opposed to union.

[9] Habitually absent.

[10] In the process of resigning his peerage. His successor took his seat at the end of the session.

[11] In his last illness.

[12] For some reason disenchanted with the court.

[13] Reputedly in prison.

[14] Too aged and ill to attend.

[15] Died in 1706, probably before the session.

[16] In favour of union.

[17] Possibly influenced by his son's being given Mar's regiment.

[18] Excused on account of his indisposition.

[19] Voted in other divisions.

[20] Died during the session. His heir a minor.

[21] Sir James Stewart and Sir John Anstruther are the only two certain abstainers amongst those who attended parliament. Neither agreed with union. Stewart was allowed to keep his post on condition that he abstained. Anstruther was persuaded by Rothes to abstain (SRO, GD220, R, Rothes to Montrose, 21 Dec. 1714). Dundas and Sir Robert Anstruther had similar voting patterns which might have been the result of the like persuasion.

[22] Adhering to the protest against the presence of troops seems to have been his sole recorded action during this parliament.

[23] Requested that his name be allowed to appear in the printed lists although as chancellor he did not vote under normal circumstances.

[24] He had received £50 out of Queensberry's union fund.

APPENDIX B[1]

The following table shows the distribution of the £20,000 paid out by the court at the time of the union parliament.[2] Recipients are classified according to political interest. Any arrears due to the recipients are also shown as far as they can be discovered, for purposes of comparison. The full total of Scottish arrears at the union exceeded £250,000.[3]

Ministers	Recorded arrears	Received
Queensberry	£26,756 9s 0½d	£12,325
Seafield	£2,535 5s 7d	£490
A. Cockburn of Ormiston	£1,354	£200

Court peers		
Balcarres	None stated	£500
Dunmore	None stated	£200
Eglinton	£942 3s 1$\frac{5}{6}$d	£200
Findlater	£100	£100
Fraser	None stated	£100
Forfar	£2,013 17s 9$\frac{3}{6}$d	£100
Glencairn	£4,886 5s 7$\frac{2}{6}$d	£100
Kintore	£2,600	£200
Forbes	£1,938 12s 5d	£50
Banff[4]	None stated	£11 2s

Argyll interest		
John Muir (Ayr)	None stated	£100
J. Campbell of Mamore	£300	£200
W. Stewart of Castle Stewart	£75	£300

Squadrone and allies

Tweeddale	£2,577 15s 7d	*£1,000*
Roxburgh	None stated	*£500*
Montrose	None stated	*£200*
Marchmont	£2,250	*£1,104 15s 7d*
Sir W. Anstruther of that ilk	£350	£300
Alexander Wedderburn[5]	£400	£75
Sir A. Campbell of Cessnock	£50	£50

Cromartie interest

Cromartie	£4,000	£300
Sir K. Mackenzie	None stated	£100
R. Mackenzie of Prestonhall	£400	£200

Country peers

Atholl[6]	£1,500	£1,000
Elibank[7]	None stated	£50

Others

Sir W. Sharp of Stoneyhill	£450	£300
Patrick [*sic* for William]		
Cultrane (Wigtown)	None stated	£25
Major J. Cunningham of Aiket[8]	None stated	£100

Notes

[1] This originally appeared as an appendix to my article 'The union of 1707 as an episode in English politics', *EHR*, 1xxxiv (1969). Permission has kindly been given for its reproduction here.

[2] Lockhart's list and his account of the transaction appears in *Lockhart Papers*, i, 262–72. Evidence concerning the £20,000 given to the commissioners of accounts appears in *CJ*, xvii, 207 *et seq*. For the apparent lengths to which the court went to preserve secrecy see SRO, GD 45, sect. i, 175. The list given here excludes the payment of £60 to the messenger who carried the treaty, which seems to have no political significance.

[3] Arrears on the Scottish civil and military lists as accounted for at the union are in BL, Add. MSS 35904. The account is not necessarily complete, so the fact that no arrears were stated is not proof that none were due. Some arrears

might not have qualified for inclusion in the civil list. John Muir, for example, was a customs collector before the union and his arrears might have been connected with that position.

[4] Had asked for 'encouragement' to make the journey to Edinburgh. See above, p. 257.

[5] Under-secretary in the new party administration of 1704–5. An excise commissioner after the union.

[6] See above, pp. 258–9.

[7] See above, p. 258.

[8] Engaged in security duties at the time of the union. See above, p. 285.

BIBLIOGRAPHICAL NOTE

There would seem to be little point in listing manuscript sources, printed collections and pamphlets since all which proved useful have been mentioned in either text or footnotes and most of them are familiar enough. The same applies to secondary works.

For those who would like to acquaint themselves more fully with the differing views of the union of 1707 some suggestions for further reading might be helpful. Work on the subject has tended to divide into two streams. The traditional main stream sees the union as, if not inevitable, at least the product of virtually irresistible economic forces in Scotland together with England's need for security. In this view union appears as a carefully planned policy and a triumph of statesmanship. Those belonging to this school have, to a greater or lesser degree, acknowledged the existence of human failings as expressed in politics but have regarded them as wholly subsidiary to the main line of causation. Such views will be found in J. Mackinnon, *The Union of England and Scotland* (London, 1896), P. Hume Brown, *The Legislative Union of England and Scotland* (Oxford, 1914) and W. L. Mathieson, *Scotland and the Union, 1695–1747* (Glasgow, 1905). This tradition very probably reached its peak with G. M. Trevelyan, *England under Queen Anne*, vol. ii, *Ramillies and the Union with Scotland* (London, 1932), who saw union as a monument to whig vision and statesmanship. Trevelyan's views were accepted by G. S. Pryde in *The Treaty of Union of Scotland and England, 1707* (London, 1950). And to this list, on the evidence of his occasional writings, must now be added Professor Hugh Trevor-Roper.

In the past two decades some dissent from the traditional interpretation has been expressed. The primacy of the economic motive has been denied as in, e.g., A. M. Carstairs, 'Some economic aspects of the union of parliaments', *Scottish Journal of Political Economy*, ii (1955).

Stress has been laid on the part played by sheer political motives and attendant corruption. The idea that the union was 'probably the greatest "political job" of the eighteenth century' has been forcefully expressed by W. Ferguson in 'The making of the treaty of union of 1707', *SHR*, xliii (1964), his *Scotland: 1689 to the Present* (Edinburgh, 1968) and, more recently, and even more emphatically, in his *Scotland's Relations with England: a Survey to 1707* (Edinburgh, 1977).

T. C. Smout closely examined the Scottish economic background to the union and in his *Scottish Trade on the Eve of Union, 1660–1707* (Edinburgh, 1963) and an article, 'The Anglo-Scottish union of 1707. i. The economic background', *Economic History Review*, xvi (1964), concluded that the state of the Scottish economy has to be emphasised in any study of the causes of the union. Later, without necessarily retracting this view, he has in 'The road to union' in *Britain After the Glorious Revolution*, ed. G. S. Holmes (London, 1969), attempted a moderate synthesis of these conflicting views, doubting whether, in the last analysis, the motives which produced the union can ever be fully elucidated.

As a result of the controversy over devolution the topic has become almost incandescent. Both unionists and nationalists have indulged in some over-excited polemics concerning the union of 1707 and historians have been infected. Dr Ferguson would certainly have no objection to being looked upon as a nationalist and his strong feelings show in his *Scotland's Relations with England* as no doubt he intended they should. Professor Trevor-Roper has championed the cause of the United Kingdom against the nationalists, though his brusque unionism, however entertaining, tends to be offensive to Scots, nationalist and unionist alike. His occasional pieces on the subject, e.g. 'England and Scotland, 1707–1977', *The Listener*, 3 March 1977, and 'The ideal of the covenant', *Times Literary Supplement*, 9 September 1977, place him firmly in the tradition of whig historiography on this topic.

Ample general bibliographies are provided in G. S. Pryde, *Scotland from 1603 to the Present Day* (London, 1962), W. Ferguson, *Scotland: 1689 to the Present*, Rosalind Mitchison, *A History of Scotland* (London, 1970) and T. C. Smout, *A History of the Scottish People* (London, 1969). A great deal of illumination is also to be found in the footnotes to Ferguson, *Scotland's Relations with England*.

INDEX

Members of the Scottish parliament whose names appear only in the lists in the appendices have not been included in the index.

Abercromby, Patrick, 223

Patrick, 223
Aberdeen, George Gordon, first earl, 79, 216, 275
Adams, William, 225
Africa Company, Scottish, *see* Scotland
Agricola, 3
ale, twopenny, 238, 291
Alves, William, 93 n. 138
Annan, 278
Annandale, William Johnston, first marquess, 17, 45, 53–4, 58, 84, 101, 116, 126, 128, 130, 134, 137, 138, 140–1, 143, 145, 148, 172, 173, 255, 280 and n. 135.
Anne, queen of England and Scotland, 1, 22, 31–2, 47, 49, 62, 69, 73, 74, 75–6, 87, 121, 127, 133, 137, 143, 149, 163, 165, 166, 167, 172, 173, 175, 177 n. 99, 178, 179, 218, 302, 304, 310, 314
Annesley, Francis, 164
Anstruther, Sir John, 275
Anstruther, Sir William, of Anstruther, 95 n. 152
Arbuthnot, John, 236
Argyll, Archibald Campbell, tenth earl and first duke, 15, 17, 19–22, 23, 45, 53–4, 57, 58, 61, 76, 327

Argyll, Archibald Campbell, third duke, *see* Islay
Argyll, family interest of the dukes, 11, 13, 257, 276
Argyll, John Campbell, second duke, 69, 74, 81, 118, 126–41, 145–51, 172, 173–5, 177 and n. 99, 256, 259, 260, 261, 265, 282, 291, 294, 295, 300, 314
Arran, James Douglas, earl, *see* Hamilton
arrears, Scottish civil and military (the 'bygones'), *see* Scotland
Ashe, Edward, 308
Atholl, family interest of the marquesses and duke, 11, 13, 19, 22, 70
Atholl, John Murray, first marquess, 17, 46
Atholl, John Murray, earl of Tullibardine (1696), second marquess and first duke, 11, 12, 17, 18, 19, 46–7, 49, 51–2, 55, 61–3, 68, 69–71, 75, 78, 81, 83 n. 73, 85, 86, 87, 88 and n. 104, 89, 101, 103, 115, 116 n. 11, 118, 145, 148, 150, 171, 203 n. 34, 205, 213, 257, 258–9 and n. 30, 271, 276, 280, 285, 289, 292

Baillie, George, of Jerviswood, 74, 75–6, 79, 80, 81, 86, 94 n. 143, 95, n. 152, 118, 119, 126, 130, 131, 133, 136, 144, 146, 147, 165, 175, 216, 217, 218, 256, 262–5, 267, 271, 272, 294, 295, 296, 301

Baillie, William, of Lamington, 95 n. 152

Balcarres, Colin Lindsay, third earl, 68–9, 257

Balmerino, John Elphinstone, fourth baron, 280, 288

Banff, George Ogilvy, third baron, 257, 277

Baltic, Scottish trade to, see Scotland, economy of

Bargany, lords, 12

barons, estate of, see Scotland, parliament of

Balhaven, John Hamilton, third baron, 75, 77, 88–9, 95 n. 152, 116 n. 11, 133, 146 n. 205, 149, 207, 243, 260, 287, 297

Bennet, William, of Grubet, 46, 95 n. 152, 118, 265

Berwick-on-Tweed, 82, 285

Black, William, 227–9

Blantyre, Walter Stewart, sixth baron, 280

Blathwayt, William, 43

border, the Anglo-Scottish, 4, 202, 305

Boyle, David, of Kelburn, see Glasgow

Boyle, Henry, 175

Breadalbane, John Campbell, first earl, 12, 79, 206

Brodie, George, 217

Brodie, James, of Brodie, 95 n. 152

Bromley, William, 163–4

Bruce, Sir Alexander, see Kincardine

Bruce, Patrick, 95 n. 152

Brydges, James, 167

Buchan, David Erskine, ninth earl, 255

Buckingham, John Sheffield, first duke, see Normanby

Burchett, Josias, 43

Burnet, Gilbert, bishop of Salisbury, 80, 120 n. 40, 168, 304

Burntisland, 282, n. 146

Bute, James Stewart, first earl, 93 n. 138, 275

Caesar, Charles, 166, 302

Calamy, Edmund, 224

Carlisle, 304–5

Carmichael, John, second baron (earl of Hyndford, 1701), 21

Carstares, William, 19, 31, 42, 74, 95, 96, 116, 119, 127, 162, 168, 183, 211, 282

cattle trade, Scottish, see Scotland, economy of

cavalier party, see Scotland, parliament, parties in

Chamberlen, Hugh, 145 n. 203

Charles I, king of England and Scotland, 5, 80

Charles II, king of England and Scotland, 5, 6 and n. 19, 14, 197, 204, 209

Chester, 307

Child, Sir Josiah, 208

Church of England, see England

Church of Scotland, see Scotland

Clarendon, Edward Hyde, first earl, 5

Clerk, Sir John, of Penicuik, 295

Clerk, John, younger, of Penicuik, 14, 91, 93 n. 138, 176, 177 n. 99, 186–7, 239, 295, 299

Club, the, 8, 23

coal trade, Scottish, see Scotland, economy

Cockburn, Adam, of Ormiston, 19, 45, 89, 124–5, 133, 137–8, 140, 141, 145, 170, 177, 257, 265, 267, 272, 327

Cockburn, John, younger, of Ormiston, 95 n. 152, 165, 266

colonies, Scottish, see Darien; Scotland, colonies

Colvill's case, see Scotland post nati

commons, house of, see England, parliament

commonwealth, the, 5

Compton, Spencer, 302

convocation of Canterbury, 9

court, English, *see* Anne; England, court in; Godolphin; Marlborough

court, Scottish, *see* Scotland, parliament, parties; Queensberry

Cowper, William, first baron, 1, 121, 168

Cromartie, Sir George Mackenzie, first viscount Tarbat and first earl, 40–3, 44, 45, 46, 49, 51–2, 55, 56–7, 62, 68 and n. 4, 70, 75, 78, 79–80, 82, 90, 91, 94, 95, 99, 115, 116 n. 11, 117, 176, 180, 183, 216, 234, 236, 257, 277, 311

Cromwell, Oliver, 3, 5

Culross, 282 n. 146

Cultrane, William, 93 n. 138, 278

Cunningham, Alexander, 41, 266, 308

Cunningham, major James, of Aiket, 285

customs collection, English, 198, 208–9

Cutts, John, first baron, 256

Dalrymples, the, 17, 19–20, 21, 42, 46, 74, 91–2, 136, 137, 206, 235

Dalrymple, Sir David, 92, 176

Dalrymple, George, 93 n. 138

Dalrymple, Sir Hugh, president of session, 92, 136, 176, 216

Dalrymple, Sir John, *see* Stair

Dalrymple, John, styled lord (later second earl of Stair), 177, 255

Dalrymple, William, of Glenmuir, 93 n. 138

Darien project, 18–19, 24, 34–5, 94, 199, 201, 204, 206–13, 215, 217, 219, 304, 314

Dartmouth, William Legge, third baron and first earl, 120, 121

Defoe, Daniel, 235–6, 239 n. 173, 240–5 and n. 209, 269 n. 90, 282, 283, 285, 289, 290, 305, 306, 309

Devonshire, William Cavendish, first duke, 31, 71 n. 22

Dickson, Sir Robert, of Inveresk, 327 and n. 4

Doddington, George, 169

Donaldson, James, 238–9

Douglas, Alexander, of Egilshay, 93 n. 138

Douglas, Archibald, of Cavers, 18

Douglas, Archibald Douglas, third marquess and first duke, 62

Douglas, lady Mary, 174

Douglas, Robert, 93 n. 138

Douglas, Robert, of Strahendrie, 95 n. 152

Douglas, William, of Dornoch, 93 n. 138

Duffus, James Sutherland, second baron, 93 n. 138

Dumfries, 220–1, 278, 283

Dumfriesshire, 45

Dundas, Robert, of Arniston, lord of session, 95 n. 152, 177

Dunfermline, 282 n. 146

Dunmore, Charles Murray, first earl, 50, 93 n. 138, 257, 258–9 and n. 30

Dupplin, Thomas Hay, sixth viscount (earl of Kinnoull, 1709), 93 n. 138, 176, 273, 277

Dutch, the, 104, 164, 205, 231; wars, 5, 197, 204

East India Company, *see* England

Edgar, Alexander, 95 n. 152

Edinburgh, 277 n. 124, 283–4, 285; castle of, 46, 117, 255

Edward I, king of England, 3

Eglinton, Alexander Montgomerie, ninth earl, 75

Elgin, 278

Elibank, Alexander Murray, fourth baron, 257, 258, 327

Elliot, Sir Gilbert, 134

Elphinstone, John Elphinstone, eighth baron, 93 n. 138

England:
court in, 58, 67, 70, 72, 74, 79, 80, 87, 90, 91, 101, 103, 130, 205, 255–6, 259, 301; and Scottish management, 73–5, 135; and the treaty policy, 139, 141–2, 144–5, 151; whig pressure, on, 166–8; and union, 162–5, 169–71, 189,

259–70, 298–302, 313–4, *and see*
Anne; Godolphin; Marlborough
Church of, 10, 303, *and see*
    convocation of Canterbury
East India Company in, 188,
    207–9, 243–4
parliament, 205, 207
    acts of: navigation, 5, 198, 207;
        settlement, 1701, 24; alien,
        1705, 121–3, 151, 163, 168,
        203; regency, 1706, 166–8;
        union, 1707, 302–5
    commons: and union proposals,
        24–5, 302–3, 305; and the
        'Scotch plot', 71; attack on
        Godolphin, 1704, 120; state
        of parties in, 123, 163–5,
        alien act in, 122–3;
        invitation to Sophia, 166–7;
        regency bill in, 167–8; and
        customs regulation, 1707,
        307–10
    lords: 184, 282; and union
        proposals, 24, 303–4 and n.
        263; and the 'Scotch plot',
        71–2, 73, 80, 117; attack on
        Godolphin, 1704, 119–20;
        alien act in, 122–3, 163; state
        of parties in, 163–4; regency
        bill in, 166–7; bill for securing
        the Church of England, 303;
        and customs regulation, 1707,
        307–10
    parties in:
        tories, 10, 23–5, 32, 33, 39–40,
            48, 67, 120, 123, 163, 179,
            183
        whigs, 22–6, 32, 33, 37, 48, 63,
            163–5, 208, 255; junto
            lords, 63, 71–2, 73, 74, 76,
            77, 82, 89, 91, 92–3, 103–4,
            116, 117, 118, 119–39
            passim, 138 n. 159, 142, 147,
            148, 151–2, 162–70 *passim*
            and nn. 10, 37, 176–7,
            182–3, 189, 219, 267, 268,
            269 n. 90, 270–1, 291–2,
            298–302, 305–10 *passim*,

312, 314, 327; *and see*
    Halifax;   Somers;
    Sunderland; Wharton
plantations, 203, 209, 227–8, 229,
    231; illegal Scottish trade to,
    208, 209, 228; Scottish access to,
    140, 180–1, 182, 184
Royal Africa Company in, 188,
    207, 208, 292
Royal Navy, 237
episcopalians, Scottish, *see* Scotland
Erskine, James, of Grange (lord of
    session), 217, 255, 273

Fairfax, Blackerby, 26, 234
Falconer, Sir James, of Phesdo, 98
Ferguson, Robert, (the 'Plotter'), 68,
    72
Fife, 18, 81, 297
Fifteen rising, 313
Findlater, James Ogilvy, third earl,
    23
fisheries, Scottish, *see* Scotland
Fletcher, Andrew, of Saltoun, 56, 59,
    145–6, 147, 148, 227, 228, 229–30,
    273, 288, 289, 292
Forfar, Archibald Douglas, first earl,
    94
Forty-five rising, 313
France, 58–9, 205; wars against, 32,
    198, 199, 204
Fraser, Charles Fraser, fourth baron,
    257
Fraser, Simon, 63, 68–9, 73

Galloway, James Stewart, fifth earl,
    93 n. 138, 255, 277, 278
Garnock, John Crauford, first
    viscount, 93 n. 138
George, prince, of Denmark, 46
Germany, 229
Glasgow, 50, 118, 126, 177, 197, 274,
    278, 283, 313
Glasgow, David Boyle, first earl, 14,
    93 n. 138, 95, 98, 134, 136, 176, 224
Glencoe, massacre of, 206, 304

Gloucester, William, duke of, heir to the thrones of England and Scotland, 22

Godolphin, Sidney Godolphin, first earl, 24, 31, 39, 42, 47–8, 51, 57, 67, 70, 73, 77–96, 102, 104, 114, 117–23, 126, 128–36, 141–2, 143–5, 147, 148, 149, 151, 162, 164, 166–70 and n. 59, 171, 172, 175, 179, 189, 205, 213, 255–6, 259, 260–8, 269, 271, 272, 277, 283–5, 291–2, 296, 297–8, 299, 301, 303, 305–6, 308–10, 311, 312

Graham, colonel James, 149

Graham, Mungo, of Gorthie, 327

grain trade, Scottish, see Scotland, economy

Granby, John Manners, styled marquess of (duke of Rutland, 1711), 177

Grant, Alexander, younger, of Grant, 217, 255, 327 and n. 4

Grant, Ludovic, of Grant, 217, 327

Green, Thomas, master of the *Worcester*, 132–4, 222, 269 n. 90

Greg, William, 149

Haddington, Thomas Hamilton, sixth earl, 95 n. 152, 125, 136, 265, 266, 295, 297

Halifax, Charles Montague, first baron, 24, 92–3, 103, 120, 121, 151, 162, 169, 175, 300, 303, 305

Hamilton, family interest of the dukes, 12, 18, 70

Hamilton, Andrew, governor of New Jersey, 203

Hamilton, Anne, duchess of, 11, 12, 211

Hamilton, James Douglas, fourth duke (formerly earl of Arran), 11, 12, 14, 15, 18, 19, 22, 36, 46, 49, 53, 56, 57, 62, 71, 75–6, 78, 81, 83 n. 73, 84, 86, 87, 88–9, 91, 95–6, 97, 98 and n. 174, 100–3, 115, 125–6, 127, 144, 145, 146, 148–51, 171, 213, 262, 268–70, 271, 275, 276, 277, 280, 283, 285–9, 294, 296, 297

Hamilton, lord John, see Ruglen

Hamilton, presbytery of, 224, 282

Hamilton, William Douglas, third duke, 11, 16, 21

Hamilton, Sir William, of Whitelaw (lord of session), 21, 42, 54–5, 95 n. 152, 118, 124, 206

Hanmer, Sir Thomas, 167 n. 35

'Hanoverians', Scottish, see Scotland, parliament, parties

Harley, Robert, 42, 91, 96, 117, 135, 141, 149, 163–4 and n. 13, 166, 167, 168 and n. 39, 169, 170, 259–60, 268–70 and n. 90, 285, 286, 301, 305–10

Haversham, John Thompson, first baron, 120, 123, 163 n. 10, 304

Hay, lord John, 70, 255

Hay, lord William, 266

Henry, VIII, king of England, 3

Hepburn, John, cameronian leader, 285

Hertford, 168 and n. 39

Herries (or Harries), cameronian leader, 283

Hodges, James, 224, 230, 241–2

Holland, see United Provinces

Home, Charles Home, sixth earl, 49

Home, earls of, 12

Home, Sir John, of Blackadder, 95 n. 152

Hope, Sir Archibald, of Rankeillour (lord of session), 255

Horsbrugh, Alexander, of Horsbrugh, 93 n. 138

Houston, Sir John, of Houston, 95 n. 152

Howe, John Grubham ('Jack'), 24, 123

Hume, Sir Andrew, 118

Hume, Sir David, of Crossrig (lord of session), 288

Inverkeithing, 282 n. 146

Islay, lord Archibald Campbell, first earl (later third duke of Argyll), 142, 177, 256, 313

Italy, 307

James IV, king of Scotland, 3
James I and VI, king of England and Scotland, 3, 202
James II and VII, king of England and Scotland, 14, 23, 25, 197, 204
Jamieson, William, 264
Jedburgh, 278
Johnston, James ('Secretary'), 17, 18, 23, 33, 44, 78, 79, 80, 81, 83, 85, 86, 89, 95 and n. 152, 96, 98, 99, 101, 115, 120, 121, 126, 130, 131, 139, 143, 147, 162, 176, 206, 209, 211, 217, 256, 261, 262, 265, 267, 268, 271, 294, 296, 298, 301, 302, 306–7
Johnston, Sir Patrick, lord provost of Edinburgh, 283
Johnston, Robert, 278
Johnston, William, 278
junto lords, see England, parliament, parties

Kellie, Alexander, Erskine, fourth earl, 93 n. 138
Ker, lord Charles, 146
Ker, John, of Kersland, 285
Ker, lord Mark, 266
Kilrenie, 277 n. 124
Kilsythe, William Livingstone, third viscount, 288
Kincardine, Sir Alexander Bruce, fourth earl, 45, 280, 287
King, William, archbishop of Dublin, 164

Lauderdale, John Maitland, first duke, 5, 6 and n. 19, 203, 204 and n. 39
Law, John, 145 n. 203
Lennox, Charles Lennox, seventh duke (also sixth duke of Richmond), 118
Leven, David Leslie, fifth earl, 45, 81, 87, 91, 92–3, 98, 100, 115, 117, 130, 134, 135, 186, 255, 283, 294, 297, 299
linen, Scottish, see Scotland, economy
Linlithgow, 274, 278
Littleton, Sir Thomas, 303

Lockhart, George, of Carnwath, 75–6, 150, 165, 177 and n. 99, 186–8, 189, 239, 258, 266, 281, 285–6
lords, house of, see England, parliament
Lothian, William Ker, second marquess, 177
Loudoun, Hugh Campbell, third earl, 137, 281
Lowndes, William, 43, 308

Mackenzie, Sir George, of Rosehaugh, 220
Mackenzie, Roderick, secretary of the Africa Company, 20, 70, 132
Mackenzie, Roderick, of Prestonhall, 41, 46, 55, 98
MacLean, Sir John, 69, 72
malt tax, see Scotland
Mar, John Erskine, twenty-third and sixth earl, 12, 13, 93 and n. 138, 98, 103, 116–17, 145, 149, 150, 162, 167, 173, 176, 183, 217, 255, 256, 265–6, 272, 274, 283, 296
March, William Douglas, seventh earl, 46, 50, 93 n. 138, 254–5
Marchmont, Patrick Hume, first earl, 18, 23, 37–8, 40, 42, 45, 53, 55–6, 76, 89, 98, 118, 122, 123, 128, 130, 148, 171, 176, 205, 211, 212, 216, 257, 260, 261, 262, 266, 272, 290, 293, 295, 301, 327
Marischal, William Keith, eighth earl, 21, 145
Marlborough, John Churchill, first duke, 32, 46–7 and n. 36, 73, 79, 91, 99, 126, 164, 167, 168, 172, 177, 217, 256, 266, 269–70, 285, 298–9, 308–10
Marlborough, Sarah, duchess, 47, 179, 266
Maxwell, Sir John, of Pollock, 45, 89
Melville, George Melville, first earl, 13, 17, 18, 45, 115–16
merchants, Scottish, see Scotland, economy
Mitchell's club, 49
Molesworth, Robert, 164 n. 13

Montgomery, Francis, of Giffen, 311
Montgomery, Hugh, 177, 274, 278
Montrose, James Graham, fourth marquess, 14, 73, 84, 118, 125, 126, 131, 136, 255, 265, 266, 267, 282, 295–6, 297, 299, 327
Morison, William, of Prestongrange, 93 n. 138
Morton, James Douglas, eleventh earl, 14, 93 n. 138, 98
Murray, Sir James, of Philiphaugh, 12, 14, 21, 32, 37, 43, 50, 103, 125, 130, 134, 137, 138, 172, 176, 198, 288
Murray, John, of Bowhill, 93 n. 138

Nairn, Sir David, 78, 82, 171, 173, 175, 296
New Galloway, 282, n. 146
New Jersey, 203, 209
new party, see Scotland, parliament, parties
Newcastle, John Holles, third duke, 164 n. 13, 165–6, 169, 177, 179, 189
Nicolson, William, bishop of Carlisle, 163 n. 10, 183
Nisbet, William, of Dirleton, 272
Normanby, John Sheffield, first marquess (then duke of Buckingham), 24, 32, 179, and (as Buckingham) 163, 303
Northesk, David Carnegie, fourth earl, 12, 93 n. 138, 133
Nottingham, Daniel Finch, second earl, 25, 32, 39–40, 41, 44, 48, 51, 58, 62, 67, 68, 71–2, 120, 163 n. 10, 179, 263, 300, 303, 304

Ogilvy, Sir Alexander, of Forglen, 124–5
Orkney, George Hamilton, sixth earl, 18, 182, 218, 274

Packington, Sir John, 167, 225, 302
Papillon, Thomas, 208
parliament, English, see England, parliament

parliament, Scottish, see Scotland, parliament
Paterson, William, 170 and n. 59, 203 n. 34, 209, 219, 238, 275
Perth Amboy, 209
Peterborough, Charles Mordaunt, third earl, 24
plantations, English, see England, plantations
Polwarth, Patrick Hume, styled lord, 266
Portland, William Bentinck, first earl, 31, 80, 205
Portugal, 307
posti nati, see Scotland, post nati
presbyterians, Scottish, see Scotland, parties and presbyterians
Primrose, James Primrose, first viscount, 93 n. 138
Pringle, John, of Haining, 93 n. 138

Queensberry, family interest of the dukes, 11, 12
Queensberry, James Douglas, second duke, 12, 14, 15, 17, 18, 19–22, 23, 32, 34, 35, 36–8, 40—7, 50–63 passim, 67–70, 72, 73–4, 76, 77–9, 81, 82, 89–93, 98, 101, 102–4, 115–17, 126–8, 129 and n. 100, 130, 137, 143 and n. 189, 145–8, 151, 162, 171–7 passim and n. 99, 179–80, 198, 205, 211, 212, 213, 234, 235, 243, 254–9 and n. 26, 265, 270, 271, 273, 276, 277, 278, 283–4, 286, 293, 294, 296, 299, 300, 301, 302, 314, 326, 327
Queensberry, William Douglas, first duke, 17

Ramsay, George, C-inC, Scotland, 254–5
Randolph, Edward, 208, 209
Reay, George Mackay, third baron, 327
Ridpath, George, 223, 267
Rochester, Laurence Hyde, first earl, 24, 32, 38, 123, 163, 303, 309

Rollo, Robert Rollo, fifth baron, 93 n. 138

Rose, Hugh, of Kilravock, 217

Rosebery, Archibald Primrose, first earl, 93 n. 138, 255

Ross, William Ross, twelfth baron, 79, 116 n. 11

Rothes, John Leslie, ninth earl, 18, 56, 75–6, 79, 80, 81, 86, 95 n. 152, 97, 115, 118, 125, 147, 148, 262, 264, 265, 266, 275, 295, 297, 301

Roxburgh, John Ker, fifth earl, 18, 56, 58, 59–60, 61, 75–6, 79, 80, 81, 86, 95 n. 152, 99, 115, 118, 119, 120, 124–5, 126–9, 130, 133, 144, 145–6, 165, 175, 216, 217, 235, 257, 261 and n. 36, 262–5, 266, 267, 272, 295–6, 297, 299

Roxburghshire, 18

Royal Africa Company, see England

Royal Burghs, see Scotland

Royal Navy, see England

Ruglen, John Hamilton, first earl, 18, 95 n. 152

salt trade, Scottish, see Scotland, economy

Scarborough, Richard Lumley, first earl, 71 n. 22, 178, 304

'Scotch plot', 62–3, 68–9, 71–2, 73, 75–6, 88, 91–2, 101, 103, 117, 135

Scotland:
  admiralty board in, 1695, 206
  Africa Company, 46, 181–2, 187–8, 202, 205, 206, 207, 212, 221, 239, 266, 292, 295, and see Darien project; parliament, acts
  arrears, civil and military ('bygones'), payment at the union, 256–9, 336–7
  Church of, 78, 128, 130, 224; commission of the general assembly, 224, 229, and see presbyterians
  colonies, 209–10, and see Darien project
  Darien project, see Darien project
  economy of, 7, 197 n. 2, 197–205,

213–20, 312–13; merchants, 140, 198–244 passim, 277–8; trades (Baltic, cattle, coal, Dutch, fish, French, grain, linen, salt, tobacco, West Indies, wool), 58–9, 197 n. 2, 200–1, 213, 229, 237, 240–1, 244, 275, 276–7, 313

episcopalians, 9–10, 33–4, 41–2, 45, 49–51, 67, 206, 225, 280

exchequer, 46

government under William, 8–9, 16–26

jacobites, 13, 63, 97, 116 n. 11; suspected, 38–9, 67, 140; and union, 226, 273–81 passim, 286; attempted invasion, 1708, 310, and see cavaliers

limitations policy, 56, 58–9, 60, 80, 94, 96–8, 101, 103, 147, 214

malt tax, 313

parliament, 221, 229, 282, 292 n. 198
  acts of, succession, 1681, 55; trade act, 1693, 206–7; for the Company of Scotland trading to Africa and the Indies, 1695, 23, 205, 207, 208; security, 1696, 32; supply, 37, 99, 100, 102, 116; ratifying the queen's title, 1702, 37; appointing union commissioners, 1702, 37; reinforcing claim of right, 1703, 54–5; anent peace and war, 1703, 57, 59, 67; security, 1703, 57–8, 59; wine act, 1703, 57–8, security, 1704, 85, 98–101, 116, 119–21, 222; wool act, 1704, 101–2; treaty act, 1705, 148–52, 171; fisheries, 1705, 146; council of trade, 1705, 146–7, 149, 150; union, 1707, 287–92; church security, 1707, 280–1, 292
  barons, estate of, 85, 101, 103, 146–7, 277, 293
  members of, 97, 214, 224, 226, 273–81, 293–4, 295–6, 326–34
  parties in, 273–81

cavaliers, 48–50, 53–5, 59, 60–1, 83, 97–8, 139–40, 145, 147, 148, 273–81 *passim*

country party, 13, 15, 18, 24, 33–6, 39–45, 49, 51, 52–6, 69–70, 75–6, 77, 81, 83, 86, 87, 95, 96–102, 139–40, 145, 176, 179, 212, 214, 215, 226, 260, 261, 273–81 *passim*, 287–92, *and see* Baillie; Fletcher; Hamilton; 'new party'; Rothes; Roxburgh; Tweeddale

court, 49, 53, 77–8, 146, 147, 148–51, 171–5, 178, 214, 215, 285–6, 273–81 *passim*, 287–98, *and see* 'old party'; Queensberry; Seafield

'Hanoverians', 55–6, 87, 92–3, 98, 122

'new party' (*squadrone volante*), 75–6, 78–102, 115, 116 n. 11, 124–36, 133–4, 137, 143–5, 144, 145–51, 171, 172, 173, 222, 260–8, 269 n. 90, 271–2, 292–9, 305, 312, 327

'old party' (old court), 77, 78–9, 83, 87, 91, 93–5, 98, 100, 115–17, 121, 123–4, 133–40, 165–6, 169, 171–8, 189, 216, 254–6, 269 n. 90, 292–9, 312

'presbyterians', 9–10, 33–4, 38–9, 42, 45, 50, 53–5, 61, 76, 77, 171, 276

politics in, 10–16, 36, 273–81

post nati, 203 and n. 34, 207

presbyterians, 206, 220–1, 223–6, 276, 280, 282, *and see* Church of

privy council, 46, 50, 132–4, 172, 197, 201

Royal Burghs, 216–7, 230–1, 277–8 and n. 124, 282 n. 146, 282–4, 293

succession policy, 55–6, 72–4, 76, 79–96 *passim*, 103–4, 117, 121, 138–42, 144, 145, 162, 173, 179, 221, 226, 286, 288, 294, 301, 303

treaty policy, 97–8, 138–42, 148–52, 168, 214, 279–80

Scott, James, of Logie, 327 and n. 4

Scott, William, 278

Seafield, James Ogilvy, first earl, 1–2, 23, 42–3, 44, 48–52, 53, 55, 56–7, 61, 63, 68, 70–1, 75–96, 97, 99, 100, 101, 102, 114, 115, 116 n. 11, 117–18, 119, 124–32

passim, 132–4, 135–6, 141–5, 150, 162, 163, 168, 172–3, 179 n. 111, 205, 207, 211, 254, 255, 257, 261–2, 272, 273, 276, 277, 288, 296, 297–8, 311, 314, 326

Selkirk, Charles Douglas, second earl, 18, 43, 69, 95 n. 152, 127, 146 n. 205, 260

Seton, William, younger, of Pitmedden, 96–7, 219, 233–4, 238, 327 and n. 4

Seymour, Sir Edward, 25, 167 n. 35

Shakerley, Peter, 307

Sharp, John, of Hoddam, 93 n. 138

Shepheard, Samuel, 307

Shrewsbury, Charles Talbot, first duke, 205, 305, 308

Sinclair, John, younger, of Stevenson, 95 n. 152

Smith, John, 120, 163, 167

'sneakers', 123, 164

Somers, John Somers, first baron, 71 n. 22, 119–20, 122, 151, 163, 165, 166, 169, 183, 298, 301, 303, 305

Somerset, Charles Seymour, sixth duke, 31, 71 n. 22

Somerset, Edward Seymour, first duke, 3

Sophia, dowager electress of Hanover, 79, 166–8 and n. 31, 286

Spain, 307

Spence, Thomas, 234–5

Spittal, James, 95 n. 152

Spottiswoode, John, 234

Spreull, John, 231–2

squadrone volante, *see* Scotland, parliament, parties

Stair, John Dalrymple, first earl, 14, 23, 37, 68–9, 74, 91–2, 136, 137,

138, 172, 176, 177, 183, 206, 217, 255, 274, 276, 277, 300
Steele's tavern, 75
Stewart, Sir James, of Goodtrees, lord advocate, 53, 164–5, 275
Stewart, John, of Sorbie, 93 n. 138
Stewart, Robert, of Tillicoultry (lord of session), 20, 93 n. 138, 177, 255
Stewart, Walter, of Pardovan, 274, 278–9
Stewart, William, of Castle Stewart, 93 n. 138
Stirling, 282 n. 146
Stuart, James Edward, prince of Wales, 72, 140
Sunderland, Charles Spencer, third earl, 71 n. 22, 298, 301, 305, 309
Sutherland, William, 278
Sutherland, John Gordon, sixteenth earl, 277
Swinton, Sir John, of Swinton, 327

tack, the, 123
Tarbat, George Mackenzie, first viscount (then earl of Cromartie), see Cromartie
Teviot, Sir Thomas Livingston, first viscount, 327
tobacco trade, Scottish, see Scotland, economy
tories, see England, parties
Townshend, Charles Townshend, second viscount, 71 n. 22, 308
Tudor, Margaret, 3
Tudors, 3
Tullibardine, John Murray, earl (then marquess and duke of Atholl), see Atholl
Tweeddale, John Hay, first marquess, 14, 17, 18, 23, 28 n. 19, 96, 204 and n. 39, 205, 206, 207, 209 and n. 64, 211
Tweeddale, John Hay, second marquess, 18, 19, 22, 44–5, 46, 49, 54, 56, 60, 70, 71, 75–6, 78–96 and n. 152, 115, 116, 118, 124, 126, 128, 131, 133, 137, 222, 257, 264–6, 172, 197, 304

Union of England and Scotland:
earlier developments: united crowns, 3–5, 214, 220; Cromwellian, 5, 201, 202; earlier union projects, 2–6, 47, 67, 140, 177–82, 204–5; motives for, 2–8, 22–6, 162–6, 178, 189, 204–5, 218, 226, 233–5; obstacles to, 6, 26, 177–82; proposed 'federal' union, 183–4, 227
treaty of 1707: negotiations for, 122, 166–71, 177–8, 180, 182–9; commissioners for, 175–7, 188–9, 294–5; arguments for, 218, 226, 233–45; arguments against, 220–33; propaganda concerning, 215–45 passim; terms, 166, 169–70, 180–8, 239–40, 290–1, 300; 'explanations' of, 244, 290–2, 303; extra-parliamentary opposition to, 282–6; ratification, 279–81 and n. 138, 276, 287–92; 302–5, 326–34; presentation of to queen, 1, 189; effects of, 307–14; as an achievement, 314
United Provinces, 229, 277, and see Dutch
Urquhart, John, 93 n. 138

Vernon, James, 119, 305

Walpole, Sir Robert, 172
Webster, James, 225
Wedderburn, Alexander, 82
Wemyss, David Wemyss, fourth earl, 12, 255, 277
West Indies, 209, 244
Westminster, treaty of, 1674, 197
Wharton, Thomas Wharton, fifth baron and first earl, 71 n. 22, 120, 130, 167 n. 35, 169, 175, 176–7, 268, 303
whigs, see England, parliament, parties

Wigtown, 277 n. 124, 278
Wigtown, John Fleming, eighth earl, 277
William III and II, king of England and Scotland, 8–11, 16–26, 31–2, 47, 69, 205, 206, 209, 210, 212, 254, 314
Wisheart, William 224

wool trade, Scottish, *see* Scotland, economy
Worcester, the, 132–4, 269 n. 90
Wright, Sir Nathan, 121
Wright, William, 221–2

Yester, Charles Hay, styled lord, 44, 81